THE POLITICAL THEATRE

ERWIN PISCATOR

AVON
PUBLISHERS OF BARD, CAMELOT AND DISCUS BOOKS

The pictures in this edition were first published in 1929
by Adalbert Schultz, Berlin.
The one volume format was done by Werner Rebhuhn

THE POLITICAL THEATER was originally published in German as
Das Politische Theater

AVON BOOKS
A division of
The Hearst Corporation
959 Eighth Avenue
New York, New York 10019

Copyright © by Rowohlt Verlag Publishing Co.,
in Reinbek bei Hamburg, 1963
Published by arrangement with Rowohlt Verlag Publishing Co.
Library of Congress Catalog Card Number: 78-58463
ISBN: 0-380-40188-6

First Avon Printing, November, 1978

AVON TRADEMARK REG. U.S. PAT. OFF. AND IN OTHER COUNTRIES, MARCA
REGISTRADA, HECHO EN U.S.A.

Printed in the U.S.A.

TRANSLATOR'S NOTE

The present translation follows the original edition of *Das Politische Theater*, which was published by the Albert Schultz Verlag, Berlin, 1929. The material which on that occasion appeared with occasional double columns and frequent insets in various typefaces has been presented in the order established by Felix Gasbarra for the abbreviated, revised edition published by the Rowohlt Verlag, Reinbek/Hamburg in 1963. Where new material from the revised edition has been interpolated, I have indicated this in the notes.

I wish to thank Dr. Walther Huder (Curator of the Piscator Center), Ilse Brauer and Hannelore Ritscher for their patient assistance at the Akademie der Künste in West Berlin, Dr. Ludwig Hoffmann for access to material at the Deutsche Akademie der Künste in West Berlin, Dr. Ludwig Hoffmann for access to material at the Deutsche Akademie der Künste in East Berlin, and the Deutscher Akademischer Austauschdienst for generously supporting my research.

Hugh Rorrison

CONTENTS

FOREWORD

This book was written and published in 1929.

At a time when there was the greatest unrest in all spheres of life.

At a time which was torn and split by the crassest political, social and intellectual conflicts. At a time when every man who could see beyond his own personal interest had to feel committed, could not avoid seeing it as his duty to define and stand by his principles.

By 1929 it was already clear that a considerable number of Germans had learned nothing from the FIRST World War. Delusions of national greatness—one of the main causes of that war—were spreading to an extent that gave cause for alarm and were being turned into a political formula by the National Socialists. The chaos that would ensue if this "movement" ever came to power was clear beyond any shadow of doubt to anybody who had read Hitler's *Mein Kampf*. But how many people had read that tedious rubbish? Was it really as few as was maintained after 1945 in Germany? It seems to me that not a few Germans *wanted* chaos inasmuch as they wanted Hitler: and not *not* wanting Hitler was tantamount to wanting him.

At any rate by 1929 the fronts were already clearly drawn. A single glance at the turmoil provoked in the streets by the Nazi terror was proof of that.

On September 6 I opened the second Piscator-Bühne in the Theater am Nollendorfplatz in Berlin with Walter Mehring's *The Merchant of Berlin*, which not only laid bare the disastrous background to inflation but also—in the fate of an individual Jew (!) —prophetically sketched the inevitable predicament of anyone who has any truck whatsoever with the economic and political speculations of fascism in its various shades. The notion of a unified antifascist front of all the workers which Ernst Thälmann proclaimed on August 24, 1930 in his *Program for the Social and National Liberation of the German People* was the thought behind the writing and staging of *The Merchant of Berlin.*

Something resembling a unified front did come into being in response to the production, only it was directed against Mehring and myself. From the far Right to the center Left the press screeched its rage or incomprehension at the public: Mehring's play was salt in an open wound . . .

The consequence of this was a unified front in boycotting us. Manfred Georg wrote at the time, "If there were a prize for unpopularity it could have been awarded here." The lesson to be learnt was that anybody who wants to lose his popular appeal has only to tell the populace the truth. So the second Piscator-Bühne had to close its doors almost as soon as it opened them.

This book was assembled in hectic sessions during rehearsals for *The Merchant of Berlin.* It was intended to clarify and lend force to the struggle we were waging on the stage. For the new theatrical style that we had developed to give artistic form to our revolutionary view of the world, the *epic* or political style, was at that time still meeting with widespread rejection and misapprehension. Official aesthetics proved to be unable and therefore unwilling to deal fairly with it. Each production demonstrated the critics' helplessness when faced with the means we employed to turn the antique shop in which a world that was gone was gathering dust into a blacksmith's workshop in which our present world throbbed and could be hammered into shape.

So at a time (1929) when the artistic success or failure of our theater could be equated with success or failure of our political views, the successful reception of the form and content of our work in the theater could not be left to chance. A definitive explanation and elucidation of the basic facts of epic, i.e., political theater, was essential. This book was written as a consequence.

That we could not stop fascism with our theater alone was abundantly clear to us all from the outset. What our theater was supposed to do was communicate critical responses which, translated into practical politics, might possibly have stopped this fascism. That Germany later preferred the irrational mysticism of the Third Reich to our clear and precise critique was not our fault, even if it was the cause of our personal tragedy. As late as 1932 I went to the Soviet Union to shoot a film (*The Revolt of the Fishermen of St.*

Barbara, after a story by Anna Seghers) which took up the idea of a unified politico-social front again. Unfavorable circumstances, however, prevented us from completing the film before events made it superfluous: Hitler had worked faster . . .

Today the stylistic concepts of epic theater are well established, thanks not least to the activities of my friend Brecht. So is this book, once a manifesto˙and a manual for instruction, now an historical document? A document certainly, but still a topical one, it seems to me. The justification for epic techniques is no longer disputed by anyone, but there is considerable confusion about what should be expressed by these means. The *functional* character of these epic techniques, in other words their inseparability from a specific content (the specific content, the specific message determines the means and not vice versa!) has by now become largely obscured. So we are still standing at the starting blocks. The race is not yet on . . .

Seen in this light this chapter of *German* theater history should not be without interest for American readers, for the subject of this book is an attempt to answer the eternally topical question which Brecht formulated as follows. "How can the theater be entertaining and instructive at the same time? How can it be taken out of the hands of intellectual drug traffic and become a place offering real experiences rather than illusions? How can the unliberated and unknowing man of our century with his thirst for knowledge and freedom, the tortured and heroic, misused and inventive man of our terrible and great century, himself changeable and yet able to change the world, how can he be given a theater which will help him to be master of his world?"

Erwin Piscator

PREFACE

In principle it is superfluous to start a book by explaining what its purpose is. Nevertheless, for personal reasons, I feel bound to write a few lines of introduction.

My name appears frequently in the following pages, sometimes as the object of critical or derogatory remarks, often as the object of (partly excessive) words of praise. I should not like to create the impression that this book was written to satisfy my personal vanity. I am, of course, as pleased as anyone would be when his work has some effect, and I am doubly pleased when that effect is positive. But for me the cause itself is the important thing. For ten years, impeded by failure, misunderstanding and inadequacy, I have consistently tried to make an impact in a specific direction. It seemed time to record the beginnings and the development of this movement, and to mark and list the milestones along the route, before they crumble amid the rubble of time. In the course of a few months, hampered by day-to-day work and the preparations for a new theater, I have been able to provide little more than a loosely connected assemblage of data, experiences and discoveries. So the comprehensive work I had in mind when I sat down has not come into being.

I still hope that important elements for a dramatic theory of our times can be extracted from the copious material I have assembled. If is particularly important that the theater, the most transient of all the arts, which leaves nothing behind but a few inadequate photographs and vague memories, be caught in print if it makes claims to historical significance and progressive development.

For that reason the theoretical discoveries that have been made deserve to be recorded just as much as the facts and events. Today it is more necessary than ever, in view of the utter planlessness, the eclecticism and the general uncertainty which predominate in theatrical productions, to map out a clear line, to dissociate ourselves from misinterpretations and bandwagon followers, and to extract the essential core of our movement and set it down in exact terms. And finally, it seemed to me necessary to demonstrate the close connection between our work and the process of social revolution which has been going on in Europe, particularly in Germany, with growing intensity over the last ten years. Neither the fact that these things happened, nor the form in which they appeared on the stage, is a matter of chance. They are the natural and logical outcome of a struggle whose beginnings lie in the social and economic roots of our times. If the theater is ever to find its way back to its true purpose and become a cultural center, a point of social crystallization, a living factor in a human community which is worthy of the name, then it must follow the path which has been described here, stage by stage, for the first time; but at the same time it must not lose touch with the general historical development.

This book is the product of a collective effort. The notes made in the dramaturgic office of the Piscator-Bühne under the management of Felix Gasbarra and Leo Lania provided the framework. The ideas themselves arose as the group worked together, and had only to be formulated. For this I want to thank all those who took part, whether their names appear in this book or not. In spite of sacrifices and disappointments our work, which is compounded of elements of deprivation and human misery, has repeatedly given us satisfaction and fresh courage, since basically it springs from an optimistic view of life: the belief in progressive development.

Berlin, July 1929.   *Erwin Piscator*

INTRODUCTION

Erwin Piscator was born at Ulm, a village near Wetzlar, on December 17, 1895. Six years later his family moved to Marburg, where he went to school. He then decided to go on the stage and in 1913 went to Munich as a *Volontär* at the Court Theater. Such unpaid trainees could, and still can, be taken on to get first-hand experience of any aspect of theatrical work, and Piscator as an aspiring actor was given walk-on parts such as Astolf in Heinrich von Kleist's *Die Hermannschlacht* (*Hermann's Battle*). In a later letter to the actor Friedrich Kayssler, he tells Kayssler that he had written to him without response in 1914 asking for acting lessons, and John Willett suggests that he actually took lessons from Ernst von Possart (1841–1921), an actor, director and Intendant whose name is associated with elaborate, carefully mounted productions of the classics in what, after 1914, came to be deprecatingly regarded as the plush, declamatory *Hoftheaterstil*. Piscator also studied literature, art history and philosophy at Munich University, where he attended Artur Kutscher's theater seminar.

Early pictures from the Piscator family album document a conventional middle-class life style, typified by a shot of the family shop in Marburg in 1911, "Carl Piscator, Woollens, Cloth And Knitwear, Ready-Made Suits And Working Clothes." Piscator stands unsmiling with his father in the doorway, while his mother and brother look out of the upstairs windows. Later Piscator poses in schoolboy dignity with two friends on a walking tour, resplendent in straw boater and wing collar, and later still we see a clean-cut, thoughtful student in the Marburg Court Photographer's 1913 studio portrait. Curiously enough the series of conventional pictures continues until 1917, when the shorn, raw recruit of 1915, at attention complete with spiked helmet and fixed bayonet, reappears in uniform, posed with officerly casualness beside an armchair on which his lap dog reclines. This was an image which Piscator was later at pains to shed, as the snapshots he includes here show *(Photos 1, 2, 4, 5 & 6)*.

In 1915 he was drafted, and his experiences at the front made acting, the theater, indeed art in general seem trivial and irrelevant, and eventually converted him to communism. In later years he was to make an anecdote of his conversion: During a lull in the fighting one day he was playing chess with his buddy in the trenches. His partner went off to relieve himself, and when he failed to return Piscator went to look for him. He found him in the latrines with his head blown off and his brains spattered on the walls. A sniper had picked him off when he inadvertently raised his head over the edge of the trench. Piscator came to blame the system for the random senselessness of the killing and for the brutalization which enabled men to rifle the pockets of fallen comrades without a qualm. The ruling classes who were running the war were discredited, and communism seemed to offer a new, egalitarian social order. Like many of the Expressionist generation Piscator embraced it, and by 1918 he was firmly on the side of the antimilitarist left wing, to the point of becoming an impromptu soldiers' councilor in the closing stages of the war, and it was from this vantage point that he viewed the German Revolution and the Weimar Republic which followed it.

By September 1918 General Erich Ludendorff, second in command in the military administration which effectively controlled Germany throughout the war, recognized that defeat on the Western front was imminent and began to engineer the transfer of power to a civilian government which would negotiate an armistice and, he rightly calculated, take the blame for losing the war. Prince Max of Baden became chancellor, aided by Philipp Scheidemann of the SPD (Social Democratic Party), and during October they sought peace, exchanging notes with President Wilson. But on October 30 the naval high command, in contravention of the spirit of these negotiations, ordered the German fleet to sea to engage the Royal Navy. The crews of two ships, the *Helgoland* and the *Thüringen* mutinied at the thought of further senseless and unnecessary bloodshed, and the operation was called off, but the situation developed its own momentum. The sailors elected councilors to represent them and sent emissaries to the major centers of population, where they were welcomed with open arms. Workers' and soldiers' councilors were elected everywhere, and within five days Germany was in the hands of the revolutionaries. This was not the result of a communist or socialist conspiracy, but a spontaneous outburst of democratic, pacifist, republican feeling after the protracted hardships of war. Piscator himself stresses the spontaneity of these events; nobody in his unit knew, he says, who had suggested that councilors should be elected. This spontaneity was to be the undoing of the revolution. The Kaiser was in the process of abdicating, the military leadership was discredited with its officers powerless, but the Left which was thrust into power was divided within itself and unable to grasp its chance.

2

The established parliamentary party of the Left was the SPD (Sozialdemokratische Partei Deutschlands). It had shed its long tradition of internationalism and pacifism in the heady patriotism of August 1914 when its Reichstag members decided by ninety-six votes to fourteen in a predebate vote to approve the War Loan. In the Reichstag the party then backed the War Loan unanimously, and the Kaiser responded by declaring that he now knew no parties. As subsequent issues of credit became necessary the SPD was unable to command unanimous approval and in 1917 its dissenting members formed their own party, the USPD or Independent Socialists. This party embraced the whole spectrum of the prewar SPD from revisionists like Eduard Bernstein to Karl Liebknecht and Rosa Luxemburg, the international revolutionaries of the Spartacus League. Many SPD supporters who now identified the party with the warmongering government transferred their loyalty to the USPD. Bitterness reigned between the two groups. The USPD considered the SPD to have betrayed the working classes, and the SPD viewed the USPD as traitors and subversives (Friedrich Ebert's word for it: a pigsty), a view shared by the government, which stripped the Reichstag members of the USPD of their parliamentary immunity.

By November 9, 1918 events forced Prince Max of Baden to place power in the hands of the SPD leader Friedrich Ebert, whose second-in-command, Scheidemann, proceeded to proclaim a Social Democratic Republic to the crowd outside the Reichstag. This embarrassed Ebert since the Kaiser had yet to abdicate. Later in the day Karl Liebknecht, who had been released from prison in October, proclaimed a Socialist Republic to the crowd outside the palace. In the face of the restive population in the streets and the disorganization and conflict among the politicians of the Left, Ebert, a traditionalist whose policy was limited to reinstatement of the prewar parliamentary system with his own SPD majority in control, struck a secret bargain with General Wilhelm Groener of the High Command. Ebert was to shackle the radical and revolutionary Left and put an end to the "silly business of the workers' and soldiers' councilors," in return for which the SPD would be given the support of the army as soon as it could be reorganized.

Ebert was now playing a double game, secretly in league with the surviving military hierarchy, although the broad mass of the people who had overthrown the monarchy and placed power in SPD hands had rejected the military decisively in November. The imperial civil service and justiciary, which like the army were hostile to the republic, were also left intact. A first attempt to install a military presence in Berlin collapsed when troops moved into the city

3

on December 10 spontaneously disbanded for Christmas after being addressed by Ebert. Various incidents showed which way the wind was blowing. The People's Naval Division, which was regarded as the elite corps of the revolution, briefly occupied the Reichstag and took City Commander Otto Wels hostage when their pay was withheld just before Christmas. Ebert gave orders for army units from Potsdam to attack the division's quarters in the Marstall (royal stables), but the operation was called off in the face of massive popular support for the sailors. The crowd at the funeral of sailors killed in this incident carried banners reading, "Who killed the sailors, name them we can, Ebert, Landsberg and Scheidemann." At the end of December the USPD members left the provisional government and were replaced by Wissel and Gustav Noske from the right wing of the SPD. The Spartacists left the USPD and formed the KPD, the German Communist Party, so the fragile unity of the Left was in ruins.

The mood among the workers who saw the revolution crumbling began to change. In January an attempt to dismiss the USPD chief of police in Berlin, Emil Eichhorn, brought the USPD, the KPD and the Revolutionary Shop Stewards together in a revolutionary committee which called out a demonstration to support Eichhorn. Once the people were in the streets they expected action, a contingency which the committee had astonishingly failed to plan for. Individual groups organized the occupation of newspaper offices and main stations, and on Monday, January 6 of what came to be known as Spartacus Week, Ebert, at Noske's instigation, called out the troops to restore order. They proceeded to do so in house-to-house fighting involving considerable brutality, as the army settled its score with the Reds. When, for example, six spokesmen emerged under the white flag from the besieged *Vorwärts* building to seek terms, one was sent back to demand unconditional surrender. The remainder were shot. On Saturday the right-wing Freikorps who had mustered on the outskirts marched into Berlin at Noske's request. On Sunday Karl Liebknecht and Rosa Luxemburg were tracked down by a squad of soldiers and taken to the temporary headquarters of one of the Freikorps at the Eden Hotel where they were beaten up before being taken out and shot. Rosa Luxemburg's body was thrown into the adjacent Landwehrkanal, while Liebknecht's was delivered to the mortuary as that of an unknown man. The revolution now had two martyrs. Liebknecht had been a bogey to the SPD and the Right since he voted alone against the War Loan on December 4, 1914. He was arrested and imprisoned on May 1, 1916 for starting a speech on the Potsdamer Platz with the words, "Down with war!" Rosa Luxemburg, a penetrating theorist and a brilliant orator whose radical views terrified the SPD and the bourgeoisie was a leading political figure from the turn of the century. She spent most of the war in jail, one year for a prewar political offense and two years preventive detention. Like Liebknecht she exerted little influence on the events of the German Revolution, apart from founding the communist newspaper *Die Rote Fahne* (*The Red Flag*) and writing its editorials. She and Liebknecht were persecuted and murdered because they, more than anyone else, embodied the spirit of the revolution. Georg Ledebour, who was at least as active on the January Revolutionary Committee as they were, was acquitted after his arrest on January 9.

Ebert continued to mop up resistance, and by mid-1919 the SPD was in full control of a bourgeois republic, but its conduct of operations alienated and embittered the radical Left, among them Piscator, who felt that Ebert, Scheidemann, Noske and the SPD had sold out the workers. They were, in the words of Kurt Tucholsky's song, radishes in the garden of the German Republic, red on the outside, but white underneath.

Back in civilian life Piscator gravitated to Berlin while these events were unfolding. He made contact with Wieland Herzfelde, whom he had met during the war, and who introduced him to the Berlin Dada circle, which was more radical and committed than the original Zurich group had been. George Grosz and John Heartfield later became his designers, Franz Jung and Walter Mehring his writers.

At the end of 1919 Piscator went to Königsberg (now Kaliningrad) and with Oscar Lucian Spaun founded the Tribunal in a municipal hall. A preliminary announcement in the *Königsberger Hartungsche Zeitung* stated that the theater's name was its program, its direction and its commitment in one. Frank Wedekind, August Strindberg, Carl Sternheim, George Bernard Shaw, Molière, Heinrich Mann, Rabindranath Tagore, Paul Claudel and Maurice Maeterlinck were lined up for the season, and the style of presentation was to be determined by the content of the drama, but Man was to be central with the setting no more than an accompanying chord. The paper cautiously welcomed the new enterprise, and the first production, Strindberg's *Ghost Sonata* directed by Spaun in an Expressionist set with white door and windowframes against a black background, was favorably reviewed. Piscator directed the second production, a double bill with Wedekind's *Death and the Devil* (*Tod und Teufel*) and Heinrich Mann's *Variété*, and the paper praised the direction, noted that the actors had a lot to learn and

5

suggested that the company might find its salvation in comedy. The paper pronounced the last two productions, Wedekind's *Castle Wetterstein* and Georg Kaiser's *The Centaur*, poor and finally catastrophic. First nights were delayed, the repertoire was rearranged at short notice, cheap matinees were introduced, indeed the whole enterprise bore signs of improvisation and lack of capital, but the paper records no scandal. In fact, rather than going out in a blaze of public indignation, it seems to have petered out. The theater closed for a week on February 20 because the hall was needed for a trade fair. Four days before it was supposed to reopen on February 29 with *The Centaur* the *Hartungsche Zeitung* commented:

"We hear that the Tribunal, an intimate theater which was set up in the Gebauhr room of the municipal hall has had to close down for various reasons. Artistically what they were trying to do was not without a certain charm, but it was doomed from the start by the inadequacies of its actors. This theater was one of the many 'wild' foundations in the realm of the arts with which Königsberg has been blessed of late, which correspond to no identifiable need, and fail to take existing conditions and requirements into account."

Piscator had gained six weeks of experience as manager and director, and in that short time the company had exhausted its capital and its good will.

I
FROM ART TO POLITICS

My calendar begins on August 4, 1914.

From that day the barometer rose:
13 million dead.
11 million maimed.
50 million soldiers on the march.
 6 billion guns.
50 billion cubic meters of gas.

What room does that leave for "personal development"? Nobody can develop "personally" under these conditions. Something else develops him. The twenty-year-old was confronted by War. Destiny. It made every other teacher superfluous.

Summer, Munich, 1914. I was an unpaid trainee at the Hoftheater and was studying philosophy, German and art history at the university.

The Hoftheater did mainly classical drama, with a bit of Wildenbruch, Anzengruber, etc. They considered Ibsen, Rosenow's *Kater Lampe*, etc., boldly progressive. Two trends disputed the field. On the one hand Lützenkirchen (one of Possart's followers), on the other Steinrück, who represented the Berlin Moderns.[1] There was no attempt at experimental drama or staging.

1. The Hoftheater (Royal Court and National Theater) was the official repertory theater in Munich until 1918, when it was renamed the Bavarian State Theater.

At the Kammerspiele Hauptmann, Strindberg and Wedekind dominated the repertoire.[2] Oscar Wilde, the French, and modern drawing-room plays were thrown in, mainly for commercial reasons.

But events rolled towards us. The avenues that were open differed in no essential particular in the face of a future we all sensed but none of us admitted. We succumbed limply to the Call of the Nation; it became the right thing to do, though it eventually turned into a hysterical, neurotic fixation.

Nobody can say I am not a "Good German." Ours is an old Church family and I was educated in the spirit of true patriotism, but I know that my father, a convinced German patriot to this day, trembled at the thought of my conscription, and was overjoyed when I was rejected on general physical grounds at the first medical.

Patriotic! My eyes shone like any other German boy's when the fifes and drums marched past on the Spiegelslustberg (in Marburg on the Lahn) on the Kaiser's birthday. I did not like school. The dryness of the pedagogues of those days, the petit bourgeois education drove me to thoughts of my own outside the compulsory school subjects. I went my own quiet way with two friends. They painted, I wrote poems.

My parents had come from the country; I had been born there. Five years among farm-workers. Marburg, with its twenty thousand inhabitants and its fraternity students—who felt like "Higher Beings" with their fathers' money and their little colored hats—seemed like the big city in those days. We lived in the twisting streets of the old town among workers, tradesmen and professional men.

I did not go to the preparatory school which in those days was attached to every high school, but to the local school. This was my

---

Piscator dismisses it as out of date in 1914. (Ernst von Wildenbruch's historical dramas were in vogue in the 1880's, Ludwig Anzengruber's Austrian folk-dramas were written in the 1870's, and Ibsen's social plays were widely produced in the 1880's.) Ernst von Possart (1841–1921) was its director from 1893 to 1905. With the revolving stage devised by his technical director Karl Lautenschläger he brought its productions of the classics (Shakespeare, Schiller) to a pitch of perfection in choice illusionistic sets with lavish use of carefully rehearsed extras. Mathieu Lützenkirchen (1863–1924) was one of his actors. Piscator mentions that although Lützenkirchen was fifty, he was still playing romantic leads (Hamlet, Romeo, Goethe's Tasso and Clavigo). Albert Steinrück (1872–1929) by contrast was a masculine actor of rugged appearance whose performances in heavy roles (Lear, Othello, Dr. Schön in Wedekind's *Earth Spirit*) were praised by knowledgeable critics, among them Herbert Ihering. Steinrück was at the Hoftheater from 1908 to 1920.

2. The Kammerspiele (Chamber Theater) was founded in 1911 as a home for modern plays on an intimate scale.

father's express wish, coming as he did from a simple family who lived in patriarchal peasant style. Their guiding principle was true Christianity as far as circumstances allowed them to practice it. (When it comes to the faults of others, understanding, kindness, tolerance and complete disregard for the outside world, politics or ambition for high office etc., I have known no more simple people or better Christians than my grandparents and my father's brother.)

I have no desire to write a family chronicle at this point. But to underline the fact that you do *not* have to be of Jewish extraction to be a communist, I would like to quote the following statement:

Die Welt am Montag, Berlin. Extract from the edition of March 1, 1927. Erwin Piscator: Your letter states: "A section of the press is spreading the rumor that my real name is Samuel Fischer and that I am a Jewish immigrant from Eastern Europe. Unfortunately, this is not the case. I would not even have commented on it, were it not that my opponents have been using this as an argument against my work. Perhaps those gentlemen who show such an interest in my personal family tree would honor me with a visit, so that supported by "my" old bibles I can show them that those same bibles were translated by my ancestor Johannes Piscator, Professor of Theology, first in Strasbourg and then in Herborn (Nassau). His new translation was intended as an improvement on Luther's version. The edition appeared in 1600 and, together with two hundred other works of the same author, aroused very considerable interest."

Even if I am somewhat different from Johannes Piscator I believe that a few drops of the same serious, humorless Protestantism (with a later admixture of Huguenot blood) still flow in my veins. The ministry, however, into which my father would gladly have sent me, held no attraction. A different pulpit seemed more important to me.

Of course I ran into strong opposition as soon as I uttered the wish to go into the theater. I heard everything that I myself tell actors today: Forget about the theater as a profession—it is chancy and difficult. Even people with real talent have trouble making the grade. It's a jungle of envy and malice. I can still hear my grandfather saying, with a long stress on the "sch": "So you want to be a *Schauspieler?*" as one might say *gypsy*, *hobo* or the like.

Nietzsche, the scourge of the middle classes, and Wilde, the aesthete and snob, and all those in the last fifty years who ironized, attacked or interpreted this morbid bourgeois society helped me to escape from the middle classes, to shed my petit bourgeois background.

9

From my library: Heinrich Mann, Thomas Mann's *Death in Venice,* Tolstoy, Zola, Werfel, Rilke, Stefan George, Heym, Verlaine, Maeterlinck, Hofmannsthal, Brentano, Klabund, Strindberg, Wedekind, Messer's *Psychology,* Wundt, Windelband, Fechner, Schopenhauer, et al. Also Otto Ernst, Conan Doyle, A. De Nora.

The dominant overall mood was that typical, morbid, resigned *Weltschmerz* which had survived from the end of the century, an indolent tolerance that contrasted remarkably with the feverish political and economic activity of the times. I had, of course, no idea at all of how things were connected: Socialists seemed to be men with Mephistophelian beards and big red caps. Without even knowing whom or what one was supposed to be against, there seemed to be no choice but to swim with this broad current.

Now: all Germany cheered, enthusiasm for war. Nothing but volunteers all around. Except for me. By instinct, not from conviction. The masses appeared in the streets of Munich, boozed, made speeches. At one such speech—we were all standing hat in hand, and for the umpteenth time the National Anthem was being belted out (your own courage sent icy shivers down your spine)—suddenly I heard two true sons of Munich say, "Just look at him, hasn't taken his hat off, he's a spy!" The man was told to take off his hat but (like a fool) he ran away instead across the Stachus (as the Karlsplatz was called). Everyone else after him bellowing, "A spy! A spy!" He is caught and badly beaten up. And now the mob—its enthusiasm knowing no bounds—moves on to its "beloved king." Meanwhile, soldiers, bedecked with flowers, march to the station. Wild confusion, which repelled me and left me uninvolved; as indicated by a poem written in those first days of August:

Denk an seine Bleisoldaten[3]

Musst nun weinen, Mutter, weine—
War dein Knab, als er noch kleine
Spielte mit den Bleisoldaten,
Hatten alle scharf geladen,
Starben alle: plumps und stumm.

3. *Remember His Tin Soldiers.* Time to cry now mother, cry now— / He was your boy when he was small, / He played with his tin soldiers, / Who carried loaded guns, / They all died, quickly and quietly. / Then the boy became a man, / And himself became a soldier, / Took his place out in the field. / Time to cry now, mother cry now— /When you read: "Died like a hero." / Think of those tin soldiers . . . / Who carried loaded guns . . . / They all died: quickly and quietly . . .

Ist der Knab dann gross geworden,
Ist dann selbst Soldat geworden,
Stand dann draussen in dem Feld.

Musst nun weinen, Mutter, weine—
Wenn du's liesest: "Starb als Held."
Denk an seine Bleisoldaten . . .
Hatten alle scharf geladen . . .
Starben alle: plumps und stumm . . .

And so it seemed the more incomprehensible to me at the age of twenty, that a whole generation that had conducted a prolonged discussion about intellectual freedom and the development of the personality should suddenly, without the slightest resistance, capitulate to the general mass hysteria, that with few exceptions the entire intellectual elite of Europe rose as one man in the defense of their "Cherished Heritage" which they had till then viewed with some skepticism, a defense they conducted more often with the pen than with the pistol. They rose against "enemies" like Tolstoy and Dostoyevsky and Pushkin and Zola and Balzac and Anatole France and Shaw and Shakespeare, and went to war with Goethe and Nietzsche in their knapsacks. And so this generation set the seal on its own spiritual bankruptcy. Whatever they may have thought and whatever they may have done it became evident on August fourth that all they had thought and done was as nothing.

We young men had no leader to restrain us, no one to whose humane words we might cling. I and many more like me were filled with boundless disappointment. We had no experience and were filled with uncertainty. And yet in 1912 and in 1913, and oddly enough for no apparent reason again in April 1914, I had had premonitions of the war which I recorded in lines like the following:

Krieg![4]

(Aus einem Gedicht)

Ich fühle ihn.

— — — — —

4. *War!* (From a poem) I feel it / — — — — — — / War!—?— / Who says war? An outcast brood of thoughts / counts up blast-torn eyes, / Throats agape with fear, / Bullet-smashed, blood-mangled guts / In the pent-up pain of a hundred years, / A million abjured nights of love! / War? / Plead loud: Make war on war! /

— — — — —

Krieg!—?—
Wer nennt Krieg? Nestverscheuchte Gedankenbrut
Zählt zerrissene Augen,
Angstaufgebrochene Kehlen,
Kugelzerfetzte, blutdurchwühlte Unterleiber
In angestautem Schmerz von hundert Jahren,
Milliarden vorentsagten Frauennächten!
Krieg?
Fleht auf: Krieg dem Kriege!
— — — —

But a solitary individual protest against the war seemed senseless to me, and when I received my draft papers, I obeyed them as a "call of destiny." The thought of refusing to do military service never even occurred to me. The Kaiser's words, "I no longer recognize Parties among us," and the conviction with which the Social Democrats obeyed him, completed my confusion.

It was never leaked to the public that on the third of August at the decisive meeting of the Social Democratic members of the Reichstag a motion to vote against the War Loan had been introduced by Ledebour, Lensch and Liebknecht[5]; that in Neukölln 300 workers had demonstrated against the war and had been arrested, or that Rosa Luxemburg had had a fit of hysteria when it was announced that the War Loan had been approved by the SPD.

In January 1915 I trudged on command across the icy barrack square at Gera, in those days still dressed in blue and red; my collar was five inches too big, the seat of my pants hung to my knees and one of my shoes was an eight and the other a seven; a crumpled forage cap sat on my head (it was only when an officer rapped me on the ear that I realized you could wash these caps) and we were worked over thoroughly ("Break the bastards' balls"). Our great hour was being worthily prepared. The small-timers were in charge. It was against them that we turned first:

How did these people—bricklayers, butchers and the like—dare to act as the minions of militarism, as N.C.O.'s and corporals, how could they boast about their treatment of those timid souls who retreated like snails into their shells at the first contact, those who knew only too well why their bodies were decked out in carnival colors: because they might die in them. Die—Do you hear that? Yes, I mean you, N.C.O.'s and corporals, cattle drovers in uniform. Do you know what dying means to a

5. Paul Lensch and Georg Ledebour were two of the minority of Social Democrats who shared Karl Liebknecht's pacifism.

man? No, a thousand times no! Peasants like you calculate the amount of seed from the amount of dung, while the sky is blue and the sun has turned into a crown—why can't we take the butts of our rifles and smash in the bullheaded skull of one of these destroyers of our souls?

Oh, the system is fine, and the torture clearly works: the yoke sits firmly on everybody's neck, yet they need only realize that together they make up the State, that they constitute the power, that without them the State is a torso without limbs, round and smooth as a billiard ball!

We are waiting for that day to come, dear N.C.O.'s.

From my diary, February 1915

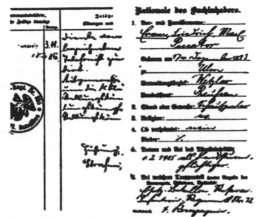

Page of Piscator's army I.D. card

We moved into the Ypres salient. The Germans were in the middle of their celebrated 1915 spring offensive. Gas had been used for the first time. The bodies of English and German dead lay stinking under the sad gray Flanders sky. Companies had been decimated and we were to refill their ranks. Before we were pushed into the front line, we were moved up and back again. As we started our second advance, the first shells came over and we were ordered to scatter and dig ourselves in. I lie on the ground, my heart beating fast as I try, like the others, to get underground as quickly as possible with my spade. The others manage it but not me. The N.C.O. crawls up to me cursing:

"Get on with it, damn you!"

"I can't get down."

N.C.O.: "Why not?"

"I can't."

He, scornfully: "What do you do for a living?"

"Actor."

The moment I uttered the word *actor* among the exploding shells, the whole profession for which I had struggled so hard and which I held so dear in common with all art, seemed so comical, so stupid, so ridiculous, so grotesquely false, in short so ill-suited to the situation, so irrelevant to my life, to our life, to life in this day and age, that I was less afraid of the flying shells than I was ashamed of my profession.

A little episode, but meaningful for me then, and meaningful ever since. Art—true, absolute art—must measure up to every situation and prove itself anew in every situation. I have since gone through more and worse things than the shellfire in the trenches at Ypres, but at that time my "personal profession" was leveled like the trenches we occupied, lifeless like the corpses around us. Art need not shy away from reality, and this was demonstrated to me at the time by *Aktion*, a little magazine published by a group of people who, although they did not really know how things were connected, did manage to scratch the true face of the war on the walls of their shelters, did bellow their protest. But their cries were swallowed up by the exploding shells, and their figures were engulfed in the smoke. My poems had already brought me into contact with *Aktion*, which under Pfemfert was alone in Germany in taking a line which opposed the obligatory enthusiasm for the war.[6] (At this point I must pay homage to stubborn old Franz Pfemfert, in spite of the way he afterwards undid all his own good work.) Pfemfert was gagged by censorship, but he nonetheless collected these voices and at least tried to give an indication of how things really were. He concluded an anthology of poems written in the field with the words: "I set up this book, this refuge for a homeless idea, in opposition to the times . . . ." A first attempt to fight the political fight with artistic means.

After two years in the trenches I was moved to a staff post. First I was with an air squadron. Then I volunteered for a new front-line theater which was being set up. This appealed to me more because it enabled me to practice my profession. At this time I still kept my

6. Franz Pfemfert (1879–1954), creator and editor of *Aktion*, a magazine for politics, literature and the arts which provided a platform first for early Expressionist verse, then for war poetry. At first a communist, Pfemfert in the 1920's became involved with splinter groups on the far Left. He dismissed the work of the Piscator-Bühne as trendy, pseudoproletarian confections for bourgeois snobs, and accused the KPD of opportunism for supporting it. In 1961 Piscator broadcast a generous reappraisal of the political significance of *Aktion* to mark its fiftieth anniversary. (cf. P. Raabe: *The Era of Expressionism*, London, 1974, p. 181 ff.)

14

profession separate from the ideas which were taking hold of me more and more strongly.

Eduard Büsing, the organizer and future director, received me leaning back elegiacally in civilian quarters, while a young man with full lips and most unmilitary bangs sat in front of him. His dreamy adolescent face was a complete contrast to his pretentious arrogance. He treated me quite superciliously. Büsing introduced him as a poet, whereupon he recited a few of his lyrical poems to us. At that time he was the editor of the magazine *Neue Jugend*, to which, among others, Johannes R. Becher, Ehrenstein, Huelsenbeck, Georg Trakl, Landauer, E. J. Gumbel, Theodor Daübler, George Grosz, Else Lasker-Schüler, Hans Blüher and Mynona contributed.

By the time we both left, we were friends and so we have remained. His name was Wieland Herzfelde; later he became director of the Malik Press.

The front-line theater was set up. And the troupe, at first made up only of men, operated from Kortrick. From there we went along the front, pushing as far forward to the troops, who were resting behind the lines, as the front allowed. A remarkable paradox: to see theatrical performances in cities demolished by shellfire, and not "sublime art" either, but *The Spanish Fly, Hans Huckebein, Charley's Aunt, The White Horse Inn*, and the like. Besides young *bons vivants*, I had to play comic roles. Comic old women were always played by a soldier who had one eye, and part of his teeth shot away. The soldiers doubled up with laughter at the very sight of him. Later on women joined the troupe, but there was no change in the repertoire. "Art" served here only to entertain (even today it is often said that "people who have been worked to exhaustion during the day need relaxation in the evening"). I tell this story about the front-line theater not because there is anything specially significant about one group of soldiers acting for another group of soldiers, but because it illuminates the total madness of the times, the way in which art was degraded into vulgar trash in the face of life and death.

Does the Red Army, you will ask, not engage in warfare, and does it have no front-line theater? Yes it does have a front-line theater, but it is precisely here that the difference lies. Its front-line theater need have no compunction about being the standard-bearer of the ideological aims of an army at war. (What remains to be decided is whether it is the artist's duty at such times to be in the theater or in the trenches. But that is a decision for the People's Commissars for War and for Education.)

Up to that time literature had put life into focus for me, but the war had reversed this relationship: from that time on life put literature into focus. On the one hand the war had sucked up every memory of earlier times like a giant vacuum cleaner. I was forced to "start again from scratch." But what I now took up was not art, was not even schooled by art, it was life schooled by experience.

I say this because people see me, indeed every artist, as a product of my artistic ancestry (which is naturally quite justified). And whereas today they say I have borrowed from the Russians, that I am a pale reflection of Meyerhold, they once said I was a pupil of Reinhardt (I must have picked it up somewhere). [7] All quite wrong. Since I first came to Berlin in 1918—and consequently did not see Reinhardt at his peak—and even then only saw plays on subjects of little interest to me, there can be no question of his influencing me. I was naturally also uninfluenced by his Munich productions (any influence there might have been was negative).

Drawing by George Grosz for the animated cartoon in *Schwejk*

7. Individual Piscator productions occasionally prompted comparison with Reinhardt. Reviewing Gorky's *Lower Depths*, which Berlin had seen in 1903 in Reinhardt's version and in 1922 in Stanislavsky's Moscow version, L. Sternaux writes, "Piscator's new production outshines these two without trying to hide what he has learnt from Reinhardt and the Russians. All the intimacy in his production derives from this school, the shadows of old have served as models for his figures. He often overdoes the modeling of these figures, to the detriment of the overall picture which spreads itself in truly Slavic breadth, and that too comes from the school of Reinhardt and the Russians." (*Berliner Lokal-Anzeiger*, 11.11.1926.) In Meyerhold's work for the Soviet October Theater we find many of Piscator's techniques: projected captions, ramps and platforms in *Mystery Bouffe* (1919); iron scaffolding, cars, machine guns, communal *Internationale* as finale in *The Earth in Turmoil* (1923); three projection screens with captions, linking commentary and quotations from Lenin and Trotsky in *Give Us Europe* (1924). Piscator's contention that similar aims led them to similar solutions simultaneously has yet to be disproved. News from the Soviet Union did filter through, and in 1927 pictures of Meyerhold's work appeared in J. Gregor and R. Fülop Miller's *Das Russische Theater*.

Only one acting personality stands out during this period: Albert Steinrück, whom I considered during my Munich years to be an actor of genius, and whose creations at the time (*Woyzeck, Kater Lampe, The Jester's Supper* and Hermann the Cheruscan) remained alive in my memory long after the war.[8] Filled with intellectual tension in spite of his physical bulk, bull-necked with red muscles bunched on his round face: that was Steinrück in those days—fit, versatile, man of the world, painter, friend of writers, aware of problems of the times, the type of actor I would still like to find today.

Art and politics were two separate roads which ran parallel for a long time, in fact, until the year 1919. My feelings had, of course, changed. Art for its own sake could no longer satisfy me. On the other hand, I could see no meeting point for these two roads, at which a new concept of art would emerge, activistic, combative, political. The change in my feelings had still to be encompassed by a new theory which would clearly formulate everything which I now dimly perceived. For me the Revolution produced that new theory.

As clearly as day followed night, the word *peace* remained the beginning and the end of all things for the soldiers. They talked of nothing else. Peace regulated all that we did. It was the end, salvation. And the longer we waited for it, the more we longed for it. But it became less and less clear where it was to come from or who was to bring it. And since we had no solution, we hoped for a miracle. This miracle came: It was the news of the Revolution in Russia. And it became more glorious when the second Revolution took place with the broadcast "to everyone":

The People's Commissars' Broadcast
(Fragmentary version)

Tsarskoe Selo, 11.28.1917

To the peoples of the countries at war!

The victorious Revolution of the workers and peasants in Russia has put the question of peace to the top of the agenda. . . . Now the governments of all classes, of all parties, of all the warring countries are invited to give a categorical answer to the question whether or not they will work together with us to negotiate an immediate truce and a general

8. In Büchner's *Woyzeck* Steinrück played the victimized, unbalanced, proletarian hero, in Kleist's *Die Hermannschlacht* the brutal, chauvinistic Hermann, and in Sem Benelli's *The Jester's Supper* Chiaramontesi, a Florentine renaissance prince. In Emil Rosenow's Saxon dialect comedy *Kater Lampe (Lamp the Cat)*, which he directed on November 11, 1914, he played Neubert, a toy manufacturer.

17

peace. The answer to this question will determine whether we shall proceed to a new winter campaign, with all its misery and terror, and whether the bloodbath in Europe will continue. . . . This is the first question on the agenda. The peace which we offer will be a peace between peoples, it will be peace with honor reached by general understanding and will enable every people to develop its culture and economy in peace. The Revolution of the workers and peasants has published its program for peace. . . . The Government of the victorious Revolution is still without the recognition of professional diplomacy. But we ask the peoples themselves whether their thoughts and hopes are reflected by their reactionary diplomatists, whether the peoples will allow diplomacy to ignore the tremendous possibilities for peace which the Russian Revolution has opened up. The answer to this question . . . [*interference*] . . . "Down with the winter campaign! Long live Peace and Brotherhood among Nations!" People's Commissar for Foreign Affairs: Trotsky; Chairman of the Council of People's Commissars: Ulianov Lenin.

Gigantic hopes hung over all further events. Their consequences stretched well beyond the end of the war. Causes which had lain unseen in the background were suddenly illuminated. That indefinable thing which had till then seemed to be "destiny" suddenly assumed tangible form, its beginning and its sources became sober, unheroic, clear. We realized that a crime had been perpetrated, and with this realization we were overcome with great anger at having been the playthings of anonymous forces. (What I later wanted to demonstrate in *Rasputin* was the all-powerful soul of the petite bourgeoisie which controlled the fates of nations in those days!) The opposition to a culture which had allowed itself to be enslaved by political and economic principles of this "order."

At this point we could not yet recognize the motive forces within the Russian Revolution. We did not understand their meaning in the context of the great revolution which was to come. Because of the military collapse and the German victory on the Russian front, we believed that we were close to the conclusion of peace, and at the same time we trembled at the thought that peace would mean the doom of the Russian Revolution. (I still remember that I once expressed this view in Pfemfert's bookshop when I came home from the front, and I now attribute our estrangement and the open hostility between us later to that remark.)

The November days came. The air was full of rumors: "The French are surrendering—divisions at the front are joining hands in brotherhood—sailors have run up the red flag." Soldiers stood at every corner, strolled around deep in discussion and then suddenly there was a call—no one, apparently not even the officers, knew where it came from—to form councils of workers and soldiers.

I was in Hasselt in Belgium with the theater. The first meeting took place in our barracks. The speakers were all officers and the tenor of the speeches was, "Let's keep law and order, stick together, obey only our former superiors, the army must be brought back into the fold," etc. Finally the padre, whom I personally knew to be one of the worst scourges of the soldiers, got up. We were now all "brothers in Christ," "his brothers," and "joined by the common love of all men for all men, and by our duty to our homeland." And this from a man who had always put every man jack who failed to give him the regulation salute on a charge. (He himself was a very arrogant specimen of the servant-of-God-in-officer's-uniform on the German side of the war.) This was going too far; I dislike making speeches, but at this point I felt compelled to intervene, and the speech I made—my only one in the whole course of the Revolution—leveled many accusations at the representatives of Christianity, and at this one in particular. The Great War was a crime, and they had not hindered it as they should have done. Once again they lined up on the side of the officers. The memory of four years of subjection and suffering provided me with words which captivated the thousand soldiers present. A real soldiers' councilor had taken over from the officers' councilor and a deputation demanded that the General hand over his sword.

Return to Germany. The first stop was home. When I got back to Marburg my library, my exercise books, the furniture in my room were still in their old places, but the foundation of bourgeois security had fallen out from under them. The objects floated in the air, like the rooms of houses that had had an outer wall shot away. But my troubles were as solid as those of the Europe who wept over her corpses and her lost riches. Nightmare. November, wet and rainy. The remnants of an army littered the streets. Business was bad. Including my father's, and his capital, which was partly invested in War Loans, dwindled rapidly in the months that followed. It was Kaiser Wilhelm's state and Karl Helfferich's catastrophic financial policies that had completed the expropriation of the middle classes and had conned their supporters out of their trust and their capital—not those of the Weimar Republic that came into this sad inheritance. But the unfortunate Republicans went on deceiving themselves. They were not guiltless and they added to their own guilt by refusing to recognize their error, by succumbing to their own reactionary convictions and sanctioning the real guilty men later. Bad and stupid, but consistent. Only I could not understand this; when I looked about me, everything here seemed as pointless, as hopeless and as senseless as it had four years earlier.

I was frantic to get to Berlin, the "Bastion of Bolshevism." I thought vaguely about my profession, but I had no idea how and where I should practice it.

BERLIN, JANUARY 1919.

Wild confusion in the streets. Debating clubs on every street corner. Massive demonstrations of workers and fellow travelers meet one another on Unter den Linden, in the Wilhelmstrasse, Communists and Social Democrats grouped in parties. They hold their placards straight and high above their heads, with inscriptions: "Up with Ebert—Scheidemann!" and "Up with Karl Liebknecht and Rosa Luxemburg!" They were all in the grip of a curious excitement. Wild abusive speeches flew back and forth. And woe betide any placard that fell into the hands of the other party! It was smashed on the edge of the pavement.

I once saw a wonderfully exciting struggle: Communists had penetrated the ranks of a Social Democratic parade. About thirty fists reached for the shaft of the disputed placard. But since the rival forces were equal, the placard did not waver. It stood unmoving above the heaving scrimmage. Then it slowly toppled; however, a quick-witted Socialist jumped up and tore the placard from its shaft and it was cast away over the heads to be raised at another point. From a thousand throats came the roar: "Up with Ebert— Scheidemann!" and just as angrily a cry resounded from the other side: "Down, down, down!" re-echoing from corner to corner. Quickly another cry gathered strength: "Up with Liebknecht!" Everybody ran to a street corner where a cab had been halted. Liebknecht was sitting in it. He was forced to speak: a speech close to events, packed with arguments, trembling with personal experience. It stands above his corpse in my memory like a living, gleaming flame which even blood cannot extinguish. That evening the first shots rang out.

In Berlin I saw Herzfelde again. He introduced me to his circle: his brother Helmut (later known as John Heartfield),[9] George Grosz, Walter Mehring, Richard Huelsenbeck, Franz Jung, Raoul Hausmann. Most of them belonged to Dada. There was a great

9. Helmut Herzfelde (John Heartfield, 1891–1968) translated his name into English as a gesture against the jingoistic anglophobia he saw around him in World War I. He was a graphic artist and is best remembered for his satirical photomontages.

deal of discussion about art, but always in relation to politics. We came to the conclusion that if art were to have a meaning at all it must be a weapon in the class struggle. Full of memories of what lay behind us, our hopes of life deceived, we saw the salvation of the world in terms of ultimate logic: the organized struggle of the proletariat, seizure of power. Dictatorship. World revolution. Russia was our ideal. The stronger this feeling became, the more clearly we inscribed the word "action" on the banners of our art, since instead of the victory of the proletariat we had hoped for, we saw it suffer one defeat after another. (So we abandoned our first exalted feelings and undertook the hard unemotional struggle.) We lowered Liebknecht into his grave, the spokesman of the will to peace, whose voice had reached us in the trenches over the intellectual barbed-wire entanglements erected behind our backs. And Rosa Luxemburg. The road to Golgotha: Unter den Linden, the Marstall, the Chausseestrasse. . . . The streets of Berlin ran red with the blood of thousands of proletarians, and we had to face the fact that their murderers were the very people whom we had looked to throughout the war for our salvation: the Social Democrats. As one man we joined the Spartacus League.

I had committed myself politically in the full awareness of what I was doing, but what was remarkable was that I was still thinking in terms of practicing my profession in a regular fashion. More or less in the way in which Kanehl always asserted that he kept his political views separate from his profession—he directed plays for Rotter.[10] "Even the politically organized workers produce coal for capitalist industry." This thesis is untenable. But I never managed to persuade Kanehl, whose courageous political views and clear, frank poems precluded any suspicion of double-dealing, that words are not bricks but have a meaning—one meaning in *Lizzie, the Cocotte* and another meaning in *Hoppla, Such is Life!*

Even then, I would already have placed art in the service of politics, if I had only known how. Up to this point our group, with the exception of Grosz, whose incisive political drawings had pioneered the way, had produced nothing but the Dada performances which had been laughed at and rejected in bourgeois circles. The demolition of art was begun by the Dadaists under the slogan, "Art is shit." We attacked the art-loving "Kurfürstendamm public" with recitations of simultaneous poems of the most incom-

10. Oskar Kanehl (1888–1929), writer, member of the *Aktion* circle, active in far Left groups after the war. During the Weimar Republic Alfred and Fritz Rotter built up a theatrical empire, the Rotter Konzern, which became synonymous with vulgar, mindless, profiteering show biz.

21

prehensible sort, using toy revolvers, toilet paper, false beards and poems by Goethe and Rudolf Presber.[11]

But the carryings-on had yet another significance. These iconoclasts cleared the decks, they changed the notation, abandoned the bourgeois position they had grown up in, and returned to the point of departure from which the proletariat must approach art.

While the emotional elements of 1918/19 subsided and the concrete political demands took on sharper contours, while the Dadaists for their part stripped art of feeling or—in the terminology of the day—"cooled it off," "froze it," a new invasion of emotion came from the O-Mensch dramatists.[12] This drama was, of course, also a "revolution," but a revolution of individualism. Man, the individual, rebelled against Fate. He appeals to his fellows, as "brothers." He wants the love of all men for all men, humility of every man towards every other. This drama is lyrical, i.e., undramatic. These are dramatized lyrical poems. In the misery of war, a war which in reality had been a war of machines against men, they sought a way through negation toward the "soul" of man. So these dramas were deeply reactionary, a reaction against the war, but against the collectivism of war too, a reaction in favor of a newly found concept of the ego and of certain elements in prewar culture. Ernst Toller's *Transfiguration (Die Wandlung)* was typical of this trend and was its biggest success.[13] It was a mixture of personal experience (lyrical), destiny (dramatic), politics (epic). The predominance of the "poet" in Toller, who formulated not facts but judgments, evaluations, ethical abstractions, and these "poetically," explains why it became neither a clarion call nor a contemporary play which transcended its own time, nor an "eternal value" in the sense of pure art.

When in the winter of 1919/20 I opened a theater of my own in Königsberg which, significantly enough, was called the Tribunal, I planned a production of *Transfiguration* which was to differ in principle from the Berlin production in that the settings were to be constructed as realistically as possible (the reality of the war as I had

11. Rudolf Presber (1868–1935), editor of a popular magazine, *Die lustigen Blätter (Pages of Fun)* and writer of humorous trivia.

12. *O-Mensch*, literally "Oh-Mankind" plays, were lyrical dramas whose theme was the moral regeneration of humanity. Kaiser's *The Burghers of Calais*, Hasenclever's *Antigone*, Unruh's *A Generation* and Goering's *Naval Encounter* are examples of the genre.

13. *Transfiguration* showed the transformation of a young man from a patriotic warrior into an idealistic advocate of the Brotherhood of Man. It was the first piece of full-blooded Expressionism to succeed in Berlin (Tribüne, 9.30.1919, dir. Karlheinz Martin, Fritz Kortner in the lead).

actually experienced it). I even reworked the language in order to suggest to Toller (may he forgive me, the blackness of this thought is unknown to him to this day!) how he might free his style of its lyrical Expressionism. The Expressionist School provided no pointer for me. I was already too deeply committed politically. We put on Strindberg, Wedekind and Carl Sternheim. Toller was in preparation. Our programmatic declarations—indeed, our very theater—aroused opposition in bourgeois and student circles, and when I wrote a polemic in the program attacking a critic, public and press were so incensed at me that I had to close the theater.

When I got back to Berlin, matters had separated themselves out more clearly. Dada had become more malicious. The old anarchic attitude to middle-class materialism, the rebellion against art and other intellectual institutions had become more extreme, had indeed almost taken the form of a political struggle. The magazine *Jedermann sein eigener Fussball* had been an impertinent attempt to "épater le bourgeois." *Die Pleite,* edited by Grosz and Heartfield, had thrown down the gauntlet to bourgeois society.[14] The drawings and poems were no longer determined by artistic postulates but by political effectiveness. The content determined the form. Or better: Forms with no aim of their own were given a content which attacked a specific target, which in turn gave them a clearer, sharper shape.

I too now had a clear opinion on how far art was only a means to an end. A political means. A propagandistic means. A pedagogical means. Not only in the sense of Dadaists, but in any event: away with art, make an end of it! (We won't argue about the level of talent above which artists and laymen are entitled to use this slogan.) There were in Berlin people who had introduced these ideas into the realm of the theater. Karlheinz Martin, Rudolf Leonhard and Hermann Schüller, a former student of theology who was now the organizer of the Proletarian Theater.[15]

14. *Jedermann sein eigener Fussball (Every Man His Own Football)* was a Dada satirical magazine edited by Wieland Herzfelde in 1919. Only one number was published and the police seized it as soon as it appeared. *Die Pleite (The Bankruptcy,* 1919–24) was a politico-satirical magazine.

15. Karlheinz Martin (1888–1948), Expressionist director in Berlin, first at the Tribüne, then with Max Reinhardt, specializing in large-scale productions at the Grosses Schauspielhaus. 1928–33 Intendant at the Volksbühne. Rudolf Leonhard (1899–1953), writer and communist, cofounder (with Martin) and dramaturg of both the Tribüne and the first Proletarisches Theater. Piscator later produced *Sails on the Horizon,* his only successful play. Went to Paris as a journalist in 1927. Hermann Schüller (1893–1948), writer and member of the League for Proletarian Culture (Bund für proletarische Kultur), which sponsored the first Proletarisches Theater. (cf. p. 37).

Program for *Ghost Sonata* (1/10/1920)

As a member of the Spartacus League, which later became the United Communist Party (VKP), I expected their support. A new theater had come into being.

We had a more radical program than Leonhard's group. Less art, more politics: proletarian culture and agitation rooted in the principles of all the elements of the proletariat. Now, ten years later, a group comes along and makes the discovery of this solution once again—and imagines itself to be heaven knows how radical in so doing: In the old days we were in the midst of crises, nowadays things are (relatively!) stable. Systematic work is what is needed. It is more difficult than ever to keep the interest in our struggle alive.

You can see from the following chapters how difficult it was for me, with the best will in the world, and how mixed my success was in putting my aims into practice. But am I to blame? I never evade serious criticism. But the interpretation of my work is part of its effect. A judgment can eat its way in, a prejudice can nullify the entire effect. Especially the effect of a theatrical performance with its limited time. Even when we remove it from the jurisdiction of the critics' instinctive judgments and place it on another plane.

Maximilian Harden once wrote that I drew my effects from peripheral zones. By that, Harden, the politician, meant: from politics.

For me that is both an advantage and a disadvantage. The following stages show how I sought to bring it about:

1919/20 Tribunal, Königsberg.
1920/21 Proletarisches Theater, Berlin (halls).
1923/24 Central-Theater, Berlin.
1924/27 Volksbühne, Berlin.
1927/28 Piscator-Bühne, Berlin.
  1929 Piscator-Bühne, Berlin (reopened).

INTRODUCTION

Having sketched his experiences and the formation of his political attitudes up to 1920, Piscator now outlines the previous development of political theater before launching into his account of his own attempts to translate his convictions into theatrical terms. He begins with the foundation of the Freie Volksbühne (Free People's Stage) in 1890, which marked the second phase of the independent theater in Germany.

The death of Friedrich Hebbel (1813–63) marked the end of the classical tradition of historical drama in Germany, though it lingered on in the bombastic, patriotic costume pieces of Ernst von Wildenbruch (1845–1909). By the 1880's, in response to the trivialization of the theater as well as to developments abroad (Zola, Ibsen), the need for realism and objectivity in art began to preoccupy progressive literary circles. Constructive ideas were at a premium, and there was little general agreement about the form and subject of the new drama, although it was broadly assumed that it should be serious and instructive. By about 1884 Otto Brahm (1856–1912), a literary critic and one of the clearer heads in the Naturalist camp, began to champion Ibsen as the dramatist to revive the German theater. His efforts attracted wider support after a specially licensed charity performance of *Ghosts* at the Berlin Residenztheater on January 9, 1887.

Neither the official nor the commercial theater was interested in Ibsen's social plays, which furthermore the censor was reluctant to release for public performance, so in 1889 a group of progressive critics set up the Freie Bühne (Free Theater) as a Berlin counterpart to Antoine's Théâtre Libre in Paris and placed artistic control in the hands of Otto Brahm. In an appeal to "the art-loving public in Berlin" the theater stated its aims:

> "It is our united aim to set up a stage independent of the existing theaters, but not in competition with them, which will be free from the restrictions of censorship and the pressures of commerce. It will present a season of ten performances of modern dramas at one of Berlin's leading playhouses, plays which, though of outstanding interest, are outside the scope of the existing theaters. The selection of plays and the style of production will promote the aims of a new living art, avoiding virtuosity and empty routine."

Among the performances in the 1889/90 season, cast with leading Berlin actors and given at noon on Sundays at the Lessing-Theater, were *Ghosts*, Hauptmann's *Before Sunrise (Vor Sonnenaufgang)* and *The Coming of Peace (Das Friedensfest)*, the brothers Goncourt's *Henriette Maréchal*, Tolstoy's *The Power of Darkness*, Anzengruber's *The Fourth Commandment (Das vierte Gebot)* and Holz and Schlaf's *Die Familie Selicke*. The second season offered a similar selection of European Naturalists which rapidly established themselves in the regular theater, so the Freie Bühne ceased to function regularly. Naturalism received the final seal of approval when Brahm became director of the Deutsches Theater in 1894.

The aim of the Freie Bühne was to propagate modern drama among its subscribing members (900 by the end of the first season). It was an avant-garde club for connoisseurs and, though the lower classes were the subject of some of the new plays, it was not part of the program to bring these plays to the masses.

Its progress had, however, been noted among the workers' educational and discussion groups, upon which the Social Democratic groundwork was concentrated while Bismarck's antisocialist legislation was in effect (1878–90), and on July 29, 1890 the Freie Volksbühne (Free People's Theater) was founded at a meeting of 2,000 workers at the Böhmischer Brauerei. It was—like the Freie Bühne—a society. A nine-man board of governors, consisting of left-wing intellectuals as well as workers and trade unionists, was responsible for the policy and repertoire. It, too, was to produce a season of special productions, and a small monthly subscription of 50 pfennigs would entitle each member to a seat, drawn by lot, for each play. Given the political situation, the society's aims had to be cultural and educational; it was to bring art to the people. This is borne out by the repertoire for the first two years, where Ibsen and Hauptmann stand beside Schiller and Lessing. Bruno Wille, the first chairman, rejected right-wing allegations that the enterprise was inspired by political motives while at the same time asserting that the repertoire contained plays "alive with the struggle of the times, concerned with the problems of the present," an attempt to face both ways at once.

When the antisocialist legislation lapsed in 1890 the overriding need for the SPD to present a unified front disappeared and the Party became less tolerant of sympathizing intellectuals. This led to a rift in 1892 when Wille and his faction left the Freie Volksbühne and set up the Neue Freie Volksbühne. Franz Mehring became chairman in Wille's place and the repertoire of modern and classi-

27

cal plays with a sociohistorical content continued as before. The exodus of the independent intellectuals generated considerable bitterness; Marxist historians see the independents as an 'obstacle in the way of forging the Freie Volksbühne into an instrument in the class struggle, whereas non-Marxists accept Wille's individualistic claim that he could advance the interests of the people without submitting himself to the dogma of a party. Wille's claim, on opening the Neue Freie Volksbühne, was that the aim of bringing culture to the people had been subordinated to party politics at the Freie Volksbühne, and he intended to keep the flame alive.

The Freie Volksbühne first mounted its own productions at the Ostendtheater and the Belle Alliance-Theater, but soon reached an agreement with Oskar Blumenthal, whereby it also took six performances of plays from his repertoire at the Lessing-Theater, thus taking the first step toward its later role as a block-booking organization. In 1895 the Freie Volksbühne had 7,600 members and the Neue Freie Volksbühne 1,000, and the authorities decided that they (and the Freie Bühne) were too big to be exempted from censorship, so they went into voluntary liquidation.

In 1897 the two societies were reconstituted. As they grew steadily they lost sight of their original aim of providing serious, instructive theater to the working classes and became a specialized booking agency within the commercial theater. The Neue Freie Volksbühne, for example, grew to 37,000 between 1905 and 1909 on the strength of its special matinees at Max Reinhardt's fashionable theaters. In 1910 the two societies cooperated in setting up the Neues Volkstheater with a permanent company in the former Theater in der Köpenicker Strasse, and in 1914 they opened an up-to-date new theater, the Volksbühne on the Bülowplatz. The two societies were formally reunited with a joint membership of 80,000 in 1920.

The Volksbühne lost its sense of social commitment in the decade before the Great War, which was dominated by the opulent, sophisticated theater of Max Reinhardt. Stylish classics and choice celebrations of symbolist pieces (Maeterlinck, Hofmannsthal) were performed for fashionable audiences, and, apart from the lone voice of Wedekind, social protest was not heard again until the emergence of Expressionism in 1917. Expressionism was essentially the younger generation's strident rejection of the materialism of its domineering elders (Sorge's *The Beggar*, Hasenclever's *The Son*), and against the brutality of war (Toller's *Transfiguration*). It developed in theaters in the provinces, especially at Frankfurt and Darmstadt. In 1917 Das junge Deutschland (Young Germany) and

28

Das jüngste Deutschland (Youngest Germany) were founded at Berlin and Munich, respectively, both offering a series of special matinees to provide a forum for new Expressionist writing. Das junge Deutschland was sponsored by Reinhardt and between December, 1917, and August, 1920, produced new plays by authors like Sorge, Hasenclever, Unruh, Goering, Lasker-Schüler, Kokoschka and Kaiser, but the long tradition of realistic acting at the Deutsches Theater militated against full-blooded Expressionism which was introduced to Berlin only by Karlheinz Martin's production of Toller's *Transfiguration* at the Tribüne in 1919. The Tribüne, which still stands in Berlin today, had opened with a manifesto preaching the Expressionist ideal of a New Humanity, and when it disintegrated Martin and Rudolf Leonhard transferred this ideal, which Piscator criticizes for its lack of a coherent political framework, to the first Proletarisches Theater, which is the subject of Chapter III.

II
ON THE HISTORY OF
POLITICAL THEATER

Political theater as it developed in the course of each of my undertakings is neither a personal "invention" nor the result of the social
regrouping of 1918. Its roots reach back deep into the last century.
It was then that the intellectual situation of bourgeois society was
penetrated by forces which, either by design or by their mere existence, decisively altered that situation, in part even destroying it.
These forces came from two directions: from literature and from the
proletariat. And at the point where they met a new concept arose,
Naturalism, and a new form of theater; the *Volksbühne*, a stage for
the people.

It is curious how long it took the workers' organizations to come
around to a positive attitude to the theater. They used all the media
of communication which bourgeois society offered; they created (if
only on a modest scale) a press of their own. They entered Parliament and made their contribution to affairs of state. The theater
they disregarded.

How did this come about? On the one hand, the intensity of the
trade unions' political struggle absorbed all their energy, there was
nothing left for cultural tasks, no strength to bend cultural factors to
their ends. On the other hand—and this was of decisive
importance—the proletariat of the 1870's and 1880's was, in artistic
matters, still under the spell of bourgeois standards. The plain man
saw the theater as a "Temple of the Muses," to be entered in

white tie and tails and in a mood of appropriate elation. It would have seemed scandalous to him to hear anything about the "ugly" daily struggle, about wages, working hours, profits and dividends amid the red plush and gold stucco of these magnificent halls. The newspapers were the place for that kind of thing. In the theater feeling and soul should reign supreme, opening up visions of a world of Greatness, Beauty and Truth far beyond everyday life. Theater is for high days and holidays. On the other hand, workers can rarely afford it in any case. The very prices of the Berlin theaters made them the prerogative of the affluent. Culture, cultural situation—this is an equation which for this society can most quickly and clearly be expressed in figures.

During the struggle to have *The Weavers (Die Weber)* passed by the censor, L'Arronge, the Director of the Deutsches Theater, based his case on the fact that the seat prices in his theater were far beyond the means of the sectors of society on which *The Weavers* might have had an inflammatory effect.[1]

This changed decisively when the Freie Volksbühne was founded (Bruno Wille, G. Winkler, Otto Erich Hartleben, Kurt Baake, Franz Mehring, Gustav Landauer, and others). It was patently clear that their aim was to provide good theater at low prices while at the same time promoting culture. "Six months after the first Freie Bühne performance (the model for this new establishment was Antoine's Théâtre Libre in Paris), Dr. Bruno Wille, writing in the *Berliner Volksblatt*, a Socialist newspaper, appealed to the masses to unite in support of an independent people's theater, and of the idea of a theater which would not offer merely trivial entertainment and flabby drawing-room wit, but which would serve art in its quest for truth" (Siegfried Nestriepke, *The Theater through the Ages* [*Das Theater im Wandel der Zeiten*], Berlin, 1928). An ideal program, but, alas, idealistic as well. The adoption of a new slogan, "Art for the People," does not mean the abandonment of the bourgeois intellectual position. The concept of art espoused by bourgeois society is left quite intact. The fact that every dramatist has something specific to say to his own time, something which cannot be passed on from one generation to the next without comment, is over-

1. On March 3, 1892, the censor refused to license Hauptmann's *The Weavers* for public performance because the portrayal of Dreissiger, the mill owner, was "calculated to provoke class hatred." The play was released only in 1894, though there was a club performance (outside the censor's jurisdiction) at the Freie Bühne on February 26, 1893. L'Arronge's case was based on the fact that *The Weavers* is a historical play. Seat prices were an incidental argument.

looked. It is not the problem but the form which provides the criterion.

At this stage it would perhaps have been premature to use art as a political factor or to have employed artistic means in the service of the workers' movement. The time was not yet right. It was enough to bring together two eminent social factors—the theater and the proletariat. The proletarian classes now appear for the first time as consumers of art, and not only as little groups or single individuals but in large organized masses. By the time the two theater clubs were amalgamated they had a total of 80,000 members, which was ample proof of the cultural receptiveness of the mass of the workers, in spite of the theory prevalent among the ruling classes, who cast them in the role of "uneducated rabble."

In contrast to the organizers of the theater club, the Berlin trade unions viewed the new establishment as part of the class struggle. They instinctively recognized in the new theater a cultural bastion of their movement, but they did not see the practical implications of this development. It is true that Brahm wrote, "The idea of founding a Freie Volksbühne came from the Socialists. The gathering which decided to put the idea into practice was a Socialist one . . . and this had a decisive effect on the nature and significance of the new undertaking" (Freie Bühne, August 6, 1890). But the directors of the club soon lost their footing.

The discrepancy between the original aims and the practical achievements widened and finally led the right wing to form a splinter group called the Neue Freie Volksbühne. Both undertakings were eventually amalgamated in 1920 in the Volksbühne.

This foundation is inseparably linked with the literary trends which predominated in the German theater in the 1890's. This is not the place to analyze the social and revolutionary components of Naturalism. But it is quite impossible to explain the rise of Naturalism as a mere literary fashion as many bourgeois art historians have tried to do. Naturalism marched under the banner of "Truth, nothing but Truth!" But what was truth at that time? Nothing other than literature's discovery of the people, of the Fourth Estate. In all other literary periods the "people" either provided comic figures, as in the tearful plays of the 1880's which typed the craftsman as the hero of the "Rise of the Able Man," or else provided the tragic individual figure, as in Büchner's *Woyzeck;* in German Naturalism the proletariat as a class appears in the theater for the first time *(The Weavers, The Selickes, Hanna Jagert).*[2]

2. *Die Weber* (1892), Gerhart Hauptmann's study of degradation and abortive revolt among the Silesian weavers in 1844. *Die Familie Selicke* (1890), sordid Berlin milieu piece by Arno Holz and Johannes Schlaf. Grown-up daughter Toni re-

But Naturalism is far from expressing the demands of the masses. It describes their condition, and restores a proper relationship between literature and the state of society.

Of course, Naturalism is not revolutionary, not Marxist in the modern sense. Like its great predecessor Ibsen, it never got past stating the problem. Cries of exasperation stand where we should hear answers. Only in the epic genre (Zola) did Naturalism formulate a picture of a social order which was destined to supersede the present one. Is it presumptuous, or modest, for me to see in Naturalism one of the roots of our movement in the theater? I know that every revolution is inclined to draw up a list of its ancestors and often exaggerates some tendency in an effort to build up a tradition for itself, to provide itself with an intellectual basis. However, the point at issue here is not to what extent the works of Naturalism have retained their validity for the present, but what effect they had in their own day. Even if some exponents of Naturalism utterly rejected any kind of political commitment (within the socialist camp itself there have been voices which have denied that there was any real socialism in the early works—Mehring),[3] this does not detract from the function of Naturalism as a whole. But for one historical moment, Naturalism did turn the theater into a political platform.[4] And it is not a matter of chance

nounces the chance to be a country preacher's wife and stays at home to hold the family together. Mainly on Christmas Eve as the family waits for drunken father while the tubercular youngest wheezes. *Hanna Jagert* (1893), a class comedy by Otto Erich Hartleben. Proletarian Hanna and her fiancé are socialists, an offense for which he is imprisoned. She becomes platonically involved with middle-class factory owner Könitz, who sets her up in a shop. She then becomes the mistress of his aristocratic friend, von Vernier, but refuses to marry him and retains her shop to show that her actions are those of an emancipated woman, and not a social climber. Final ironic twist: she gets pregnant and *has* to marry him.

3. Franz Mehring (1846–1919), socialist writer and critic, member of the Spartacus League and founding member of the German Communist Party. Reprinted in the German Democratic Republic as a classic of socialist literary criticism.

4. On the effect on the authorities: "It goes without saying that a play like this would have inflammatory effect on a large section of the metropolitan public in times like the present. The public would compare the conditions which are used in the play to justify the revolt with present conditions, and they would find similarities. The constitution of the State and the order of society as they existed in 1844 still exist today; Social-Democratic agitation reinforces the conviction that the predominance of the so-called capitalist order of society necessarily involves the exploitation of the working classes. The Social-Democratic press has already pointed out that this play is a powerful piece of agitation . . . and it is to be feared that the lowest classes of society would be carried away by the effect of the action on the stage, with its echoes of the slogans with which they are bombarded daily by the Social-Democrats, and would revolt against the existing order." (From the response to the appeal lodged on February 4, 1893, against the censor's ban on *The Weavers*, Police President von Richthofen.)

that the time which brought the proletariat into dramatic theory and into the organization of theater also began to revolutionize the technical side of theatrical presentation. The introduction of electrical stage-lighting came in the eighties, and the revolving stage was invented at the end of the century. So everything conspired to create a new concept of theater.

But the movement reached its climax in the course of this initial phase. It almost seems as though destiny had linked this development with the evolution of the major political factor of the day, the Social Democratic Party. There was rapid growth in the organization, a process of formal development and refinement, followed quickly by the degeneration of its intellectual substance into sheer stereotype. The forces of the opposition were still rooted in the world of the bourgeoisie, but they had shown signs of developing in new directions before they exhausted themselves without striking a decisive blow.

A technical revolution which began in England heralded the reorganization of society. The machine is conquering Europe. It is putting an end to sweated labor and cottage industry, and welding the proletariat together in factories and industrial slums. An industrial proletariat is growing up. From now on this will determine the development of society and it will not leave the most social of the arts, the theater, unaffected.

Of course, the theater of this period, which Sternheim nicknamed the Plush Age, never quite severed its connection with society. Strindberg and Wedekind had raised questions of sex, marriage, and the revision of our moral code for discussion. With hindsight we can now see that this involved a loosening or disintegration of the forms of communal life which had shown themselves to be ossified—this at a time when all forms of communal life were beginning to be changed by economic pressures. But this was clearly a revaluation in terms of existing classes. High society remained insulated. The factory worker who earned 60 pfennigs an hour preferred to go to his local movie theater (these were just appearing at the time), for there he occasionally saw at least a shred of something that was recognizably his own life. Wedekind's dictum "The

---

On the effect on the proletariat: ". . . during the fourth act [of *The Weavers*] there was as great a ferment among the audience as on the stage. People could scarcely contain their displeasure, the sympathy which the author had stoked up. A storm threatened to break loose, and it could be restrained only with difficulty. A noisy tumult erupted in the middle of the act and held up the action for minutes, reverberating around the house like a cry of rage at the misery of humanity." (From a newspaper account) [E. P.]

flesh has its own spirit" and Strindberg's "Mankind is to be pitied" meant as little to him as the telegramese of Sternheim's aphorisms or George Kaiser's structured ecstasies.

In the first place, the war does not permit us to raise any objections to the state of society. It not only demonstrates how utterly hollow and insignificant the last twenty years have been in artistic terms, it also shows us how astonishingly adaptable the production of art is. *The theater is militarizing itself.* One hundred percent holders-out-to-the-end and final-victors are discovered among the classes.[5] Shakespeare becomes Pan-German. At a later stage directors of theatrical revues bring on field messes every evening, and Claire Waldoff[6] promises every man on furlough what he can't have from her. Ballet dancers in tutus wag their bottoms and coo at the audience, "We'll hold out, we'll hold out, for the sake of the Kaiser and Hindenburg!" Both art and kitsch proved that when they had to show their true colors they preferred the colors of the ruling classes.

The forces which carried on the further development of political theater came from another direction: from "War-Expressionism" (dating only from the end of the war, and even then only in a very tentative form). In 1917 "Young Germany" *(Das junge Deutschland)*, which was founded by Heinz Herald (under the patronage of Max Reinhardt), staged its first two war plays.

Reinhard Goering's *Naval Encounter (Seeschlacht)* was put on as a matinee at the Deutsches Theater. Unruh's *A Generation (Das Geschlecht)*, a vague treatment of the social forces active in the war years, followed shortly afterwards.[7] No need to stress that in both plays the problem remains unsolved. The suggested way out is to do your duty until you fall ("Gunnery must have been closer to our hearts," says Goering in *Naval Encounter)*, or else to go to pieces. Weak attempts to come to grips somehow with the vast subject.

The official theater, including the Volksbühne, is silent. While the workers on the streets are being driven back with machine guns and flamethrowers, while houses shake as the columns of tanks and infantry move into Berlin from Potsdam and Jüterbog, the curtain is going up on the fate of *Henry the Fourth of England* or on Shakespeare's *As You Like It* (Reinhardt) in front of half-empty or-

5. Official propaganda encouraged the Germans during the Great War to hold out *(durchhalten)* until the final victory *(Endsieg)*.

6. Claire Waldoff (1884–1957), actress and cabaret singer known for her gravel-voiced rendering of saucy Berlin songs.

7. *Naval Encounter* by Reinhard Goering (1887–1936) shows a near mutiny in a gun turret under fire. *A Generation* by Fritz von Unruh (1885–1970), a rhetorical, antimilitarist piece, showed a family destroyed by the passions unleashed by war.

chestras and empty balconies. However, the groups which had formed the intellectual opposition during the War and who now felt that the revolution had given them their chance seized the initiative. At the beginning of 1919, "The Tribüne" is founded at the "Knie" [Ernst-Reuter-Platz] in Charlottenburg. Karlheinz Martin produces Ernst Toller's *Transfiguration*. But this theater soon loses its ideological significance and takes its place in the ranks of the commercial theater.

Martin, disturbed by current events, tries to repeat the experiment elsewhere. The first "Proletarian Theater" comes into being, but it collapses after a single performance.

"In the Spring of 1919 in Berlin the Proletarisches Theater was founded by Arthur Holitscher, Ludwig Rubiner, Rudolf Leonhard, Karlheinz Martin, Hermann Junker, Alfred Beierle, Alfons Goldschmidt and others. The intention was to create the first theatrical instrument of the cult of the proletarian in Germany in a collectivist form. The Philharmonic Hall was chock-full for the first production (it was also the last) of Kranz's play *Freedom (Freiheit)*. The organizers had to make do without a normal stage and willingly accepted this because they believed that they could stage their plays anywhere using the most modest resources. Just as it was intended that the work should be anonymous, so that not even the names of the actors were published, so too the props were kept as simple, unobtrusive and essentially proletarian as possible. The production was a success, although the play had a sentimental ending, reminiscent of Tolstoyan humility. The whole tendency of this theater was like this play, only half proletarian. It was not topical theater at all in terms of the demands of the proletariat."

Alfons Goldschmidt

This initiative, which almost came to fruition, was then developed by more lively spirits from the old Dada circle who had clearer political intentions. These men began to work on a political propaganda theater with clear revolutionary slogans. I refer to the Proletarisches Theater founded by myself and my friend Hermann Schüller in March, 1919.

INTRODUCTION

Piscator returned to Berlin and in the autumn of 1920 founded the Proletarisches Theater with Hermann Schüller (1893–1948), a writer who had been a member of the Bund für proletarische Kultur, the first postwar attempt by left-wing intellectuals to organize cultural affairs for the masses. When the Tribüne, the theater which gave Berlin its first real taste of idealistic Expressionism with Toller's *Transfiguration*, disintegrated after some of the company refused to perform the play for striking metalworkers, its director, Karlheinz Martin, and dramaturg, Rudolf Leonhard joined the Bund and under its auspices formed the first Proletarisches Theater, with professional actors. Their aim was to break the cultural stranglehold of the bourgeoisie, while preserving "the eternal works which sublime spirits, past and present, have bestowed on mankind."

On December 14, 1919, Martin directed Herbert Kranz's *Freedom (Freiheit)* on the platform of the Philharmonic Hall with an angular, semiabstract cardboard backdrop in the style developed at the Tribüne to indicate the prison cell in which the four acts take place. Eight condemned deserters and protesters, named simply as three Sailors, three Soldiers, Woman and Anarchist, cast around for a means of escape, even suggesting that the Woman offer herself to the guards as a bribe. The keys are surrendered in confusion by one guard, only to be thrown away after the Anarchist has demonstrated that the only gesture morally compatible with the selfless pacifism for which they stand condemned is resignation and self-sacrifice. The terse, heightened dialogue abounds with stage-directions like "visionary," "with an unreal smile" and "quite solemn and noble." The actors appeared anonymously and the audience was instructed not to applaud. The critic of the *Rote Fahne*, which had pronounced *Transfiguration* counterrevolutionary, since it preached the brotherhood of man, exploiters and exploited alike, now pointed out that *Freedom* represented the anarchist position, individual self-realization through self-sacrifice. Both the Bund and its theater collapsed soon after this performance.

Piscator's Proletarisches Theater was conceived from the start by contrast as an agitprop (agitation + propaganda) group with the sole aim of developing class consciousness and proletarian solidarity for the struggle ahead, and Piscator pioneered the material which by 1928 was being used by agitprop troupes in virtually every German town: short sketches in brief, simple scenes with typed characters and dialogue larded with direct appeals to the audience to respond to the communist message. He toured the working-class quarters of Berlin with a small group of actors and helpers doing one-night stands in halls and meeting rooms.

The opening production comprised three sketches: *The Cripple, At the Gate* and *Russia's Day*. The first demonstrated that the limbless veterans who begged daily in Berlin were the discarded victims of capitalist exploitation; the second exposed the use of concentration camps for communist prisoners in Hungary. Workers' revolutions had been crushed in Poland, Finland and Hungary in 1918, and in the spring of 1920 there was an abortive military coup d'etat (Kapp *Putsch*) in Berlin. Then in April counterrevolutionary units from Poland and Finland invaded the Soviet Union, the bastion and symbol of communism. These three sketches, Germany's first agitprop, were a response to the threat of counterrevolution.

Russia's Day is the only script to survive. In it the individual figures are symbols of political forces. World Capital appears as a character and other groups are represented by types (Diplomat, Officer, Preacher, etc.) who mouth rapacious, capitalist clichés in a dialogue in which capitalist assertion alternates with revolutionary exhortation.

World Capital [dressed in a giant moneybag with a stockbroker's top hat]: I am World Capital. Silence! [*To the Diplomat*] Have you given orders for force to be used ruthlessly against anyone who infringes the sacred rights of property? Speak up!

Diplomat: Your Majesty's power embraces the entire world that has been bestowed upon man. But Your Majesty's omnipotence is gravely threatened by the masses of the workers in their struggle for power.

World Capital: Trample the masses underfoot!

Officer: Yes, sir. Well-drilled men, field guns, bombs, machine guns, poison gas!

Preacher: In the name of the Lord God, blessed be thy name.

Diplomat: It is clear that freedom for the masses would be the downfall of us all.

World Capital: Downfall? Anybody who is not with me is against me. I will smash my enemies.

Officer: Blood! Blood!

Preacher: In the Lord's name.

Diplomat: Naturally we will use any means at our disposal to ward off our downfall. We will shrink from no method that could help us . . . no matter what atrocities are involved. . . . Let me remind you of Hungary, of the Ruhr. We have always succeeded with the White Terror.

World Capital: White Terror? Good, excellent. Squeeze them till they are bled white, that is the surest method.

This is crude, propagandistic caricature with a few factual allusions (Hungary, Ruhr) thrown in, sensational rather than enlightening, except in the most partisan terms.

The play begins with distant strains of the "Internationale" and ends with the workers chanting, "Fight! Fight! Fight! Everything for Russia!" The Diplomat is kicked off the stage. Turnpikes symbolizing European national frontiers are smashed, and, as the final climax, actors and audience sing the "Internationale" together. The whole performance is calculated to provoke indignation and class feeling and stimulate audience participation.

These plays were performed in halls with minimal stage facilities, so the sets were as rudimentary as the script. A few props, some black drapes and a couple of spotlights would be transported in a handcart. For *Russia's Day* the stage was enclosed by drapes with a map of Europe as a backdrop *(Photo 7)*. There was a turnpike painted with the flags of Europe on each side of the stage, one with a placard "East," the other with "West" above it. John Heartfield was the designer, and, in an anecdote interpolated into the 1963 edition of *Das Politische Theater* (p.48), Piscator jocularly credited him with founding epic theater:

The following incident shows how we put these performances together: John Heartfield, who had agreed to produce a backdrop for *The Cripple*, was as usual late with his work and appeared at the back of the hall with his backdrop rolled up under his arm when we had reached the middle of the first act. What then happened might have looked like a director's gimmick, yet it just happened. Heartfield: "Stop, Erwin, stop! I'm here!" All heads turned in astonishment toward the little man with the red face who had just burst in. We could not simply go on, so I stood up, abandoned my role as the cripple for the moment, and called down to him: "Where have you been all this time? We waited almost half an hour for you [*murmur of agreement from the audience*] and then we had to start without your backdrop." Heartfield: "You didn't send the car! It's your fault! I ran through the streets, the streetcars wouldn't take me because the cloth was too big. When I finally managed to board one I had to stand on the platform at the back, and I almost fell off!" [*Increasing amusement in the audience.*] —I interrupted him: "Calm down, Johnny, we have to get on with the show." —Heartfield [*highly excited*]: "No, the cloth must be put up first!" And since he refused to calm down I turned to the audience and asked them what was to be done, should we continue to play, or should we hang up the backdrop? There was an overwhelming majority for the backdrop. So we dropped the curtain, hung up the backdrop and to everybody's satisfaction started the play anew. (Nowadays I refer to John Heartfield as the founder of the "Epic Theater".)

The exclusion of the bourgeois press has deprived us of information about other performances, though the *Rote Fahne* reviewed Jung's *The Kanakans (Die Kanaker)* in positive terms, singling out a realism of presentation which aimed to make the stage events look like the real thing. A couple, embracing as the curtain goes up, turns to the audience as if startled by its intrusion. The theme is exploitation. A Japanese entrepreneur persuades a German to dismantle his factory and ship the plant to Japan, where profitability is higher. The workers are disunited in the face of the loss of their livelihood, some of them already preoccupied with the threat of eviction from their homes, but they are eventually mobilized and occupy the empty factory. The bourgeoisie—manager, police and courts in collusion—plans countermeasures in a drawing room, to caricatural musical accompaniment as in a silent movie. The workers are surrounded and come out docilely. Some are taken out and shot as looters. The rest, the program augurs, face further exploitation and starvation. A philosophical debate between Lenin and H. G. Wells was interpolated into the middle of the play to set the events in the context of the class struggle, with Lenin persuading Wells that the only escape from Kanakanism lies in proletarian solidarity in the struggle against the bourgeoisie. (The Kanakans apparently ate members of their own South Sea Islands tribe, solely from fear of being eaten by them—an apt metaphor, according to Jung, for the thinking behind the bourgeois class war against the proletariat.)

A few of the actors were professionals like Piscator; the rest were amateurs. Piscator wanted to break down the barriers between the professionals and the workers and weld the whole group into a team with common political convictions and objectives. The venture was to be backed by a club of subscribers, but it was soon in financial trouble. The seats were cheap, free to the unemployed. The German Communist Party withheld its support. The official line was that theater was Art, and propaganda was propaganda, and the two were not compatible. This echoed the arguments used in the Soviet

Union by Lenin and and Lunacharsky against proletcult theorists like Bogdanov and Kerzhentzev who favored a new approach to art at a level the proletariat could be expected to understand. Piscator's problems were further complicated by police harassment and the venture folded quietly in April, 1921. Piscator could now claim to have firsthand knowledge of what it felt like to play to the working classes.

III
PROLETARIAN THEATER
1920/21

Discussions Concerning Proletarian Theater

The propaganda section of the Proletarisches Theater in Berlin-Halensee has sent us the following document: "A committee of the revolutionary workers of Greater Berlin has been founded to support a proletarian theater with a view to making it the propaganda platform of the revolutionary workers of Greater Berlin. The members to date are: The Cultural Committee of the Independent Social Democratic Party of Germany (USPD), of the Communist Workers' Party (KAP)—the representative of the German Communist Party (KPD) could only contact us a few days later and will present himself at the next session—of the Free Workers Union, of the General Workers Union, of the "Friends of Nature" (a workers' hiking club), of the International Association of War Victims, and of the Council for the Unemployed. The Central Office of Shop Stewards also pledged its support.

The Committee invites all organizations who support the dictatorship of the proletariat to attend its second session, during which the articles of the association and its program will be discussed. The session will take place on Tuesday, September 7 at 6 P.M. in the Trades School, Schicklerstrasse 5–6."

(Notice in the press)

Comrades!
You are about to see *The Cripple (Der Krüppel)* [1]

1. The Proletarisches Theater opened on October 14, 1920, the third anniversary of the October Revolution, in Kliem's Dining Rooms, a traditional meeting place for

Proletarisches Theater
Bühne der revolutionären Arbeiter Groß-Berlins
Geschäftsstelle Halensee, Karlsruher Str 27.   Telefon: Pfalzburg 4515

Genossen und Genossinnen!

Die Seele der Revolution, die Seele der kommenden Gesellschaft der Klassenlosigkeit und der Kultur der Gemeinschaft ist unser revolutionäres Gefühl.

Das proletarische Theater will dieses Gefühl entzünden und wach halten helfen.

Die Erlebnisse, die sozialistische Kunst in uns hervorruft, stärken das Bewußtsein vom Ernst und von der Größe der geschichtlichen Sendung unserer Klasse.

I. Programm-Ausgabe.   20 Pfg.

Program booklet for the *Proletarisches Theater*

The capitalists' war for which the proletariat has worked and is still working has destroyed millions and left millions begging on the streets. Who helps them? The middle class perhaps, flippant, nasty, oozing charity, each according to type, who walk past these cripples on the other side of the pavement, salving their conscience with remarks about do-nothing rabble, and calling upon the State to remove these offenses to public decency from the streets?

Do you sympathize with the anger of these cripples?

There you stand. You—a worker who may tomorrow get the boot from your employer. You, the unemployed, thrown on the street because there are no more profits to be made. To you, the workers, we say: Solidarity with your unemployed comrades.

To you, the unemployed: form a revolutionary central organization for the unemployed! Elect political councilors for the unemployed.

Nobody can help you but yourselves.

Either socialism—or the decline into barbarism.

At the Gate (Vor dem Tore)—of a camp where your comrades are imprisoned in Horthy's Hungary.

Does the hireling who guards its gates have a proletarian conscience, can the woman, the political prisoner, the tortured comrade make him change his mind, and persuade him to join the revolution?

And if he kills the White officer, the camp commandant, will you, comrades, stand by the soldier, because you know that revolutionary acts of violence are justified even if someone gets killed, and that we can save ourselves only by our own deeds, and that the soldier's act is a symbol of those deeds? The capitalist world is building up its economic and military strength as fast as it can to beat Russia down. Russia is the solid rock in the turmoil of world revolution. *Russia's Day (Russlands Tag)*—the day of decision is upon us. Either active solidarity with Soviet Russia in the course of the coming months—or international Capital will succeed in annihilating the custodians of world revolution. Either socialism, or decline into barbarism.

This appeal, which was distributed as a pamphlet and was also used as our program, states all that need be said about the nature and intentions of the Proletarisches Theater. It was not a question

---

the workers in Berlin. There were three short plays on the program: *The Cripple*, by Karl August Wittvogel (attributed on the program to Julius Haidvogel); *At the Gate*, by Andor Gabor (attributed to Ladislaus Sas on the program); and *Russia's Day*, by Janos (Lajos) Barta (attributed to a Proletarisches Theater script collective). Gabor and Barta, whose names also appear on the projected repertoire for the Proletarisches Theater as E. Sass and L. Barta, were Hungarian refugees. In Hungary the workers under Communist leadership had seized power and set up the Hungarian Soviet on March 28, 1919. On April 10 Rumanian troops crossed the border and helped to put down the soviet and set up a fascist regime under Admiral Horthy. Many fled from Hungary like Gabor and Barta, but it is thought that 20,000 people were killed and 70,000 interned during the ensuing White Terror.

of a theater that would provide the proletariat with art, but of conscious propaganda, nor of a theater for the proletariat, but of a Proletarian Theater. This was where our theater differed not only from the Volksbühne, whose club membership size we wanted to achieve ourselves, but also in important aspects from the proletarian theater of Martin and Leonhard. We banned the word *art* radically from our program, our "plays" were appeals and were intended to have an effect on current events, to be a form of "political activity."

The directors of the Proletarisches Theater must aim for simplicity of expression, lucidity of structure, and a clear effect on the feelings of a working-class audience. Subordination of all artistic aims to the revolutionary goal: conscious emphasis on and cultivation of the idea of the class struggle.

The Proletarisches Theater wants to serve the revolutionary movement, and therefore has a duty to the revolutionary workers. A committee chosen from these workers will ensure that its cultural and propagandistic aims are realized.

It will not always be necessary to give priority to the message the author intended. On the contrary, as soon as the public and the theater have worked together to achieve a common desire for revolutionary culture, almost any bourgeois play, no matter whether it demonstrates the decay of bourgeois society or whether it brings out the capitalist principle with special clarity, will serve to strengthen the notion of the class struggle and to add to our revolutionary understanding of its historical necessity. Such plays could well be preceded by an introductory lecture which would prevent misunderstanding or an undesirable effect. In certain circumstances the plays could also be altered (the conservative personality cult of the artist need not concern us) either by cutting the text, or by building up certain scenes, or, where necessary, even by adding a prologue or an epilogue to make the whole thing clear. In this way a large part of world literature can be pressed into the service of the revolutionary proletariat, just as the whole of world history can be used to propagate the idea of the class struggle.

The style used by the actor, the writer and the director must be wholly factual (similar in style to the Lenin or Chicherin manifestoes, whose easy, flowing rhythm and unmistakable simplicity produce a considerable emotional impact). Everything that is said must be unexperimental, un-Expressionistic, relaxed, subordinated to the simple, unconcealed will and aims of the revolution. For this reason all Neoromantic, Expressionist and similar styles and problems, emerging as they do from the anarchistic, individualistic, personal needs of bourgeois artists, must be eliminated at the outset.

There must of course be no failure to exploit the new technical and stylistic possibilities of recent movements in the arts, so long as they serve the artistic aims we have described, and do not serve some stylistic purpose of their own as part of some private artistic revolution or other.

In all problems of style the guiding principle must be whether the vast circle of the proletarian audience will derive some benefit from it, or whether it will be bored, or confused, or even infected by bourgeois notions. Revolutionary art can emerge only from the minds of the revolutionary workers. It will be the work of a character that was formed in common toil and in the common struggle by the selfless will of the masses. The workers' instinct for self-preservation will see to it that they achieve cultural and artistic freedom in the same measure as political and economic freedom. And this intellectual liberation must be Communist in character to correspond to the material liberation.

Two fundamental principles emerge for the Proletarisches Theater. The first relates to the fact that as an organization it must break with capitalist traditions and create a footing of equality, a common interest and a collective will to work, uniting directors, actors, designers and technical administrative personnel, and then uniting these people with the consumers (that is, the audience). It will gradually be able to do without "professional actors" as it accumulates players from its own audiences. These players will cease to be dabbling amateurs, for the first task facing the Proletarisches Theater is to spread and deepen the understanding of the Communist idea, and this cannot be restricted to the activities of one professional group but must become the concern of a wider community in which the public has just as important a function as the stage. The first condition is that the actor must have a completely new attitude to the theme of the play in question. He can no longer set himself above each role, or be indifferent to it, any more than he can be totally absorbed in it, abandoning his own conscious will. Just as the Communist politician must deal with political or economic problems, or any other social question, according to an immutable scale of common humanity in each case, and just as every individual in a political gathering must become a politician, so the actor in each of his roles must make every word, every gesture an expression of the proletarian, Communist idea, and in the same way each spectator, wherever he may be, whatever he may be saying or doing, must act in a fashion which stamps him unmistakably as a Communist. Skill and talent will not produce this result. The second task facing the Proletarisches Theater is to make an educative, propagandistic impact on those members of the masses who are as yet politically undecided or indifferent, or who have not yet understood that a proletarian state cannot adopt bourgeois art and the bourgeois mode of "enjoying" art. The method of utilizing traditional literature which I mentioned at the outset should become the accepted method of doing this. In these old plays we still find the old world with which even the most sheltered among us are familiar, and here too we shall see that all propaganda starts off by using the existing state of affairs to point to the desirable state of affairs.

This brings the writer face to face with an important task. He too must cease to be the autocrat he has always been in the past, and must learn to put his own ideas and original touches to the back of his mind and concentrate on bringing out the ideas which are alive in the psyche of the masses. He must cultivate trivial forms which have the merit of being clear and easily understood by all, and he must learn from political leaders. Just as they have to sense and interpret in advance the forces and tendencies which are developing within the masses, and not to sugar-coat for the masses a policy which is historically and psychologically alien to them, or is only familiar to them because of evil practices in times past, so the writer must become the point at which the proletarian will to culture crystallizes, the flint on which the workers' desire for truth will ignite.

Erwin Piscator

(*From Der Gegner (Malik Verlag)*, special issue devoted to the Proletarisches Theater, October, 1920)

The repertoire which we drew up never appeared in practice. Playwriting lagged behind the developments that were taking place in the theater, both ideologically and structurally. All the writers who shared our convictions were still in the throes of post-Expressionism, and were not in a position to give us what we needed for our theater. With the exception of the work of Franz Jung, which was politically the most advanced, and was also constructed on novel lines.

Projected Repertoire for the Proletarisches Theater

E. Sass, *The Wife Comes Home (Die Frau Kommt nach Hause)*, *At the Gate (Vor dem Tore)*, plays by a Hungarian Communist, written for the Proletarian Theater in Budapest at the time of the dictatorship of the Budapest Soviet.
J. Barta, *The Gray House (Das Graue Haus)*, produced at the Proletarian Theater in Budapest.
N. Garami, *Toward Salvation (Der Erlösung entgegen)*.
Verhaeren, *The Dawn (Les Aubes)*.
Gasbarra, *Prussian Walpurgis Night (Preussische Walpurgisnacht)*.
Rutra, *The Deed (Die Tat)*.
Leo Matthias, *Unfettered (Die Entfesselung)*.
Paul Zech, *The Wheel (Das Rad)*.
Karl Fischer, *The Inheritance (Das Erbe)*.
Ivan Goll, *Death of Lassalle (Lassalles Tod)*, *Thomas Münzer*.
Trantner, *Arrest (Die Haft)*.
Toller, *Masses and Man (Masse-Mensch)*. [2]

2. Of the projected plays, only *At the Gate* was staged, and of the authors listed, Goll, Toller, Verhaeren and Zech have their niches in literary and theatrical history; the rest have disappeared without trace.

Time and again what we received were "plays," fragments of our times, sections of a world picture, but never the whole, the totality, from the roots to the ultimate ramifications, never the red-hot, up-to-the-minute present, which leaped to overpower you from every line of the newspapers. The theater still lagged behind the newspapers, it was never quite up to date, it never intervened actively enough in the events around it, it was still too much of a rigid art form predetermined and with a limited effect. What I had in mind was a much closer connection with journalism and with day-to-day events.

We were convinced that it was purely a matter of the script and proceeded to concoct a script of our own. Our point of departure was the topical relevance of the Russian problem to the attitude of the independent onlooker. The drama was called *Russia's Day* and was a collective effort.[3]

Proletarian Theater

In November Gorky's *Enemies* was on the program.
There will be one more performance on December 12 in the Great Hall of the Philharmonia at 3:00 P.M.
Performance dates:
> Neukölln: Sunday, 12.5., at 8.00 P.M. in Kliems Banqueting Rooms.
> East: Saturdays, 12.11 and 12.18., at 8.00 P.M. in the Parkaue School Hall.
> North: Thursday, 12.9, at 8.00 P.M. in the Pharussäle.
> Moabit: Wednesday, 12.15., at 8.00 P.M. in the Moabit Gesellschaftshaus.
> Center: Sunday, 12.12., at 3.00 P.M. at the Philharmonia, Bernburger Strasse.
> Sunday, 12.19., at 3.00 P.M. in the Beethoven Hall, Cöthener Strasse.
> Sunday, 12.26., at 3.00 P.M. in the Beethoven Hall, Cöthener Strasse.

Prices: 6 marks for nonmembers of workers' organizations, 5.50 marks if booked in advance. For members of workers' organizations 3.50 marks or 3.20 marks if booked in advance. Members of the Proletarisches Theater free! Membership cards to be shown at the box office. Unemployed persons 1 mark. New members may join at the box office or any ticket outlet.

---

3. At Piscator's request, Janos (Lajos) Barta wrote *Russia's Day* in German (of which he had an imperfect command) in five days. Piscator's collective then reworked it, with the author's agreement, and inserted allusions to the current German situation.

The Proletarisches Theater performed in halls and assembly
rooms. The masses were to be met on their own ground. Anybody
who has ever had anything to do with these rooms and their little
stages which scarcely even deserve the name, and who knows the
smell of stale beer and men's toilets, the little flags and banners left
over from the last beer festival, can imagine the difficulties which
faced us as we attempted to put over our idea of a theater for the
proletariat.

The sets were primitive, as one might imagine. But in view of
the new tasks facing the theater, these simple, hastily painted can-
vases underwent a change in significance.

In *Russia's Day* there was a map which made the political meaning of the play's setting clear from the very geographical situation.
This was no longer purely "decor," but also sketched in the social,
politico-geographical and economic implications. It had a part to
play. It obtruded into events on the stage and came to be an active
dramatic element. And at this point, the performance began to
work on a new level, a pedagogic level. The theater was no longer
trying to appeal to the audience's emotions alone, was no longer
speculating on their emotional responsiveness—it consciously appealed to their intellect. No longer mere élan, enthusiasm, rapture,
but enlightenment, knowledge and clarity were to be put across.

Our original intention was to do without middle-class actors.
Apart from a few professionals who shared our political convictions
I worked mainly with proletarians. It seemed to me important to
work with men who believed as I did, that the revolutionary
movement was the motive force, the center of their creative activity. Because of the fundamental idea of the proletarian theater, I set
great store on forming a community which shared not only human
and artistic but also political values.

The demand that is heard these days within many workers' cultural organizations, especially in the proletarian theater groups—that only proletarian actors should be used—is comprehensible and even necessary
from their point of view. But to elevate this demand into a principle for
the whole revolutionary theater in general seems in the light of my practical experience to be a mistake. The first thing we require of an actor is
characterization: the ability to bring a figure to life in terms of its inner
logic. It cannot even be said of the proletarian that he can always act a
proletarian character convincingly. But as soon as an amateur is faced
with the need to create a character from a milieu which is foreign to
him, he invariably overacts, and gets caught up in exaggerated man-

49

nerisms. The soundest convictions on the part of the actor do not guarantee that he will in fact achieve the political effect a character is intended to produce. In such a case, an actor who has worked out for himself the essentials of the role will achieve the effect we need, even if he has no "political convictions" himself. —It seems to me that there is a second, more important requirement: the actor must have an intellectual grasp of the role quite apart from the quality of his technique. The figure must be created from the inside, from its intellectual, political and social substance rather than from its external appearance. The actor must be sure of his function within the structure of the play. Only when he has comprehended this will the actor be able to play his part with objectivity, and not merely in the fashionable sense of the word; he must be objective in that he serves a common objective.

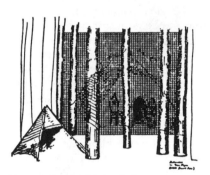

Design by Lázló Moholy-Nagy for the *Proletarisches Theater* production of Upton Sinclair's *Prince Hagen*

All the collaborators in the Proletarisches Theater dedicated themselves without reserve to the cause. The motives were not financial—we were all constantly having to do without our wages—nor personal ambition—more often than not the actors involved were not even mentioned on the program. It was other motives that kept us going as we attempted for a full year to establish our theater with no outside help. We brought out six productions (Jung, *The Kanakans* [*Die Kanaker*] and *How Much Longer, Bourgeois Justice, You Whore?* [*Wie lang noch, du Hure bürgerliche Gerechtigkeit?*]; K. A. Wittvogel, *The Cripple*; Upton Sinclair, *Prince Hagen*; Gorky, *Enemies*; *Russia's Day*; some of them major plays which took weeks of rehearsal. Some of them compared favorably with what the normal theater offered (Gorky's *Enemies*, and Jung's *The Kanakans*) or were at least as good. But nonetheless, on principle, we permitted no bourgeois critics in our theater.

The Proletarisches Theater was supposed to be supported by a theater club like the Volksbühne. Our 5,000–6,000 members were recruited mainly from the General Workers Union, the Communist Workers' Party (KAP) and the Syndicalists.

The German Communist Party (KPD), or at least its spokesmen, were so cool toward us from the beginning that some effect on the general body of their members had to be expected. Instead of recognizing that something was happening here which had the appropriate propagandistic aims, rejected the bourgeois concept of art and at least set out to lay the foundations of new (proletarian) art, the critics in the *Rote Fahne* applied standards drawn from bourgeois aesthetics to our work and demanded a standard of performance from us which tallied exactly with bourgeois notions.

"There is no basic objection to the idea of a proletarian theater [sic!] and we have to admit that a need for a proletarian stage may exist. . . . We read in the program . . . that this is not supposed to be art but propaganda. . . . The intention is to put the proletarian, Communist idea on the stage so that the effect will be propagandistic and educative. The intention is not to 'enjoy art.' To this we would like to say: In that case, why choose the name theater? Let us call a spade a spade and label it: propaganda. The name theater commits you to art and to an artistic level of performance! . . . Art is too sacred a thing to lend its name to *propagandistic concoctions!* . . . What workers need *today* [1920!] is for art to be strong. . . . Such art can even be *bourgeois* in origin, *but it must be art.*"[4]

Rote Fahne, October 17, 1920

And even after making this demand for "art," bourgeois art if necessary, they could turn round and equate art with—street fighting.

"In addition, the present acute state of the class struggle precludes contemplative and hedonistic art forms; for in such times art as truth does not find expression in word or tone, but in deeds. The way to serve the great figures we see in our past is not to mutilate them but to extract from them the elements that transcend time. It is not in the Proletarisches Theater that a new art will come into being, but in the workers' councils, the Trades Unions and the street fighting. . . ."

This continues a tradition which stemmed from classical bourgeois definitions and served the Volksbühne for decades as a guideline; even today it has not yet completely disappeared. Central to this issue is the question of eternal values in art, a question which Marxists should not even pose. Thanks to the work of Trotsky, Bogdanov, Kerzhentzev in Russia, and Diebold, Ihering,

4. Brackets and italics by E. P.

Kerr, Anna Siemsen and others in Germany[5] and not least as a consequence of our own practical work, a revision of bourgeois aesthetics has begun, which must eventually lead to the establishment of a new concept of art.

Although the proletariat felt the necessity and importance of our undertaking, it proved to be too weak economically to support it in the long run. On many evenings our houses were full to the last seat and yet the takings for the evening failed to cover our expenses (since the unemployed had, for the most part, only to show their cards to be admitted free).

Then there was the additional burden which constant, niggling police intervention imposed on our work. We were unable to get a regular license from the chief of police. No wonder, for the chief of police was—a Social Democrat (it was humiliating enough that it had to be the *Rote Fahne* which gave him the formula with which he finally rejected our application).

Resolution

During the performance of *How Much Longer, Bourgeois Justice* at the Proletarisches Theater a resolution was drawn up which protested in the strongest terms the measures taken by the chief of police against the Proletarisches Theater. The theater's customers are incensed that any theater or movie house, or club or music hall can get a license, even if it can be proved that they are presenting nothing but kitsch, while the Proletarisches Theater, a workers' enterprise which is trying to counteract the harmful influence of trashy pictures, vaudeville and the like among the workers, is to be suppressed by refusing it permission to perform.

They wish to point out to the chief of police that he has no right to forbid stage performances because of their content, that he is not competent to pronounce judgment in matters of artistic form, and that the police have to observe the regulations laid down by the Bühnengenos-

5. Bernhard Diebold (1886–1945) was regarded as the most influential critic outside Berlin. He wrote the theater notices for the middle-class, democratic *Frankfurter Zeitung*. As FZ correspondent in Berlin he took an interest in the development of Brecht and Piscator. Alfred Kerr (1867–1948) was the deadliest critic in Germany. A leftish, middle-class liberal, he lent his support as theater critic of the *Berliner Tageblatt* to Toller and Piscator. Herbert Ihering (1888–1977) was the most authoritative critic in Berlin. He regarded the theater as a political factor, a formative influence on public opinion, and his reviews in the *Berliner Börsen-Courier* between 1918 and 1933 encouraged the progressive and committed younger generation of the day. Anna Siemsen (1882–1951) was a teacher, political activist and publicist in the Weimar Republic, author of *Political Art and the Politics of Art* (*Politische Kunst und Kunstpolitik*, 1927). The two Soviet theorists' work was available in German, A. Bogdanov's *Art and the Proletariat* appearing as *Die Kunst und das Proletariat* in 1918, P. M. Kerzhentzev's *Creative Theater* as *Das schöpferische Theater* in 1922.

senschaft and the Bühnenverein,[6] who have said that a license should be issued. They further point out to Herr Richter that his taste for censorship would be better employed at the Alexanderplatz Cinema, at the vaudeville halls on the North Side, or at the nightclubs and floor shows on Friedrichstrasse and in the West End, and that he is supposed to close stage shows which blatantly indulge the sensuality of a shady public, ruthlessly exploit their performers and turn their actresses into prostitutes.

They ask Herr Richter whether he intends to refuse a license to the Proletarisches Theater if it applies under the new dispensation.

Leaflet announcing the opening of the *Proletarisches Theater*

The last performance of the Proletarisches Theater took place in April, 1921. However large or small the positive gain from this first year may have been, one result was achieved: the theater had moved into the top spot among the propaganda media at the dis-

6. The Deutsche Bühnengenossenschaft, founded in 1871, is an organization representing the interests of the employees of the German theaters. It may be compared with Equity. The Deutsche Bühnenverein was founded in 1846 by Theodor von Küstner as a combine to protect the interests of the theaters as employers. The original thirty-two members agreed not to engage actors who were under contract to another member theater.

posal of the proletarian movement. It had taken its place alongside Parliament and the press as one of the revolutionary movement's modes of communication. But at the same time the theater as an artistic institution had undergone a change of function. It now had an aim again which was socially relevant. After having functioned in a rut for a long time, isolated from the forces of the times, it had once more become a live factor with some bearing on new developments.

"What is basically new about this theater is the curious way in which reality and the play merge into one another. You often don't know whether you are in a theater or in a public meeting, you feel you ought to intervene and help, or say something. The dividing line between the play and reality gets blurred. . . . The public feels that it has been given a look at real life, that it has been watching a piece of real life and not a piece of theater . . . that the spectator is involved in the play, that everything that is going on on the stage concerns him."

Rote Fahne, April 12, 1921
(Review of Jung's *Kanakans*)

INTRODUCTION

A season elapsed before Piscator returned to the professional scene in Berlin and took over the Central-Theater, a shabby, unfashionable theater with 1,000 seats, which had been built as the Reunion Theater in 1861 in the Alte Jakob Strasse. At the turn of the century it specialized in Berlin farce, and Martin Zickel, Piscator's predecessor, had presented vaudeville, operetta and the like. Hans José Rehfisch (1891–1960), Piscator's partner in the enterprise, was a playwright in Berlin in the twenties, and a lawyer, judge and legal adviser to a film company besides. He was president of the Association of Dramatists and Composers (1931–33, and again 1951–56, after his return in 1950 to the Federal Republic). Rehfisch was arrested by the Nazis in 1933 and on his release in 1936 went via Austria to England, where he worked for the BBC. In 1945 he moved to the United States, where he taught the course for directors at Piscator's Dramatic Workshop.

Piscator is more dismissive of his work at the Central-Theater than were the critics. Herbert Ihering, reviewing Tolstoy's *The Power of Darkness*, was one of several who approved of bringing serious drama at low prices to a house associated by the public with light entertainment. A public that was uneducated *(ungebildet)* might have an unspoilt *(unverbildet)* palate for strong meat, and the plays at the Central-Theater were more important than the literary experimentation with which the Neues Volkstheater was at the time preoccupied. Ihering felt that the Tolstoy production, however, concentrated too much on naturalistic detail and missed the spirit of the original, showing "poor folk" rather than "folk possessed."

Romain Rolland's *Le Temps viendra* (1903) dealt with an episode from the Boer War and raised such issues as imperialism and its links with capitalism (Lord Clifford, a thinly veiled Lord Roberts, has an agent of a gold-mining company on his staff), concentration camps and the treatment of enemy civilians. In the second act an Italian fighting for the Boers and a Scottish sentry shoot one another, then die in one another's arms after making a plea for European brotherhood and humanity. The play was generally felt to be long-winded and rhetorical, but it had enough topical substance to touch the pacifist feelings of the audience, and was positively reviewed. Gorky's *Smug Souls*, sometimes known as *The Philistines*, was also well received, Max Osborn noting that the young company made up in fresh and infectious enthusiasm for what it lacked in technique.

In his review of *The Power of Darkness* Moritz Loeb commented that the production would have been more effective had there not been an icy blast blowing from stage to auditorium, so that the audience had to contend with hot eyes and cold noses as well as Tolstoy—which may corroborate Piscator's claim to having sold the central-heating system to pay off the theater's debts.

IV
CENTRAL-THEATER
1923/24

The only entry on the positive side of the balance sheet when the Proletarisches Theater closed down was the 4000–5000 members; but we had to offer them theatrical performances if we were to keep them.

While I was on the lookout for some way of doing this, I ran into Hans José Rehfisch who had the Central-Theater on his hands. It was to cost three million, of which one million was payable immediately and the rest in three months. We paid off the rest after two months by stripping out some old central-heating pipes and selling them to the scrap merchant on the corner. This was the time when inflation was at its height.

The previous director, Zickel, had been given a large number of members of the Volksbühne for his operettas. They left us these members at the start, but as soon as the people in charge of the Volksbühne noticed that this venture too was showing political ambitions, they withdrew them. This was my first conflict with the Volksbühne.

The venture did not follow as clear and simple a line as the Proletarisches Theater. Looking back today, I can see that this period really represented a retreat from the position I had already achieved. But only because the venture never reached its full potential. Our intention was to move toward a political message from a broad artistic base. Our repertoire included Gorky, Tolstoy and

Romain Rolland (in a sense we were drawing closer to the *O-Mensch* type of drama). But I had accepted Franz Jung's *Annemarie* for a later production, and I intended to put on a political revue.

The Central-Theater was really set up in opposition to the Volksbühne and was to be a sort of proletarian Volksbühne. This being so, we had no choice but to draw on the lower and middle sectors of the bourgeoisie, for it had been shown that the revolutionary proletariat was in no position to support a theater without the official backing of the parties.

The actors' strike of 1923, which we were the sole theatrical undertaking in Berlin to support, marked the end of a phase in the activity of the Central-Theater. The Bühnengenossenschaft had authorized us to play on, and this gave rise to certain conflicts. Gorter, in whose name our license had been issued, did not agree with our attitude and sacked the whole company, but the only result was that we had to re-engage the actors he had fired half an hour later. I directed three plays: Gorky's *Smug Souls*, Rolland's *The Time Will Come* and Tolstoy's *The Power of Darkness*. In doing these three shows I was, as it were, catching up on a stage of my development which I had missed during the Proletarisches Theater. These were thoroughly naturalistic productions in which I tried to achieve the greatest possible realism in acting and decor.

In the Autumn of 1924, the theater passed into the hands of the Rotter brothers.[1] For me the final result of these years was that I now had a firmer foothold in Berlin's theatrical life. This was balanced by the fact that I had lost what was, for me, a considerable sum of money.

1. Alfred and Fritz Rotter had three theaters in 1924. With a policy of star names in undemanding vehicles they built up a chain of nine theaters in Berlin. It collapsed in 1932.

INTRODUCTION

In 1924 the Volksbühne needed a director for Alfons Paquet's *Flags (Fahnen)*. Piscator chanced to be available and was given the job, and this was to have consequences which the management, possibly lulled into a sense of false security by the relative tameness of Piscator's work at the Central-Theater after the radical commitment of the Proletarisches Theater, cannot have foreseen. The Volksbühne had drifted through the postwar years untouched by political and social upheavals, and by 1924 had produced only four plays that could be said to face contemporary issues, Kaiser's *Gas*, Toller's *Masses and Man*, Andreyev's *King Hunger* and Lunacharsky's *Don Quixote*. It was soon to be reminded of its socialist beginnings as the contention of Siegfried Nestriepke, the general secretary from 1920 to 1933, that the Volksbühne, like art itself, was politically neutral, was challenged from the Left. In this chapter Piscator puts the case for a committed Volksbühne, basing his argument substantially on Herbert Ihering's pamphlet, *The Betrayal of the Volksbühne* (1928).

The Volksbühne was staid and institutionalized by the time it opened its theater on the Bülowplatz in 1914 with Bjornson's *When the Young Wine Blooms* (not, ominously, as planned, with Goethe's *Götz von Berlichingen*, which was postponed because of technical faults in the revolving stage). Its choice of directors was unenterprising. First Emil Lessing, formerly Otto Brahm's right-hand man, but by now a relic from the bygone age of Naturalism. Lessing failed, the war halved the membership to 35,000, and the governors turned to Max Reinhardt, whose reputation as the most successful impresario and director of the century was still at its height. Ihering points out that at this time Leopold Jessner, who was soon to make the Staatstheater one of the most progressive stages in the Weimar Republic, was available and even keen to take over the Volksbühne. From 1915 to 1918 Reinhardt had a free lease of the theater, and in return he became responsible for the repertoire and reserved half the seats for Volksbühne members. The Volksbühne am Bülowplatz became part of the Reinhardt organization, indistinguishable from its other parts. Productions were transferred from the Deutsches Theater, so the Volksbühne saw

Reinhardt's celebrated classics, *The Merchant of Venice, Hamlet, As You Like It,* Schiller's *Wallenstein* and Goethe's *Faust,* Lessing's *Minna von Barnhelm* and Molière's *Le malade imaginaire,* and his equally celebrated stars, Werner Krauss, Emil Jannings, Helene Thimig and Auguste Pünködsy and many more, though often the stars had given way to a second cast before the plays reached the Volksbühne. There were modern plays, too, like Karl Schönherr's *A People in Distress (Ein Volk in Not)* and Hofmannsthal's *Everyman,* and there were large-scale pieces like Sophocles' *Oedipus* and Vollmoeller's *Miracle* which were later to be shown on arena stages. Some productions—*The Tempest* was one—were mounted at the Volksbühne before going to Reinhardt's other theaters. The Volksbühne had come a long way since 1890 and was offering its membership culinary theater at its best. It was providing "Art for the People" in accordance with the motto carved on the facade. Yet there were many who felt it incongruous that the members should be absorbing the patriotism of Kleist's *Hermann's Battle* and the tearful symbolism of Hauptmann's *Ascension of Hannele (Hanneles Himmelfahrt)* while the munitions factories were on strike in 1918.

Reinhardt's successor at the Volksbühne was Friedrich Kayssler (1874–1945), who was director from 1918 to 1923. Kayssler had been with Brahm and was one of the first members of Reinhardt's company at the Neues Theater. He was an introverted, melancholy actor who projected himself into his parts, notably the title roles in Kleist's *Prinz Friedrich von Homburg, Faust* (alternating with Josef Kainz) and the first German *Peer Gynt.* His *Notes for Actors* show a high-minded aestheticism: "Art is a land of miracles . . . a land for free souls. . . . The actor puts himself into a state where he is unconscious of life, and then a different, artistically enlightened consciousness awakes, the consciousness of the human dream figure he wants to create, and as this dream figure he acts consciously, in the truest sense of the word." During his directorship at the Volksbühne Kayssler built up a homogenous company and presented a repertoire which was German without being chauvinistic. He produced great drama from Aeschylus to Hauptmann with pious humility, setting it in pristine purity before the receptive people. There were no gratuitous experiments.

He opened with Immermann's *Merlin,* which had waited since 1832 to be staged. It offered him a plum part as Merlin. The director was Ludwig Berger, who was to become a distinguished director and later make films in Hollywood. Kayssler gave Berger a second chance to develop his fluid, musical brand of Expressionism with minimal decor in Shakespeare's *Measure for Measure;* then Berger joined the Reinhardt organization. Kayssler also gave Jürgen Fehling, whose directing graced the German stage until 1950, his start. Fehling came to the Volksbühne as an actor and got his first chance to direct with Gogol's *Marriage* in 1919. He demonstrated a masterly touch with comedy at the Volksbühne—*Comedy of Errors,* Shaw's *Captain Brassbound's Conversion,* Raimund's *Peasant as Millionaire (Der Bauer als Millionär)*—and set the seal on his reputation with Hauptmann's *Rats (Die Ratten)* before joining Jessner's Staatstheater as a first-rank director in 1922. Kayssler's achievements were not negligible. He did not measure up to the standards of Ihering and Piscator, but he was never invited to, nor did he ever suggest he would.

Fritz Holl was a provincial actor and director who came to the Volksbühne via Stuttgart and Düsseldorf. He was a lesser man than his predecessors and a bland purveyor of culture, directing Heiberg's *Tragedy of Love* and Strindberg's *Dream Play* while Piscator sought to turn the Volksbühne into a political platform. He was director from 1923 to 1928.

V
THE POSITION OF THE VOLKSBÜHNE
From Max Reinhardt to Fritz Holl

Where did the Volksbühne stand at this point, when the intellectual problems were greater and the struggle harder than any the organized workers had ever faced before? Where was the body of drama it could have produced with the resources placed in its hands by a membership which was numbered in the thousands? Where was the gleaming blade, forged to cut the Gordian knot of capitalist contradictions and slice away its own misery? It was hanging on the wall in the best room behind the red plush sofa. "For goodness' sake, children, don't touch it; it's an heirloom. And besides, you might cut your fingers." The Volksbühne had abandoned every last vestige of aggressiveness, it had been absorbed and digested by the bourgeois theater system. The war failed to open a new era for the Volksbühne, unless it was the era of its final and irrevocable capitulation to the ruling powers.

Its public, too, had changed. The lower and middle reaches of the bourgeoisie predominated, the "bread-and-butter brigade." The workers had virtually disappeared. Only in the institution of the supervisory committee, whose members had and still have to be organized on a political or trade-union basis, did traces of the old proletarian tradition remain. It was only later, during my spell as a director at the Volksbühne, that events demonstrated how restrictive an element that body's whole attitude had become; it was using its power to combat the revolutionary elements in its own ranks, instead of trying to halt the creeping morass of the petite bourgeoisie.

The period up to 1924 saw the Volksbühne as just another of Berlin's many theaters, its plays and its style of production indistinguishable from normal, commercial show business. A pompous building was erected on Bülowplatz, with costly wood paneling in the parquet and the most up-to-date equipment behind the curtain. The one hundred and forty thousand members exceeded the capacity even of this house and additional stages had to be opened. From the outside it presents an image of power and solidity, of sound organization and purposeful cultural vitality.

To what use is all this put? The club is still dominated by the old guard who fought their first battles at the time of the Socialist Law, Naturalism and police harassment.[1] Baake, Undersecretary of State in 1918, Springer, Neft, the former plumber's apprentice who at one time had carried the entire Volksbühne around in his coat pockets, the list of members in the right-hand one, the funds in the left, and finally Nestriepke, at one time a specialist on trade unions and author of a standard work on the German trade union movement. By their sides the many-headed management committee, the artistic committee under the spiritual guidance of Julius Bab, and the supervisory committee. All these combined to determine the course of the Volksbühne. All sound men, and deeply convinced of the need for their work: "Art for the People."

Are they never beset by the merest glimmering of what they have to answer for if they raise the concept of art up like a cliff of brass? Do they ever doubt their own infallibility as, with their coarse bureaucrats' hands, they dish up to the people what they decree to be "art"? If you ask what that is, you are told: it is what elevates man, opens up for him loftier worlds, heightened experience, freedom of the soul, new emotional depths; it is what lets him forget the daily grind, and bears him up to the loftiest pinnacles of Mankind.

Can one blame this outfit, which has been "managing art" up there for twenty years in the same way as it managed the woodworkers' and metalworkers' union or sold barley and sauerkraut to the masses in coop stores—can one blame these men because their eyes

---

1. Bismarck promulgated a special law on October 21, 1878, against tendencies in the Social Democratic movement which "constituted a threat to public order." It enabled the police to disband organizations, extradite propagandists and confiscate publications. Socialists no longer had the right of assembly. This "Socialist Law" expired in 1890.

could not see beyond their own times, because they retailed art to the masses as a consumer item, believing in all good faith that hygienic packaging and low prices are everything? Should they in 1900 have thought more clearly, analyzed more acutely or been more competent sociologists than the clearest heads in the Marxist school? This epoch had never taken stock of the situation, nor seen any reason to submit its heritage to a merciless revision. Millions might stand against society, dozens of articles might daily analyze the conflicts between the classes and every last root of their relationship to one another, and yet as soon as the word *art* was spoken a reverential silence descended. The fight was being fought on all fronts, and it was only on the third front, the cultural front, that the opposing forces were still falling into one another's arms, either in ecstasy or in tears. This was sacred ground. The noise of conflict stopped at the box office. If humanity had ceased to exist everywhere else, it survived here, the one and only beatific, all-embracing church wherein all differences of class and education disappeared.

What could be more convenient than to hire the best men in the field for this consumer group? They could afford to pay for the Rotters' ideal: we use only the best butter. There were three stages along this road. Herbert Ihering in his pamphlet "The Betrayal of the Volksbühne" defined them as follows:

Reinhardt:. . . no way of bringing him into contact with the Volksbühne. Max Reinhardt represented the opposite principle. Max Reinhardt: an inspired theatrical prodigal. He delighted in the effects he created. He dwelt on the lingering taste of his own magic. Max Reinhardt was the most colorful theatrical talent of all time, intuitive, improvising effortlessly, giving and taking new ideas. Max Reinhardt put plays on for people for whom the theater was a luxury, a delicacy, the finest adornment of existence. Max Reinhardt was the genius who presided over the final culmination of grand bourgeois theater, his every achievement incomparable, his artistic versatility inexhaustible—Max Reinhardt and the Volksbühne? It was wartime of course: the artistic and technical personnel and the audience were fused into one, it became more and more difficult to raise objections. The continued existence of the Volksbühne was placed in jeopardy. The need for a supply of performances in difficult times was what seemed to make the sellout to Max Reinhardt comprehensible. But comprehensible only if those responsible had been aware that this was an act of desperation, embarrassing when it happened, and a mistake in terms of the future. An embarrassment that had to be rectified, a mistake that would have to be corrected. But the management had tasted blood. The maneuver appealed to it. It seemed significant. It was not seen as a sidetrack, but as the way ahead. So the Reinhardt years were less serious than was the blindness of the management to their consequences. This is why they were a turning point for the Volksbühne, a break in the movement, a betrayal and the first stage of decline. . . .

Kayssler:. . . The classic at the Volksbühne. To put it another way: one of the established greats. A priest of the cult of acting. A templar of the theater. Art as an act of worship, the stage as a cathedral. The public trod the sacred ground in felt slippers. Not a sound. Pray silence for the words of the Master. Gentle slumber. The silence of the grave.

Sublime funereal art—without a doubt the correct aim for a stage intended to satisfy the seething masses. A public that is used to taking part in political gatherings and floodlit sports meetings is supposed to come here to listen, to listen in silence and maintain an attitude of reverence. What an imposition! Hundreds must hold their breath, just to enable one egocentric actor to air his soul. Hundreds of spectators must suffer so that one artist's wounds may bleed. The actor as Therese von Konnersreuth[2]—what more cruel misunderstanding could befall a people's theater . . .

Holl:. . . Kayssler had at least tried to exercise some control over the great hunchback; we are now faced with the spectacle of one shapeless effort after another. The goings-on at the Volksbühne resemble the play of form and color in an abstract film. From the right-hand corner a sharp triangle shoots into a circle in the middle, the circle dents, the triangle flattens itself. Circle-management and triangle-Holl move around one another, collide, interchange, slide past one another, separate and rejoin. To what end? For the sake of an ever-changing pattern of form and color. At one moment it is *Midsummer Night's Dream,* then it is *The Dissident Czar (Der abtrünnige Zar),* then it is *Peer Gynt,* then *Volpone* and finally *Dear Augustin (Der liebe Augustin),* or even *Tragedy of Love (Tragödie der Liebe).*

The quotations above could give rise to the impression that the responsibility for the development of the Volksbühne lies with certain artistic directors or with particular authorities. These pages are intended to show the contrary. I have already indicated that neither the times nor the organization were ripe, but art was not ripe either. Where had it come to a standstill? Where had the drama come to a standstill? Where had the writers come to a standstill? The power of

2. Theresa Neumann (1898–1962), born at Konnersreuth in the Palatinate, was stigmatized during Lent, 1926, and is reputed to have had visions of the Passion every Friday, church festivals excepted, from then until her death. When he was in America in 1928, Max Reinhardt tried to get backing to film her life in Hollywood. The coming of talkies put an end to the idea.

the drama, of the producers, directors, political advisers, of the administration and, last but not least, of the public, all these powers had conspired to ensure that the Volksbühne would slumber in perpetuity. No side produced an initiative. Nestriepke himself had come to grief with a program tinged with politics in the Neues Volkstheater,[3] which the Volksbühne had taken over from Goldberg to run as an annex, and the management held this against him for a long time. "Society," to which the public who frequented the Volksbühne belonged, had no interest in revolutionary art.

But those who might have felt called upon to speak out were confronted with the plea: Give us the plays that the broad mass of our public wants to see. What is clear is that the tactic for the day was not reform but revolution: educate the public, against its will, if necessary, take it in a storm of activity by persuasion and by your own sense of mission.

We who had once regarded art as an end in itself, who had once supported art's claims to be omnipotent in comparison to the realities of the day, were now marching against that very idea under the slogan, "No more art!" We had experienced the alteration of every direction, the relativity of all styles, the destruction of all forms. Walls of piled-up bodies as the frontiers of Germany to East and West. We ourselves, hopelessly exposed to chaos year after year. Into all our longings came death. What grand, unrestricted right had we to make pronouncements, and what duty bound the others to listen in respectful silence? The generation which had to follow the passion of art and politics from one station to the next until the bitter end bore within it the ineradicable realization that form and content, art and politics are inseparable to the last fiber. The present generation, and possibly tomorrow's generation, will not realize this. But we know. The synthesis of art and politics implies final responsibility, implies placing every means, including art, at the service of the highest human aims. Once this had been realized, there was no way out. The tables at which a potbellied age had indulged itself, without asking where the dishes were coming from and what was in them, were overthrown. Even if we found everything comprehensible (without excusing it) there was no way out from now on. The Volksbühne had to make up its mind where it belonged, and from that time on it, and the men at its head, bore the full burden of responsibility.

3. The Volksbühne used the Neues Volkstheater in the Köpenicker Strasse as an annex from 1921 to 1922. The first "special literary production" there was P. Zech's *Brotherhood (Verbrüderung)*. This was followed by a series of forgotten plays by forgotten names, the best-known M. Brod and W. Schmidtbonn.

INTRODUCTION

The next three seasons made Piscator's name in the Berlin theater. He directed eleven plays at the Volksbühne and one at the Staatliches Schauspielhaus, and he staged two mass revues for the Communist Party, with occasional free-lance productions in Berlin, Hamburg and Munich besides. His first play at the Volksbühne was *Flags* by Alfons Paquet (1881–1944), a respected journalist, essayist and travel writer whose journeys had taken him as far afield as Siberia and the United States and who had been one of the first Germans to visit the Soviet Union, where he saw Meyerhold's work in Moscow in 1919. Paquet was a believer in the brotherhood of man who took a sympathetic interest in all progressive political movements. Latterly he lived as a free-lance writer in Frankfurt, where he was killed in an air raid.

Flags was a historical play with topical appeal. It was based on the abortive campaign for the eight-hour day among immigrant workers in Chicago in 1886 which culminated in the Haymarket Affair. A shorter working day had been a political issue in Germany since the end of the war, and in December 1923 the Marx administration, under pressure from the unions and the SPD, had passed legislation establishing the eight-hour day, but the employers' lobby and the Deutsche Volkspartei ensured that it had so many loopholes that it remained the exception rather than the rule. The play touched a nerve, though the program, with typical Volksbühne caution, stated that it was not intended to further any party policy, and that persons viewing it through partisan eyes would be disappointed.

Paquet's script began with a "Prologue on the Puppet Stage," in which the puppeteer sketched in the characters and functions of the principal figures in verse couplets. Piscator turned this into a *Moritat*. Slides of the historical figures were projected on a screen behind the proscenium arch while a balladeer (Fritz Hannemann) with a pointer stood below and sang the comments, lines like (Judge Gary):

> Calvinist, psalms fill his Sunday hours,
> Moloch yet, who living flesh devours.

There were also two projection screens mounted at either side of the proscenium arch on a level with the gallery, where slides were projected to comment and enlarge upon the action. Piscator, with Paquet's enthusiastic concurrence, planned to use film for the play, but technical problems intervened. Piscator called these screens "blackboards, for purposes of reporting, and documentation." Between scenes captions were projected in the manner of the intershot titling of silent movies, the court scene (scene 12) being entitled "Condemned to death." There were exclamations, too. "The police threw the bombs themselves" flashed up as the framed men were convicted. Newspaper cuttings and telegrams were projected to make events seem more real, and pictures of a menacing revolver or the departure of the factory boss were used to make the ambivalence of certain events clear. Piscator's intention was to fuse audience and stage action and turn the performance into a public meeting, but the reviews suggest that both public and critics were perplexed by this first attempt to combine film and live action. The one exception was Alfred Döblin, who discerned the beginnings of a new type of theater.

> "The open, folksy character of the whole thing was clear. This is not a play for aesthetes. Here one man's feelings are appealing to the feelings of others. . . . These imperfect achievements gave me great pleasure— and not just me but the general public."
>
> (*Leipziger Tageblatt*, 6.11.24)

Apart from the use of projections, the production style was realistic. City noises and drums offstage were used during scene changes.

The subject of *Flags* is Brechtian (cf. *St. Joan of the Stockyards*): tycoons and proletariat, graft, corruption and exploitation in Chicago. The theme is class justice. Cyrus MacShure, the city boss, bribes the police to plant a bomb and frame the labor leaders during a demonstration. These men are then tried and convicted by a prejudiced, petit bourgeois jury of clerks and managers before Judge Gary, an establishment, law-and-order man. Piscator stated in 1963 that the author had assembled the events objectively into a dramatic comic strip, thus justifying its subtitle, *An Epic Drama*. The script has twenty loosely linked, naturalistically written scenes with the characters clearly divided into good and bad and the action predictable from the outset. The first and second acts mainly depict the struggle between labor and capital in public places (demonstrations, newspaper offices, police headquarters, MacShure's offices), but the third act, mainly in prison, slides into sentimentality. In the

68

seventeenth scene the four condemned men take leave of their families and friends. Lingg, a German immigrant, reminisces about the green hills of Hesse before biting into an apple-size bomb his wife chances to have kept in her handbag. Engel takes leave of his daughter, telling her he has to take a long trip and asking her to be a good girl while he is away. Spiess, the socialist journalist, rejects the ministrations of Rev. Bolton and is then visited by Nina von Zahnd, a society girl who falls for him, then marries him in absentia, with his written concurrence. She even gate-crashes Mac-Shure's celebration party to take up subscriptions for an appeal fund. Nina enters the cell, expensively dressed, bearing roses, and wishing she could be an angel of beauty to please him. Spiess affects to cold-shoulder her and she exits calling him a thankless case, whereupon he comments, "Thankless! Good, she's cured." The sentimental slide was then arrested by a hanging scene onstage, when the men speak only a few laconic words. The final scene at the cemetery made it clear that this reversal for the workers was but a momentary interruption of the march of social progress.

The opportunity to direct Paquet's *Flags* gave Piscator his first chance to work on a well-equipped stage. The Theater am Bülowplatz with its 1,800 seats was among the biggest in Berlin. The stage could be raked mechanically and adjustable rostra were built into the 20-meter revolving stage. The resident designer, Edward Suhr, built a composite revolving set for the play's nineteen scenes *(Photo 10)*. (Piscator cut the first scene of the script but otherwise contented himself with expunging the anarchist lines in accordance with communist policy of cultivating a respectable image of the proletariat to counter tales of revolutionary atrocities which had wide currency in the Weimar Republic.) Paul Fechter remarked that the set scarcely stopped revolving. It had been divided into segments by low, cutoff walls behind which was a backdrop of towering, reeling city blocks. A deep vista through streets would alternate with a closed courtroom scene. For the eleventh scene there were two levels, the conspirators meeting in a cellar while police spies listened on the floor above, the lights picking-out the levels alternately from the overall gloom in which the events were plunged. Two striking effects were singled out by the critics. The last scene of act 2 and the first of act 3 (12 and 13) were run together, so the audience heard the verdict on the five accused, heard their last words of contempt for the proceedings, then saw the court emptied as a drop fell behind the three judges who were standing downstage. Three attendants divested them of their robes to leave them standing in white tie and tails, ready to turn to Mac-

Shure's cynical celebration banquet which was revealed in progress as the drop behind them went up. The positive message of the play was in the finale. Downstage a young worker read the funeral oration, while about a hundred extras behind the scenes chanted responses. In the center of the stage stood a coffin which floated up on the hands of twenty-five extras concealed in the catafalque. On the cue, "Flag of scarlet silk, emblazoned with golden emblems, with hammer and sickle, dear and holy flag," huge red flags sank from the flies, and the curtain fell on the word "Freedom."

Flags marked the start of Piscator's attempt to mechanize the theater and expand its range as an instrument for conveying information and as a weapon for propaganda. Reflecting in 1963 that it was in this production that he began to develop what later became known as epic theater, he went on to define his aims at the time:

> "Briefly, it was about the extension of the action and the clarification of the background of the action, that is to say, it involved the continuation of the play beyond the dramatic framework. A didactic play *(Lehrstück)* was developed from the spectacle-play *(Schaustück)*. This automatically led to the use of techniques from areas which had never been seen in the theater before."

The public and critics, as has been observed, had difficulty in accepting the new mixed media, but the production as a whole gripped the emotions of the audience. Even Monty Jacobs, who had no hesitation in finding the play a rabble-rousing potboiler, recognized the director's achievement:

> "Paquet's hand quivers uncertainly, but Piscator's fingers have a firm grip. The Volksbühne was favored by a flash of insight when it hired a young director who had the power to face the task. He pulled the loose sequence of nineteen scenes together, and, supported by Edward Suhr's sets, he created the atmosphere of Chicago, an atmosphere of oppression and joylessness. He let the city thunder behind the scenes, he freed the humanity of the speakers from the enveloping verbiage. Only the superfluous gimmick of the projections showed that Piscator still has to steel himself to surmount the flaws in his writers."
> (*Vossische Zeitung*, 5.27.1924)

As a director, Piscator had arrived.

VI
FLAGS

Art Desecrated
by Leo Lania

Some days ago a French publisher's catalogue came into my hands
which listed last year's most successful literary works. To my astonishment I observed that, in the classical land of the novel, social-critical
pamphlets and journalistic reports predominated at this time. Among the
books which had the highest circulation and biggest impact we find,
among others, *Prisoners' Hell (Die Hölle der Sträflinge)*, an account of
the prisons in Cayenne by Londres, *Cocaine*, a trip around the dens of
vice among the Paris nightclubs, *Interviews with Clowns*, etc.
"Americanization" is now beginning to impress its stamp on French literature, too, and one can see that the general decline in interest in novels
and poetry, in so-called "pure" art, about which German publishers are
complaining, is not fortuitous and is not a result of economic conditions
in Germany, but has its causes deep in the process of social change
which we are all witnessing.

Clearly the average reader today no longer has the leisure and inner
composure to read thick novels. But what is more important is that he is
too closely entangled in the web of the daily struggle to be able to escape
to the inadequate island haven of "pure art." The times we live in today
have people more firmly in their grip than any past age, and these times
are more exciting, romantic, colorful and dramatic than anything the
poetic imagination could dream up. Social revolution is on the agenda
and makes insistent claims on our attention. There is no way in which
you can fail to see or hear it. It dominates the hour. It flushes the pale
dreamers and unworldly fantasts out of the remotest hideaways, knocks
the pens from the fingers of professional poets and writes the mighty,
awful and heroic drama of our lives itself. The de-romanticization of art

71

has prepared the way for the romanticization of everyday life, and the way leads from "pure art" to journalism, to reporting, from poetry to truth, from the invention of sentimental fables or dabbling in the secrets of psychology to insistent, true-to-life descriptions of the exciting mysteries of prisons, factories, offices, machines, added values and the class struggle.

At the Berlin Volksbühne a drama is now being performed which, in spite of the heat of summer, has full houses every night, while all the other theaters are empty and abandoned. It is called *Flags*, and its author, Alfons Paquet, is widely known as an essayist and sensitive writer of travel books. *Flags*, which was written in 1918, is a direct response to the Revolution, a loosely connected series of scenes that radiate the heat and the stirring rhythms of those days. The play is set in Chicago in the eighties and deals with the well-known anarchist trials, which at the time sent a storm of indignation through the whole civilized world.

At that time the workers in Chicago struck the first blow for the eight-hour day and, thanks to the sympathy which their struggle against the trust magnates aroused, captured an important position, only to be thrown back immediately by the combined offensive of the police and the capitalists. Cyrus MacShure, the boss of Chicago, with 10,000 workers under his rule, bought out the police and the justiciary and infiltrated *agents provocateurs* into a peaceful workers' meeting where they staged a bombing, at which point the strike leaders were arrested and condemned to death by Judge Gary. This was for Gary the start of an honorable career which took him to the presidency of the American Steel Trust, where to this day he is working for the benefit and prosperity of American capitalism.

A drama from the lives of the workers, the kind of thing that has happened almost annually since then in every country, to the point where we are hardened to such happenings. But precisely for this reason the Chicago workers' struggle has become a symbol with general validity, so that this play enacts the struggle, the grief and suffering of the workers in our times.

In the opening minutes, comparisons with *Danton* and *The Weavers* spring to mind.[1] These comparisons are not only sterile, they are quite misplaced. The difference between this play and these works is that here we are not given a picture of a specific milieu, nor a psychological analysis of the hero. The author consciously avoids any kind of artistic treatment and lets the naked facts speak for themselves. The play has no "heroes" and no "problems," it is one long epic of the struggle of the proletariat for freedom, it is a play with a message. But because the author is a poet, a fighter in the cause of truth and justice, warm life pulses through the figures in the play, there are people with flesh and

---

1. Hauptmann's *Die Weber*, about the Silesian weavers' revolt in 1844, had been directed by K. Martin in 1921, Romain Rolland's *Danton*, which deals with Robespierre's elimination of his political rival Danton in 1794, by Reinhardt in 1920, both productions at the Grosses Schauspielhaus.

blood on the stage. And for that reason this "dramatic novel" *is* a work of art.

The production at the Volksbühne was designed to bring out a clear, simple line. The director had had the original and happy idea of using film to back up the play. There was a prologue at the start of the show which gave character sketches of the workers' leaders, the trust magnate and the police officers, while at the same time pictures of these characters were projected on the screen. The effect of the titles which were flashed on the screen to link scenes, as they are in the movies, was less happy. The director fortunately avoided any kind of Expressionistic experiment and managed his army of fifty-six actors excellently well, if one makes allowances for the technical problems of scene-shifting. The effect was profound and prolonged.

If the workers came across less convincingly than the middle-class characters in the production, it was the fault of the writer, not of the actors. This is where the only flaw in the play emerged, a flaw which is to be found in almost every play about the lives of the workers. With the exception of Sinclair, no writer has yet been able to create true-to-life industrial workers. *Jimmy Higgins* is the supreme achievement in this field. The lumpen proletarians and vagabonds that Gorky introduced into literature, and Hauptmann's miserably deprived weavers, are individualized, are removed from the sphere of the typical into the human sphere, because they are single beings, individual entities, so that the writer can get inside their feelings. The modern worker, when he is put on the stage in his uniform condition, has a disconcerting effect. You get "the radical," and "the doubting Thomas" and "the revolutionary," instead of men with all their weaknesses and virtues and contradictions. But perhaps the reason for this is that the average worker has not yet awakened to a life of his own, still lives his life today as a small part of the larger masses, and will only develop his own individuality fully when these masses have successfully concluded their great struggle for freedom.

When I wrote this article in the summer of 1924, only a few months had passed since the spectre of inflation flitted through Germany; the ground was not yet firm under our feet. Economic insecurity had an effect on people's minds. New slogans had been devised which seemed to obviate the need to give a precise meaning to the bright new concepts. We had *Americanism, Tempo, New Objectivity, Reportage.* Words, words. They fluttered up, got into circulation, and we used them, pleased to have anything at all that we could lay hold of, that we could rely on, but quite soon these new concepts became as worn as old pennies—they became catch phrases before they had time to develop into concepts.

To anticipate this development in those days under the shadow of inflation was impossible. *Flags* was a clear and unambiguous sally into unexplored territory. This is true both for the drama and for the theater. I felt this and tried to formulate my ideas in the article in the *Wiener Arbeiterzeitung.* But only today, five years later, is it possible to check the accuracy of my impressions at the time, and to compare my formulations with the experiences of the years which have since passed.

Flags as a drama represented the first consistent attempt to get away from the established pattern of dramatic action and put the epic progression of events in its place. Seen in this light, *Flags* is the first consciously epic drama—and it is only logical that the play's subtitle should state this. Having said this, we will refrain for the moment from assessing how successfully Paquet fulfilled all the requirements of epic drama as we know it today from the works of Döblin,[2] Joyce, Dos Passos (in the domain of the novel) and from Brecht and the works staged at the *Piscator-Bühne*. (To give an example, the principle was most successfully put into practice by us in *Schwejk* and in the first act of *Boom*.)

In his broad epic presentation of the subject Paquet aimed consistently at baring the roots of the case. The production had a direct and powerful impact, people forgot that the case was twenty years old and related it directly to present-day events; this "general validity" was achieved only because the production stripped the subject of its particular historical associations and emphasized the social and economic background. So *Flags* was in a sense the first Marxist drama, and this production was the first attempt to make the forces of materialism tangible and comprehensible. At this point analogies to *Storm over Gotland* and *Rasputin* become apparent.

The theoretical significance of the first use of projections was something which I could not fully grasp at the time. It was a mode of expanding the subject on the stage and illuminating the background of the action and I thought it was an interesting arabesque; it was only after a few years of practical work that I came to realize that the titles between the scenes, which I had felt were "less happy," were in fact the most important aspect of this production. (By this I do not mean that it always takes ten years to determine exactly what is important about a production or an artistic event—it can sometimes take longer.)

The screen on either side of the stage, where Piscator ran a commentary to point out the message of the play, represented a didactic principle which was developed and perfected in later productions. The film in *Storm over Gotland*, in *Hoppla*, the calendar in *Rasputin*—they all tie in with the screens which were used for the first time in *Flags*: not only as a pedagogic device, but as a means of lifting the whole drama from its original level and making it a play with a message on a higher level.

And did people get the message from this message-play? Theories usually come after the event. Yet, like all theories which fail to grasp the social implications in their totality, but set the problem of form above content, the statement that "epic drama" is the only currently valid form of drama can be accepted only with reservations. Since everybody who subscribes to the idea has a different approach, everybody understands something else by it. Alfred Döblin wrote the following about *Flags*:

2. Alfred Döblin (1878–1957), experimental novelist, remembered for *Berlin Alexanderplatz*.

"Paquet intentionally dramatized the anarchist rising in Chicago in such a way that the final picture stood somewhere between drama and prose fiction. It is a mistake to call this a defect. You cannot reproach a mule because it is neither a donkey nor a horse, it can only be bad if it is a bad mule. Paquet is not the first man to explore this intermediary area of the drama-novel. A whole group of youthful dramas of recent years falls into this category. Each one evolved its own special form, and each was dismissed as a mongrel. This intermediary form always occurs where an icy feeling prevents the author from being involved in the fate of his characters or in the course of the action. Plays with a message will then tend to be dramatic novels and the flame of inspiration will be epic rather than lyrical. This is—I hasten to add—not the only way in which dramatic novels occur.

I should like to think that this no-man's-land is very fertile: it will always be sought by those who have something to say or something to show, and who are not at ease with the stage at which drama has now petrified. This form in turn petrifies all dramatic composition. At the time of Aeschylus the drama-novel was still the matrix from which drama sprang, and it can be so again. In our times, the film, the dramatic narrative in pictures—who can find an adequate name for it?—points in this direction."

In 1924 Alfred Döblin saw this new direction in *Flags*. He saw that "this new mode, which was separate from conventional, merely artistic form, was form and spirit of our spirit."

In 1929 in his essay "The Construction of Epic Works" Döblin takes this to its logical conclusion: "I . . . consider the liberation of the epic from the book to be difficult and yet necessary, especially from the point of view of language. The book is the death of real language. The most important formative forces within language elude an epic writer who does nothing but write. 'Down with books' has long been my slogan, but I see no clear path for the present-day writer of epics to follow, unless it be the path to a—New Stage."

I was now able to develop a type of direction which, years later, was proclaimed by others to be "epic theater."[3] What was it all about? Briefly, it was about the extension of the action and the clarification of the background to the action, that is to say it involved a continuation of the play beyond the dramatic framework. A didactic play was developed from the spectacle-play. This automatically led to the use of stage techniques from areas which had never been seen in the theater before. It had started, as has been mentioned, in the Proletarisches Theater. At the Volksbühne I could see what tremendous possibilities the theater offered if you had the courage to extend your forms of expression. I had broad

3. The following passage was interpolated in the revised edition of *Das Politische Theater*, Hamburg, 1963.

projection screens erected on either side of the stage. During the prologue at the beginning, in which the play was introduced with character sketches of the figures who were to appear, photographs of the persons in question were projected on the screen. Throughout the play I used the screens to connect the separate scenes by projecting linking texts. To my knowledge, it was the first time that projections had been used in this way in the theater. Apart from this I restricted myself to staging the play, which had a cast of fifty-six, as clearly and objectively as possible.

All the ingredients of success seemed to be there, and today I cannot even say exactly why it was that, two days before the performance, the bits still refused to fit together. During the dress rehearsal the space around me became more and more empty. The people who had pleaded to be allowed to be present at the great event disappeared one after the other. It became more and more lonely around me. The techniques I have mentioned not only failed to convince, they were completely without effect, and the actors went from bad to worse, so that when the curtain fell I took a slip of paper and wrote on it the word *shit*. Then I took my briefcase and went up the spiral staircase until I heard voices raised behind a door. It was Holl, the artistic director, the managing director Neft and my friend Paul Henckels, the actor who had been so successful at the *Central-Theater* in my production of Romain Rolland's *The Time Will Come*. I only heard one sentence: "This is the worst thing we've ever done! What made you take this man on? Simply awful!" With determination I strode in, laid my promptbook on the table and said, "Gentlemen, I share your opinion." I told them I had prepared the play thoroughly but had obviously failed to achieve what I had in mind, and consequently wished to resign as director. This was turned down, as was my second suggestion, namely, to postpone the first night for a week. I was seized with desperation and declared that when the day's performance was over I would rehearse the whole show with all the technical apparatus until the curtain went up on the first night. This was granted. I went back downstairs to the stage and spoke to the actors who were dressing, explaining my plan to them. They agreed, and so we rehearsed from one in the morning until the next evening, in fact, until after the time the curtain was scheduled to rise. So there was a postponement of the first night, although it was only half an hour.

As the performance went on the audience's approval became more and more noisy. And after three large flags of mourning had been lowered from the flies over the final scene, a thunder of applause broke loose which was almost revolutionary in character. For Paquet, for me, and for everybody involved the evening was a major success. In the review I have already mentioned—and it was typical of many—Lania wrote:

> "At the Berlin Volksbühne a drama is now being performed which, in spite of the heat of summer, has full houses every night, while all the other theaters are empty and abandoned. . . . *Flags*, which was written in 1918, is a direct response to the Revolution, a loosely connected series of scenes that radiate the heat and the stirring rhythms of those days. . . . The effect was profound and prolonged."

Much as I enjoyed my personal success—whatever people might say against me, this was something like a breakthrough for me at one of Berlin's major theaters—it was the success of the new venture which really pleased me. Once again the way ahead seemed clearer, a way which would lead to political drama and to the hotly disputed technical revolution in the theater. But we were not there yet. The first thing I turned my hand to was more political agitation by theatrical means.

Design by Edward Suhr for Gorky's *The Lower Depths*

INTRODUCTION

The Communist Party was now beginning to overcome its reservations about Piscator's work and commissioned him to write a political revue with Felix Gasbarra (1895–), a journalist whom Piscator had recognized as a combative kindred spirit on meeting him in the back room of an East End bar in 1920. Gasbarra published *Prussian Walpurgis Night,* "a grotesque puppet-play in *Knüppelreim,*" as the ninth in the Malik Publishing House's *Collection of Revolutionary Stage Works* in 1922, and he was an editor of the Communist satirical paper, *Der Knüppel (The Cudgel),* whose moving spirits were George Grosz and John Heartfield. Gasbarra was Piscator's mentor, an orthodox Communist placed in his entourage by the party to keep him in line. Together they compiled the *Red Revue,* which was first performed on November 22, 1924. It was then repeated fourteen times in different parts of Berlin before the Reichstag elections on December 7.

The May elections in 1924, overshadowed by deflation and unemployment, produced a swing to parties of the extreme Left and Right. The Communist membership of the Reichstag rose from seventeen to sixty-two, and the National Socialist Freedom Movement, standing for the first time, took thirty-two seats, of which ten went to Hitler's Nazis. By December the first dollar loan under the Dawes Plan had produced a drop in unemployment and a palpable upturn in the economy. Knowing this would benefit the center, the Communists campaigned vigorously, but could retain only forty-five seats.

The text of the *Red Revue* is lost, but its general lines can be reconstructed. The theme was class injustice in Germany, accompanied by a prophecy of the eventual triumph of communism. Edmund Meisel's overture was a rousing medley of communist songs. As the lights dimmed, an argument developed in the audience. The two contending parties, a wholesale butcher and a pieceworker, argued their way down the aisle and onto the stage, where they remained throughout the show, commenting on the successive sketches from the bourgeois and proletarian standpoints, respectively. Nightclubs and champagne bars were set against workers' slums, paunchy capitalists and braided porters against limbless veterans, profiteers against the exploited, poverty against plenty. In one sketch a high-court judge sentenced a Communist candidate to prison. Slides of interiors of German prisons were shown. A team of workers swinging Indian clubs symbolized the vitality of the proletariat. In another sketch, "The Electoral Boxing Match," pairs of bourgeois (i.e., non-Communist) politicians, Wilhelm Marx and Noske, Ludendorff and Stresemann, sparred with one another until Max Hölz, a professional agitator who led several Communist risings in the early twenties, climbed into the ring and quickly knocked out the other contenders. A sketch entitled "The Revenge of the Bourgeoisie" showed slides and film of Noske's brutal military suppression of the workers in 1919 *(Photo 9)*. It was followed by rousing speeches from actors representing Lenin, Liebknecht and Rosa Luxemburg, whereupon the whole assembly stood and sang the "Internationale" together. This was (like the appearance of Lenin) Piscator's artistic signature. It was used again as a finale in *In Spite of Everything* and as a theme tune in *The Robbers*, and if the writers omitted it, the audience spontaneously put it back *(Hoppla)*.

The presentation of propaganda had become more sophisticated since the days of the Proletarisches Theater. Music, songs, acrobatics, projections, statistics, instant drawings and short sketches were used to put the message across. The *Red Revue* established a standard for agitprop revues against which all subsequent productions were measured.

The music was by Edmund Meisel (1874–1930), soon to become a prominent composer of musical scores for films with *Berlin, Symphony of a City* and the German releases of the *Battleship Potemkin* and *October* to his credit. Meisel pioneered special scores for specific films. *Potemkin* was his masterpiece, and his music was recorded with choir and orchestra, the subtitles being shouted as voice-over. Of *Potemkin*, Kurt London wrote:

"His expressionistic style, turning first and foremost on rhythm, was many stages in advance of the films for which he composed. His musical accompaniment for the Russian film *Battleship Potemkin* marked him out as a pioneer in film music. The film made a deep impression wherever it was shown, but there is no doubt that this impression was to no small extent enhanced by the music. It is significant that several European countries which allowed the film itself to pass the censor forbade

79

the music to be played. Its really provocative rhythm was liable to lash the revolutionary instincts latent in audiences to boiling point."

(*Film Music*, London, 1936)

Meisel was Piscator's musical director at the Theater am Nollendorfplatz from 1927 to 1928.

VII
R.R.R.

R.R.R.: Red Riot Revue. Proletarian political revue. Revolutionary revue.

Not a revue like those Haller, Charell and Klein were doing, with shows imported from America and Paris.

Our revues came from a different source. Their predecessors were the evenings of entertainment I had staged with the International Workers Aid (I.A.H.)[1] That was the positive source. Apart from that, the form of the revue coincided aptly with the formal disintegration of bourgeois drama. In a revue there is no unity of action, effects are lifted from any areas which can be made to connect with the theater; the revue is untrammeled in its structure and at the same time quite naïve in the directness of its appeal. *Flags*, which we had chopped up into a series of separate scenes, was already a revue in its way.

The idea of using this form for purely political ends had long been in my mind; with a political revue I hoped to achieve propagandistic effects which would be more powerful than was possible with plays, where the ponderous structure and problems tempt you to psychologize and constantly erect barriers between the stage and

---

1. The International Workers Aid was set up in 1921 at Lenin's instigation. The committee was to organize relief for the Soviet Union, which had been devastated by drought and civil war. The organization eventually became a kind of European-Soviet friendship society.

the auditorium. The revue offered a chance of "direct action" in the theater.

Each number was to be hammered home; the theme of the evening was to be shown not by one example, but by dozens: *Ceterum censeo, societatem civilem esse delendam!* ["But I think civil society must be destroyed"] There were to be variations on the theme, so that it could escape no one. To this end we needed variety. The audience had to be brought face to face with the examples, and these had to provoke question and answer, they had to be concentrated—a quick-fire series of examples had to be brought to bear, and driven into the columns of figures. Thousands are learning this, you should too! Do you think it concerns only the others? No, it concerns you, too! This is typical of the society in which you live, you cannot escape it—here it is again, and here again! And this was to be done by quite unscrupulous exploitation of all the possibilities: music, songs, acrobatics, instant cartoons, sport, projections, films, statistics, sketches, speeches.

The Reichstag elections of 1924 provided us with a point of departure. The Communist Party asked for a public performance. (The notion had begun to catch on. The masses wanted to see a slice of life with their own eyes at their conventions, and the Party had grasped the need to use the stage as an instrument for propaganda.) I compiled the text with Gasbarra, who was sent to me by the Party. We put together old material and wrote new material to go with it.

Much of it was crudely assembled and the text was quite unpretentious, but this very fact enabled us to add up-to-the-minute material right to the end.

" 'Red Revue.' The masses made their pilgrimage to it. When we arrived, hundreds were standing on the street trying in vain to get in. Workers were fighting for seats. In the auditorium everything was packed full and the air was thick enough to knock you over. But the faces shone as the audience waited at a fever pitch for the show to begin. Music. Lights out. Silence. In the audience two men were fighting, upsetting those around them. The dispute moved to the central aisle, the lights went up on the stage and the two belligerents climbed up on to the stage in front of the curtain. They are two workers discussing their positions. A man in a top hat joins them. Bourgeois. He has his own view of life and invites the two men to spend the evening with him. Curtain up! Scene One. The points are made one after the other. Ackerstrasse — Kurfürstendamm. Slum dwellings — champagne bar. The porter glittering in blue and gold — the beggar who has lost his limbs in the war. Potbellies and heavy watch chains — a man selling matches, another collecting cigarette butts. Swastika — assassin — yes, we have no bananas — national anthem. And between the scenes: screens, movies, columns of statistics, pictures! New scenes. The crippled begger is thrown out by the porter. A crowd in front of the restaurant. Workers force an entry and wreck the joint. The public joins in. And how they whistle, scream, rage, shout encouragement, wave their arms and participate in spirit . . . unforgettable!"

Jakob Altmeier, in "How It Began:
The Story of the Piscator Theater,"
Frankfurter Zeitung, April 1, 1929

The pedagogic aspect of the *Red Revue* was given a new theatrical twist. Nothing was left unclear, or ambiguous and without effect, the connection with current political events was pointed out at every turn. The "political discussions" which at the time of the elections dominated conversations in factories, workshops and on the street had to be incorporated into the action on the stage. We took the figures of the *compère* and *commère* from the old operetta and changed them into the typical "Proletarian" and the typical "Bourgeois." Then we put them together in a loosely constructed plot where they kept the show moving and interpreted the individual scenes.

In developing the projections, I worked in the same direction as I had done in *Flags*.

The music had a particularly important function. And here I must point out that in Edmund Meisel, whom I had previously met on several occasions at functions staged by the International Workers Aid, we had found a musician who knew what it was all about: the musical line had not only to illustrate and provide a background, it had also to pursue its own independent and conscious political line: music as a positive element in the drama.

"Tens of thousands of proletarians, men and women, have seen this revue in their own districts in the last fourteen days: in the Pharussäle, in the Hasenheide, in Lichtenberg, in the Sophiensäle and in other big meeting rooms in Berlin. . . . The effect of the scenes on the expectant and excited audiences is without parallel. Such mass appreciation—indeed, mass participation—is found in no other theater."

Franz Franklin in the *Rote Fahne*, December 8, 1924.

The revue made its mark. But in spite of this and even with the lowest possible outlay for each evening (500 marks, I think), it was a financial failure. The huge numbers of unemployed, the poor financial organization and so on, prevented the Party from putting the revue company on a permanent footing.

But the immediate consequence was the emergence of the proletarian groups which now formed all over the country.[2] The *Red
Revue* became a permanent concept in the arsenal of agitation and
has remained in the movement to the present day.[3]

2. Hundreds of theater groups have since sprung up all over Germany, using the
cabaret-revue form for political agitation, sometimes with great success: among
others, *Rotes Sprachrohr* (The Red Megaphone), *Rote Blusen* (The Red Shirts), *Rote
Raketen* (The Red Rockets), *Die Nieter* (The Riveters), *Galgenvögel* (The Jailbirds),
etc. [E. P., 1929]

The visit of the "Blue Shirts" from the Soviet Union in 1926 seems to have
provided as important a stimulus as Piscator's activities to the agitprop movement.
Rotes Sprachrohr was attached to the KJVD (Young Communists of Germany). It
was a Berlin group, as were the *Rote Raketen* and the *Rote Blusen*. *Die Nieter* were
founded in Hamburg after the visit of the "Blue Shirts." The actors were recruited
from the workers at the Blohm & Voss shipyards, which accounts for the group's
name.

3. At this point, Piscator in 1963 incorporated chapter ix of the 1929 version
(entitled "The Proletarian Amateur Play") into chapter vii. As a result, chapter x of the
original edition becomes chapter ix in the revised second edition and the numbering
of the following chapters is changed accordingly.

Erwin Piscator's family history.

Top right: Erwin Piscator aged 35.

Center: As a child.

Below: Johannes Piscator's Bible translations and commentaries (about 1600).

Erwin Piscator 1915-18.

In Flanders.

In hospital at Lophem (Belgium).

In the trenches at Ypres.

Proletarisches Theater 1920.

Above: Scene from *Russia's Day* Designer: John Heartfield.

Right: Scene from *The Cripple* by K. A. Wittvogel. In the title part: Erwin Piscator (seated).

R.R.R. (Red Riot Revue) 1924.

Scene of execution by firing squad.

Flags by Alfons Paquet.   Volksbühne 1924.

Model for *Flags* Designer: Edward Suhr.

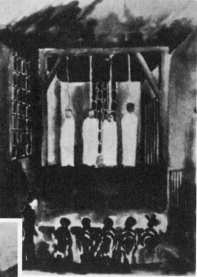

Design by Edward Suhr (execution scene in Act 4).

Final scene in *Flags* (flags lowered over the coffin from the flies).

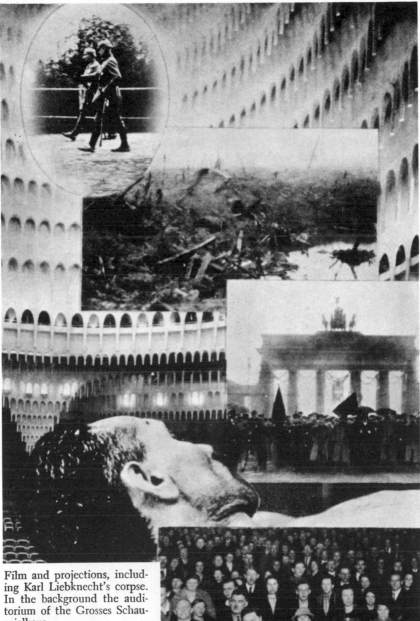

Film and projections, including Karl Liebknecht's corpse. In the background the auditorium of the Grosses Schauspielhaus.

Right: Spectators with Edmund Meisel at the conductor's stand.

Tidal Wave by Alphons Paquet.   Volksbühne 1926.

Piscator with Hübler-
Kahla filming exteriors
for *Tidal* Wave.

Scene from Act 1 (sale of St. Petersburg to the
English).

Combination of film and
live scene.

The Drunken Ship by Paul Zech.   Volksbühne 1926.

Background projection (cartoons by George Grosz).   Room in Paris.

Cáfe in Aden.

Jail in France.

Sails on the Horizon by Rudolf Leonhard.   Volksbühne 1926.

Designer: Traugott Müller

"Praktikabel": Ship on the revolving stage.

The Lower Depths by Maxim Gorky.

Designer: Edward Suhr

INTRODUCTION

Eight months after the *Red Revue* Piscator and Gasbarra were invited to stage a political piece for the Communist Party's annual convention. They had been preparing a large-scale, open-air revue on the theme of revolution from Roman times to the present, a kind of mass festival *(Massenfestspiel)* of the type first seen in the Soviet Union in 1919 (e.g., Meyerhold's *Storming of the Winter Palace*, 1920). The Leipzig Workers' Educational Institute (ABI) had taken up the idea in Germany and commissioned *Spartacus* for the 1920 trade-union convention, and Josef von Fielitz had marshaled 900 performers in Roman dress on the grass and on specially built steps and rostra in a cycle stadium in front of 50,000 spectators. *Poor Conrad (Der arme Konrad)*, then Ernst Toller's *Szenen aus der französischen Revolution, War and Peace (Krieg und Frieden)* and *Awakening (Erwachen)* followed annually until 1924. These were largely historical pageants on socialist themes in which the workers were deployed as crowds by the director, and in spite of attempts to graft drama onto the pageantry, for example with Berta Lask's *Thomas Münzer* at Eisleben in 1924, the productions were discontinued in Leipzig before Piscator and Gasbarra conceived their more elaborate version for Berlin.

In the event the grand project was abandoned, and Piscator and Gasbarra took the German revolution, which would have been its last episode, and in three weeks put together *In Spite of Everything (Trotz Alledem*, the title being taken from a proclamation made by Karl Liebknecht after the collapse of the Spartacus rising and shortly before his assassination). It was a string of sketches presenting the communist view of German history from the declaration of war to the death of Liebknecht. There was no scenery, and events took place on the ramps and niches of a terraced platform on the revolving stage, illustrated and counterpointed by old slides and newsreel clips *(Photo 5)*. The script, which was entirely based on historical documents, is lost, but the list of scenes that follows, taken from the program which is reproduced on page 95 has been amplified with material from the police report of the revue, as quoted by Ludwig Hoffmann and Daniel Hoffmann-Ostwald in *Deutsches Arbeitertheater 1918–33* (Berlin, 1972, pp. 170–74).

Scenario

1. Berlin awaits war / Potsdamer Platz.
   Von Wildhagen, von Falkenhausen / Schulze, Lehmann, Franz, Willy, Paul / Newspaper-seller, Berlin public.

A newspaper-seller is selling a news extra: "Heir to Austrian throne assassinated at Sarajevo." Social Democrats and right-wingers among the bystanders discuss the chances of war.

2. Meeting of the Social Democratic parliamentary party on July 25, 1914.
   Ebert, Landsberg, Scheidemann, David, Langlen, Bauer, Haase, Barth, Dittmann, Ledebour, Liebknecht / Comrades in the parliamentary Party.

Liebknecht raises a lone voice against a possible war.

3. In the Imperial Palace, Berlin, on July 25, 1914.
   Reich Chancellor von Bethmann-Hollweg, War Minister von Falkenhayn, an orderly / Proletarians, bourgeois.

Wilhelm II signs the declaration of war on Russia and addresses the people from the balcony.

4. Meeting of the Social Democratic parliamentary party on August 2, 1914.
   Ebert, Landsberg, etc. / Party comrades, proletarians.
   Film shows mobilization and the departure of the troops.
   The massacre begins.

The SPD votes to approve War Credits, Liebknecht voices his opposition.

5. Meeting of the Reichstag on December 2, 1914. (Second vote on War Credits.)
   Reichstag members of all parties / voices: von Bethmann, Reichstag President Kämpf, Liebknecht / Ebert, Scheidemann, Noske, Ledebour, Liebknecht.

Liebknecht defies the SPD line and votes alone against War Credits.

6. In a Berlin shell factory.
   Franz, Willy, Paul, Gustav, the factory owner / workers of radical and moderate views.

Radicals demand a strike, the owner threatens to have them drafted, they capitulate.

7. May 1, 1916 / Potsdamer Platz
   Proletarians, Liebknecht, policemen, Becker and Rothke, a police inspector.

Antiwar demonstration instigated by the Spartacists. Liebknecht addresses an antiwar demonstration with the words, "Down with the war! Down with the government," and is arrested on the spot.

8. Landsberg's speech on May 11 when Liebknecht was deprived of his parliamentary immunity.
   Landsberg / the Reichstag.

Landsberg refuses in the name of the SPD to intercede for Liebknecht.

9. Liebknecht before a court martial on August 25, 1916.
   Liebknecht's voice.
   Film: The massacre continues (authentic shots of World War I battles).

Liebknecht reasserts his pacifism and calls on his hearers to oppose the war.

10. In a shell hole.
    German soldiers, one officer, one French officer.
    Film: But the proletariat refuses to go on being exploited.

Russians rise (October Revolution). Lenin speaks.

11. The 1918 munition workers' strike / January 30 / In Treptow Park.
    Paul, Willy Adolf, Gustav, striking workers, Ebert, Dittmann, a police inspector, policemen.

Ebert addresses the strikers and is shouted down.

12. Berlin awaits the Revolution / Potsdamer Platz.
    Von Wildhagen, von Falkenhausen, Schulze, Lehmann, Willy, Paul, newspaper-seller, Berlin public.

A news extra is being sold and bystanders discuss the possibility of revolution.

13. November 9 / In the Reich Chancellor's Palace.
	Ebert, Scheidemann, Bauer, Landsberg, Noske.
	On the street.
	Proletarian demonstrators, Liebknecht.

Ebert and his colleagues discuss how to salvage the monarchy, while Liebknecht proclaims a socialist republic to workers and soldiers outside.

14. Reich Chancellery / Landsberg's office / December 5.
	Landsberg, Corporal Krebs.

Landsberg is briefing Krebs, "A Spartacus demonstration is planned in the Chausseestrasse. There will be a shot from the crowd and that will be the signal to open fire—with machine guns into the crowd."

15. Chausseestrasse / December 6.
	Spartacus demonstration. The Rotherz battalion.

The shot and machine-gunning of the crowd indicated in the previous scene. (This first counterrevolutionary putsch by the military, who also demolished the offices of the *Rote Fahne,* was beaten off by workers and the revolutionary naval division.)

16. *Rote Fahne* editor's office.
	Liebknecht, Rosa Luxemburg, Karl Radek, Franz, Willy,
	one compositor, one worker.

Liebknecht, Radek and Rosa Luxemburg discuss the next moves. The Spartacists failed to prepare adequately for the first Reich conference of councilors and were taken by surprise when the delegates voted for an assembly to prepare a constitution, thus effectively ending the power of the workers' and soldiers' councilors. This and the foundation of the German Communist Party at the Spartacus League's conference on December 30 seem to have been the substance of the discussion.

17. Reich Chancellery / Ebert's office / January 9, 1919.
	Ebert, Scheidemann, Braun, Landsberg.

Here, too, the next moves are discussed. Noske has promised to send troops. This is the prelude to Spartacus Week.

18. On the Alexanderplatz.
	Franz, Willy, Paul, armed workers.

The workers await the decision of the leadership.

19. Sitting of the "Committee for the Revolution" / 11 January.
    Rosa Luxemburg, Liebknecht, Ledebour, the revolutionary shop stewards, the Independents.

The Independent Socialists state willingness to negotiate with Ebert and Scheidemann. Liebknecht protests. The delay and indecision demoralize the militant workers and enable Ebert to bring up troops.

20. The storming of police headquarters.
    Willy, Franz, voices.

Police headquarters are taken. Spartacists are seen defending a room they have occupied in the building. Troops burst in and mow them down.

21. The final evening / January 15.
    Rosa Luxemburg, Liebknecht, citizens' militia.

Rosa Luxemburg and Liebknecht are arrested in hiding by men of the Freikorps.

22. Foyer of the Eden Hotel / The same evening.
    White Guardsmen, Trooper Runge, von Pflugk-Hartung / Rosa Luxemburg, Liebknecht.

A lieutenant captain makes it clear to Runge that the government wants Rosa Luxemburg and Liebknecht dead. Runge is to take them into the Tiergarten, pretend to have a breakdown and ask them to get out of the car. They are then to be shot "trying to escape."

23. Tiergarten / At the Neuer See.
    Two passers-by, voices: Runge, von Pflugk-Hartung, Liebknecht.

A car draws up at the Neuer See. Liebknecht gets out, takes a couple of steps and is gunned down.

Finale. March-past of the workers. Liebknecht lives!

About fifty Red Front fighters march on and take up formation on the stage with eight flags.

Closing speech: Ruth Fischer / Final song all together.
Technical direction: *Franz Dworsky*

Lighting: *Paul Hoffmann*

The *Rote Fahne* carried an enthusiastic review by Otto Steinicke which congratulated Piscator and the organizers. He had reservations about the portrayal of historical figures; the characters of Rosa Luxemburg and Liebknecht had been confused with one another, and in particular the former's cogent reasoning and the latter's warmth and fiery rhetoric were missing, while SPD figures like Noske, Landsberg and Scheidemann had not been painted black enough. The bourgeois press had also been invited, and Fritz Engel in the *Berliner Tageblatt* also commented on the characterization. The acting was no more than weak impersonation of known figures, poor photographs that fell far short of the fierce caricatures that could be seen on the Soviet stage. Everybody agreed that Piscator had generated enthusiasm and turned the Grosses Schauspielhaus into the theater for the masses that Max Reinhardt had tried in vain to achieve. The combination of film and live scene was now accepted and Steinicke singled it out as sensationally successful. With this revue, proletarian theater, after years of theoretical wrangling, had come close to being a reality.

VIII
THE DOCUMENTARY PLAY

The first production in which the text and staging were based solely on political documents was *In Spite of Everything* (Grosses Schauspielhaus, July 12, 1925).

The play grew out of a mammoth historical revue I was to put on in the spring of that year for the Workers' Cultural Union at a midsummer festival in the Gosen Hills [on the southern outskirts of Berlin]. The revue—I commissioned Gasbarra to put the text together—was to show briefly the revolutionary highlights of the history of mankind from the Spartacus rebellion to the Russian Revolution, and to be a summary in instructive scenes of the whole development of historical materialism. We planned on a grand scale. There were to be 2000 participants; twenty gigantic spotlights were to light up the natural arena, massive symbolic props would illustrate the separate passages. (A sixty-five-foot battleship would represent British Imperialism.) I had moved nearby to Schmöckwitz to be able to keep a constant eye on the work. The scenario had been worked out and the general outline of the music, again by Edmund Meisel, was ready, when the Cultural Union, prompted by Ernst Niekisch (who is, after several changes of loyalty, currently a pioneer of national "socialism"), suddenly had political reservations. While negotiations were still in progress, the German Communist Party asked us to put on a performance in the Grosses Schauspielhaus for their Berlin Conference. The form and content of the thing had not been determined, but were to be worked out at a meeting at the Central Office the next day. The idea of having this performance stemmed from Ernst Torgler, a Communist member of the Reichstag, and an old friend of ours from the days of the *Red Revue*.

I talked with Gasbarra about what we should do. To transfer our show from the Gosen Hills to the Grosses Schauspielhaus was not feasible. On the other hand, we had gotten so used to thinking on a vast historical scale during the weeks of work on our revue, that the idea of using a ready-made play seemed unsatisfactory. Gasbarra suggested that we should take an extract from what we had already put together, perhaps turn the period between the outbreak of war and the murder of Liebknecht and Rosa Luxemburg into a separate revue. The revue took as its title Liebknecht's phrase "In spite of everything" to show that the social revolution continued to take place, even after the terrible disaster of 1919.[1] The plan caused head-shaking among senior party officials at the meeting, because we intended to have figures like Liebknecht and Rosa Luxemburg portrayed on the stage. Many felt that our plan to include members of the government in the revue (Ebert, Noske, Scheidemann, Landsberg, etc. was dangerous. They finally consented, because nobody came up with a better suggestion, but remained skeptical—all the more so since we had barely three weeks left till the day of the performance.

The show was a collective effort. The separate tasks of writer, director, musical director, designer and actor constantly overlapped. The scenery was built and the music composed as we wrote the script, and the script itself emerged gradually as the director worked with the group. Different scenes were put together simultaneously in different parts of the theater, sometimes even before a definite script had been worked out. Film was to be combined organically with live action on the stage for the first time. (As planned, but not carried out in *Flags*.)

The way I combined apparently contrasting art forms features prominently in the critics' discussions and in the general public's appraisal of my work. For my part, I did not consider this aspect of the thing so important. The technique has been rejected out of hand, or praised to the skies, but rarely accurately appraised. The use of film clips followed along the same lines as the use of projections in *Flags*. (Not to mention the fact that the general idea of transforming the stage with film goes back to my time in Königsberg, though the stress then was still on the decorative pos-

1. The disaster of 1919 was the assassination of Karl Liebknecht and Rosa Luxemburg and the collapse of their Communist revolutionary movement in Germany.

92

sibilities.) All I did was to extend and refine the means; the aim stayed the same.

Later it was often maintained that I got the idea from the Russians.[2] In fact, I was quite ignorant of what was happening on the Soviet stage at this time—very little news about performances and so on came through to us. Even afterwards I never heard that the Russians had employed film with the same function I had had in mind. In any case, the question of priority is irrelevant. It would merely prove that this was no superficial game with technical effects, but a new, emergent form of theater based on the philosophy of historical materialism which we shared. After all, what do I consider the essential point of my whole work? Not the propagation of a view of life through formal clichés and billboard slogans, but the presentation of solid proof that our philosophy and all that can be deduced from it is the one and only valid approach for our time. You can make all sorts of assertions, but repeating assertions does not make them more true or effective. Conclusive proof can be based only on scientific analysis of the material. This I can only do, in the language of the stage, if I can get beyond scenes from life, beyond the purely individual aspect of the characters and the fortuitous nature of their fates. And the way to do this is to show the link between events on the stage and the great forces active in history. It is not by chance that the factual substance becomes the main thing in each play. It is only from the facts themselves that the constraints and the constant mechanisms of life emerge, giving

Stage for *In Spite of Everything* in the Grosses Schauspielhaus, Berlin

2. Piscator's name was often linked with Meyerhold, who by 1925 had also used constructivist, tubular sets, captions and slogans, film and projections.

a deeper meaning to our private fates. For this I need some means of showing how human-superhuman factors interact with classes or individuals. One of the means was film. But it was no more than a means, and could be replaced tomorrow by some better means.

The film used in *In Spite of Everything* was documentary. From the archives of the Reich which were made available to us by one of our contacts, we used authentic shots of the war, of the demobilization, of a parade of all the crowned heads of Europe, and the like. These shots brutally demonstrated the horror of war: flame thrower attacks, piles of mutilated bodies, burning cities; war films had not yet come into "fashion," so these pictures were bound to have a more striking impact on the masses of the proletariat than a hundred lectures. I spread the film out through the whole play, and where that was not enough I projected stills.

For the basic stage I had a so-called "Praktikabel" built, a terraced structure of irregular shape with a raked platform on one side and steps and levels on the other. This structure stood on a revolving stage. I built the various acting areas into terraces, niches and corridors. In this way the overall structure of the scenes was unified and the play could flow uninterrupted, like a single current sweeping everything along with it.

The abandonment of the decorative set was taken a stage further than in *Flags*. The predominant principle was that of a purely practical acting structure to support, clarify and express the action. Freestanding structures, a self-contained world on the revolving stage, put an end to the peep-show world of the bourgeois theater. They can also be set up in the open. The squared stage area is merely an irritating limitation.

The whole performance was a montage of authentic speeches, essays, newspaper cuttings, appeals, pamphlets, photographs, and film of the War and the Revolution, of historical persons and scenes. And all this was in the Grosses Schauspielhaus that Max Reinhardt had once used to stage classical (bourgeois) theater.[3] He, too, probably sensed that the masses had to be reached—but he came to them from the other side with foreign wares. *Lysistrata*, *Hamlet*, and even *Florian Geyer* and *Danton's Death* were no more than circus performances, blown up and coarsened. All Reinhardt did was to inflate the form. Actual involvement of the masses in the audience was not a conscious part of his program,

3. Max Reinhardt converted the Circus Schumann into the Grosses Schauspielhaus in 1919. With its thrust stage and 3,000-seat auditorium, it was his bid for mass audiences. Sometimes called "the theater of the five thousand," which had been its capacity as a circus.

94

Program for *In Spite of Everything*

and never amounted to more than a few ingenious touches from the director.

Nor did Karlheinz Martin's use of "Expressionist movement" achieve this, either with classical drama or with *The Machine-Wreckers (Die Maschinenstürmer)*—it worked only in *The Weavers*.[4] In our case arena and stage were fused into one. In this there

4. *The Machine-Wreckers* by Ernst Toller was produced at the Grosses Schauspielhaus (6.30.1922) by Karlheinz Martin. It was based on Cobbett and the Luddite Movement in England. The set was a huge machine with pistons, flywheels, drive shafts and steam vents, devised by John Heartfield. The workers posed and gesticulated in front of this monster. Hauptmann's *The Weavers* is set in Silesia, and the separation of Upper Silesia from Germany was being debated at the time of Martin's production (6.20.1921), so its audience impact was partly political.

was one decisive factor: Beye had organized block bookings for the trade unions that summer. Class-conscious workers were sitting out front, and the storm broke. I had always been aware that we were not filling the house, and had wondered how we could actually reach this mass audience. Now I had them in my hand—and even today I still see that as the only real possibility for mass theater in Berlin.

For the first time we were confronted with the absolute reality we knew from experience. And it had exactly the same moments of tension and dramatic climaxes as literary drama, and the same strong emotional impact. Provided, of course, that it was a political reality ("political" in the original sense: "being of general concern").

I must admit that I myself was tense with apprehension as that evening approached. The tension was twofold: how would the interacting and interdependent elements onstage actually work, and would the effect that I was after come off to any degree?

The dress rehearsal was utter chaos. Two hundred people ran around shouting at one another. Meisel, whom we had just converted to Negro music, was conducting a loud, incomprehensible, fiendish concert with a twenty-man band, Gasbarra kept popping up with new scenes (until I put him in charge of the projectors), Heartfield stuck out his jaw and began to paint every single prop brown from top to bottom, none of the film clips came in on cue, the actors did not know where they were supposed to be half the time, and I myself began to be overwhelmed by the masses of material that still had to be fitted in. People sitting out in the auditorium during that rehearsal went home at 3:00 A.M. with no idea of what had happened on the stage. Even the scenes that were ready no longer pleased us. One thing was missing—the public.

On opening night there were thousands in the Grosses Schauspielhaus. Every seat was taken, steps, aisles, entrances were full to bursting. The living masses were filled from the outset with wild excitement at being there to watch, and you could feel an incredible, willing receptivity out in the audience that you get only with the proletariat.

But this inner willingness quickly turned into active participation: the masses took over the direction. The people who filled the house had for the most part been actively involved in the period, and what we were showing them was in a true sense their own fate, their own tragedy being acted out before their eyes. Theater had become reality, and soon it was not a case of the stage confronting the audience, but one big assembly, one big battlefield, one massive demonstration. It was this unity that proved that evening that political theater could be effective agitation.

The drastic effect of using film clips showed beyond any theoretical consideration that they were not only right for presenting political and social mechanisms, that is, from the point of view of content, but also in a higher sense, right from the formal point of view. The experience we had had with *Flags* repeated itself. The momentary surprise when we changed from live scenes to film was very effective. But the dramatic tension that live scene and film clip derived from one another was even stronger. They interacted and built up each other's power, and at intervals the action attained a *furioso* that I have seldom experienced in theater. For example, when the Social Democratic vote on War Loans (live) was followed by film showing the first dead, it not only made the political nature of the procedure clear, but also produced a shattering human effect, became art, in fact. What emerged was that the most effective political propaganda lay along the same lines as the highest artistic form.

"Grosses Schauspielhaus . . . Main Scene: A plenary session of the wartime Reichstag. . . . Text from the shorthand minutes of the Reichstag. I happened to have been in Berlin on holiday during that session and had witnessed it all. Here Bethmann-Hollweg (in his general's uniform) was on his feet once more, thanking God for endowing our fields so fruitfully again that year. At the end of the session, the Members fought over single bread coupons. The thousands in the theater laugh, shout in contempt, stamp their feet, wave threatening fists. At another point a soldier from the pioneer corps (standing below the rostrum) in shabby battledress shouts down the speaker—Karl Liebknecht. Then we see Liebknecht in the streets distributing pamphlets and speaking against the war. He is arrested, and as the mob lets him be taken away without protest, cries of anguish and self-accusation are heard in the audience.

From the *Frankfurter Zeitung*, April 1, 1929 ("How It Began")

Rote Fahne, July 14, 1925: "These were magnificent scenes: as the voices came from the masses, and the actor-workers interrupted with shouts! Just let the bourgeois theater directors with their underpaid, overworked staffs try to emulate this!"

Jacob Altmeier in the *Frankfurter Zeitung:* "And that was the overall impression it left. With all its exaggeration and tendentiousness, one no longer stepped uncomprehending into the street that night. Jessner might work wonders with *The Death of Wallenstein (Wallensteins Tod)* or *The Prince of Homburg (Prinz Friedrich von Homburg)*, and Reinhardt might spread heaven at our feet with *Twelfth Night*, or with Elisabeth Bergner, and yet when you stepped out into the city after the show, it was a jungle and you were lost. . . . But after a revue like this you felt as if you had had a bath. You had new strength. You could swim and row in the streets. Traffic and lights, the roar and the machines all made sense."

Neue Berliner 12 Uhr: "For the opening of the Communist Party Conference, workers and actors under the guidance of E. P. are staging dramatized world history in the Grosses Schauspielhaus. Scenes of war and revolution crammed together with a kind of wild power, with a gaping, tattered message, but with an almost unexpectedly moving personal effect, at least when bald, factual events were being shown. Political convictions . . . their fanatical, touching and sacred expression merges to produce something with climaxes which in some mysterious way achieve the same visible result as high dramatic art."

Welt am Abend, July 17, 1925: "And yet it seems to us that it is not the intention but the effect that makes art. Here it must be said that this revue got across to its public and produced dramatic climaxes such as we rarely see, and then usually only in works of dramatic genius."

After the second evening had drawn such a flood of people that hundreds could not get in, I tried to get them to keep the show going for at least fourteen days, if only to cover our costs. And Torgler supported this energetically. Thousands were being spent on propaganda posters which were by now so familiar to people that they had no effect. But the authorities were afraid to take the risk, and so for the umpteenth time it was my bitter experience, in spite of success and approval, in spite of massive audience support that any bourgeois theater might have envied, that even this stage in the development of the political theater achieved no real outward progress.

INTRODUCTION

Piscator rounds off the account of his political revues with a refutation of left-wing objections to the direction that his experiments were subsequently to take at the Piscator-Bühne. Much of this criticism was based on the Soviet proletcult ideas, especially the notion that proletarian art could develop only out of the proletariat itself. Berta Lask's review of *Das Politische Theater* (*Linkskurve*, 1930, no. 1, pp. 19–20) states that there were two strands of political theater in Germany in the later twenties, and Piscator's was the sterile one.

> "He [Piscator] is of the opinion that the last ten years saw a unified development of 'political theater,' closely linked to Piscator's own fate. Even in retrospect he cannot see that this was the case only in the first few years after the war, after which a point came when 'political theater' developed on the one hand into a proletarian revolutionary theater, and on the other into the Piscator-Bühne. The former has developed steadily, in spite of difficulties, whereas the latter has collapsed spectacularly every two years."

Berta Lask's main objection was that the plays at the Piscator-Bühne had ideological shortcomings which no feat of direction could overcome, but she also objects to Piscator's bland self-exoneration, observing ironically that the fault always seemed to reside in the stage that had failed to foresee the advent of Piscator, rather than in the director who failed to take account of the existing stage.

The existence of critical views like this among influential literary figures of the Left explains the lengths to which Piscator occasionally goes to justify his theatrical practices.

IX
THE PROLETARIAN AMATEUR PLAY

Our repeated forays into new territory were not without consequences in another quarter. The proletariat began to experiment.
There is, unfortunately, no space in the present book to go more
fully into this important and interesting theatrical phenomenon
which grew out of the proletariat itself. I only mention it because
there have been constant attempts by certain groups, that would
be happy only if there were a revolution every three months, to
make out that my work and that of the proletarian groups are contradictory. In fact, no such contradiction exists. Indeed, this way of
looking at the problem is quite wrong. You cannot use proletarian
amateur groups as a stick with which to beat the revolutionary professional theater. In the first place, the development which this theater has followed in my enterprises to date shows that it developed
out of the proletarian amateur propaganda play. Secondly, the two
types of theater are fighting on different sectors of the cultural front
and they consequently face different tasks. Compared with the revo-
tionary professional theater, which is tied to one place by its complexity and size, the theater groups and theater companies which
sprouted up in their hundreds all over Germany can spread propaganda through the whole length and breadth of the working classes. The professional theater, on the other hand, can attract sectors
of the community which would otherwise be untouched by our
movement. (This apart from the possibilities of major experiments
in the fields of writing, acting and staging.) It would be worthless to
attempt to establish which task is the more important. I consider

the proletarian amateur play, provided it is clear in its pursuit of political and propagandistic aims and does not attempt to mimic the professional theater, to be just as important and valuable as my own work. The forms which I devised for the first *Red Revue* (cf. pp. 86–89) have proved to be right for what the proletarian amateur groups are trying to do.[1] Their main task is to develop and deepen these forms. Both the revolutionary professional theater and the revolutionary amateur theater are moving toward a proletarian cultural theater, and this will be the form the theater will take in the cultural life of a socialist community once the economic and political foundations have been laid.

I do, however, consider it quite wrong when these groups with their inadequate technical and acting resources attempt to "stage plays," that is, to transfer to their own predicament a type of drama which is too full of problems and psychological complexities as it stands, and which in addition has grown out of the modern bourgeois theater system. This means that they are reversing the steps I have already taken in the course of gaining experiences that were clearly valid not only for myself, but for others as well.

But the view that is understandably often heard in proletarian amateur circles, that more attention to the form, more use of the full range of technical apparatus, and the employment of professional actors detracts from the political or revolutionary effectiveness of the theater—this view is, at least in this crude form, misguided. What is then the correct view? Amateurism has one great strength: its plays are freestanding, without predecessors or followers, and this gives an inner freshness, an intuitiveness, a lack of professional polish. The undiminished originality of a first attempt with all its inadequacies, but also with the surging energy of new untapped resources. This is what I should like to capture in all my work with the so-called "revolutionary professional theater." I detest routine performances, professionalism and rigidity. But can the freshness of amateurism be sustained in the long run? I have observed that proletarian actors whose technical attainments are straightforward and undifferentiated succumb much more easily to the temptation to repeat an effect they have once used successfully, simply because the range of possibilities professionals have at their fingertips is not available to them, and that amateurism after its first beginnings is in much more danger of hardening into a hollow unconvincing routine, with the sole difference that this routine is on a lower level than the professional routine.

So what are the arguments against using professional actors, stage machinery, and the whole institution of the theater? They are just as absurd as the contention that a revolutionary magazine must on

101

ideological grounds be produced on Gutenberg's handpress instead of on a modern rotary press. The important thing is always the aim: the best performance is the most effective propaganda. And if I have achieved anything at all, I think it is that I have placed the total apparatus of the theater in the service of the revolutionary movement and adapted it to the aims of the movement. In so doing I have given the theater itself, in purely theatrical terms, new possibilities.

INTRODUCTION

Piscator's next major production at the Volksbühne, and the first play he selected for himself after being put on contract as a staff director, was Alfons Paquet's *Tidal Wave* (*Sturmflut*). In the twenty-one months that had elapsed since *Flags* he had, besides the two political revues, directed seven other productions, which will be dealt with in the next chapter. Paquet had published a novel, *The Prophecy* (*Die Prophezeiung*, 1922), with substantially the same plot and characters as the play. He had spent six months in Moscow in 1918, and, without being a propagandist, was keen to promote sympathetic understanding of the Soviet Union, and both of these works attempted to show the political forces behind the Revolution in terms of typical figures in a farfetched, fictitious situation. *Tidal Wave* presents ten scenes of love and intrigue in postrevolutionary St. Petersburg. The city is in the hands of the proleteriat under the leadership of a sailor, Granka Umnitsch, who is presented as an impetuous, charismatic son of the soil. Ssarin, a renegade revolutionary, lands with Orville, a British agent empowered to buy the city for the Russia Company, which plans to industrialize it after resettling it with Europe's unemployed lumpen proletariat. The dikes are breached and the city flooded. Granka, urged on by his new mistress, Rune Lewenclau, a Swedish aristocrat, amazon and adventuress, closes the deal for 5 billion and hands over the money to the assembled international socialists who disperse to promote world revolution. The negotiations are handled by a local Jew, Gad, whose boat capsizes as he is leaving. Granka is injured rescuing him, but retires to the woods with Rune and his band to pursue a Tolstoyan idyll in later scenes of bear hunting and folk dancing. By act 3 Granka is rumored to be debilitated or even dead and Ssarin, pursuing his own vision of a future constitutional and democratic Russia, tries to win Rune and her followers for his purposes. Rune prevaricates. Granka hears of the plight of the proletariat under the new regime and returns disguised as a worker. Ssarin shoots Orville, who has served his purpose and is now threatening bloody repression of the restive populace. In the final scene the people repossess the city and Granka confesses to the masses in front of the Winter Palace that his country idyll was an error. Ssarin makes his bid for power, but Granka's leadership is reaffirmed by popular acclamation. He lets Rune depart, welcomes the penitent Gad's commercial skills to the revolution and condemns Ssarin to prison for treason, but Ssarin shoots himself with the consoling thought that the Russians are free again so he has at least achieved part of his dream. The final note is jubilant—victory for Granka Umnitsch.

Paquet's characterization is flimsy. Orville, for example, is a stock Englishman, touring with a Baedeker, a camera, an unshakable belief in the civilizing mission of British parliamentary democracy and an amused contempt for the natives. At the same time he symbolizes capitalist imperialism, with a touch of White Terror. The Russian characters represent revolutionary attitudes or factions but are also emotionally involved with one another. Ssarin's ex-mistress, Awdeja, is an unswerving, lucid bolshevik who is now a passionate admirer of Granka. Granka has an affair with Rune. Ssarin makes a pass at Rune, possibly for tactical reasons. Rune eventually rejects Granka because her blue blood allegedly rebels against the plebeian in him. Of these figures, Paquet in his foreword states that only Ssarin is based on a real person, Boris Savinkov. Granka can be identified with Lenin only in that he is the leader of the Revolution.

Piscator could not use Paquet's original script, so it was reworked by the company and author in rehearsal. (The published version bears marks of haste, and, since it includes film clips in the stage directions, is probably based on the promptbook.) Paquet had used the October Revolution as a foil for a romantic anecdote, and this emphasis had to be reversed. To do this, Piscator used film between (and occasionally during) scenes to inject a factual note.

Edward Suhr designed a permanent set which was modified by props carried on and off between scenes while the film was running. A transparent screen mounted on a stepped black frame which masked the entire stage bisected the revolving stage, which consequently could not be used (Photo 17). Behind the screen four projectors were mounted in front of the cyclorama, behind which a special control box had been constructed. At the back of the screen was a rostrum with steps at either end for shadow play (also used in The Drunken Ship, cf. Photos 18, 19, 20). A similar rostrum, 1 meter in front of it, accessible from the back up steps right, left and center, and also from the front up angled steps center and half-right, served as an acting area, representing a quay in St. Petersburg (scene 1) or high ground in the woods (scene 7). For scene 2 the equestrian statue of Peter the Great was set against the screen, and in scene 5 a truck with furniture rolled on as Gad's house, while dollar and pound signs were projected overhead. The props were simple and the colors muted to tone in with the film, and here, as in *Flags*, the overall lighting level was, to judge from the photographs, low.

The projections in *Flags* had been documentary, and some of the film in *Tidal Wave* had the same function. Granka's broadcast "to everybody" was punctuated by shots of crowds in Shanghai, riots in Rio and dock strikes in New York. To show the consequences of Granka's dereliction of duty his love affair in the forest was counterpointed by shots of factory chimneys, strikes and street fighting, and maps and tables of statistics. There were also new effects, some of them using film specially shot by J. A. Hübler-Kahla, a Viennese movie comeraman who learnt his trade with Joe May and Ernst Lubitsch. These could be part of the decor like the clip of the raging sea which led into the opening dialogue on the St. Petersburg waterfront, or the crowd shots which stretched away behind the stage crowd in the final scene *(Photo 16)*, or they could be expository like the clip of Granka transmitting orders in a radio tower before he appears on the stage, or the exploding destroyer (accompanied incongruously by a tinny thunder sheet) before a German sailor is rescued in scene 3. They could also pursue a character after his exit, as when Granka quarrels with Rune in scene 7 and is then seen striding away through the trees and into the mist. The voice of Lloyd George on the radio was accompanied by footage of one of his speeches, and Gad's decision to unload his Russia Company shares was followed by a clip of panic on the New York Stock Exchange. The reception of the film was mixed, ranging from Moritz Loeb's ecstatic praise in the *Morgenpost* to Hans Knudsen's hope that Piscator had now got it out of his system in the *Ostdeutsche Morgenpost*. H. Ihering devoted his column in the *Börsen-Courier* to *Tidal Wave* on two successive days (February 22 and 23). He was positive but critical, and suggested that Piscator's film had the same flaw as the text, a tendency to slide into sentimentality:

> "The switch from acoustic to visual has a power I had never imagined. . . . The new medium is such a substantial innovation that any vagueness in its application immediately strikes false emotions. Granka on the tower, China, the sea—the unbourgeois grandeur of the work is spread out before us. Granka ambles off sadly and the decline into bourgeois sentimentality begins. Film in plays should stick to documentation and never try to touch the emotions."

Among the actors, Heinrich George as Granka was singled out by several commentators, among them Alfred Mühr, who characterized one episode in detail:

"Simple bearing, firm and upright, but broad and built like a wall.— George greets the German, then learns that the German navy has been sunk [at Scapa Flow] and will not be joining him. He sees red. Wide eyes in a face swollen with fury. One, two steps toward the German. Wham! A blow to the side of the head. George walks past him as he falls, his feelings relieved.—Then an abrupt change.—The German is a friend and ally after all. With a few halting words, George's hand goes out hesitantly to the German, he wants to apologize. His hand quivers, seeks the other's. Powerful acting without words. George embraces the German, runs his fingers through his hair, then cuts off the emotion and turns to deal with the business at hand."

Deutsche Zeitung, 2.22.1926

Moritz Loeb noted that George was surpassing himself from one role to the next, and Herbert Ihering singled out his sober clarity and manly decisiveness, observing that the actors at the Volksbühne were delivering their lines under Piscator with a crisp, objective clarity and freedom from sentimentality that was a welcome change from the false discretion and false tears elsewhere on the Berlin stage.

With all its flaws the evening was an event, the premiere watched by celebrities, among them Asta Nielsen sitting sphinxlike in the stalls. Moritz Loeb summed it up: "All the episodes burn with the holy fire of the cause, fanned by a director who can keep up the tension through the most verbose passages."

X
A PARAPHRASE ON THE RUSSIAN REVOLUTION
Tidal Wave (Sturmflut): Volksbühne, 1926

Meanwhile I had signed a firm contract for several years with the Volksbühne which gave me the right to choose the plays I wanted to direct. From lack of time the first play I chose was *Tidal Wave* by Alfons Paquet, though I was fully aware of the weaknesses of the play.[1]

> Contents: The revolution triumphs. But there is no money to carry it through. So Granka Umnitsch, the leader, sells St. Petersburg to an old Jew who resells it to England. Granka and his band take to the woods. At this point there is a lovers' quarrel between him and a Swedish woman who goes over to the opposition party, represented by Ssarin, a White Guardsman. Granka returns to St. Petersburg in secret, incites the proletariat and conquers the city back for the Revolution.

"It is not the history of a revolution. Not a description of Lenin's life. Not a picture of Soviet Russia. Not even a milieu-piece. . . . It was not a matter of copying reality, but of capturing the motive forces of our times in a few figures . . . in images which would awaken in us the feelings that reality awoke." (Alfons Paquet in the preface to *Tidal Wave*, book edition.)

1. The preceding paragraph was inserted in the 1963 edition.

"Poetry" instead of reality, symbol instead of document. Feelings instead of insights. Very well: let us see whether a poetic play is more convincing and consequently more powerful and effective than a political play.

On the Relationship of Symbol and Reality

Symbols are concentrated reality, unambiguous ciphers for weighty or complex matters. The sign of a culture which can afford to abbreviate its material into shorthand, which is clear in its mind about its own concepts and therefore only needs to hint at them. Typical of the initial and the final phase of an epoch. But symbols are not trademarks, labels. Symbols must not become clichés of reality. The moment a symbol can be measured by the forces which it represents it begins to display its inadequacy. Symbols stand most effectively for things past or yet to come, both of which defy exact measurement. They are never a substitute for reality, which even in its most banal form has the power of symbols. Historical climaxes are symbols in their total concrete reality. A mistake to subtract concrete detail from such subjects: this does not achieve an intensification but merely deprives it of substance.

But *Tidal Wave* showed us that any attempt to depoliticize political subjects or to "elevate them into poetry" is bound to lead to half measures (inconsistency). So *Tidal Wave* proved to be a step backward after *Flags* and *In Spite of Everything*.

"There is a gulf between the effect of this story and the effect of the presentation of the actual, documented facts. The gulf runs through the characters who in the first instance have a private existence, in the second instance are exponents of political ideas and in the third instance are symbols, though it is never made clear what they are to convey as private persons, what as politicians and what as symbols. In *Flags* Paquet limited himself to the unpoetic but powerful and effective document. In *Tidal Wave* (the very title is meant partly in a literal and partly in a symbolic sense) he blurs the edges . . . he gives . . . an extensive political typology . . . but he individualizes his typology and subsequently expands it."

H. Ihering, *Börsen-Courier*, February 22, 1926

Few poets can stand a confrontation with the totality of the real world. Why didn't Paquet disregard the material and attempt, as he had done in *Flags*, to analyze this gigantic upheaval right to its roots in terms of a small sector of the Russian Revolution, a task which in itself would have been big enough if he had limited himself to historical documents? Do we not have too much respect for language as a medium, and too little respect for the material, for the event in itself? Paquet himself has no answer to this question. He observes, as if this were quite a new discovery, that "Granka is not Lenin himself. Lenin never 'took to the woods.' Lenin was never subject to Tolstoyan fits . . . Lenin never sold St. Petersburg . . . Lenin never for a moment lost contact with the masses. . . . Lenin never . . . let himself be influenced by a love affair . . . He was never a rustic primitive, etc." So the whole thing merely blurred the events and figures, it was not "intensification" but dilution and confusion.

" . . . whereas everything which was staged as revolutionary or tendentious drama derived its effect from Literature, from unadulterated Art. Where Paquet is weak, it is not because he is not a poet but because he is too much of a poet."

H. Ihering, *Börsen-Courier*, February 22, 1926

This weakened the message of the play. So we could not achieve the political effect we wanted. (A. Paquet: "I did not write tendentious plays, or plays of ideas. I am only trying to achieve with contemporary means effects which can be achieved only by 'timeless' art. . . . I believe that right up to the last minute I subjugated myself to no law other than artistic laws.")

In a sense this ran counter to the new function for the theater which I had made people accept in my previous work. And when Paquet says of his overall treatment of the subject: "Call it romanticism if you like: that is the right of poetry!"—then, for my part, he forces me to say today as I did then: wrong! To apply romanticism to this subject today, in our times, is to do art injustice, not justice.

On the Relationship of Truth and Tendentiousness

Two contradictory elements? Not at all. They are completely identical in an era in which truth is revolutionary. The tendentious is a much maligned concept, sometimes becoming synonymous with untruthfulness, or at least with distortion of the truth in a certain manner to a certain end. I have never had any time for "tendentiousness" of this sort, for twisting, distorting, diluting the facts. On the contrary! I would always prefer to demonstrate a truth "at the expense of " a tendentious message, to show reality, to expose causes, if only the tendentious message did not always emerge automatically, of its own accord, so to speak, in the course of my demonstration. The most powerful tendentious message possible is inherent in the raw, objective, untouched reality; and it seems to me that nowadays not only the most powerful revolutionary sentiments but also the highest artistic ability are required to present reality on a new level.

Film

In this production we took a big step forward in terms of working up and polishing the film scenes. For the first time it was possible to shoot lengths of film especially for the play. This meant that the film clips represented a greater contribution to the working of the play.

> "The problem of dimension also obtrudes on the stage. Film is no longer . . . a trick or a stylistic nuance. . . . The film has a dramatic function."
> H. Ihering, *Börsen-Courier*, February 22, 1926

But though we managed to give the film itself a more precise function, we could not in practice prevent its being influenced by the unbalanced structure of the plot. The personal events in the play were unavoidably reflected in the form of purely personal events in the film and onstage.

> "We had three and a half weeks to produce *Tidal Wave*. Alfons Paquet had worked on the play for a year—had written a book—a drama and a novel at the same time—of epic breadth . . . whereas the climaxes of the dramatic passages demand sudden tensions and a rapid succession of events. The play had been strongly influenced in the writing by stage technique . . . but as soon as it came into contact with a stage we saw that this was a case where staging had to take new forms, and where, conversely, more than in other plays, the subject had to be closely adapted to the new resources in acting and technique which our stage afforded. A complete reconstruction began, so that one can say with justification that this play was recreated on the stage. The work presented us all with new—or at least unusual—problems. I could not direct the play according to a preconceived plan or a conception which had been fully thought out in advance, I could not, as was usually the case, have the complete production ready in my mind. The actors could not see the total complex of their own roles until the last days of rehearsal—they had to use their imagination to fill out new avenues and new twists as they occurred, and to form and intensify them. (In this way we are seeing a new company emerge here, a company whose members each make an independent contribution to the common task. Paquet had the experience of seeing important new connections emerge in moments of intuitive cooperation by all concerned. The structure changed, it had to be

torn apart and put together again. Of course, this was not always to the advantage of the play's poetic qualities, but it was an occasion when the laws of the stage suddenly seemed to all of us to have become the laws of life. Life—this life, today's life—had to be harnessed, had to be captured at all costs; this submerged every other consideration.)"

(E. P. in an essay in *Der Neue Weg*, April 16, 1926)

The play, therefore, had to be revised during the rehearsals. My head was full of the events of the Russian Revolution, and I was aware of all the political and social overlaps and connections, I knew all the problems and all the difficulties, but at the same time I had to stage a play in which everything was confused, unclear, pale and half-baked. Does anyone really believe that it was a matter of ego-bolstering or director's monomania that made me again and again take on the task of splitting a play right down to its foundations, reconstructing it, adding new elements to it and constantly demanding new lines from the tortured author right up to the first night? Or did I not have to do this if the subject was to be dealt with conscientiously, if the people who were going to see this play in the hope of finding answers to their questions were to be dealt with conscientiously? Even if it involved the danger of incompleteness, indeed, of leaving out effects? The conclusion of the article I have just cited answers these questions:

Not "Art," no: a beginning! We subordinate everything to our aim, and the aim is subordinate to the goal. Seen in this light and seen from my point of view I do, of course, criticize the present state of affairs. And so the play *Tidal Wave* was unfinished when it opened. The production

Erwin Piscator

111

was unfinished because the means with which we made our attempt were unfinished.

What does it matter to us whether content and form are given the ultimate finishing touches to create "Art"? We leave our work unfinished on purpose. We do not in any case have time for matters of formal structure. Too many new revolutionary ideas are struggling toward the light, time is too precious to wait until they are finally purified. We take the means that we find—reproach us for that if you will—and we make a provisional contribution with them!

INTRODUCTION

In this chapter Piscator briefly mentions four relatively conventional productions at the Volksbühne, and then goes on to outline his work with the actors in evolving a style appropriate to political theater.

His second production at the Volksbühne was a double bill, Alfred Brust's *South Seas Play* (*Südseespiel*) as an exotic curtain raiser for Eugene O'Neill's *Moon of the Caribees*. O'Neill was not infrequently performed in Berlin in the later twenties, and the critics were generally impressed with Piscator's version. Moritz Loeb noted that the production brought out O'Neill's "torrid atmosphere, vibrant temperament and glowing life energy," and asked why the Volksbühne didn't use Piscator more. Herbert Ihering, however, rejected O'Neill as a sentimental pastiche of Hauptmann, Toller and Kaiser, and found the production noisy and ragged. F. Leppmann reviewed the *South Seas Play* in terms reminiscent of Reinhardt:

> "Piscator . . . put all manner of ethnographically and geographically accurate exotica on display. Day and night alternated magically, stars twinkled and faded, dancers writhed, muffled drumbeats approached, rhythms faltered and might have seemed outlandish if they had come before our new dance music."
>
> (*Berliner Zeitung*, 12.22.24)

These plays enabled Alfred Kerr to refer to Piscator as the Volksbühne specialist in nautical matters when he later staged Leonhard's *Sails on the Horizon*.

Piscator then directed *Who Weeps for Juckenack?* (Wer weint um *Juckenack?*) by his old partner at the Central Theater, Hans Rehfisch. This was a tragicomedy about a civil servant who seems to be dead when the play starts, then appears in the fifth scene, wild-eyed, having been sent back to life because nobody wept at his death. Juckenack, a dedicated lawyer, and a bachelor without family ties, now tries indiscriminately to ingratiate himself by helping others. He gives money to down-and-outs, and gets mugged. He signs over his capital to his landlady's niece, Lina, then turns away when she reciprocates by unbuttoning her blouse. He burns an incriminating file on Edmund Walter, a would-be poet and check forger. Lina falls for Walter, who zooms into high finance on the strength of her capital. Juckenack is offered his money back with interest, but with no gratitude. When he dies again at the end of the play, a mysterious agent from the Charon Insurance Company appears and picks up Walter's crumpled check to give it to a tubercular girl in a garret as a gift from her mother's childhood sweetheart. Thus Juckenack will get his tears.

The writing is cool and ironic, but Piscator objected to the naïve, unworldly hero and preferred the minor figures as social types: Lina for instance, a flapper who has already been a maid, had an affair with her employer, served a short sentence for theft and even been briefly on the streets. A victim of capitalism? Or Walter, a ruthless, up-and-coming capitalist. With its fanciful introduction of the revenant and Juckenack's bourgeois quest for an emotional justification for his own existence, this was not Piscator's sort of play, but it was creditable of its kind. A largely rewritten version was produced in Hamburg in 1951 and appears in Rehfisch's *Ausgewählte Werke*.

Rehfisch became one of the most frequently performed authors of the next five years with *Nickel and the 36 Just Men (Nickel und die 36 Gerechten), Duell am Lido, Razzia, The Gynecologist (Der Frauenarzt)* and *Die Affäre Dreyfus*.

Razzia is a Berlin tragicomedy in which a working-class family is ruined after a minor offense (the mother gives short weight at her vegetable stall on the Wittenbergplatz) because they refuse to plead guilty and to accept the system in order to minimize the penalty. The prostitution, which offended the Grossdeutsche Theatergemeinschaft in 1926, was marginal when the play was staged at the Schillertheater. Lucie, the daughter, whose looks are good enough for the chorus line or a penthouse on the Ku'damm, prefers honest poverty until the final act, when she tarts herself up to lure into a trap the policeman who has been the undoing of her mother. A melodramatic ending to a play which is otherwise a realistic plea for social justice.

Contemporary critics noted that Rehfisch followed stage fashions. *Razzia*, written in Berlin dialect, can be seen as a Volksstück, and *The Gynecologist* and *Dreyfus* were Zeitstücke, appearing when these genres were in vogue.

Piscator's next production was *Sails on the Horizon (Segel am Horizont)* by Rudolf Leonhard (1889–1953), a dramatization of a brief news item that appeared on November 7, 1924. The crew of a Soviet ship whose captain had disappeared mysteriously in Port Talbot elected his wife, the only woman on board, to command the ship on the voyage home. Leonhard first built up erotic tension. In act 1 men visit the bridge on flimsy pretexts while Captain Angela tries to keep her mind on the job. "What would have happened in 1917 if Lenin had done what he fancied?" she asks. By the end of act 2 a sailor has burst into her cabin, and she convenes the ship's council while two other sailors restrain him. The ship's council decides that if she were to choose another husband it would take the heat off the situation, so she chooses the helmsman, a male chauvinist whose pride prevents him from accepting, then the ship's idiot, Kaleb, who is thrown overboard in a scuffle which follows. In the final act the helmsman makes a bid for the captaincy, fails and jumps overboard. After these chastening events Captain Angela explains her husband's disappearance. When he realized that she was attracted to two of the men, he went ashore to a brothel and there committed suicide and was discreetly disposed of by the management. "Is comradeship between men and women possible?" she has asked at the outset. Now that the air is cleared, the answer is yes, and they set course for the Soviet Union in serene solidarity.

It was a thin, long-winded piece, full of breathless dialogue and Expressionist soul-searching, with occasional conventional theatrical twists. There were twenty-five scenes, and Traugott Müller, working with Piscator for the first time, built a system of steps, gangways and rostra to represent the superstructure of a sailing ship. Two masts completed the picture (*Photo 21*), and the whole structure revolved to offer a variety of acting areas and facilitate inventive grouping at different levels. (The same basic structure was used again that summer for *In Spite of Everything* and two years later for *Storm over Gotland.*) The revolving stage also simulated movement, as when the ship, all problems solved, put about and headed for home in the last scene, a visually powerful moment, according to Piscator.

At the end of the season Piscator directed W. Schmidtbonn's *Help, A Child Has Fallen from Heaven! (Hilfe, ein Kind ist vom Himmel gefallen!)* for the Volksbühne at the Central-Theater, and in the 1925/26 season he directed H. Johst's *The Joyous Town (Die fröhliche Stadt)* and Strindberg's *Rausch* at the Munich Kammerspiele, both with sets by Otto Reigbert, his old designer at the Königsberg Tribunal. These were followed by E. Ortner's *Michael Hundertpfund*, which was performed at the Berlin Tribüne; this bucolic thriller served mainly to retain Heinrich George, the big, plebeian actor (one of the Berlin heavies of the twenties) whom Piscator had used for the first time in *Who Weeps for Juckenack?* and now wanted to use in *Tidal Wave* at the Volksbühne.

After *Tidal Wave* he directed *The Drunken Ship (Das trunkene Schiff)* by Paul Zech (1881–1946). Zech was an Expressionist poet and a translator. He had studied at Bonn and Heidelberg and then turned to manual labor and spent two years as a miner. He was interned in 1933, and his books were burned. On his release in 1934 he immigrated via Paris to Argentina, where he died. His play was a dramatic biography of Arthur Rimbaud and it took its title from the French poet's best-known poem. It showed sixteen "stations" in the French poet's life, from his meeting at seventeen with Paul Verlaine (anarchism, homosexuality) to Africa (shady arms deals, anticolonialism) and back to Europe to die full of regrets in a scene called "Haven." Again, it was the story of a bourgeois individualist, but Piscator decided to set the poet's life against his times, the Paris Commune and the Third Republic in France, and for this he used film and projections by George Grosz. It was the first time the two men collaborated extensively. The curtain went up to reveal a screen on which the title was projected. This then went up to reveal a triptych of screens *(Photos 18, 19, 20)* with mobile side sections for back projections of cartoons by Grosz. Herbert Ihering commented:

> "In this way he could suggest both the place and the thoughts behind the screen. He illustrated the content and the reality, the idea and the location. He gave both the historical background and its relevance to the present. In one scene we saw the date 1871 in red figures over the revolt of the Commune. On another occasion we saw a cafe on the left, the Grande Place in Brussels in the middle and ships and a ticket for a steerage passage to Algiers on the right. The screen passed through time and space.
>
> "Changes were made with the curtain up. The stage crew was not concealed. This is fine, but the lights must be controlled so that we do not confuse the actors with the stage crew at the beginning and end of the scenes. Even so, the effect is excellent, though it comes very close to being empty artistry. It would be a great pity if Erwin Piscator's very real talents were to be sidetracked into the wrong scripts, if the only director who sees the theater as an instrument for the people were to be unwittingly seduced by special artistic effects into thinking that directing is an end in itself."
>
> *(Berliner Börsen-Courier, 5.22.26)*

In the 1926/27 season Piscator directed Schiller's *Robbers* at the Staatliches Schauspielhaus, followed by Gorky's *Lower Depths* at the Volksbühne. He then returned to the Munich Kammerspiele where he staged a rousing version of a now-forgotten play by Heinrich Mann, *The Hospitable House* (Das gastliche Haus) with jazz music and a noisy elevator in the center of the stage. His designer was Otto Reigbert. The season then ended with Welk's *Storm over Gotland*, Piscator's swan song at the Volksbühne.

XI
THE CRAFT

The nature of my profession, my lack of independence, naturally prevented me on occasion from completing a whole season with the kind of plays that my political convictions called for. (Even when we managed to clear away all the other difficulties, we were left with the intractable problem of finding plays which were consistent and at the same time successful, a problem which later beset us during the year of the Piscator-Bühne. Nonetheless, I was careful to ensure that our plays made no concessions to the commercial theater. "I had a free hand in staging them." The problems here were not "political," but "human." My task was to arrange and bring out the background, and then to insert the personal and the individual into it. Various new methods of doing this presented themselves and I tried out effects which later became widely accepted. There were plays by Eugene O'Neill: *Moon of the Caribees*, Hans José Rehfisch: *Who Weeps for Juckenack? (Wer weint um Juckenack?)*, Rudolf Leonhard: *Sails on the Horizon (Segel am Horizont)*, Paul Zech: *The Drunken Ship (Das trunkene Schiff)*, Maxim Gorky: *The Lower Depths*.

It is interesting to see how Rehfisch, in real life a cold-blooded lawyer, can immerse himself in the involved abstractions of figures of his own invention, working off his own (lyrical!) complexes as soon as he turns to "creative writing." You can always expect him to come up with something good when he is working in a detached vein. The characters in his plays who are well drawn are precisely the ones with whom he is in no

118

way connected, apart from having visualized them sharply and clearly—and these are not the lyrical, intuitive heroes, but the secondary figures. Yet, although he is capable of handling a social theme in terms of these characters, he always bungles the opportunity by focusing everything on the hero who, incidentally, is invariably fashioned after the basic character of whatever actor Rehfisch chances to be writing for at that particular time (so the theme is robbed of objectivity from two sides). To this day Rehfisch has not realized which form suits his gifts, or what the content of his writing for the theater should be.

Rudolf Leonhard, lyric poet and aphorist, armed with wit and even sarcasm, manages to make an intellectual thesis of the most physical of acts—coitus, or murder, or a fistfight (though he himself refuses to this day to believe it). In spite of his tendentious distortions he contrives to reveal several facets of every fact. But where his friend and mentor Georg Kaiser translates real events into an intellectual-linguistic form, and so creates a coherent new structure, Leonhard lets his message and content crumble into a mosaic. *Sails on the Horizon*, which to my astonishment I was able to persuade the Volksbühne to accept, had all the strengths and weaknesses of a play built with the elements that this analysis has isolated: sound convictions and a proper conception of the problem (a woman as ship's captain, surrounded by men, who despite the severest proletarian discipline cannot free themselves from their sexuality. A conflict in which their duty, their binding relationship to the collective finally manages to triumph).

In Paul Zech's work, too, there were points at which he was beginning to come to grips with the stuff of the times (the war of 1870, the Paris Commune, the Third Republic in France, the whole transitional period of French history from which a figure like Rimbaud is inseparable). But he, too, unfortunately never got beyond individual psychology, and even there he could not see the anarchism of the individual clearly enough for the good of the play; here again the dramatist transfers his own lyrical feelings, and projects them on his fellow poet Rimbaud.

The Lower Depths proved that the stage can be topical. The play dictated its own terms. In this early naturalistic work Gorky had painted a picture of a milieu which was conceived in terms of types, according to the conventions of the day, but which still remained narrowly circumscribed. In 1925 I could no longer think in terms of a small room with ten miserable people in it, but only on the scale of the vast slums of a modern city. The subject of discussion was the slum proletariat as a concept. I had to widen the confines of the play to embrace this concept. What a disappointment it was when I invited Gorky to cooperate on this project and he refused to help! It was precisely the two moments in the play which we modified to this end which were the most effective in the theater: the opening scene, the snoring and wheezing of a crowd fills the whole stage, the city awakens, streetcar bells ring, then eventually the ceiling is lowered in and closes the room off from its surroundings, and then comes the tumult, not just a little private fight in the backyard but a whole quarter rebelling against the police, a rising of the masses. Throughout the play my aim was to translate the spiritual anguish of the individual into general terms wherever possible and to make it typical of the present, to open the confined space (by raising the roof) out into the world. The success of the production proved I was right. (Alfred Kerr commented that this production restored the subject to view again.) The guiding principles, which were political, had brought forth an effect which was right in theatrical terms.

The productions which interested me most were *Sails on the Horizon* and *The Drunken Ship*. In the former the main prop (ship) had a function of its own which turned the weak ending of the play into one of the most powerful dramatic moments.—In *The Drunken Ship* projections were used in a new form. They showed the world in which the play was set through drawings of the major social and political events by George Grosz. The action took place in a space bounded by three huge screens on which the appropriate pictures were projected at suitable moments. (Originally, I wanted these three screens to be constructed in the shape of a prism on a revolving mount.) In *The Drunken Ship* I also used film during the sea-crossing, not just as an illustration, but as a pictorial representation of Rimbaud's fevered fantasies.

During this whole period my work with actors was very valuable for me. The Volksbühne had, over the years, put together quite a number of good actors, although they did not form what I would have considered an integrated ensemble.

Gradually the kind of cooperation which my productions required transformed them into a human and artistic, and in a certain sense also a political, community, and the majority of them took part in the 1928 secession and have remained involved in political theater since that time: Genschow, Hannemann, Kalser, Steckel, Venohr, etc.[1] Particularly fruitful was my work with Heinrich George, an imaginative actor with great certainty of instinct who was prepared (in spite of Ehm Welk) to come to the aid of the author and the director alike.

1. Fritz Genschow, Leonhard Steckel, Erwin Kalser, Albert Venohr and Karl Hannemann all later joined the Piscator-Bühne company. When it collapsed in 1928, Genschow formed a political collective on his own account from the actors who were thrown out of work. His *Gruppe junger Schauspieler* toured with P. M. Lampel's *Revolt in the House of Correction*, an indictment of the treatment of young offenders.

In the course of time something approaching a new style of acting developed within my productions—hard, unambiguous, unsentimental. At the same time a new concept established itself concerning the task facing the actor in creating a role. Away from stock characters, from the practice of touching in the outline of a character, but away, too, from the overdifferentiated characterization which reaches down into the deepest crevices of the soul, as it was practiced under Kayssler, in particular. Were I asked to put a name to this style I would call it in the first instance Neorealist (not to be confused with the Naturalist style of the nineties).

The actors cannot be separated from the overall style, from the dominant ideas and convictions of a theater. In Russia an actor from the Meyerhold Theater cannot act at the Tairov Theater nor can he work with Stanislavsky.[2] The gulf between the generations is just as great as the gulf between the styles of the different theaters as reflected in their themes, plays and authors. Our generation has consciously set itself up in opposition to the inflation and the overvaluation of emotion. Such transformations naturally cannot be achieved overnight. I never took less time over the transformation of the actor than over the transformation of stage technique. To suit the open construction of a stage built of wood, canvas and steel, the actor's manner must also be unfalsified, hard, unambiguous and open. What makes children or animals so effective in the magnified eye of the film camera? It is the naturalness of movement and gesture which goes beyond the *actorly achievements* of even the greatest actors. Of course, we do not require professional naturalness, but a performance so scientific and so clearly analyzed by the intellect that it reproduces naturalness on a higher level and with a technique just as intentional and calculated as the architecture of the stage. Every word must be as central to the work as is the center to the periphery of a circle. That is, everything on the stage is calculable, everything fits together organically. So keeping the overall effect of my work in mind, I see the actor in the first instance simply as fulfilling a function, just as do light, color, music, scenery, script. How well he fulfils it depends on how gifted he is. At any rate, I am not prepared to turn my theatrical aims upside down on his behalf.

It must be admitted that the value of the actor's personality is a separate entity which has nothing essential to do with his function,

2. On recent Russian theater, J. Gregor and R. Fülöp-Miller's *Das russische Theater* (1927) and Alexander Tairov's *Das Entfesselte Theater* (*The Theater Unbound*, 1923) were available in German. Tairov's company visited Berlin in 1923, Meyerhold's in 1930.

and therefore represents a separate aesthetic element. Where this personal value occurs as an aesthetic stimulant in its own right, it is of no use to us (just as a very beautiful rococo writing table is of no use in a functionally furnished living room). For the actor it is not a matter of intensifying his personal individuality by means of his ability as an actor, but of putting across his human qualities in relation to his artistic-political function. That you can produce good theater with good actors is self-evident. Anyone with a modicum of talent should be able to do it. But—and this is a decisive factor which I as an "expert" have observed—the actor who is aware of his function grows with it and takes his style from it. He no longer needs the inspiration of the moment or elaborate stock business; he need only act out (in a higher sense: naïvely) his own spiritual and physical substance to be effective. I find it remarkable that the Press first discovered an "actor's director" in me with the production of *What Price Glory?* (Theater in der Königgrätzer Strasse, March, 1929). In fact, I have always been an actor's director, even if it was in an entirely different sense from the one accepted as standard by the critics until now.

As early as 1923 the *Deutsche Zeitung* made the following comment on my production of Romain Rolland's *The Time will Come (Le temps viendra)* in the Central-Theater: ". . . acting . . . of a quality that many Berlin stages would do well to emulate. Not a star system loaded with big guns, but a company deeply moved by the dramatist's power and wealth of experience right down to the smallest bit part. Yet at the same time firmly controlled by a director who can keep everybody in the right place. The way this slender, still quite youthful Erwin Piscator can impose his will is astounding. If you compare his direction with the laxity that allowed things to slide and actors to go their own sweet way . . . in Shakespeare's *Richard II* at the Deutsches Theater recently, then Piscator's achievement goes up a few more points. Here is a man who knows what he wants and has a team of capable, accomplished actors, so that he has no need to bother about singing solo tenors. With glowing enthusiasm they go out to do their best not for themselves, but for the author, and with their modest resources they have created an impression that has more claim to real artistic value than the tortured artistic humbug which plagues the spectator with its eternal search for new gimmicks, all of which has become the fashionable thing for Berlin productions. Here—everything is clear-cut: yes or no."[3]

I see in the craft of the actor a science which belongs to the intellectual structure of the theater, to its pedagogy. In contrast to

3. The preceding paragraph ("As early as 1923 . . . yes or no.") was inserted in the 1963 edition.

the artistic-balletic, to the *commedia dell'arte* which is still being used, albeit in a modified form, by the Russian theater, we make the constructive aspect of thought our point of departure.

INTRODUCTION

Piscator's reputation was growing. Leopold Jessner (1879–1945), the progressive Intendant who had introduced Expressionism to the state theater in 1919, gave him a contract for three productions at the Staatliches Schauspielhaus. The first—and last—of these was Schiller's *The Robbers* (*Die Räuber*), which opened in a heavily cut and rewritten version on September 11, 1926.

The Robbers (1778) was Schiller's first play. It is an archetypal romantic melodrama in which Spiegelberg, the villain, persuades Karl Moor, the noble but temporarily mildly dissolute student son of Count von Moor, to take to the woods at the head of a band of robbers. It is his response to being cut off by his father, who has been falsely persuaded by his evil second son Franz, that Karl has disgraced the family name. Karl eventually sees the error of his gesture, rights the injustices generated by a complex plot, and, in a final idealistic flourish, surrenders to a penniless father of eleven who will collect the reward on his head.

The play's passionate idealism had early attracted the label "revolutionary," and Piscator set out to reinterpret it in contemporary revolutionary terms. He altered the first two acts, pruning figurative language, and turning Karl Moor, the romantic hero, into a romantic fool. Spiegelberg, the treacherous villain, became a lucid proletarian revolutionary, an interpretation which impressed Kurt Pinthus:

> "The only actor who struck the right note for the production was Paul Bildt as Spiegelberg, in baggy trousers and brown bowler, with Trotsky's face, gold-rimmed spectacles on a sharp nose and a reddish goatee beard, a fanatical, ambitious Jewish intellectual, speaking with sober pathos, but with such precision that every word was clear."
>
> *(8-Uhr-Abendblatt)*

He was to be the yardstick against which the other characters could be measured in modern political terms. With his cane and bowler, Spiegelberg derived from Charlie Chaplin, whose *Gold Rush* was running in Berlin. Old Moor was transformed from a pathetic old eighteenth-century sentimentalist into the choleric, domineering patriarch of Expressionist nightmares, a brisk, fit, irascible specimen of the ruling classes, brandishing a riding crop. The robbers became proletarian revolutionaries in cloth caps, and Piscator's handling of them in the crowd scenes was the real strength of the production *(Photo 26)*.

Traugott Müller, the designer, enclosed the stage in a cyclorama and erected a freestanding construct for Moor's castle. It was painted gray, had ramps, ladders and electric lights, was bristling with guns and owed much to Eisenstein's *Battleship Potemkin*, which was first screened in Berlin with music by Edmund Meisel on May 8, 1926. The set portrayed a brutal somber, fortified place from which the aristocracy imposed its rule of force *(Photo 9)*.

There were various acting levels, and one scene could be made to flow into another by simply cross-fading the lights from one area to another, without the interruption of a curtain, which, Piscator felt, inevitably dispelled some of the tension that had already been built up in the audience. The different levels could also be used to play two or even three scenes simultaneously, with various characters on the stage at different places but unaware of each other's presence. Most of the intrigue in the castle was handled in this way. In the fourth scene (II, 1 & 2) Franz in the lower room disguises Hermann and instructs him to bring a false report of Karl's death while Graf Moor sleeps in the room above. Amalia enters Graf Moor's room and the two indulge in some touching mutual consolation. Then Hermann goes up, followed after an interval by Franz, and reports Karl's supposed death. Hermann goes off and Franz goes back downstairs to listen to the results of his plan. Old Moor faints. This visual juxtaposition of the deceiver and the deceived illuminates the text. Franz's intrigue culminates in scene 8 (IV, 2, 3 & 4). Franz downstairs tries to bribe first Hermann (unsuccessfully) and then Daniel (apparently successfully) to murder Karl, who has by this time returned home incognito. Daniel off. The lights come up on Karl in the upstairs room, where Daniel joins him and tells him the truth about his brother. Daniel off. Karl above and Franz below now each delivers a monologue, speaking their lines alternately in a kind of stichomythia. Then Amalia appears at stage level in the garden. We now have three characters at different levels, oblivious to one another. She has been moved earlier by Karl's voice but only gradually realizes who he is, and by the time she dashes upstairs he has gone and we hear his horse departing.

This simultaneous technique made the lines incoherent and hard to understand. The actors were visibly listening for their cues.

However, Piscator rejected the melodrama of the Franz-Amalia-Karl triangle; he knew the absurd effect of simultaneous declamation from Dada and was unconcerned about the meaning of the words.

For the robber scenes a forest came in from the flies. This left a narrow strip of the forestage with an entrance up steps at the right, where the robbers made their stirring appearances. A picture taken at rehearsal shows the actual layout *(Photo 26)*. Scene 5 (II, 3) will serve as an example. In this scene Roller returns, having been saved from the gallows, and then the court officer (whom Piscator substituted for Pastor Moser) at this point appeared with the offer of a conditional pardon, which was rejected with derision. Kurt Pinthus describes this passage:

"Each incident built up, pausing only once to dwell pointedly on Spiegelberg's attempted putsch, to the first big robber scene, which should be cherished in theater history as a pointer to the future, a masterpiece of precision in the interplay of carefully controlled crowds and exuberant solo speeches. The robbers erupted onto the stage to pulsing jazz rhythms, punctuated by the "Internationale." The motley band of proletarians disappears into the woods, which tower in gloom, regrouping again for the frenzied symphony of the Roller scene; a constant flux of controlled movement, the robbers' gestures and actions precise, the main characters' lines delivered with exactitude; interrupted once by the fermata of the court officer (instead of Pastor Moser, a court officer in khaki appeared), only to bubble over again into the disciplined tumult of a finale that had the audience on the edge of their seats, exhilarated, involved."

(8-*Uhr-Abendblatt*)

This scene was the climax. When it ended, lights went up to tumultuous applause for the intermission. The second half of the evening, in which the romantic intrigue was worked out, offered none of the stirring possibilities of this demonstration of proletarian solidarity. It was so heavily cut that the entire performance took only two hours.

The press response to Piscator's production was mixed. Of the fourteen reviews I was able to find, the *Rote Fahne* was jubilant, seven gave qualified approval, two (Alfred Kerr and Monty Jacobs) took a detached view but felt the evening was a failure on aesthetic and theatrical grounds, and three (Paul Fechter, Erich Krafft and Franz Servaes) from the conservative, not to say right-wing, press were appalled at Piscator's mutilation of the German cultural heritage, as was Karl Kraus. There was no subsequent scandal in the press, and Carl Ebert does not recall any political repercussions, but Intendant Jessner had to write one of his many letters to his superiors to defend Piscator and himself, and the production ran for only twelve performances, half the usual run.

This production was part of a continuing search for a modern style for the classics in the Weimar Republic, now that the bombast of the court theaters and the charm of Max Reinhardt belonged to the past. Brecht's version of Christopher Marlowe's *Edward II* (1924) and Erich Engel's production of *Coriolanus* (1925), which had reduced the hero to a calculating politician, had preceded it, and Jessner quickly followed up with a political *Hamlet* (12.3.1926). Jessner was not a party propagandist, but he was an opponent of the nationalist and monarchist enemies of the Republic on the Right, and his production parodied the monarchy and militarism, so that English critics concluded that Claudius was Kaiser Wilhelm II and Polonius was Bethmann-Hollweg. Herbert Ihering, who preferred the classics to be scrutinized rather than celebrated, analyzed the role of the classics in the German theater in a pamphlet, *Reinhardt, Jessner, Piscator, oder Klassikertod? (RJP, or the Death of the Classics?*, Berlin, 1929, reprinted in H. I., *Der Kampf ums Theater*, Berlin, GDR, 1974), which Piscator quotes to support his case.

XII
INFLUENCES WHICH OUGHT NOT TO EXIST

Spiegelberg

Spiegelberg was the figure who replaced film, the globe, and the conveyor belt in *The Robbers (Die Räuber)*; he was my dramatic gimmick, my regulator, my barometer. I had the "nerve" to use this little man to test whether Karl Moor might not perhaps be a romantic fool and the gang of brigands around him simply robbers in the most straightforward sense of the word, albeit embellished with all the subtleties of a poetic imagination, and not communists at all. It was a death-defying dramatic leap, but nobody saw it. Of course, it must be stated that I made one great mistake: I should have had only that one man move through the play with his almost timeless cutaway coat, his dirty brown bowler hat and his Charlie Chaplin cane, and all the other characters should have been dressed by way of contrast in historical costumes, such as any schoolboy would recognize, and not in the timeless costumes they actually wore. It is curious how serious this little man became, true Schillerian villain that he is, as I picked out the ideological threads which connected him with his companions in crime, and with the world about him. How tragic he became when all his humorous and "roguish" arabesques were trimmed away, how thoroughly he carried out his revolution—he, the man who had no real father in a lordly palace in the background, who was no handsome, tenor-voiced hero, who had none of the attributes of the "beloved" leader! How harshly and unrelentingly fate forces him to use any means he can devise in order to pursue his logical path to the bitter end. He became the representative of the problem-ridden social situation we find ourselves in, the liaison between today and yesterday. He unmasked Schiller's pathos, he unmasked the ideological weakness of the background, but he did honor to the dramatist by coming alive for a modern audience—he alone—while the world which surrounds him is dead. Schiller's magnificent poetic passages are, of course, still superb; the robbers' song is like wondrous music. The palace: a composite set, castle, property and power, wonderful monologues are woven together into a trio of hate, revenge, love, loyalty and penitence—as in the fabric of Grand Opera. And this all has a validity and a sphere of its own, it intoxicates, it makes the heart beat faster. Art! Yes, and true, true Schiller, the most wonderful of German dramatists! In *The Robbers* and in *Love and Intrigue (Kabale und Liebe)*, he is a bourgeois revolutionary and consequently far too revolutionary for the present-day bourgeoisie. Even if I had not used Spiegelberg to sound his depths, Schiller would still have been explosive enough to knock many generations of bourgeois society out of their clogs. Unfortunately, as far as the proletariat is concerned the man has been dead for a hundred years.

"Frontbann-Räuber. [1] A short time ago the newspapers announced that the Staatstheater intended to put on Schiller's *Robbers* in modern dress. An experiment of purely artistic character. But our nationalists are quite worked up about it. They namely take the view that modern robbers can be presented only in the guise of nationalistic assassins, Rossbachs, etc., and so the *Deutsche Zeitung* speaks in today's morning edition without further ado of the magnificent *Frontbann-Räuber."*

(From *Vorwärts*)

1. The *Frontbann* was a paramilitary, right-wing organization which in 1924–1925 took over the mantle of the *Wehrverbände*, uniformed associations formed in Germany after the debacle of 1918 to rekindle the flame of "national defense." "Rossbachs" were presumably men like Gerhard Rossbach, a right-wing officer who had been active in one such group, and had fought against the Communists in the Ruhr.

The production of *The Robbers* in March and Jessner's production of *Hamlet* in September of the year 1926 raised the problem of classical plays in the modern theater. Academic critics were especially interested in this issue, and Ihering in particular dealt with it fully in his pamphlet, *Reinhardt, Jessner, Piscator, or the Death of the Classics?* Ihering, who treated the question in close conjunction with the social structure of the times, and was consequently only one step away from abandoning bourgeois modes of thought and going over to a Marxist system, was of necessity faced with the problem of the "content" of classical drama. And in particular with the relationship of that content to his own times:

"It was clear that even Schiller could not remain untouched by the great reappraisal of cultural values. Schiller, who always had an instinct for major subjects from world history, for the objective content of the drama, had to be freed from Goethe's influence. . . . The only trouble was that they attempted to do this with *The Robbers*, a play which was not written under Goethe's influence.[2] But this attempt contrived to reveal the relationship of Schiller's problems to the present day. In the first two acts of *The Robbers*, Erwin Piscator toned down the role of Karl Moor, the revolutionary by personal inclination, and played up the role of Spiegelberg, the systematic revolutionary, the man of revolutionary convictions. This required brutal changes in the original text—a dangerous move, and quite uncharacteristic of Schiller. But the production did raise one fundamental problem. This version of *The Robbers*, ostensibly a demonstration of the absolute authority of the director over the dramatic text, in fact signals the passing of the director who applies his own conception to the play, the passing of the director who indulges in formal experiments. Although the second part of this version of Schiller was downright bad, the production as a whole was significant in that it used a classical text to bring substance and content back to the theater in place of the usual empty aesthetic flourishes.

". . . It caused repertories to be revised. Not that it was significant for the classical stage in that it solved the problem of staging and presenting the classics themselves. But it was important for the old plays in that it brought them into contact with modern writing, with the modern problem play, and thus made Schiller fruitful once again for the present day."

Herbert Ihering in "Death of the Classics?"

It is possible to revitalize classical plays, to bring them close to us, only if one places them in the same relationship to our genera-

2. Schiller wrote *The Robbers* between 1778 and 1780 while he was at school in Stuttgart. His friendship with Goethe dated from 1794.

tion as they once had to their own generation. This is not a matter of formal business (modern costume, Hamlet in morning dress, a castle like a modern fortification, etc.). The formal aspect of the staging is only a means of expressing a particular intellectual attitude (as it always should be). This was also the guiding principle in my production of *The Robbers*. For me, the intellectual target is and will always remain the proletariat and the social revolution. This is the barometer against which to measure my work. Inner spiritual problems should not be discussed in an airless void. They can be fruitful only when an aim is present, an aim which is socially relevant. Ihering is right in placing the problem of the public's needs in the foreground. But who constitutes this public? In the Staatstheater it consisted of the readers of the conservative-democratic and liberal-reactionary press. They applauded loudly and were filled with excitement as the band of robbers stormed ahead, only to read in the papers the next morning that "the nation's most cherished heritage had been dragged through the mud." What conclusion do we draw from this? It is not possible at this time to speak of a public which has an intellectual need or is intellectually unified. The bourgeois public is so self-contradictory, so split and divided within itself, that it is scarcely possible to use its intellectual needs as a guide. Not so the proletariat. It does choose and reject with the unadulterated instinct of its class. And, although its members were not sitting in the orchestra of the Staatstheater, it was for this public that I staged *The Robbers*.

In an extensive article in the *Frankfurter Zeitung* (July 2, 1929), Bernhard Diebold turned Ihering's question mark into "the sleep of the classics." Diebold is against bringing classical drama radically up to date and suggests that "the classics should be banned for five years—then our tongues will be hanging out for classical plays." Instead of restructured classics, he says I must turn out "homemade" plays until his dramatists appear on the scene.

> "It is certain that the modern stage with the public's present weak-mindedness and total lack of character is more in need of cool, objective plays reflecting social realities than of vague poetic experiences, but it is also true that one cannot deep-freeze warm classics as Piscator has done; what is required are not variants of Coriolanus and Karl Moor, altered in form and content until they are aesthethically unrecognizable, but quite simply new plays from new authors.
> A de-heroified Karl Moor does not give Schiller a new life upon the ruins of himself; when Spiegelberg is made the moral hero, Schiller finally and unquestionably dies the death of the classics. . . . A Spiegelberg drama cannot be derived from Schiller, but must be written

anew—say, by Brecht. Or else we must turn to Piscator himself as a writer and ask for a homemade piece from him."

Bernhard Diebold in "Death of the Classics"

This is in my opinion a question to which there is no simple answer. The growth of a type of drama whose form and aims are suited to our theater is a process which cannot be separated from the general development of society in our times. The content, the problems and even the forms, cannot be chosen à la carte. The question of theatrical demand is also a prime consideration and until two years ago the bourgeois theater had no reason to raise social, far less, revolutionary, topics for discussion.

I feel I am not being immodest when I say that the emerging "boom in revolutionary drama" is one of the results of my own work. All at once, after the year of the Piscator-Bühne, topical drama, that is to say, drama with a contemporary social message, was a consumer item and something which no self-respecting theater could do without. A demand had been created and the producers hastened to meet it. No "dramatists" have yet been produced, but speculators have taken advantage of the boom. This phenomenon naturally has nothing to do with the slow, gradual growth of true revolutionary drama. Tomorrow these same men will be working in the realm of individual psychology or romanticism, according to public demand. The plays that Diebold has in mind, even if he fails to express this clearly, will draw their strength from the same ground upon which revolutionary theater stands. Separate from public "demand," but aiming to meet the needs of the masses.

At the time of my production of *The Robbers*, I made a statement of principle concerning the second question: to what extent is it possible or permissible to revitalize classical drama?

Fundamental Principles

If a generation existed that was fully conscious of its own times, that generation would already have outlived itself. Or at least the life of all earlier epochs would have been absorbed into the present to a point where there would no longer be a problem of "renovating the classics," just as Shakespeare relegated to oblivion everything which preceded him. The live components would have been absorbed, the others cast aside and extinguished. Our own times would be strong enough to match past experiences with present ones, so that not only the structure but also the major part of the content of classical plays would appear superfluous, empty, indeed, almost ridiculous. (Consider the progress from the stagecoach to the airplane, from the letter which takes weeks to deliver to telegraphy and even television: consider the advance in the techniques of warfare from 1814 to 1914, the difference between the petit bourgeois provincial capital and international capitalism and the proletarian Internationale.) But the din of reality has deafened us. A generation before us saw its ideals crumble beneath its feet on the day of the shots at Sarajevo, and the present generation has been forced back against the wall by the pressure of events. The blow was hard. We have to get our breath back slowly and formulate the steel conclusions of our experiences amid the shellfire.

Meanwhile, the "Moloch theater" must be fed (the needs are internal as well as external), and there is a feverish search through the literature of the past for components which might be pressed into service. So let us list briefly the principles which will enable us to face the future unresigned and full of hope.

1.

In determining whether or not it is justifiable to doctor classical plays to the needs of the modern theater, it is wrong to advance parallels from other areas of the arts. The fact is that our attitude to painting and sculpture is that of a detached visitor to a museum—unfortunately! But works for the stage, everybody is agreed on this, must offer more than purely historical and etymological interest, and must be related to the actual experiences of each successive generation of the theater public.

2.

In contrast to the lyrical poem, which owes its timeless quality to the uniqueness of the way it touches our sensibilities, a uniqueness which reverberates down the centuries, the dramatic work of art is closely bound up with its own times (with few exceptions), as is shown by its dependence on all the elements of the day, of the society of the day and that society's economic problems. (At every stage of culture the theater stood and fell by its own "topicality.") Time, as it passes over such a work, brings one element or another of the play into focus and lets the rest sink into the shadows. Every living epoch finds in past epochs certain components which appeal to it and brings them to light once more.

3.

The director cannot be a mere "servant of the work," since the work itself is not something rigid and final. Once it has been brought into existence, it grows with the times, takes on a patina of age and assimilates the contents of later minds. The task which presents itself to the director is to find the point of view from which the roots of the dramatic creation can be revealed. This point of view cannot be established by gratuitous cleverness, nor can it be chosen at will: it is only when the director is conscious of being the servant and exponent of his times that he will be able to fix the point which is common to him and to the decisive, formative forces of the epoch.

4.

What is the nature of such a standpoint? It can be determined either artistically or ideologically. But only in the latter case will one find a relationship to the work of art which is convincing not only for the particular case but also for those who will mold the future. An artistic standpoint on the other hand is not only purely external, it is bound to lose itself in a myriad of fortuitous combinations.

5.

Where does this fortuitous element begin? In our weakness. In our lack of clarity. In our failure to make a choice, in our uncertainty, in our failure to recognize what has already been theoretically or intuitively achieved. It begins with speculation on financial success, on public recognition, on personal originality. It begins with our failure to confront the absolute, which requires an intellectual commitment at every second and forever. It begins with an attempt to camouflage the gaps in our own experience and imagination. It begins with the avoidance of the direct methods which require deeds; with a retreat into "solutions" which are mere nuances.

6.

In its most fruitful periods the theater was deeply involved with the community, but today, at a time when the great masses of the people have been awakened to political life and quite rightly demand that the state should be reformed according to its ideas, the fate of the theater, if it is not to be the dainty prerogative of the upper class, must align itself through thick and thin with the needs and requirements and tribulations of the masses. In the final estimate its task is to make the people who stream into the theater aware of what is slumbering in their unconscious, vague and incoherent.

To sum up: Were war and revolution the great forces which transformed our lives, our experience and our view of the world? If they were not, then art has no justification. Every attempt to erect a human culture, every attempt to bring man closer to his fellows and to make men familiar with the world seems futile.

Quite simply, without pathos, without enmity, without prejudice, impartially, in a moment of truce: what is this thing called Art? What are its elements? Are its elements not the wishes of the human heart, and are its requirements not the conditions of a clear and rational mind? And do these wishes and requirements not grow with each day we live? Are not the things which remained unfulfilled in centuries past growing to insatiable proportions? Can an idol continue to exist which refuses to face up to the demands of life?

INTRODUCTION

Piscator's production of Ehm Welk's *Storm over Gotland* brought the simmering conflict between the conservative (Art for the People) and left-wing (committed political theater) factions of the Volksbühne to a head. The national Volksbühne conference at Hamburg in June, 1926, at which the Berlin section and the network of provincial Volksbühne organizations were represented, had been greeted with a demand from Arthur Holitscher that petit bourgeois tendencies be swept aside, with the *Welt am Abend* following this up with a campaign for a committed Volksbühne. In selecting Welk's play the management was trying to compromise with these demands.

Ehm Welk (1884–1966) was a journalist who had tried his hand at various trades and worked his passage to the United States and South America. *Storm over Gotland* was his first play. He was later persecuted by the Nazis, and after the war he was active in adult education and as a writer of novels and film scripts in the German Democratic Republic, where he died. His play was suggested by Fritz Holl, and Siegfried Nestriepke formulated the artistic committee's evaluation.

> "There is social criticism in the play, and it glorifies the Vitalian Brothers' revolutionary rising, but it also has undoubted poetic qualities, and promises to be effective on the stage, and it is this which makes the committee willing to accept it."

None of the critics shared the artistic committee's view, and even Paul Fechter on the right wing was dismissive:

> ". . . a good old historical drama like the ones high-school teachers used to write, with burgomasters, pirates, pious fisherfolk who have visions, girls in breeches, parts with grand passions, and a hero who is part Götz, part Wallenstein and part Don Quixote. You imagine it going down well in the old Royal Theater . . ."
>
> *(Deutsche Allgemeine Zeitung)*

Welk had written a medieval costume piece with political undertones based on the conflict between the Hansa and the Vitalian

Brothers. The Hansa was a loose confederation of German towns for the protection of foreign trade which in the fourteenth century opened up a Baltic route to Russia. The Vitalian Brothers, or "equal-dealers" *(Likedeeler)*, were a band of Hansa sailors who had mutinied and set up a protocommunist community on the island of Gotland, from which they preyed on shipping. The Hansa wiped them out in 1398, executing their two leaders, Godeke Michelsen and Klaus Störtebecker, who subsequently became pirate heroes of popular legend.

Welk's play centered on Störtebecker, an impoverished Junker, who becomes leader of the Vitalians and tries to sell them out to the Hansa in return for money and an aristocratic marriage. He is opposed by Asmus, an ill-defined figure, who sees himself as the guardian of the Brothers' creed, "God's friend, the world's foe, all equal in property and before the law." He tries to sell Störtebecker to the Hansa in return for immunity for Gotland. The Hansa is prepared to deal with and double-cross both of them, and eventually, after the complication of a love interest, wins the day.

Piscator saw the pirates as crusaders against capitalism, and cast Störtebecker (Heinrich George) as a Nazi conspirator and Asmus (Alexander Granach made-up as Lenin) as a lucid communist revolutionary. Welk's "good old knights and guilds German" (Herbert Ihering) was reduced where possible to clipped, colloquial exchanges (which George had not mastered by the first night).

Piscator used film and projections, much as in *Tidal Wave*. Traugott Müller's set was again a multilevel platform with a mast, using elements from *Sails on the Horizon (Photos 28–33)*. This was backed by projections on the cyclorama, including an old print of Hamburg for a scene in Hamburg City Hall. Ehm Welk wrote a prologue explaining the social structure of the Middle Ages which was projected on a central screen while old prints of medieval people and places were shown on tall side screens like the ones used in *Flags*. Scenes aboard ship were preceded by shots of the raging sea. But the really controversial component of the production was a film specially shot by Curt Oertel, a respected cameraman who had worked for G. W. Pabst, among others. The quality of the film was poor and was not improved when the censors cut a quarter of it two hours before the performance. The crucial sequence showed five figures marching side by side towards the camera, Asmus and Störtebecker among them. As they marched their costumes changed (reflecting the Peasants' Revolts—ie. 1789, 1848, 1917/18) to demonstrate the continuous triumphal march of social revolution—an outright provocation at least for the conservatives in the audience

136

(Photo 32). This was underlined by the closing effect, a red star rising in homage to the Bolshevik Revolution.

The production split the critics. Alfred Kerr and Herbert Ihering, for once in agreement, thought that this was a magnificent production of an indifferent play, and half a dozen others agreed with them. Kurt Pinthus, who had hitherto championed Piscator, felt it was too blatant a piece of propaganda. Paul Fechter in the *Deutsche Allgemeine Zeitung* demanded to know why the management had sanctioned such a production. Many members of the Volksbühne sent letters of protest, some accompanied by resignations. The managment took fright, dissociated itself from Piscator and cut the offending film. Piscator resigned, and the affair rumbled on and became a political issue, as the next chapter shows.

XIII
STORM OVER GOTLAND
Volksbühne, March, 1927

"The signs are increasing. The question of flags in the realm of literature is being raised for discussion." With this remark Béla Balázs (*Berliner Börsen-Courier*, February, 1927) entered the debate on "intellectual freedom" and "the salvation of pure art" which raged through the daily newspapers and the literary periodicals in the last months of 1926.

It was not by mere chance that this argument broke out so suddenly and so violently. The question of political theater which had been raised repeatedly by my productions was suddenly removed from the realm of theory and casual discussion and placed in the "humble arena of the daily political struggle," when the Volksbühne was at last forced to state its attitude to the problems of political theater—that is, to the problem of its own existence.

For some years it had been possible to disregard the principles behind my productions; now compromises were no longer possible. Three "revolutionary experiments" to ten bland unexceptionable dramas of "pure art"—the public was no longer prepared to accept the label "experimental." The public was alarmed. The public was no longer prepared to compromise. The public was beginning to realize that the individual productions at the Volksbühne were not gratuitous experiments but were connected with one another, and that we were following a specific line toward goals which were gradually becoming clearer. What were these goals? Where was the road leading?

Against Corruption of the Public by Press, Film and Stage!

Proclamation by the National Women's League

". . . A warning and an alarm . . . a warning against the immoral and inflammatory influences which have been widely disseminated among the masses in recent years and months by the three most important media forming public opinions and attitudes. These must be opposed manfully, not only with words but with decisive actions. . . .

"Alfred Mühr has spoken of a theater to reflect the Christian-National attitude. He demonstrated that every theater has its own regular audience and represents its own particular view of life, in so far as it is not a purely commercial theater. It is only Christian-National circles that have no theater. . . . This is their own fault. . . . Why are we not active, just as active as Piscator, who is on the verge of opening a communist theater in Berlin? . . . Our only demonstrations take the form of editorials, as in the case of *The Robbers*; we never actively take steps to defend ourselves. . . . The Greater German Theater Society (Grossdeutsche Theatergemeinschaft) has been called into being.[1] And thus our theater has been founded."

Deutsche Zeitung

On the left wing there was a search for a unified program. Béla Balázs wrote:

"In the *Berliner Börsen-Courier* of December 1, Herbert Ihering, one of the most determined flag bearers, reproaches Bernard Guillemin for using the poetically falsified notion of 'intellectual freedom' to disguise a total lack of conviction. Some time ago in the *Literarische Welt*, Willy Haas indulged in a little joke and demanded of the President of the Republic that he should solve the problem of flags in Germany by 'simply' doing away with all flags. This is, of course, not what he really thinks.

"Willy Haas is very well aware that we must have visible badges to make ourselves clearly recognizable, so that we lose none of our enemies. For we need our enemies to define ourselves. The *cogito, ergo sum* has long since turned into the opposite in our case. Nothing loosens and weakens our substance so much as our own thinking. Nonetheless: 'I exist, because I have enemies'—that is the statement which is valid in our social reality, and we know no other.

"A flag is a battle cry in the concrete struggle. Herbert Ihering demands one of theater critics and of the theater in general. But it almost seems as

1. The vision of a Greater Germany, embracing Germany, Austria and all lands in Europe where German is spoken, was frustrated at the Frankfurt Parliament of 1848 when the Prussian lobby managed to set up a federation which excluded Austria. The Pan-German idea continued to appeal to nationalist circles, especially after the humiliation of 1918, until it was ultimately discredited by the Nazis.

if he were asking the flag to stand up by itself. For while he writes, 'Theater critics have assumed political responsibilities' (*Lit. Welt*, No. 22), he shies away from taking this insight to its logical conclusion. For he also demands of the theater that it should be 'the mouthpiece of the unconscious will of the masses,' while in the same breath he complains that the public's renewed participation in the theater today is not the awakening of a productive conviction, but the tearing apart of that public into parties. But convictions, if they are clear and unambiguous, mean party affiliation! For 'public' and 'masses' as homogeneous elements within our society with a will of their own, be it only an unconscious will, do not exist, any more than the 'nation' in that sense exists. For the public is not torn apart by the theater, it is torn apart by its own divergent convictions, and then turns on the theater to tear it apart. There is no real conviction which is not, and be it only indirectly, political. In the theater of convictions there can be no truce. And when Ihering demands that the theaters show their flags, then he is demanding party theaters, because only party theaters have a homogeneous public, because it is only in these theaters that a real—shall we say, Dionysian contact between stage and auditorium can take place.

"And yet every revolutionary flag has been abused by common criminals in the initial confusion, and every flagcloth has been used as a cover to smuggle in the most vulgar, talentless kitsch. Yes, literary conscience is never so necessary as in times when truths are wafted in the air on flags, banner-truths to accept without thinking. In these cases we are inclined to let good convictions excuse bad art. But bad art is bad workmanship, and stands as treachery and counterrevolution in the service of the Revolution.

"The higher the flag, the higher the standards of achievement. 'Literary conscience,' aesthetic criticism and control, and appreciation of a man's mastery of his craft will not blind the onlooker to that man's convictions, where he has convictions. Nor will they lead us astray, for even aesthetic criticism is, if it is deep enough, always political. We believe that living and significant art can spring only from progressive convictions."

To this Herbert Ihering replied:

"Béla Balázs is right to take up the theme of the political obligations of literary and theatrical critics. On one page he states a self-evident truth: convictions must never become a mask for bad art.

"For that reason Ernst Toller's recent works have been rejected in these columns. But the question today is a different one. Toller's problem is rather that he wants to be too much of a poet and is not content, in spite of his lack of imagination and powers of organization, with an objective account of contemporary subjects. The problem today is one of themes and values. A revolutionary dramatist like Toller does not face up to the question of artistic values. A contemporary answer to the question of theme has already been found: Upton Sinclair gives one in his drama *Singing Jailbirds* and Leo Lania gives another in *General Strike (Generalstreik)*. In these cases aesthetic matters such as originality, plot, or form are not decisive. What is important is that the material should be well assembled and laid out, that it should be properly understood, so that the message can be put across in an objective style, as opposed to a declamatory style. The message is self-evident, inherent in the subject, and it need not be consciously injected or applied.

"Balázs has misunderstood 'theater politics.' Of course the public is torn apart, and will tear the theater apart. This is the very situation which should be clearly reflected in the overall direction of the theater, but seldom is. If the Staatstheater hands over one production to the Bühnenvolksbund and another to the Volksbühne—that is, one to the Right and one to the Left—then it will never build up a public. If the Bühnenvolksbund were strong enough to run its own theater, that would be an achievement to think about.[2] But to prop up an organization that has not the strength to support a theater of its own, and to use one of the major state houses to do it—this is suspect.

"Clear relationships! Differentiation, not admixture. In this way, a party theater can be created which will be productive in that it will be able to penetrate all social strata. The political task of theater criticism is to further the development of such a party theater until it blossoms into humanity theater, or political world-theater. But not to build this world-theater on the basis of the aesthetic assumptions of 1900, as some people would like to today."

The call for "clear relationships" as proclaimed by the Left was taken up with equal fervor—one might almost say with more acute political insight—by the Right. While the public, i.e., the middle classes and lower middle classes from whom the average audience of the Berlin theaters was recruited, had been mobilized by this discussion (whose ramifications they scarely understood) and gazed in fascination at this remarkable Volksbühne which had suddenly turned into an "affair," discussions began among the members of the Volksbühne in an attempt to achieve the self-knowledge and clarity which was being demanded so energetically by the Right and Left in the daily press. It was now the turn of the junior members of the Volksbühne to insist with increasing urgency that the Volksbühne pluck up its courage and press ahead on the path towards political drama, along which it had so far moved unwillingly and hesitantly, to its logical end. In the deliberations of the junior sec-

2. The Bühnenvolksbund was an organization set up in 1919 to promote theater in the "German-Christian-Nationalist" spirit. This was a right-wing venture, in opposition to the predominantly Socialist Volksbühne.

tions which had previously met to discuss the repertoire and the various productions, a new, aggressive tone suddenly made itself heard—the demand for topical plays, for political theater as a matter of principle drowned the usual casual debates about the strengths and weaknesses of individual productions.

Tragedy and Drama at the Volksbühne

"Discussions during the last meetings of the junior members of the Volksbühne have clearly and unambiguously formulated the basic ideas which must guide the Volksbühne from now on. The junior members of the Volksbühne are unanimous in a way that is unusual in any movement constituted from young workers, or from workers of any kind, in accepting the guiding principle that the founders of the Volksbühne, our Socialist comrades of the year 1890, also supported! The motion placed before the assembled members of the junior section of the Volksbühne on March 14 and unanimously adopted was the following:

" 'The Volksbühne, which is supported by the workers, must produce a repertory which is alive and purposeful and expresses clear convictions. The proletarian youth within the Volksbühne rejects the bourgeois concept of the neutrality of art. Since the theater is an important weapon in the struggle for the freedom of the working classes, the stage must reflect the life and the wishes of the proletariat as it struggles to put the world into a new order.'

"This is naturally at variance with the statements of the management of the Volksbühne, who sent Dr. Nestriepke to the meeting to formulate, or promise, or welcome, or threaten, or forbid anything the junior assembly might say: the management stated that the junior members did not have their sympathy; it was expected that every member of the Volksbühne would realize that *King Lear* was an ennobling experience, and if the junior members failed to be ennobled they had better get out of the Volksbühne: the reason being that the Volksbühne is and must remain neutral!

"This neutrality of art was then publicly demonstrated on March 21 in the Theater am Schiffbauerdamm in an amiably tragic manner with the first performance of the *Tragedy of Love (Tragödie der Liebe)*—a completely passive tragedy of love and marriage written thirty years ago, unreal and fundamentally irrelevant and superfluous.

"The production was rejected in unison by the entire press. Instead of writing a polemic of my own, I shall quote an extract from the pious, bourgeois *12-Uhr-Mittag-Zeitung* with which I am fully in accord.

" 'What happened at the Volksbühne on Saturday is quite incredible. A play was performed that was as dusty, as moldy, as decrepit, as outmoded as can be imagined. Presumably to point out to the protesting junior members of the Volksbühne and to everyone else who has advocated a progressive course that here the blackest reaction is still in command. Everything that is young and alive, moving and exciting, is ignored by the Volksbühne at present. But perhaps we have to go through this phase first; perhaps these farces which really have nothing more to do with true theater must be drowned in laughter and the musty trash forgotten, because the opposition movement is growing up at quite a different point and cannot but be greatly helped by these provocative actions. The Volksbühne has only to take one more step along this path to ensure that no one will take any further notice of it. It has already missed one great chance: the chance to be taken seriously.'

"How did the Volksbühne react to this crisis which became a catch phrase among the theater critics, which figured in discussions among members of the Volksbühne and was on the agenda at the meetings of the Artistic Committee? The management sent out Herr Springer, who explained to the *Weltbühne* that they knew nothing of any crisis within the Volksbühne."

Johannes Jahnke in Aufrufer, February, 1927

The conflict developed into a duel between Arthur Holitscher and Georg Springer of the management committee of the Volksbühne, a duel which was enacted in the pages of the *Weltbühne*. On March 8, 1927, Arthur Holitscher wrote the following in the *Weltbühne* under the rubric, "On the Volksbühne Crisis":

"Constant worries about the continued existence of the grandiose, to my mind, catastrophically grandiose, house on Bülowplatz and worries about the way unemployment has been causing the membership in Berlin and throughout the Reich to fluctuate wildly explain much that must seem reactionary to the discontented outsider in the running of the Volksbühne at present. This explains why the management was so jittery and opposed the 'experiments' which the discontented among us regard as the only essential aspect of its work, as the only requirement which it must fulfill, indeed, as the justification of the existence of the Volksbühne—as an element in the repertoire which is at present conspicuously absent. After every premiere of a work conceived in terms of the political convictions to which we subscribe, reflecting the proletarian attitude to current events, hundreds of letters from members pour into the Volksbühne offices, all with the same message: 'Spare us all these problems, hunger, revolution, class struggle, misery, corruption, prostitution; we have more than enough of this at our party subscription meetings, at work, at home, and in the neighborhood!'

"The political development of the organized workers in Germany, and particularly those in Berlin, whose convictions led to the founding of the Volksbühne a generation ago, runs parallel to that of the Volksbühne itself. The mentality of the limp petite bourgeoisie has developed and spread widely among the German workers. It has not only destroyed

143

their will to fight, it has also almost completely eradicated the class consciousness of the average German proletarian. The more radical elements within the German proletariat can see nothing to interest them in the Volksbühne and they stay away. They have no wish to be lulled to sleep by Art; on the other hand, they are too weak economically to create or knock together an instrument which would express their own creative impulses. The management of the Volksbühne, responsive to the instincts and the needs of the great mass of their members who follow the struggles of the times so reluctantly, indeed, even ignore them, is concerned to avoid irritating these instincts, concerned, in fact, to cater for them. A parallel development shows where this kind of thing must lead: just as the German Social Democrats are prepared to go into coalition with parties whose aims are diametrically opposed to its historical mission, merely in order to reap a few minor benefits in the form of ministerial and lesser posts, so the Volksbühne has, with the blessing of the Ministry of Culture, entered in the course of the last year into a coalition with the reactionary Bühnenvolksbund—a link which is, one might say, unnatural, and which has produced a vile compromise, a hybrid concoction, especially in the theaters whose repertoires now take into consideration both the red and the black groups of members. In the process, the Volksbühne has declined to the level of a consumers' union for theater tickets."

Georg Springer wrote an answer to this under the same rubric in the *Weltbühne*, March 22, 1927:

"The Volksbühne has neither the tradition nor the intention, nor even the possibility of equating the word V*olk* in its name with the radical-socialist trade unions. There can be no doubt that it owed its foundation to a desire to make art, and in the first instance the theater, accessible to the workers, and to the present day it considers the opening up of a path for the proletariat to our cultural tradition as its main aim. But neither in Berlin nor in the Reich does the membership of the Volksbühne stem exclusively from the proletariat; and if we were to limit our definition and consider that only those among the people who have radical-socialist convictions are entitled to an opinion and worthy of advancement, this would be tantamount to exploding the Volksbühne. According to Holitscher, the whole body of workers organized within the SPD has to be excluded from the V*olk* by definition, and since it is well-known that there are deep divisions in the ranks of the Communists in Germany at the moment, it is difficult to see exactly where this political definition of V*olk* gets us.

"We prefer therefore to cling to a notion of culture which affords artistic movement and enables us to find a community of experience among a wide range of people without coming down to the level of party differences."

But the struggle which had broken out could not be fought out on a theoretical level. The management of the Volksbühne had realized that certain conclusions had to be drawn from the revolt among its members. Naturally, not by making a clear-cut decision—but with a good old-fashioned compromise which, they hoped, would placate the opposition. This is how I came to produce Ehm Welk's *Storm over Gotland*.

The management's intentions were transparent: the content of the work was revolutionary but the action was set around 1400 and should, even in my production, be devoid of any unnecessarily dangerous topicality; it was a political play whose documentary essence had been exploited as mere spectacle.[3] But the management had overlooked one detail, a single sentence. It was printed on the title page of this work and read: "The play takes place not only in 1400."

To be sure: the author himself had omitted to develop this dramatic insight fully. In language and diction the play was still in the style of medieval historical drama; the significance of the struggle between the capitalist Hansa and the communist Vitalian Confederacy and its relationship to the present day were not clarified. A flaw ran right through the work: the gap between the author's intention, the intellectual line he was pursuing, and the watered-down "poetic" form of the piece.

The author wanted to show that the struggle between the Hansa and the Vitalian Confederacy recurs throughout the centuries under different names, so that in form and content the drama of the uprising and its collapse had a general validity. But this intention, the indication that the play was taking place "not only in 1400," had not been realized dramatically. So I made a special film outlining the political, religious and social power-constellations in the Middle Ages, to fill in the documentary background to the action of the play. Then I transformed the individuals in the drama into types by taking the various heroes and clarifying their social function, and by playing off Störtebecker, a passionate revolutionary who today would probably be a National Socialist, against Asmus, who dealt in sober facts and typified the rational type of revolutionary who appears in his purest form in Lenin. And, in fact, Asmus appeared made-up as Lenin. Störtebecker and his fellow

3. "The Conservatives accept it because it is 'traditional literature.' The young members of the Volksbühne are for it because it has a political message. This is wrong, of course. Compromises are never profitable." H. Ihering in the *Berliner Börsen-Courier*. [E. P.]

fighters appeared in the film striding toward the audience in a quick succession of historical costumes, so that the general pattern followed by revolutions and the men who have made them could, in a few seconds on the screen, be followed through the centuries up to the present day. The principles of social revolution were worked out in all their inevitability, and their universal validity from Hamburg to Shanghai was demonstrated,[4] from the year 1400 until March, 1927, the date of the performance.

The Result

"There was absolutely no question of art this evening. Politics had swallowed it up to the last morsel. Without realizing it, we had stumbled into an election meeting of Communist activists, we stood in the midst of jubilation at a celebration of Lenin. The shining star of Soviet Russia rose above the stage at the end."

Der Tag

"One of the most deeply moving shots shown by Piscator . . . one of the most unforgettable film clips is: a figure of Lenin being beheaded again and again . . . and each time the figure returns it is in a new guise and has a fresh impact. Yes, I wrote for the Russian memorial album as this man died: 'This dead man will rise again and again from the dead—in a hundred forms—until justice reigns in the chaos upon earth.' Bolshevism? Every bible has another name for it. —And then as Shanghai appeared in black and white on the screen, a storm broke loose in the house, from the orchestra to the balcony, quite unparalleled—everyone was conscious of experiencing something entirely new. One's own political attitude scarcely matters. The emotional fact speaks, speaks, cries out."

Alfred Kerr

While *Vorwärts* (Hochdorf) had been completely captivated by the art of the director and wrote: "Piscator makes us want what he wants. We cannot escape from him. We have no will to quibble with him over theory. We stand amazed, amazed at the fact that he has now given a totally convincing demonstration of the possibility of combining film and live theater"—*Der Tag* states: "The film and the action on the stage are linked in a wholly inorganic manner and constantly contradict one another."

Fechter in the *Deutsche Allgemeine Zeitung* declared: "Not even the public at the Volksbühne with its brilliantly organized claque can stand

4. The advance of the Chinese Revolution was closely followed in Germany. The People's Party led by Chiang Kai-shek at that time had the united support of the Communists and the Conservatives in China. In 1927 it took Shanghai, in 1928, Peking.

so much boredom at once," while Manfred Georg in the *Berliner Volks-zeitung* declared: "Seldom have the blinds been ripped so violently from the eyes of the average man." Kurt Pinthus talked of Piscator's "monumental direction against the grain of the dramatist Ehm Welk" and wished "that this performance, play and production alike, had never taken place," but Moritz Loeb in the *Morgenpost* was of the opinion that "with this one achievement Piscator confutes all the literati and actors who are busy producing papers and arguments against the dominance, the supposed omnipotence of the theater director."

But whereas the critics were apparently unable to agree about the effect produced by the performance, its effect on the public was of a quite consistent nature: political. Political theater had broken free from the limitations of the conventional theater, just as it had freed the drama from its author's limitations. The energies thus released flowed from the theater into the public, just as on the evening of the performance the energy had streamed down from the stage into the auditorium. Fronts were formed and began to march, conflicting views clashed violently; *Der Tag* wrote: "The management of the Volksbühne has repeatedly stressed that its aims are purely artistic, above and beyond politics. This being the case, how could it permit such a performance?" The management replied:

"The management of the Volksbühne considers that the manner in which Ehm Welk's play *Storm over Gotland* (which it had acquired for performance in the Theater am Bülowplatz) has been staged constitutes a misuse of the freedom which it is its principle to accord to the personalities entrusted with the artistic direction of the Volksbühne's theaters. Ehm Welk's play was accepted not because it had any particular political slant, but because of its inherent artistic value—it was, of course, fully appreciated that there was an implicit connection between the subject of the play and problems of the present day—but in Erwin Piscator's production, with due deference to his artistic authority, it was handled in a tendentious and political fashion and was adapted and transformed in a way for which there was no essential justification. The management of the Volksbühne wishes to state expressly that the work was exploited for one-sided political propaganda purposes without its knowledge or wishes, and that this sort of production is in contradiction to the fundamental political neutrality which the Volksbühne enjoys and is obliged to preserve. Steps have already been taken to ensure that our conception of the tasks of the Volksbühne will in future be properly respected."

The management's declaration was welcomed by the forces of reaction—from the *Mecklenburger Warte* in Rostock:

"As far as one can judge from the outside, what seems to be taking place is a counteroffensive of the idealistic elements which still exist within the Volksbühne who are now trying to free themselves from the embrace of the Jews."

—across the board to *Vorwärts:*

"The management's statement of principle was necessary to protect the fundamental idea of the Volksbühne from misinterpretation."

In order to avoid misinterpretation the management immediately took the steps its initial statement had hinted at: sections of the film were cut.

Vote of Confidence in Piscator by Members and Actors of the Berlin Volksbühne

"On Sunday evening there were stormy protests by members and spectators at the mutilation of Piscator's production of *Storm over Gotland.* At the end of the first part of the play, amid a storm of applause for the actors, there were tumultuous calls for Piscator. When the audience made no move to leave the auditorium, Heinrich Georg, who plays the role of Claus Störtebecker, asked for silence and declared (presumably in the name of all the actors): 'We have been raped; it is under constraint and against our will that we are acting without the film and negotiations are in progress but have not yet been completed.' "

Vote of Confidence in the Management of the Volksbühne

"A general meeting of the management and artistic committee of the Volksbühne after a lively discussion accepted the following motion by thirty-seven votes to four: 'The management has the full confidence of the administrative staff and of the Artistic Committee in any steps that it might take to preserve the character of the Volksbühne as a cultural organization above political partisanship.' In the face of certain rumors that negotiations have opened between the Volksbühne, the Staatstheater and the Städtische Oper to create 'organizational concentration' and merge the subscription lists, the management of the Volksbühne declares that it has no knowledge of any such plans, and has no intention of surrendering or limiting the independence of the Volksbühne."

Vossische Zeitung, March 3, 1927

My Declaration

The way in which I staged *Storm over Gotland* does not constitute a misuse of the freedom accorded by the Volksbühne to its artistic directors. It has been established and is indeed widely acknowledged that a connection exists between the subject of the play and current problems (Ehm Welk himself wrote: "The play takes place not only in 1400") and this finds artistic expression in an appropriate, contemporary manner. I do not agree that my production is merely tendentious in its effect and I maintain that artistic considerations alone governed both the coupling of film with live action, and the dramatic ideas which determined the content of the film; these artistic considerations were recognized by the management of the Volksbühne itself as well as by a large sector of the press and the majority of the public. I stand by my production, which was conceived as a totality and should be judged as such. The fact that the management has spoken out against one of its own directors is surely a unique occurrence in the history of the theater, and they have now compounded this by mutilating my production in cutting all the important parts of the film. I cannot give my consent to these measures. I herewith relinquish any responsibility for future performances of *Storm over Gotland.*

Criticism of the Management

"Now hold tight! . . . The political propaganda in Piscator's production was not at all 'one-sided' (1848, for example, hardly stands for Bolshevism)[5]—but showed on film with unquestionable justification the slow and agonized progression from slave state to people's state. Is this forbidden? Long live our strong, courageous German Republic! There is a proverb which the Volksbühne might note in regard to such a rare and outstanding director as Piscator—to wit: 'The bridegroom complains that the bride is too beautiful.'

In this case one must add: 'And he does not hesitate to disavow her afterwards.' Pity the poor bridegroom!"

Alfred Kerr, *Berliner Tageblatt,* March, 1927

Solidarity with Piscator

The management of the Volksbühne has taken a public stand against Erwin Piscator's production of Welk's *Storm over Gotland.* At the same time it has arrogantly defaced and mutilated Piscator's work with cuts of its own.

The management's attempt to justify its rigorous proceedings against the most lively and promising artist and fighter in its ranks by suggesting that he was obliged to observe "the principle of political neutrality" contradicts the spirit in which the Volksbühne was founded. The belief that in a modern play dealing with modern problems all sociopolitical

5. In 1848, in the wake of the July Revolution in Paris, there were widespread risings in Germany. These risings were liberal in character, aiming at constitutional government and popular representation. This bourgeois revolution was one of the phases through which the revolutionaries in the controversial film marched.

tendencies must be excised, or can be excised, is obviously a great mistake. Not satisfied with this, the management—in a grotesque misunderstanding of its own functions—took it upon itself to act as censor, not contenting itself with banning the result of much concentrated toil, but recklessly shortening and bowdlerizing it, so that a completely false picture of the original admirable achievement emerges.

They have interfered with the work of an artist whose talents in the field of theater reform are acknowledged even by his enemies; they have publicly abandoned him, and have belittled his incontestable service in the rejuvenation of a Volksbühne which had been becoming more and more ossified. In our opinion they should have considered themselves lucky to have a man like this in their ranks—this bold and trenchant mind, who has served and continues to serve the Volksbühne honestly.

In the face of this action we consider it our duty to assure Erwin Piscator of our sympathy and of the pleasure his work affords us, in spite of the opposition of a group of bureaucrats who seem to have forgotten their own past.

Joh. R. Becher; Bernard v. Brentano; Paul Bildt; Ernst Deutsch; Tilla Durieux; Erich Engel; Fritz Engel; Gertrud Eysoldt; Erwin Faber; Emil Faktor; Jürgen Fehling; Lion Feuchtwanger; S. Fischer; Manfred Georg; Alexander Granach; George Grosz; Wilhelm Herzog; Herbert Ihering; Erwin Kalser; Alfred Kerr; Kurt Kersten; Egon Erwin Kisch; Fritz Kortner; Leo Lania; Heinrich Mann; Thomas Mann; Karlheinz Martin; Edmund Meisel; Gerda Müller; Traugott Müller; Max Osborn; Alfons Paquet; Max Pechstein; Kurt Pinthus; Alfred Polgar; Ernst Rowohlt; Leopold Schwarzschild; Hans Siemsen; Ernst Toller; Kurt Tucholsky; Paul Wiegler; Alfred Wolfenstein.

Storm over the Volksbühne

"The Friends of Nature section of the Berlin-Fichte Sports and Athletic Club held a protest meeting at which hundreds of Friends of Nature and working-class sportsmen stated their position on the Piscator case. In a unanimously accepted resolution those present demanded that the struggle to restore artistic freedom, which the management of the Volksbühne had fettered, should be carried on, and that a fresh proletarian-socialist spirit should be injected into the Volksbühne movement."

Albert Weidner Accuses

"Piscator's staging of Ehm Welk's play *Storm over Gotland* was critically appraised in the last number of this paper by Hans W. Fischer. From an artistic point of view the production is not unassailable. Piscator is, without a doubt, a most effective director in the modern manner, but he did not have time to allow this undertaking to mature. That is regrettable. What is worse, he did violence to the play's author: rather than feel his way into the work, he pushed the author aside and distorted his play in a tendentious manner. Those who demand 'artistic freedom' for Erwin Piscator are clearly not aware that the author, Ehm Welk, left a rehearsal in protest a few days before the play opened, and that his wife let the management of the Volksbühne know that they could expect the author to make a public protest from the stage on opening night against Piscator's production. That he intended to instruct his agent to withdraw the play. And this was before the dramatist had any idea what the Soviet political films would look like, whose conflicting style ripped the production completely apart before the last act! They are probably equally unaware that Ehm Welk walked out of the theater on the first night at the moment when Piscator's Soviet Star impressed the final party political stamp on the production.

"Artistic freedom! Is that your emphatic cry, my friends? And where is the dramatist's artistic freedom in this affair? When I put this to you during the meeting at the Herrenhaus you called back: the author is in agreement with Piscator's production. In the meantime I have positively established that you were mistaken. Will you now accord the author his freedom?

"The management of the Volksbühne, responding to the pressure of protests against the party political line taken by the production, has made Holl, the artistic director of the Volksbühne, cut Piscator's Soviet appendages out of Ehm Welk's play. This unleashed a storm of protest; and it is true that the public declaration which accompanied this move was not happily worded. And, of course, it is debatable whether they had any right to do this. But if the dramatist himself, who hitherto kept his bitterness quietly to himself, had made a complaint to the Artistic Committee of the Volksbühne, would that committee not have had to defend his artistic freedom against the director's private political interpretation? Would you, dear Holitscher, as a member of the committee, have hesitated for a moment?

"If you want to put your shoulder to the wheel of the Volksbühne's Thespian wagon to help to move it forward, you must not take liberties with a dramatist's work to drive home your own message. You have to content yourself with participating in the hard, responsible work of those who have created this organization for the workers of Berlin, and have faithfully managed it under the most difficult conditions."

Ehm Welk Declares

To the Management of the Union of German Volksbühne-Associations:
Dear Sirs,

You have asked me to state my position in the Volksbühne-Piscator case. I did not want to make any statement, since this case does not greatly concern me; I see it as a private matter between management and the director. Since, however, efforts are being made on both sides to involve me, let me say the following:

I disapprove of the protests made by the management against the director because they were made on political grounds. I wrote *Storm* as a political play and agreed to a political production. I also willingly agreed with the director that the revolutionary idea should be clearly worked out, and I made no objection to the use of lighting and film, and even cooperated willingly in-this. I was also prepared to accept the rearrangement of a few scenes and, after much hesitation, the addition of new scenes.

I did protest, unmistakably and energetically, to the dramaturg, Dr. Kayser, at the rehearsals, and to Piscator in letters, against the way the text was maltreated; against the actor George, who would go through whole scenes without using a single word of the script and would extemporize nonsense and rubbish like "You don't say! Well, I'll be damned! Comrades in Hell and high water!" and hundreds of equally ridiculous expressions. And the director not only failed to correct these, he made sweeping alterations to accommodate George's antics. I protested at the way the film and the stage business were engulfing the whole play; at the way banalities, party slogans and bureaucratic jargon were inserted into the text; at the excessive number of revolutionary prophecies. So, to be precise, I did not protest because the production was political—I wanted it to be as trenchant as possible—; I protested at the way in which the style of the production had become a political and artistic end in itself, which came between the director and the text, and could only turn the director's contribution into a purely optical one which was independent of the play itself and indeed demolished the play. Everything that might have lent any depth to the characters was sacrificed to this end, and all that was left was an empty medieval costume piece. In this way, as some critics observed, the director's grandiose contribution amounted to a colossal effort against the grain of the play. In absolute terms it was highly artistic, it was more powerful and more artistic than the original text. But it was also artistically questionable when one stepped down from those despotic heights to the level where a director is expected to serve the interests of the written drama. If the play was really weak, this kind of production could not help it, but could only destroy it. Even *Florian Geyer, The Robbers* or *Edward II*—supposing the texts were unknown—could not have stood up to having the audience diverted and distracted in this way.

I have no intention of abandoning my sense of comradeship because of these experiences. And I still stand by the theatrical aims which Erwin Piscator proclaimed in his objective speech in the Herrenhaus. The fact that these aims cannot be reconciled with his handling of the production of *Storm* is of secondary importance. And if I am reluctant to place myself as a shield in front of the Piscator of *Storm*, I am much more reluctant to be used as a battering ram against him. I have explained my reasons for this.

Nobody can say, unless it be out of ill will, that I am trimming my sails to the wind in this matter—since March 23, this is impossible. I have no wish to become more involved. Since I never wished to speak out, I would like to be left out of the argument about the dangers threatening art and artists. Let me enjoy Spring and the march of the army of South China.

Yours truly,
Ehm Welk

Erwin Piscator's Correction

Even befor the play *Storm over Gotland* was accepted for production, the Artistic Committee pointed out to Herr Welk that the style of the text would have to be adapted for the production we had in mind. During rehearsals it became clear that over long stretches of the play not only the text but also the dramatic structure would have to be altered.

Herr Welk accepted this and made all the substantial alterations himself. So it is a vile lie when people say that I have done him violence.

Not only did Herr Welk agree that the play should have a political production, he even wrote in the text that the play takes place not only in 1400, and he himself points out that in the central figure of Asmus he has imitated Lenin's manner of speaking and that Störtebecker is a "Junker from the Baltic provinces, a fanatical monarchist."

He himself wrote the text to the film prologue. He helped Traugott Müller, the designer, to select pictures for projection, and he knew and approved of our ideas for the film, including the rising star.

Because we were so short of time, neither Herr Welk, nor Director Holl, nor myself, saw a finished dress rehearsal, with the result that I relinquished all responsibility the evening before we opened. I was persuaded by arguments which I do not at present wish to publish that it was necessary to open on time.

I regret that I have been forced to make this statement and that I have to reject any other formulation.

The objections that remain are all secondary; they are known to me and concern individual efforts. I would agree that I too spotted inadequacies in the play during the rehearsals which had not attracted my attention earlier because the subject matter was so powerful, and at that stage I myself finally suggested to the dramatist that he should withdraw the play before the first performance. It was at this point that the author left the rehearsal. We reached an agreement later. But it now seems quite ludicrous that people should shout about the dramatist's "lack of artistic freedom" and the director's personal dictatorship, when they ought to know that both of us have one aim in mind, to make the work a success, and they ought to know, too, how thankful everybody in the theater is to be able for once to start with something that we rarely even end up with nowadays: namely, a completed, ready-made play.

INTRODUCTION

The controversy which followed *Storm over Gotland* was not confined to the Volksbühne. The Social Democratic faction which held the Volksbühne to be above politics unexpectedly found itself in alliance with the nationalists and conservatives for whom the *Berliner Lokalanzeiger* polemicized in the press. Piscator and the communist Jugendliche Abteilungen, as the junior section was called, on the other hand, were supported by a broad spectrum of liberal opinion; refined gentlemen like Thomas Mann and Alfred Kerr, as well as Kurt Tucholsky of the *Weltbühne*, signed a letter of protest on Piscator's behalf.

In the eyes of the liberals the Volksbühne's decision to cut the controversial parts of Piscator's production constituted a step back toward censorship, which had been abolished in 1918, but which the Catholic Center Party had recently been advocating. A law regulating pornography and trash *(Schmutz und Schund)* had been passed in 1926, and though it expressly excluded plays with tendentious social and political views, Gerhart Hauptmann, at sixty-four scarcely a hotheaded radical, had pronounced it the biggest threat to intellectual freedom in his lifetime. The conservative and nationalist groups continued to press for state control of the arts, and by 1929 the police had taken the matter into their own hands and banned several plays, among them P. M. Lampel's *Poison Gas over Berlin (Giftgas über Berlin)*, which in their judgment posed a threat to law and order. In 1933, of course, ideological censorship became absolute.

At a meeting called by Piscator's supporters at the Herrenhaus, the former upper chamber of the imperial government, artistic freedom was the main theme of the discussion. Piscator describes the meeting at length. Among the speakers were Ernst Toller, Kurt Tucholsky and Leopold Jessner. Tucholsky (1890–1935), poet, satirist, social commentator and editor of the *Weltbühne*, was a former USPD supporter who had returned to the SPD, only to become a harping critic of its hierarchy and policies. Jessner (1878–1945) had been a thorn in the flesh of the conservatives from his appointment as Intendant of the Staatstheater in 1919. They had commented then that the last "Christian" theater had now fallen to the Jews. His republican and antimonarchist productions (e.g., *Wilhelm Tell*, 1919, *Hamlet*, 1926) in the former Hoftheater had given rise to questions in the Reichstag, and the renewal of his contract met with opposition both in 1925 and in 1929. Adverse criticism and political pressure finally forced his resignation in 1930, and he immigrated to Hollywood in 1933.

The rumored merger of Jessner's Staatstheater with the Volksbühne—even if it was only a matter of forming a joint booking organization along the lines of the "Reibaro," which marketed tickets for the Reinhardt, Barnowsky and Robert theaters—would have placed the noncommercial theater in the hands of the broad Left, and that at a time when Piscator was threatening to take over the Volksbühne and was under contract to do two more productions at the Staatliches Schauspielhaus. This accounts for the vehemence of the right-wing press. For the first time in the Weimar Republic, the nationalists (Deutschnationale) were represented in the Marx administration which took office in 1927, and the Volksbühne Affair prompted them to set up a theater organization of their own, the Grossdeutsche Theatergemeinschaft (Greater German Theater Society). The organization eventually produced Hellmuth Unger's *Mammon* at the Wallner Theater in January, 1928. It was later revived abortively with Nazi support but finally collapsed in September, 1930, in time to make way at the Wallner Theater for the third Piscator-Bühne. The plays it produced were trivial, sentimental Volksstücke. Even Julius Bab, the literary advisor to the Volksbühne, who was a mild critic, dismissed *Mammon* as light entertainment for lowbrows.

Both Kurt Tucholsky and Alfred Mühr, writer for the *Deutsche Zeitung* and the most influential critic on the extreme Right, refer with respect in this chapter to Soviet films whose quality was recognized right across the political spectrum in the Weimar Republic. They began to be shown in 1923, and the sensational impact of Eisenstein's *Battleship Potemkin* in 1926 brought a wave of Soviet films into the Berlin cinemas. *Potemkin*, like Chaplin's *Gold Rush* when it came out two months earlier, was hailed as a masterpiece. Herbert Ihering wrote:

> "If everything written in the last twenty years were lost, and only this film survived, mankind would still have a masterpiece to rank alongside the *Iliad* and the *Nibelungenlied*."

Pudovkin's *The Mother*, which was shown in Berlin a month before the opening of *Storm over Gotland*, also got rave notices. What impressed critics like Ihering, apart from the technique of the Soviet directors, was the unity and integrity of the films. Ihering stated:

> "In Germany we occasionally have excellent films, but we have no folk cinema because we are in political, intellectual and artistic disarray. . . . In the Soviet Union there is folk cinema because there is a dominant sociopolitical world view."

Piscator resigned and the storm at the Volksbühne died down, though there was one change. Later in the summer the Special Sections were founded to offer a progressive repertoire of Zeitstücke to the more radical of the younger members.

XIV
PROCLAMATION AT THE
HERRENHAUS

"The Piscator controversy. The left wing of the Volksbühne has arranged a meeting on Wednesday, March 30, at 8:00 P.M. in the ballroom of the old Herrenhaus to discuss: 'The Volksbühne, the living theater, and the latest events.' Arthur Holitscher will chair this protest meeting. Erwin Piscator will speak about his production of *Storm over Gotland* and about the subsequent disagreements within the Volksbühne."

(Press notice)

The following report appeared in the *Berliner Volkszeitung*:

"Between 1,500 and 2,000 people had gathered. The ballroom of the Herrenhaus was filled to overflowing; as we reported in our morning issue, a second meeting had to be held simultaneously; indignation, enthusiasm, and a determination to make political propaganda out of the situation dominated the public. They were concerned with something bigger than the 'Piscator Case.' Young people took the stand. Unanimous protests against the management of the Volksbühne, confessions of faith in tendentious drama: the time had come to decide whether the Volksbühne was to continue to be an organization which paid lip service to Left and Right in equal measure, or whether, true to its traditions, its stage would once more become the exclusive province of the working classes. The opposition at the Volksbühne forms only a minority of the members, and they should have known that the fight could be conducted only in a purely objective manner: some of the speakers were rather too concerned about the (personal) effect of their pathos.

"Arthur Holitscher opened the meeting: 'The Volksbühne is on the way to becoming a commercial enterprise—the management of the Volksbühne has declared that this protest meeting does not concern it. The Volksbühne is a weapon in the cultural struggle and we refuse to let this last weapon be snatched from our hands!'

"Erwin Kalser, on behalf of the actors of the Volksbühne, made the statement which was published in full in the morning edition. The declaration that the whole artistic personnel is behind Piscator to a man met with thunderous applause. Victor Blum spoke in the name of the extras at the Volksbühne: another declaration of solidarity with Piscator. Ernst Toller, who was greeted with loud applause, spoke on Drama—Idea—Message: 'Drama means conflict, means we must be radical if we are to be anything at all. The proletarian who walks the stage today carries a flag—and that disturbs the petite bourgeoisie. The proletarian of today is no longer a man of feeling, he is the bearer of an idea. The Volksbühne has no face, no character, has not the courage to make itself disliked.' Toller then spoke on his own account, which seemed unnecessary. (It is well-known that Toller is involved in a lawsuit against the Volksbühne, which accepted one of his plays but has failed to stage it.)

"After Toller, the next man to appear on the platform was Intendant Jessner. Loud applause.

"And after Jessner had declared his solidarity with his fellow director Piscator—applause for several minutes. For the record, Jessner denied any knowledge of a projected merger of the Staatstheater with the Volksbühne. 'Nor could I imagine that my actors would be foolish enough to refuse to work in Piscator's productions, as was stated in several newspapers. I am bound to Piscator by more than a legal contract.[1] I have no fears about Piscator the artist. Piscator must not be thrown out—he is one of the most powerful personalities in the modern theater!'

"Karlheinz Martin protested at the 'Rape of Art.'

"Erwin Piscator was greeted with thunderous applause, 'Comrades, Comrades!' At this, louder applause and shouts of 'Bravo.'

" 'My case,' Piscator declared, 'is the case of the Volksbühne—the leadership of the Volksbühne itself needs to be led—we want no retreat into the past—on the stage as elsewhere we must have commitment.'

"After this, Kurt Tucholsky spoke, and his speech was the most serious, the wittiest, the most effective and political of the evening. 'If a Berliner wants to know what year he is living in, he doesn't come to the Volksbühne; he goes to Russian films! Art without a message is unthinkable to us! In the name of justice we must have courage enough to be unjust!' Tucholsky closed his speech with a plea, 'For our own times!' "

Alarm on the Right

Berliner Lokalanzeiger

"Before you got to the top of the steps you knew what was on. A leaflet was pressed into your hand which was intended to fire Berlin with the

1. I had signed a contract to direct three plays for the Staatstheater. [E. P.]

cause of Soviet China. The fact that Piscator was prepared to face such an auditorium, to flatter it and allow it to sympathize with him, divests him of the last vestige of respect you might have been able to raise for his errant artistry.

"Intendant Jessner makes a declaration of solidarity with his fellow director. He does not seem to have taken a very close look at the people he is addressing, but at least he avoids any political allusions, unlike Karlheinz Martin, who at one time applied for the post of Director of the Volksbühne and was rejected, and who now claims the theater for the proletariat. Not that this will prevent Herr Martin from working on the stages where the Kurfürstendamm public is wont to attend. Piscator himself gets a tumultuous welcome and naturally addresses those present as 'Comrades!' He is of the opinion that the expression 'art is above politics' is a worn-out cliché, and demands that the actors should be represented on the artistic committee of the Volksbühne. (This would be tantamount to a return to the times of the workers' councils, times that are fortunately behind us.) The theater needs new political subjects, and pure, supreme art will grow organically out of the working class. So long as the present has not brought forth its own writers, dramas which point in the right direction must be pressed into service. (As, for example, *The Robbers*.) Ultimately, the choice is: Piscator or the Volksbühne. The management has made its position clear and the majority of members are behind it. *If it steps down, the Volksbühne goes up in smoke.* If it stands fast, it must expect the left wing to break away in the near future, but it will then be able to stick to its stated principle: that the practice of art is always above politics. Nobody who has the interests of *art and the Volksbühne at heart will hesitate to lend his support to the management.*"

Berliner Nachtausgabe, March 31, 1927

The conflict provoked by this production became a political struggle which spread far beyond the circles which were interested in theater and far beyond the specific artistic problem. It was fought out with terrible bitterness by the Right, whose main target was Intendant Jessner. They used the aesthetic ideology of the petite bourgeoisie in most skillful fashion to camouflage their attack on the position of power within the state. The *Lokalanzeiger's* next headline was:

The Street Rebels Against Art.

The Piscator-Shindig at the Herrenhaus—No Interest at the Volksbühne for Ernst Toller's Dramatic Nonstarter—Jessner's

Artistic Love for Piscator, the Revolutionary and Enemy of the State

"Then Herr Holitscher raises himself from the presidential chair to utter a few senile words about the Volksbühne as a political weapon. 'Political!' The word crops up frequently during the evening, and each time it is—hypocrisy, for what they mean is, in fact—Communist. Among those who declared themselves in agreement with the abuse of the Volkstheater for propaganda against the state were: Heinrich Mann, George Grosz, Bert Brecht and a number of people of no account, and Alfred Kerr, his fine nose for the beginnings of a trend having picked up the scent of the latest literary, revolutionary fad. . . .

"Then Erwin Kalser produces the shattering news that the actors are behind Piscator to a man. —The extras, rehearsed by Piscator, swear that they are, too. . . . Next, the Director of the Staatstheater:

" 'You will understand that I have no intention of expanding on the problem of the Volksbühne. The idea behind the Volksbühne is so powerful that opposition can only be of benefit to it. I do not intend today to discuss acting style, art or anything of that nature, nor even the efforts I myself am making to combat the sugar-coated style of acting, and the sugar-coated style of presenting the classics.

" 'I am here to put the record straight and to express my solidarity with my colleague Piscator. You may have read in various newspapers that this whole machination has been provoked by the intention to set up a "Reibaro" involving the Volksbühne and the Staatstheater. It was rumored that in the event that the Volksbühne were to merge with the Staatstheater, Erwin Piscator would be an impediment. At this point I must state that I have no knowledge of any such projected merger. But I can state quite definitely that from my standpoint as director of the Staatstheater I do not see that Piscator's existence would be a hindrance if such a merger were to take place.' "

And the "Epilogue":

"In the Prussian Parliament a major question from Koch–Berlin has been tabled concerning Intendant Leopold Jessner's declaration on March 22, 1927, at the meeting of protest in the Herrenhaus against the decision taken by the Volksbühne. According to the question, Jessner made a declaration of 'solidarity with his colleague Piscator' and stated that he knew nothing of any merger between the Volksbühne and the State theaters. He was able to state categorically that from his point of view as director of the Staatstheater Piscator's existence would not constitute a hindrance if such a merger took place. We would like to ask . . . whether the Ministry approves of any extension of the contract given to Piscator by Intendant Jessner, and whether a merger of the State theaters with the Volksbühne is in fact intended."

"What does the Minister for Arts intend to do?" the *Tägliche Rundschau* asks. It then provides the following survey of current opinion:

"Since the Prussian Diet is in recess the Prussian Minister for Culture has time to consider the Jessner question which the Deutschnationale have tabled. The main thing the questioner wants to know is whether Herr Becker shares Jessner's warm approval of Piscator and whether the Staatstheater is to be turned into a Piscator-Theater from time to time. In the meanwhile it has become possible for Herr Becker to study the newspapers where this major question has aroused much interest. From the *Berliner-Tageblatt* (No. 166) he could learn that democratic circles expect him to give this major question short shrift:

By reason of this Nationalist question, which is scarcely of any practical consequence, the management of the Volksbühne has found an ally, one surely not of its own choosing.

"In the *Deutsche Zeitung* (No 82) the Minister for the Arts can read that racialist circles viewed the major question tabled by the German Nationalists with pity:

What positive result can this question have? Intendant Jessner and Fritz Kortner, his top political actor, have so many hidden supporters within the government that such 'questions' are scarcely likely to disturb them. On the contrary, they feel their own views confirmed. Tabling questions is no way to carry on the cultural struggle; one must turn to intellectual weapons. The official announcement of the Jessner-Piscator Staatstheater-Volkstheater merger is only a matter of time. The Republic will have no objections. On the contrary, Jessner is its protégé. The Jessner-Piscator case will *not be solved by a pronouncement from the Reichstag.* Let us set up a theater for our own front in opposition to the theater of Bolshevism, and in this way we can put up a real, concrete defense against the methodical destruction of our cultural heritage. The enemy will not be beaten by words but by deeds: the theater of our convictions as the last bastion against the Bolshevist–Communist storm troopers in Berlin and in the Reich.

"On the other hand, if the Minister for the Arts thumbs through the *Kreuz-Zeitung* (No. 163), he will see that the Nationalists expect 'a satisfactory answer' from him:

Parliament has no small interest in learning how the Minister for the Arts views the aspirations of the director of the Staatstheater, and whether he approves plans to use State money to put antistate propaganda on the stage. The Prussian Minister for the Arts cannot avoid making an unambiguous statement about the tendencies in Jessner's policy which have become clear and which have moved into the arena of politics. We expect an answer which will be satisfactory for the future.

"And finally, the eye of the Minister for the Arts may light upon an article in the *Frankfurter Zeitung* (No. 264) because it is entitled '.Theatrical Battle.' There, among other things, one can read:

> Does a director have any right to transform the intellectual content of a drama against the dramatist's wishes, no matter how artistic or imaginative the transformation may be? Doesn't the mind of the writer still have greater rights than the man who stages his work?

"What does the Minister for the Arts intend to do to see that this theatrical battle finds a fitting ending?"

The Right Positions Itself for a Counterblow

The Republic tolerates this radical political movement, which states openly that it intends to use every means at its disposal to turn the world view of the proletariat into a reality. The main weapon is the theater. The theater of modern times, the theater of the proletariat, the theater of political and cultural demonstration. The theater according to the Russian model as it has been seen in films like *Potemkin* and *Mother*. And we? Where do we stand? Who is to stand against the theater of the intellectual Left in Germany, against the radical Volksbühne, against the use of the Staatstheater for political purposes? Who is going to demonstrate against the cultural revolution?

Alfred Mühr

As a result of this appeal, "The Greater German Theater Society" was founded in the following summer. It was intended as a political counterblow to us. "German" art was to (politically) counteract the political theater. Apart from a single performance, nothing further was heard by the public about this interesting experiment.

Pamphlet from the "Greater Germans"

Esteemed Sirs:

You will, as true Germans, have experienced difficulty in associating yourselves with the so-called cultural theaters in Berlin. The Volksbühne is putting out unmistakable Socialist propaganda sandwiched between the objective productions in its theater. The Staatstheater, too, can be savored only with caution since the productions of *The Robbers* and *Hamlet*. You can never be sure that you won't be unpleasantly surprised. Indeed, last season, family audiences in the Schiller Theater, which is part of the Staatstheater complex, quite unsuspectingly found themselves faced with urban prostitution in full, revolting, naturalistic detail in Rehfisch's *Razzia*. . . .

In an eight-month season starting at the Wallner Theater on October 1, 1927, members will be able to see one significant work each month. It is the intention to balance serious work with good, clean fun. The following series of plays has been proposed:

162

André Hofer, a Tyrolean drama by Franz Kranewitter; *Time in Bottles* (*Zeit auf Flaschen*), a topical comedy by Friedrich Freksa; *The Lantern* (*Die Laterne*), a drama of the French Revolution by F. Walter Ilges; *The Journey to God* (*Die Reise gegen Gott*), a drama of longing for the German homeland by Rolf Lauckner; *Mammon,* a peasant comedy by Helmut Unger; *Thomas Paine,* by Hanns Johst; *Katte,* by Burte; *Mother Highway* (*Mutter Landstrasse*), by Schmidtbonn.

We hope that we shall be permitted to welcome you as a member of the Greater German Theater Society.

Signed for the Professional Advisory Committee by, among others:

Lieutenant-General von Altrock (Militär-Wochenblatt) . . . *Captain Bleeker-Kohlsaat* (City Councilor and Chairman of the North Suburban German-National People's Party Club) . . . *Heinrich Förstemann* (Grand Master of the Pankgrafschaft) . . . *Lieutenant Guthmann* (Stahlhelm, Berlin Section of the Combat Troops Association) . . . *County Court Judge Jenne* (German Richard Wagner Society) . . . *Schoolteacher Kümmelberg* (Association of Large Families).

Faced with a Decision

"The least that this movement can come up with is either reelection of the management or a splinter group. It would be a crime against the idea to fail to exploit the impetus of the moment. If the lethargy of the mod-

Headlines in the nationalist press: "Communist theater on Nollendorfplatz?"

erates is too great, if the allegiance of one sector of the membership to the Bühnenvolksbund, and of another sector to a policy of silence proves insurmountable, then there must be a schism, a new, rejuvenated theater—in opposition to the Volksbühne! To compromise, to draw up pacts, to mix, to work at one moment for one 'trend,' and the next moment for a different one, would, at this stage, be the end. Piscator's production *Storm over Gotland* has divided the minds. We must not talk our way around this division."

Herbert Ihering

The Robbers by Friedrich Schidler. Staatstheater Berlin 1926.

Designer: Traugott Müller

Right: Roller is freed. Schweizer (Hardt), Moor (Ebert), Roller (Harlan), Spielberg (Bildt).

Center: Old Moor's castle. Simultaneous scene. Franz (Erwin Faber), Amalia (Maria Koppenhöfer).

Below: Rehearsal of the forest scene with the robbers.

Storm over Gotland Ehm Welk. Volksbühne 1927.

Top right: Practicable ship with raked platform.

Designer: Traugott Müller

Film Director: Erwin Piscator

Cameraman: Curt Oertel

Left: Filmed summary of the transformations of revolutions through the centuries (mass action).

Bottom right: Scene of the Vitalians' ship.

Left:
Still projection
over box set.

Scenes and film (the progression of revolutions in class types) from *Storm over Gotland*.

Below left: Heinrich George Störtebecker. *Below right*: Alexander Granach (Asmus).

Above: For *Boom*
Designer: John Heartfield
Right: opening program for *Hoppla, Such is Life!*
Designer: Traugott Müller

Above: For *Rasputin*
Designer: John Heartfield

Above: For *Singing Jailbirds*
Designer: John Heartfield

Above: For *Schwejk*
Designer: George Grosz

Left: For *The Last Emperor*
Designer: Doris Homann

Hoppla, Such is Life! by Ernest Toller. Piscator-Bühne 1927.

Three storey stage with translucent backing for *Hoppla, Such is Life!* with Piscator's silhouette (montage by Sascha Stone).

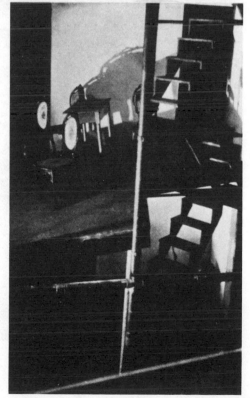

Detail of one level with the outer steps.

Hoppla, Such is Life!
Set Model
Design: Erwin
Piscator
Construction: Trau-
gott Müller

Top: Election scene.
Combination of live
scene and film (central
screen).

Center: Freestanding scaffolding set on the revolving stage. *Below*:
Simultaneous scenes in four compartments (Act 4) with back
projection.

View of the stage during rehearsals for *Rasputin*.

Above: Crownpiece of the hemisphere (suspended). In front of it the scaffolding stage for *Hoppla, Such is Life!* (standing on the stage).

Rehearsals for *Hoppla*. From left to right: Granach, Piscator, Graetz, Toller, Traugott Müller (rear).

Stage-door in the yard of the Theater am Nollendorfplatz while the set for *Hoppla* is being struck.

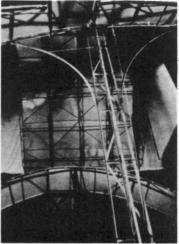

Above: View of the dome of the segmented hemispherical stage (Rasputin).

Below: Hemisphere on the revolving stage with the crownpiece raised.

Upper half of hemispherical stage with acting segments open (picture stands on its side).

INTRODUCTION

The Volksbühne Affair in March, 1927, marked an unforeseen turning point in Piscator's fortunes. Soon after his resignation he was enabled through the good offices of the actress Tilla Durieux, as will later be shown, to set up his own company, the Piscator-Bühne, with unconditional financial backing for a full season. He leased the Theater am Nollendorfplatz, a conventional proscenium theater with (according to the *Bühnenjahrbuch* for 1926) 1,100 seats, which normally housed light entertainment. His predecessor, Martin Zickel, had presented operettas, and the Volksbühne had taken blocks of seats from him. The Nollendorfplatz is in the West End of the city, not far from the Kurfürstendamm, and Piscator was accused of turning his back on the working-class quarters. He argued that he was aiming to convert the less committed elements in the bourgeoisie, and not merely to preach to the converted proletariat, and that the Theater am Nollendorfplatz was the only one available to him with adequate equipment, including a revolving stage.

In one sense, Piscator's connection with the Volksbühne was not severed. The campaign for a committed Volksbühne which had come into the open during the national Volksbühne conference in Hamburg in July, 1926, found wide support among left-wing writers and Arthur Holitscher published an article in the *Weltbühne* on March 8, 1927, castigating the supine apathy which, though more characteristic of the petite bourgeoisie, had infiltrated the working classes and sapped their will to fight. The timid protestations by the management of the Volksbühne that art must remain neutral and the willingness of the SPD to enter coalitions with parties whose aims negated socialism were symptoms of the same creeping paralysis.

This protest was taken up by the Jugendliche Abteilungen, the Young Volksbühne which had been formed in the 1923/24 season to accommodate the wishes of working-class youth organizations and trade unions, and at a meeting in July, 1927, the Special Sections were formed by the more radical youth and absorbed most of the members of the Young Volksbühne. The Special Sections were to have three productions of their own and seven productions from the general repertoire, with the proviso that the repertoire would henceforth contain Zeitstücke, plays dealing with contemporary problems. Shortly afterwards the Volksbühne concluded an agreement with the newly founded Piscator-Bühne. Its plan for three special productions was dropped, and Piscator undertook to provide five productions in their place. Though the Special Sections soared from 4,000 to 16,000 members (still only 13 percent of the total membership) after this was announced, the commitment to stage five plays and to accommodate a possible 80,000 people at reduced prices proved to be a considerable financial burden for the new company.

XV
CONTRADICTIONS IN THE THEATER
CONTRADICTIONS IN THE TIMES

1927. Everything is just as it was before the war ("Just before the next war!" as Walter Mehring sang in the song "Hoppla, Such Is Life!"). The battles against the enemy within had been fought, and fought successfully in the main as far as bourgeois society was concerned. But the peace which reigns on the surface is deceptive. The red faces are hectic and feverish. Their bank balances may be healthy, but something in the bourgeois mentality is out of joint.

Consolidation

"1927 was a boom year for Germany. The number of unemployed which during 1926 had fluctuated between 2 million and 1.5 million as a consequence of the deflationary crisis, and which had scarcely fallen even in the summer, dropped in 1927 from 1.8 million in January to 500,000 in June and July and to 300,000 by October. These were the lowest figures that we had ever seen in recent years. The number of bankruptcies declined as well: compared to 2,000 a month at the beginning of 1926, the figure stayed fairly consistent throughout the year 1927 at 400 bankruptcies and 100 businesses placed in receivership (before the war there had regularly been 800 bankruptcies a month). There was an extraordinary rise in production; crude iron, for example, rose from 22,000 tons a day in 1926 to 36,000 tons in 1927. The utilization of rolling stock on the Imperial Railways, a useful pointer to the exchange of goods, was on average 25 percent higher in 1927 than in 1926.

"The upturn had come about largely because of an inflow of foreign money which probably amounted to 4 billion marks—a record figure. In spite of the huge capital investments which the economy normally needs in periods of expansion, the interest rates had stayed relatively low. For the one and only time since stabilization the bank rate at the beginning of 1927 dropped to 5 percent, and as a consequence the Reich made the misguided Reinhold Loan.[1] Although industry complained that this was only a "boom in volume"—in other words, that their profits were not rising in proportion to the increase in turnover—1927 was definitely a good year for business. People felt for the first time that economic 'stability' had been achieved, and consequently things quietened down on the political front too. The right-wing government presented a fairly liberal face to the outside world (at the World Economic Conference in Geneva). All in all, the picture is one of consolidation."

Richard Lewinsohn (Morus)

The very fact that we should found a revolutionary stage at a moment when capitalism was in a phase of relative consolidation seemed startling. The echo awakened by the theater was a sign of the inner fragmentation of bourgeois society. The best elements, in an accurate assessment of their own spiritual existence, recognized the Theater am Nollendorfplatz as a bridge to the future. Doctors, lawyers, teachers and writers who, since they are entirely dependent on their own labors, seem by any objective criterion to belong to the working classes and yet have a thousand links with the bourgeoisie, joined our front willingly, indeed enthusiastically. The great liberal-democratic press opened its columns to their voices. There was, of course, in addition, an upper class with no political leanings which was avid for the sensation which our theater seemed to promise. A process which repeats itself constantly in history as a declining class abandons its own position, and so enables its opponents to make victorious offensives on the stage. *The Marriage of Figaro* is a classic example. The nationalistic press, to do it justice, saw the situation clearly in class terms.

1. Hjalmar Schacht, the president of the Reichsbank, stabilized the mark and put an end to inflation in 1924. Peter Reinhold, finance minister from 1926 to 1927, lowered the turnover tax 1 percent to boost trade, covering the deficit with a long-term loan. The policy failed and the government soon had to buy back its own securities.

168

"The struggle for the theater is much more than an aesthetic question . . . and so their theater will become the ultimate in fashion, the very latest thing for the chic world of the Kurfürstendamm. Cocaine is dead, long live the Piscator-Bühne. . . . But the red venture illuminates a very serious current situation and under no circumstances must we underestimate the dangers to which this theater will expose certain classes of the population. The snob is beyond further harm, and it will not reach the proletariat in the slums. But the little man without a mind of his own who falls in behind the Social Democrats' program from long habit can be turned into a radical in the provocative sense by fare like this."

Tag, August 20, 1927

"Piscator is not fighting to get himself talked about, but for a goal. With Communist theater he is fighting for the Communist type of state. . . . It is not a matter of Piscator's activities as a stage director, or of his personal inviolability."

Bremer Nachrichten, July 26, 1927

"What is necessary is that the citizens whom they hope to take by storm take stock of the situation: the fight must begin."

Oder-Zeitung, September 1, 1927

But what attitude to the Piscator-Bühne was in fact adopted by the class whose ideology it purported to express, the proletariat? The Social Democrats in general remained skeptical. They may well have feared that the growth of this theater placed a superior propaganda instrument in the hands of their bitter enemies, the German Communists. On the other hand, it was left-wing Social Democrats, in particular Seydewitz, a member of the Saxon State Assembly *(Landtag)*, who first tried to persuade the management of the Volksbühne to set up the Special Sections, which was tantamount to advocating our ideas.

The German Communist Party took a positive attitude to the venture from the beginning, although it was agreed on both sides that the Piscator-Bühne as an institution was to have no party-political links of any color and was not to be viewed as a party venture.

"The opening of a theater in Berlin under the direct control of Erwin Piscator is of greater significance than any other theater ever was. The opening of the Piscator-Bühne is the beginning of a new chapter in the public struggle for the theater in present-day Germany.

"Comrade Fritsche is unjust in his *Pravda* article when he levels the following reproach at the Piscator-Bühne:

" 'When one looks closely at the program and the actors, and also at the play by Toller with which Piscator opened his theater, one sees clearly that the whole thing betrays an ideology which is intelligently radical, and revolutionary in a petit bourgeois sense, rather than a proletarian-communist ideology.' This is the presumptuousness of a demanding theorist. And from a theoretical point of view Comrade Fritsche is naturally right. But in practice things look rather different. The political context within which Piscator had to operate in order to establish the position of his theater must not and should not be forgotten. . . . A maximal program, a one hundred percent Socialist program would be the best solution.

"But from a tactical point of view Piscator's action in engaging big names like Tilla Durieux, Max Pallenberg and others to supplement the young actors in his theater was quite well considered.

"So Comrade Fritsche's reproach, amicable though it is, seems to us misplaced. A few mistakes are possible in every venture, and among the activities of the Piscator-Bühne there are many things which may seem quite naïve to us. But we are, of course, dialecticians and dialectical materialists; we see every phenomenon in a relatively objective light, and not in an abstract light. In these circumstances a theater like Piscator's theater, whose stated aim is the revolutionary class struggle, a theater which sees itself as an advance party of the workers' movement, is something to which, in the personality of its director Erwin Piscator, we must extend the heartiest comradely welcome."

Ognev, Pravda

In fact, the founding of the theater came about without help from the Party or from Soviet Russia, contrary to the allegations of particularly well-informed newspapers. In spite of this, and without tying itself to any particular party, the Piscator-Bühne was philosophically and politically closest to the German Communist Party. If the Communist Party provided only the tiniest percentage of spectators throughout the following season, this was because the radical elements in the working classes were economically too weak.

The proletarian public appeared mainly as the "Special Sections of the Volksbühne."

What do the Special Sections of the Volksbühne want?

They are intended above all for people like you who have to serve others in workshops and offices, but who, arm in arm with your comrades in destiny, want to create a new future without oppression for yourselves and for the world; for you who see the present dominated by treacherous cultural values, but are determined to overcome these values and replace them with a new culture emanating from your brotherly convictions; for you who want to press into the service of this struggle everything which is meaningful and dynamic in the present.

And last but not least, the theater is part of this. At all times the lives of men and of nations have found a mirror in the drama, and at all times it has aided their further development. So we dare not be indifferent to the way in which life in our time is influenced by the theater.

The theater must become the instrument of our will to found a new community! It must consciously place itself at the service of the social and political ideas which are trying to bring about a transformation of present conditions. What we need is a stage which gives clear and emphatic artistic expression to the will which is alive within us.

We feel bound to the Volksbühne because it is not a commercial theater, but a theater supported by the mass of the people. We recognize the independent artistic achievement of this organization which has grown out of the working population. As its members, we want access to any manifestations of artistic creativity which are great and full of life. But our desires go beyond this, and we are looking for productions which are unabashedly one-sided and tendentious in their efforts to serve our ideas about the reordering of society.

Erwin Piscator is a director who has matured under the auspices of the Volksbühne, and the methods and artistic aims manifest in his productions of Gorky's *Lower Depths*, Paquet's *Flags* and *Tidal Wave*, in Welk's *Storm over Gotland* and in other productions have shown us how effective revolutionary staging can be and how well it can promote our aims. Now as director of an independent company of his own at the Theater am Nollendorfplatz Piscator has achieved a new freedom for his activities.

The Special Sections of the Volksbühne have given this new company under Erwin Piscator great prominence. They have offered their members only three or four performances in the Volksbühne's own house, the Theater am Bülowplatz, and one or two performances in the Theater am Schiffbauerdamm or in the Thalia-Theater (or on occasion an opera), but in addition to these there are to be five performances at the Piscator-Bühne. All are evening performances; subscriptions are the usual Volksbühne price (1.50 M. per performance).[2]

Help us to make these Special Sections of the Volksbühne strong and powerful! Do this to show how great is the desire and the will of the masses to have topical theater which exploits the latest artistic methods to provide support for the proletarian masses' struggle! To every house, to every workshop, to every office we appeal: Join the Special Sections!

The Publicity Committee for the Special Sections

A Nice Working Committee

". . . the Special Sections are an outlet for the Bolshevist tendencies in the Volksbühne."

Kreuz-Zeitung, July 14, 1927

2. I Reischsmark = $0.238 in 1927.

An Odd Decision

"The decision seems to be a tentative attempt to close the supposedly open rift between those who would like to see the theater dedicated to the education of the people, and those who demand categorically that the theater should give expression to the thoughts of the Communist Party."

Tägliche Rundschau, July 14, 1927

The Special Sections constituted a separate organization within the Volksbühne. It had developed from the "Young Volksbühne," which in its turn had been an association of young workingmen's groups within the overall membership. During the controversy provoked by my productions, the young members had become the storm troopers in the service of our ideas; at the outset they were merely a group of like-minded people, but they were soon faced with the need to work out a sound organizational framework and they ended up as a regular faction. When we founded our theater this section of the youth supported the new house and the Volksbühne agreed that the Special Sections should constitute a separate sector of the membership. The new theater gave a fresh impulse to the Young Volksbühne and provided a broader basis for their agitation, with the result that the membership of the Special Sections had reached the relatively grand total of 16,000 when the theater opened, whereas the Young Volksbühne had never managed to attract more than 4,000 members. It is a fact that these members were mainly teenagers, and it seemed all the more worthwhile and important to me to have among my regular customers precisely people who were so open to new impressions and experiences and at the same time capable of such enthusiasm. They were mainly young workingmen who were actually involved in the processes of industrial production, and were consequently extraordinarily important as a yardstick by which to measure the pedagogic value of our work.

Set against the masses of the Berlin proletariat, these 16,000 members were only a tiny flock. When one considers that the theater had from the very first day to play an important role in a struggle which was vital to the proletariat, and that our ideas had an impact far beyond the frontiers of Germany, or even Europe, then it must be admitted that the fact that only 16,000 workers were prepared to sign up with our theater for a season, that is, for five performances, virtually amounts to another failure on the part of the proletariat.

But the following confession is even more contradictory: even if more workers had responded to the call and we had managed to recruit many times this figure of 16,000, we would still have been unable to run our theater with this public alone: we could not have raised the price of admission above 1.50 marks, nor could we have covered the theater's day-to-day budget with this money alone. It was in this realization that I stuck from the very beginning to the view that a proletarian theater could be built up only as a theater for the masses, a theater for two or three thousand people. It is not possible in Berlin today for a theater that has to rely on only a purely proletarian public to cover the costs of an evening performance with a house seating 1,200 people and a daily budget of 1,800 marks.

"To belong to the Volkstheater is to deflect the German theater from its mission. They want to politicize the theater in terms of the class struggle."

Deutsche Zeitung, August 10, 1927

This contradiction in the structure of the theater is nothing more or less than a contradiction in the times as a whole: it proves to be impossible to build up a proletarian theater within the framework of our current social structure. A proletarian theater in fact presupposes that the proletariat has the financial means to support such a theater, and this presupposes that the proletariat has managed to make itself into a dominant social and economic power. Until this happens our theater can be no more than a revolutionary theater which uses the means at its disposal for the ideological liberation of the proletariat and to promote the social upheaval which will free both the proletariat and its theater from these contradictions. The fact that we were under no illusions about the contradictory aspects of our situation,[3] the fact that we felt that these contradictions did not absolve us from any responsibility, but obliged us to work out our line of thought more clearly and sharply in the light of our years of experience—these were perhaps the only substantial entries on the credit side when we founded our theater.

3. Journals like *Der Klassenkampf, Vorwärts, Die Aktion* (Herr Pfemfert's magazine) could well sneer at the "jewel-bedecked and tail-coated" public at the Piscator-Bühne. Apart from the misunderstanding implicit in these cheap sneers (who did Herr Pfemfert think bought his books on the Kaiserdamm?) the Piscator-Bühne was in no position to choose its audience. [E. P.]

INTRODUCTION

Piscator took his summer vacation in 1926 in Bandol in the south of France with four of his Berlin circle, Erich Engel, Ernst Toller, Wilhelm Herzog and Otto Katz, and one thing they discussed was the possibility of founding a theater to develop their ideas. When these idle speculations became a reality the following year the last three were to be on Piscator's payroll. The exception was Erich Engel (1891–1966), who was a pioneer of epic theater in his own right. He had directed the first performance of Brecht's *The Jungle* (later renamed *The Jungle of Cities*) in sets by Caspar Neher at Munich in 1923. This trio, Brecht, Engel and Neher, went on to produce *Man is Man* in 1928 with the lights and machinery revealed, and *The Threepenny Opera* the same year, and the partnership was revived at the Berliner Ensemble after World War II. Engel, like Piscator, had an experimental classic behind him. He had staged Shakespeare's *Coriolanus* with Fritz Kortner in 1925, isolating each scene and carrying over a single conclusion from it to the following scene.

Ernst Toller (1893–1939) was to provide the scripts for the first production at the Piscator-Bühne, *Hoppla, Such is Life!* In Bandol he was working on a "drama of the masses" *(Massendrama)* set in a proletarian quarter of Berlin, the Scheunenviertel or shantytown, at the time of the murders of Liebknecht and Rosa Luxemburg. It was never completed, though fifteen scenes were published in *Kulturwille* (No. 12, 1926) and *Volksbühne* (3.1.1927). Toller was already an established writer.

Karlheinz Martin's sensational production of *Transfiguration* at the Tribüne in 1919, which had given Berlin its first taste of full-blooded Expressionism, had made him famous. He had also played a prominent part in the abortive Munich Republic of Councils in 1919, and had become a martyr of the Left after the Republic's collapse. He narrowly escaped being shot and was subsequently sentenced to imprisonment, from which he was released in 1924. In prison he wrote *Masses and Man*, a dramatic distillation of his experience of revolution which was informed by his own humane idealism, and *The Machine Wreckers*, a Luddite drama. These were followed by *Brokenbow*, the tragedy of a mutilated war veteran, and *Wotan Unbound*, a satire on Hitler and the nationalists.

174

Wilhelm Herzog (1884–1960) was a dramatist and publicist who had edited a succession of pacifist and socialist journals, *Das Forum, Die Weltliteratur* and *Die Republik*. Piscator made him his dramaturg and planned to open the Piscator-Bühne with his revue *Down Around the State Prosecutor*, but it was not ready in time. Herzog collaborated with Hans Rehfisch in 1929 on a drama, *Die Affäre Dreyfus*.

Otto Katz was a journalist who became Piscator's front-of-house manager.

Piscator and his friends had discussed the possibility of setting up their own theater to develop their ideas unimpeded, but the scheme was no more than a pipe dream until the intervention of Tilla Durieux, a well-known actress who had been deeply impressed by Piscator's *Robbers* at the Staatstheater. Tilla Durieux (1880–1971) had made her name with Max Reinhardt from 1903 until 1911, playing contemporary femmes fatales (Wilde's *Salomé*) and demonic women in the classics (Hebbel's *Judith*). She then played similar heavy roles in various Berlin theaters until 1933, among them the name parts in Shaw's *Caesar and Cleopatra*, Wedekind's *Lulu* and Ibsen's *Hedda Gabler*. When Piscator left the Volksbühne she persuaded her prospective third husband, Ludwig Katzenellenbogen, to back him with 400,000 marks. Katzenellenbogen was managing director of the Schultheiss brewery group and the link between big business and a communist theater was not without irony. On the inside the Piscator-Bühne was jocularly referred to as the Pilsator-Bühne, Pilsator being one of Katzenellenbogen's beers.

Piscator realized that the Theater am Nollendorfplatz was a provisional solution and the techniques he had devised called for a new type of theater. He commissioned Walter Gropius (1883–1970), of the Bauhaus, who produced one of the most revolutionary and thoroughly thought-out designs in the history of the reform theater movement. It is fully described below, and, though it was never built, several models exist, one of them in the Bauhaus Archive in West Berlin. Gropius was a distinguished architect, but not a theater specialist. The only theater he built in Germany was the small, conventional but functionally decorated Jena Stadttheater in 1923. He appears to have had no part in the Bauhaus theatrical experiments by Moholy-Nagy or by Oskar Schlemmer *(Triadic Ballet)*, both of whom were working in the realm of abstract art, far removed from Piscator. Gropius cites three previous practical attempts by van de Velde, the Perret brothers, and Poelzig to rid the theater of the proscenium arch. He might have added Copeau's Vieux Colombier (1919), which had a permanent set of concrete platforms, linked by steps, with no proscenium. Henry van de

Velde (1863–1957) had built a theater for the Cologne Werkbund Exhibition in 1914 which had an adaptable stage, divided into three by two nonstructural pillars which slid on rails. It faced a rectangular auditorium without galleries. In Paris, in 1925, Auguste and Gustave Perret built a temporary theater for the Exposition des Arts Décoratifs which used van de Velde's tripartite stage divided by pillars and widened it to dominate a narrower, rectangular auditorium. Between 1918 and 1920 the Viennese architect Oskar Strnad produced designs for a "ring stage" which extended van de Velde's sliding stage to form a ring around a circular auditorium which the audience reached over bridges. In the Soviet Union, in 1926, Lissitzky produced a design for reconstructing Meyerhold's theater which had curved tiers of seating behind the proscenium, and between these and the orchestra a stage in the form of a spiral ramp accessible from three levels.

Max Reinhardt had been the first director to experiment freely with new relationships of actor to audience. In 1910 he set *Oedipus* in the ring of the Circus Schumann, and placed the chorus among the audience in the tiered amphitheater. In 1919 Hans Poelzig (1869–1936) converted the same building into the Grosses Schauspielhaus for him, with a long, low proscenium and a deep U-shaped forestage thrust out to fill the ring. In London, in 1911, Reinhardt had also converted the Olympia Exhibition Hall into a replica of Cologne Cathedral with banks of spectators around the perimeter for Vollmoeller's drama without words, *The Miracle*. In Salzburg he staged plays on the steps of the cathedral and inside the Collegiate Church, and in Venice he put on *The Merchant of Venice* in a square backing onto a canal. The Piscator-Gropius total theater was thus part of a wider search for an alternative to the proscenium theater.

Piscator also took up and expanded the idea of an experimental group within a large company, which Reinhardt had tried out with Das junge Deutschland at the Deutsches Theater. On October 16, 1927, a studio was set up at the Piscator-Bühne. This was a study group rather than the kind of theater workshop for small-scale productions that we would now associate with the term. Piscator himself considered the rehearsal process and not the final production to be the important aspect of the group's work, and its performances were matinees or late-night shows at the Theater am Nollendorfplatz, with the exception of Sinclair's *Singing Jailbirds*, which ran for two weeks at the Lessing-Theater.

The Studio's activities were divided among three groups. The first was to prepare productions of *Singing Jailbirds* and *Homesickness* under the direction of Ernst Lönner and Leonhard Steckel, respectively, and the results of their efforts are dealt with in chapter XXI. The second group was to explore the dramatic possibilities of the fairy tale but there is no record of anything having come of this. The third group was to prepare two pieces of agitation, an amnesty demonstration and a Max Hölz demonstration, though in fact it seems to have been members of the second group who took part in a Hölz matinee on November 27.

Besides these group activities the Studio was to provide training for members of the company and other actors who shared the Piscator-Bühne's aims and ideology. The lessons were to be scheduled to enable senior members of the company to participate and to teach courses on various aspects of acting. These projects were clearly conceived in a fine collective spirit and point toward later work in the United States at the Dramatic Workshop in New York. It is impossible to tell how much was put into practice, though we do know that Tilla Durieux and Alexander Granach were unable to teach their courses, so that there may be some truth in Franz Jung's allegation that Piscator's stars dodged their obligations. (F. Jung, *Der Torpedokäfer*, p. 317.) Here, too, the busy company's ambitions may have outstripped its resources, though it must be remembered that after the collapse of the Piscator-Bühne three collectives rose from the ruins, the Gruppe Junger Schauspieler, the Notgemeinschaft der Schauspieler der Piscator-Bühne, and the Piscator-Bühne (Kollektiv), all of which bear witness to a resilient corporate spirit.

XVI
FOUNDATION AND DEVELOPMENT OF
THE PISCATOR-BÜHNE

Although I had no aspirations in that direction, I had already been compelled on several occasions to take over the management of a theater. The way in which I put across my political philosophy on the stage always got me into trouble in the regular theater, so at the back of my mind I always had the idea of working in a theater of my own. Even in the summer of 1926, when I went to Bandol in the south of France with Toller to work with him on his new play *Shantytown (Scheunenviertel)* and to snatch a few weeks of relaxation while the Volksbühne was closed (besides Toller, Erich Engel and Wilhelm Herzog made the trip, along with Otto Katz, who at that time was still publicity manager at the *Montag Morgen*), we worked out all sorts of plans in the intervals between bathing, walking and working, and we discussed founding a theater and a magazine which would harness all the intellectual strength of the Left. The idle conversation of a summer's day; nobody really believed that they could come into existence six months later. For all our discussions still ended with the weighty question: who's going to put up the cash?

My position at the Volksbühne grew more problematic day by day. The performance of *The Robbers* which I had prepared for the Staatstheater was postponed.

In the days of July and August, 1926, we did not know that the coming season would work out this way, that it would begin with *The Robbers* and end with *Storm over Gotland*. And now in the spring of 1927 it had come to that. The knotty problem of financing the operation was unexpectedly solved.

I had always taken the view that a theater of the sort we had in mind must be in a position to support itself, and that the Berlin theaters were doing bad business—which threatened to turn into a general crisis that year—because the selection of plays they offered was lifeless, petrified and quite out of touch with the times. The flimsiest film reflected more actuality, more of the real excitement of the times than the stage with its ponderous dramatic and technical machinery. It was not the theater as an institution that was out of date, but the plays and the staging. A theater that tackled the problems of the day, that met the public need for a reflection of the times we lived in without flinching and without ceremony, such a theater would be of interest everywhere and would also be financially viable. (Experience has borne out these views.)

In relation to the final product, the theater requires huge capital investments. Before the curtain can go up for the first time, rent, lighting, heating, administration, technical apparatus, rehearsals, actors' salaries, sets, etc., have swallowed up a small fortune. The very existence of the undertaking and the hundreds of people involved in it depend on the success or failure of the first night. One sentence from a critic can seal its fate. I have always felt that the way Berlin theaters put all their money on a single card was less than practical. Within certain limits I wanted my own theater to be independent of this process. I had several times had the occasion to raise 50,000 or 60,000 marks to get the first performance of a show on the stage. I refused to consider doing the same again. An undertaking like mine, whose fundamental significance for the whole development of the theater was becoming more and more evident, should not be jeopardized by the fortunes of a single evening. Financial support which would underwrite a whole season regardless of success or failure was the minimum that I was prepared to accept. But even if I got that I would still have to build up my theater with archaic and inadequate technical resources; at the very best, the result could be only a shadow of my real intentions. What I had in mind was a theater machine, technically as perfectly functional as a typewriter, an apparatus that would incorporate the latest lighting, the latest sliding and revolving scenery, both vertical and horizontal, numerous projection boxes, loudspeakers everywhere, etc. For this reason I really needed a new building equipped with all the technical gadgets I would need if I was to put my new dramatic principles into practice. Such a building would, of course, cost millions.

After seeing my production of *The Robbers* in the Staatstheater, Frau Tilla Durieux had expressed a wish to meet me. From this meeting an interest in my ideas developed which finally crystallized in a desire to collaborate with me. The establishment of a theater of my own seemed indispensable if I was to get any further. There could be no question of my contract with the Volksbühne being extended, and after I had been so uncompromising and provocative in my defense of political theater and in my statement at the Herrenhaus, it would have seemed as though I was backing down if I had accepted invitations or contracts to direct plays in bourgeois theaters. So a theater of my own was essential if my activities were to be continued. Frau Tilla Durieux's good offices made it possible to raise the sum which seemed necessary to ensure one full season. It was estimated that 400,000 marks would suffice. It may sound presumptuous when I say that this solution did not entirely satisfy me. Anybody else would have considered it an unheard-of stroke of luck, but to me it seemed like a risk.

With this in mind, I completed the financial negotiations. The following season in a Berlin theater was merely a provisional solution. A new building based on a plan which Walter Gropius and I had drawn up, and which was to be built by the Bauhaus, formed the basis of our contract, and negotiations for a site near Hallesches Tor had already begun.

The Total Theater

The architecture of the theater is closely bound up with the form of the drama at any given time, or, rather, both interact upon one another. Drama and architecture together have their roots in the social form of the epoch.

The stage form which dominates the present day is that of the court theater, a form which was evolved by absolutism and has outlived its usefulness. The division into orchestra, circle, boxes and balcony reflects the social stratification of a feudalistic society.

It was inevitable that this form would come into conflict with the real purpose of the theater the moment the drama or, alternatively, the social situation changed. When I sat down with Walter Gropius to draw up a rough plan for a type of theater which would fulfill the needs of a changing situation, it was not simply a matter of expanding or complementing the technical equipment; the new form was

180

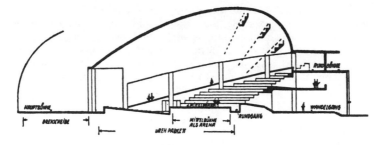

Side view (cross section) of the Total Theater

to be an expression of a new social and dramatic situation. Professor Gropius has given a better and more detailed account than I ever could of the aims and scope of his design, which, unfortunately, never got beyond the planning stage.

on the construction of a modern theater, with particular reference to the building of a new piscator theater in berlin

new thinking on constructional matters has rarely affected the spatial world of the theater. the most significant stage directors of the last generation sought new technical and spatial means of bringing the spectators into the action to a greater degree than had previously been the case, but none of the theaters quite freed itself in principle from the old perspective stage, since decorative interests rather than spatial interests dominated the minds of the architects of the time. van de velde's tripartite perspective stage for the werkbundtheater, cologne 1925, which was taken a stage further by perret in the theater for the arts and crafts exhibition at paris in 1925, and poelzig's reconstruction of the grosses schauspielhaus, berlin, which was equipped with a thrust stage extending far in front of the perspective stage, are, as far as I know, the only attempts to loosen and radically alter the ossified problem of theater construction which were actually carried out in practice.

in the history of stage building three basic spatial forms for accommodating scenic events may be distinguished: the round arena or circus, with a central acting circle on which the scenic action is staged concentrically in the round and is seen from all sides. the amphitheater of the greeks and romans, which takes half the round arena, has a semicircular acting area and a forestage on which the action develops in relief in front of a static background, without being separated from the spectators by a curtain. the perspective or picture-frame stage which uses the orchestra pit and curtain to divide the "world of illusion" on the stage from the real world of the audience and presents the stage set as a two-dimensional projection on the plane revealed by the curtains. nowadays our experience is pretty well limited to this last form of theater, the picture-frame stage, which has the great disadvantage of not allowing the

181

audience to participate actively in the separate events on the stage. if this disadavantage were overcome, the result would be a strengthening of the illusion and a revitalization of the theater. when erwin piscator entrusted the plans for his new theater to me, he made a number of seemingly utopian demands, as is characteristic of the boldness of his full-blooded temperament, all of them aimed at creating a technically refined, versatile theatrical instrument, which would fulfill the requirements of various directors, and which would to a high degree offer the possibility of letting the spectators participate actively in the events on the stage, thereby making these events more vivid for them. the problem of stage space had long exercised the minds of myself and my colleagues at the bauhaus.

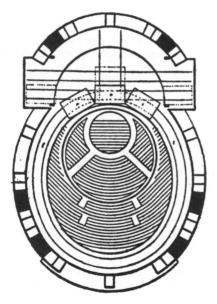

Plan: stage and auditorium

piscator's very welcome commission and the persistence of his demands produced a final solution which is now about to be built. my "total theater" (pat. pend.) offers the producer the possibility of working on a picture-frame stage, or on a thrust stage, or on an arena, or on several of these stages simultaneously during the same production. the oval auditorium stands on twelve slender pillars. behind three pillars at one end of the oval a tripartite stage has been placed, which curves around at either side to embrace the foremost rows of seats. the action can be set on the central stage, or on one of the side stages, or on all three together. a two-level horizontal "paternoster" of movable stage wagons permits fast and frequent scene changes without the disadvantages of the revolving stage. behind the pillars a walkway runs right around the auditorium, extending the side stages and rising with the tiers of seats. wagons can travel on this walkway so that certain parts of the action take place around the audience. the smaller circular area at the front of the orchestra can be lowered for dismantling the seats in the basement, and the area in front of the picture-frame stage can then be used for acting. from this the actors can go down the middle aisle into the midst of the spectators, and from there they can go down through the spectators via the walkways around the large orchestra and back to where they started from.

the shape of the house can be completely changed by turning the large revolving stage through 180°! when this is done the small circle becomes an arena with concentric rows of spectators rising on all sides! this transformation can be carried out by the machinery during the performance. the actors' access to this arena is either by steps from the basement, or along the passage which leads back to the proscenium stage when the revolving stage is in this position, or from the roof by way of frames and ladders which can be dropped in, thus permitting action on a vertical plane above the arena. the machinery for varying the acting area is effectively complemented by projections. in his productions piscator has used film quite ingeniously to reinforce the illusion created by the actors on the stage. i have paid particular attention to his demand for built-in projectors and screens in many places, since i considered projectors the simplest and most effective scenic device available to the modern theater. for in the neutral space of the darkened stage you can build with light and project slides and movies of abstract or figurative material to create scenic illusions which render real flats or stage props superfluous. in my "total theater" i have not only provided facilities for projections on the cyclorama behind all three stages with the aid of a system of mobile projectors, but also for covering the whole auditorium—walls and ceiling—with projections (pat. pend.). to this end screens can be fixed between the twelve columns in the auditorium and film can be projected onto the back of all of these screens from twelve projection boxes simultaneously, so that the spectator can find himself in the middle of a raging sea or at the center of converging crowds. at the same time a projection tower can be lowered into the auditorium to project film on the inside of the same screens. there is also a cloud machine to project clouds, stars or abstract pictures on the sky from a central point. in other words, the projection surface (cinema) is superseded by the projection space. the removal of the light neutralizes the interior of the auditorium and this space, filled with illusions created by the projectors, itself becomes the scene of events.

the aim of this theater is no longer to accumulate a collection of fanciful technical apparatus and gimmickry; everything is a means to an end: the end is to draw the spectator into the middle of the scenic events, to make him part of the space in which the events are taking place and prevent him from escaping from them under cover of the curtain. in addition, a theater architect is bound in my opinion by a duty to make the stage instrument as impersonal, responsive and versatile as possible, so that the various directors are free to develop their various artistic concepts.

it is a great space machine with which the director of the play can shape his personal work in accordance with his own creative impulses.

walter gropius, director of the dessau bauhaus

But the first problem was to find a house to work in during the coming season. It was not an easy task. There was criticism, particularly from proletarian circles, when our choice fell upon the Theater am Nollendorfplatz in the West End of the city, instead of a working-class theater in a working-class district. The self-appointed pundits prophesied that this choice alone heralded a change in political policy within the new venture. Yet all our considerations were practical ones. The Nollendorf Theater was the most suitable of all the theaters available at the time. Of the other theaters on our short list, one had too small an auditorium, and the technical equipment was so run-down that it would have cost a vast sum to repair it; the other theater lay even farther west. The Nollendorf Theater happened to have technical equipment which we could use and occupied a position which was central for our working-class patrons.

The Equipment of the Piscator-Bühne

Piscator-Bühne invitation to subscribers

Not only the individual productions, but the theater in its entirety represented an experiment, a bold sally into unknown territory: it was experimental with regard to the public, the drama, the direction, the technical equipment. And it was also—and this is crucial for the survival of the venture—an experiment in terms of commercial viability (success). Never before had an enterprise walked into such an uncertain future, in spite of all advance calculations and considerations.

How did matters stand with the written drama, the lifeblood of every theater? Plays which incorporated our ideas and at the same time retained some artistic shape were neither available nor likely to be available in the foreseeable future. We knew that the production of the sort of plays which corresponded to the ideals behind our theater was still in its infancy, that their development would be a long and arduous task which could not be brought to completion independently of the overall political and economic development. My whole activity at the Volksbühne had been nothing less than an attempt to reshape the production of plays from a social and revolutionary angle and to develop such plays and give them depth. Perhaps my whole style of directing is a direct result of the total lack of suitable plays. It would certainly not have taken so dominant a form if adequate plays had been on hand when I started. (The whole controversy about the relative responsibilities of the author and the director can in my estimation be reduced to the simple question: which of the two has it in his power to be more lucid, more convincing, more powerful and effective? Artistic energy has a duty to perfect the work in hand and that duty may not be shirked.)

So we went into action with deficiencies in two decisive components of the theater, plays and architecture; but, as often happens, our weaknesses produced positive results. A new theory emerged, a political and sociological theory of the drama. This was not a recipe for new plays, rather a new angle from which to view and adapt half-formed or totally incomplete dramatic subjects. From the lack of revolutionary architecture a new form of staging grew. These results were transitional, auxiliary measures which proved fruitful and pointed toward future developments.

Basic Principles of a Theory of Sociological Drama

1. The Function of Man

Fundamental to what I have called the "new point of view" is the situation of man, his appearance, his function in the context of the revolutionary theater; man and his emotions, his relationships, either private or imposed by society, or his attitude to supernatural powers (God, Fate, Destiny, or whatever form that force may have taken in the course of evolution)—concepts dear to dramatists and dramatic theorists throughout the centuries! But it was left to the Volksbühne, or rather to the intellectuals active within it, to present man in his purest form, as a chemically pure preparation, so to speak, and to make this a "thing-in-itself," the essential center, not only of the drama, but of the theater as a whole. The principle of "Art for the People" had been transformed by means of a detour through "human greatness" into its own diametrical opposite: "the Sovereignty of Art." It was a long road, past the stations of bourgeois individualism with their array of private torments of the soul—but what an irony that it should be the Volksbühne whose particular brand of drama pursued this road up a blind alley from which there was no way back into a social framework.

This complex of questions is very closely bound up with acting technique and it came up for discussion once more in relation to this new type of theater which was based on entirely new functional assumptions. Again and again we have to go back to the original sources of the whole movement. For we are not dealing here with a gratuitous change, but with a change which was in the first instance imposed by the social circumstances. And these circumstances were war and revolution. These were the things that changed man, his intellectual structure, and his attitude to the community in general. They put the finishing touches to the job that industrial capitalism had started fifty years earlier.

The War finally buried bourgeois individualism under a hail of steel and a holocaust of fire. Man, the individual, existing as an isolated being, independent (at least seemingly) of social connections, revolving egocentrically around the concept of the self, in fact lies buried beneath a marble slab inscribed "The Unknown Soldier." Or, as Remarque formulated it, "The generation of 1914 perished in the war, even if some did survive the shellfire."[1] What came back had nothing more in common with concepts like man, mankind, and humanity, which had symbolized the eternal nature of the God-given order in the parlors of prewar days.

The columns of troops that maintained order in their own ranks without any snarled commands as they struggled back over the Rhine in 1918 still fell far short of the kind of comradeship which thinks, acts and feels collectively, a kind of comradeship which is the ultimate aim, and not, as is sometimes claimed, the basic premise of socialism. Those troops returned to German soil with the firm intention of building a new, better, more just order, with weapons in their hands if need be; they were in fact a preliminary form of the socialist type. Smelted in the crucibles of heavy industry, hardened and welded on the forges of war, the masses of 1918 and 1919 brought their threats and demands to the gates of the State, no longer as a mob, or an ill-assorted gang, but as a new living being with a life of its own, which was no longer the sum of its individual components, but formed a new and mighty ego, spurred on and guided by the unwritten laws of its class.

Is there anyone, in the face of this vast revolution which none of us can opt out of, who can seriously maintain that we should see man, his emotions and his ties with life, as something eternal, abso-

1. Erich Maria Remarque (1898–1970), author of *All Quiet on the Western Front* (*Im Westen nichts Neues*, 1919).

lute, untouched by time? Or can it now be admitted at last that in our own century Tasso's complaints beat on unresponsive concrete rooms and steel walls, and that Hamlet's neurasthenia can expect no sympathy from a generation of grenade-launchers and record-winners? Will people finally see that "interesting heroes" are of interest only to epochs which can see their own fates embodied in them, and that the joys and sorrows which only yesterday seemed so sublime appear ludicrously irrelevant to the keen eyes of the fighting present?

The epoch whose social and economic conditions have in fact perhaps deprived the individual of his right to be a man, without affording him the higher humanity of a new society, has raised itself on a pedestal as the new hero. It is no longer the private, personal fate of the individual, but the times and the fate of the masses that are the heroic factors in the new drama.

Does the individual lose the attributes of his personality in the process? Does he love, hate or suffer less than the heroes of former generations? Certainly not, but all his emotional complexes are seen from a new angle. It is no longer one man alone, insulated, a world in himself, who experiences his fate; that man is insepara-bly bound up with the great political and economic factors of the times, as Brecht once pointedly observed: "Every Chinese coolie is forced to take part in world politics to earn his daily bread." He is bound in all his utterances to the destiny of the age, regardless of what his station in life might be.

For us, man portrayed on the stage is significant as a social func-tion. It is not his relationship to himself, nor his relationship to God, but his relationship to society which is central. Whenever he appears, his class or social stratum appears with him. His moral, spiritual or sexual conflicts are conflicts with society. The Ancients may have focused on his relationship to the Fates, the Middle Ages on his relationship to God, Rationalism on his relationship to na-ture, Romanticism on his relationship to the power of the emotions—: a time in which the relationship of individuals in the community to one another, the revision of human values, the realignment of social relationships is the order of the day cannot fail to see mankind in terms of society and the social problems of the times, i.e., as a political being.

The excessive stress on the political angle—and it is not our work, but the disharmony in current social conditions which makes every sign of life political—may in a sense lead to a distorted view of human ideals, but the distorted view at least has the advantage of corresponding to reality.

187

We, as revolutionary Marxists, cannot consider our task complete if we produce an uncritical copy of reality, conceiving the theater as a mirror of the times. We can no more consider this our task than we can overcome this state of affairs by theatrical means alone, nor can we conceal the disharmony with a discreet veil, nor can we present man as a creature of sublime greatness in times which in fact socially distort him—in a word, it is not our business to produce an idealistic effect. The business of revolutionary theater is to take reality as its point of departure and to magnify the social discrepancy, making it an element of our indictment, our revolt, our new order.

2. The Significance of the Technical Side

It has probably become clear from what has already been stated that technical innovations were never an end in themselves for me. Any means I have used or am currently in the process of using were designed to elevate the events on the stage onto a historical plane and not just to enlarge the technical range of the stage machinery.

This elevation, which was inextricably bound up with the use of Marxist dialectics in the theater, had not been achieved by the plays themselves. My technical devices had been developed to cover up the deficiencies of the dramatists' products.

Frequent attempts have been made to refute this point by objecting that true art transcends the private sphere and elevates it into the realm of the typical or the historical. Time and again our opponents have overlooked the fact that types do not have eternal validity, so that art can never do more than record the historic aspect of its own epoch along with the action. The Classical epoch saw its "eternal plane" in the great personality, an epoch of aestheticism would see it in the elevation of beauty, a moral epoch would see it in terms of ethics, an epoch of idealism in the sublime. All these evaluations were considered eternal in their own times and art was anything that provided a generally valid statement of these values. For our generation these values are exhausted, outmoded, dead.

What are the forces of destiny in our own epoch? What does this generation recognize as the fate which it accepts at its peril, which it must conquer if it is to survive? Economics and politics are our fate, and the result of both is society, the social fabric. And only by taking these three factors into account, either by affirming them or by fighting against them, will we bring our lives into contact with the "historical" aspect of the twentieth century.

Anyone who demands anything else of art in our times is intentionally or unintentionally engaged in subverting and damping our energies. We can allow neither ideal nor ethical nor moral impulses to intrude upon the scene if the real mainspring of the action is political, economic and social. Anyone who refuses or fails to recognize this is blind to reality. And the theater cannot send other impulses out into society if it is really to be the topical, representative theater of our generation.

It is not mere chance that in an age whose technical achievements tower above its achievements in every other field the stage should become highly technical. And neither is it mere chance that this technical invasion should receive an impetus from a sector which is in conflict with the social order. Intellectual and social revolutions have always been closely bound up with technical upheavals. And a change in the function of the theater was inconceivable without bringing the stage equipment technically up to date. In this regard it seems to me that we have just caught up with something which should have been done long ago. With the exception of the revolving stage and electric light the stage at the beginning of the twentieth century was still in the same position that Shakespeare had left it in: a square segment, a picture frame through which the spectator gets a "forbidden look" at a strange world. The insurmountable gulf between stage and auditorium has decisively shaped international drama for three centuries. It was a drama of make-believe. The theater existed for three hundred years on the fiction that there were no spectators in the house. Even works which were revolutionary in their day deferred to this assumption, were forced to defer to it. Why? Because the theater as an institution, as a piece of apparatus, as a house had never until 1917 been in the hands of the oppressed class, and because that class had never been in a position to liberate the theater structurally as well as intellectually. This task was taken in hand straight away and with the utmost energy by the stage directors of Revolutionary Russia. I had no choice but to follow the same path in my conquest of the theater, but in our context that path led neither to the end of the theater, nor, at least to date, to a change in theater architecture, but only to radical changes in stage machinery, which, taken all in all, amounted to the destruction of the old box form.

From the Proletarisches Theater to *Storm over Gotland* I was sustained by various sources in my attempts to put an end to bourgeois forms and replace them with a form which would bring the spectator into the theater not as a fictitious concept but as a living force. This tendency was, of course, in the beginning political,

189

and all technical means were subordinate to it. And if these means were subordinate, still incomplete, strained, overemphatic, the reason is to be sought in the conflict with a house which was without provision for them.

The House of the Piscator-Bühne

Even the house on the Bülowplatz, which ranked alongside the Staatstheater in having the most up-to-date stage equipment in Berlin, was scarcely equal to the demands which the new dramatic theories with their extended concepts of time and space made on a theater. Even there I had forced them to make considerable improvements in the machinery; three film and slide projection units were bought, and three projectors of extra-long focal length to throw images on the gigantic cyclorama. The conditions in the house on Nollendorfplatz were still worse. Its dimensions were smaller, but it had better acoustics. On the other hand, there was no cyclorama and none of the storage space we needed for our technical work. Our own modifications brought a good deal of the equipment up to a relatively high standard. For example, we were able to work with four projectors simultaneously after our new projection box had been built backstage. But the work on each new play gradually revealed to us how much was still missing, and how many obstacles were left that could be attributed to the architecture of the house.

Due to Technical Difficulties . . .
By Stage Manager Otto Richter

Many a battle has been waged over this issue and in many instances, some more plausible than others, technical difficulties have provided a scapegoat, but what were in fact the difficulties?

People are not entirely ignorant of the fact that our productions have struck out in new directions and followed courses that were different from what had hitherto been usual in the theater. It goes without saying that our production style involved entirely new stage techniques. We stand by the principle that technical advances made outside the theater should be put to service on the stage, which will no longer be a decorative stage-set but a constructive stage.

Purposeful, utilitarian.

These utilitarian stages are, of course, in the first instance experimental structures. Since the primary materials are iron, wood and transparency linen, it will be obvious that the actual building of the sets is quite a different matter from the old system. For example, in our production of

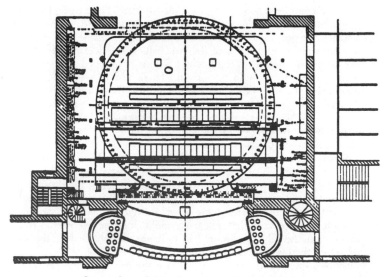

Stage plan of the Theater am Nollendorfplatz

Hoppla, Such is Life! the stage structure is an iron scaffolding: 3-inch gas piping, 36 feet broad, 26 feet high, 10 feet deep, weight over 4 tons. It is clear that this kind of structure could not be erected or even modified in a few minutes, even though it stood on the revolving stage and ran on rails.

When we started rehearsing our next play, *Rasputin*, where we used a hemispherical scaffolding set which also had to be erected daily, we ran into problems which outside observers considered insurmountable. Skillful maneuvering and precise drilling of the stagehands who built and struck the set enabled us to manhandle the two halves of the hemisphere onto the rear of the stage, though each was 46 feet broad, 25 feet high, 20 feet deep and weighed close to a ton. To get the structure ready for rehearsals next day the following routine was required:

After the end of *Hoppla, Such is Life!* sixteen men worked for three hours to move the scaffolding for *Hoppla* to the rear of the stage and bring the two halves of the hemispherical framework onto the front of the stage. Next day the men worked a similar shift to assemble the hemisphere and build the acting platforms, etc. for rehearsals. The rehearsals had to end at 4:00 and it took twenty-four men to clear the stage and set up the evening show. We kept up this daily routine for three weeks. Any repair work which had to be done on the hemisphere was carried out on the stage during the night. It was never possible to get the hemisphere fully ready for rehearsals, and the play could not be rehearsed with film, lights and scene changes as long as the set for *Hoppla* was still on the stage. The matter of space was crucial here, and we often faced almost insurmountable difficulties; these were experiments which

191

had to be completed, once they had been started. Then came the third production, *The Good Soldier Schwejk*. As an innovation: conveyor belts on which the props glide on and off; these have a considerable effect on the actor's technique. Each of the two belts was 9 feet broad, 56 feet long, 1 foot in depth. Weight about 5 tons. Equipped with dirigible rollers, so that they could be moved. These two conveyor belts were assembled at the back of the stockroom and rolled out onto the stage for rehearsals and back off afterwards. You can just imagine that every corner of the stage was utilized for the performance of *Rasputin*. In addition to the hemispherical scaffolding, we now had the two conveyor belts for *Schwejk*, together measuring 18 feet by 56 feet. The manhandling of *Rasputin* started from the front and at this point work could not be limited to fixed hours; three shifts were organized. —After the performance of *Rasputin* we did the first quarter of the dismantling of *Rasputin* and hauled the conveyor belts onto the stage with pulleys; it was then turned on the revolving stage, moved into position and connected to the motors so that rehearsals could go on next morning. In the afternoon all available personnel had to be on the spot to clear the stage and set up the evening performance.

It took sixteen men two hours to move the first conveyor belt but in the course of time we got this down to forty-five minutes.

These accounts make it clear that we had real technical difficulties to contend with, and, moreover, that they cost the company vast sums of money.

When we added things up and calculated the exact cost, it emerged that it had cost 6,491 marks to erect and strike the *Rasputin* hemisphere alone during the run of *Hoppla, Such is Life!* The same thing happened during rehearsals for *Schwejk*. Erecting and striking *Rasputin* and the preparations needed for *Schwejk* cost 4,464 marks. Nor does this sum include the wage bill for actually making the set, for all-night rehearsals, or for dress rehearsals and lighting rehearsals. You can see from these figures the huge sums of money that were spent because of lack of space, lack of workshops and preparation rooms, and the impractical layout of the storerooms and workshops.

And how can these difficulties be overcome? Since the question of space is one of the most important factors affecting our productions, it must be stated that it is quite impossible to keep an operation of this size running smoothly, without any hitches, in the accommodation available to us at the moment, whether it be stage space, storage space, workshop space or whatever other working space is needed. What we need is not a stage equipped with every gadget yet devised and some that have not yet been invented; the ideal thing for us would be a gigantic assembly shop with an array of traveling hoists, cranes, lifting gear and engines, large storage rooms and backstage area with mobile stage wagons that would enable us to put thousands of pounds on the stage in a moment at the touch of a lever, without ever resorting to muscle power or disturbing rehearsals or work in progress. How much precious time, money, muscular energy, and exhausting night-work could be saved if it were possi-

ble, to take one example, to move the whole scaffolding for *Hoppla,
Such is Life!* into a storeroom at the side of the stage in a few minutes
using electro-mechanical power, or if the revolving stage carrying the
hemisphere for *Rasputin* could be wheeled into position from the back
of the stockroom floor in a short space of time, and how wonderful it
would have been, if the conveyor belts for *Schwejk* could have been
assembled in position at the side of the stage, ready to be wheeled out at
the appropriate moment. Instead of a big elevator taking loads of several
tons, we had to manhandle loads weighing up to a ton and a half down a
narrow staircase. There should be a heavy-duty elevator for every acting
area above stage level. Workshops should be attached to the acting and
rehearsal areas to enable us to get down to some real work, and they
should be equipped with every possible machine: for technical work behind the scenes is so complex and varied that it is impossible to work
without the very best machinery. What use is a wood-workshop that can
build nothing wider than 6 feet, or a metal workshop that is too small to
accommodate an iron bar over 13 feet long? These are unpardonable
shortcomings, and they must never be repeated when buildings are converted or constructed in this day and age. These are real technical difficulties. Instead of luxurious auditoriums made of iron, concrete, glass
and fine materials, build us workshops and a stage which is equal to the
demands of modern production techniques, and much money and precious time will be saved—and most important of all: there will be no
more technical difficulties.

But even in the auditorium ideological and material problems of no
less importance emerged. How the spectators are grouped is not
without importance for a performance, whether the space is used to
break the audience into the separate units in accentuated galleries
and boxes, or is used to draw the spectators together in a single unit
(something we had experienced before—das Grosse Schauspielhaus). The court-theater architecture of the Theater am Nollendorfplatz had somehow to be overcome. The material problem
of the auditorium was more difficult. What it amounted to was that
we had to cover costs estimated to be between 3,000 and 3,500
marks each evening with a seating capacity of 1,100 places (the error
in our estimate of these costs was due, at least in part, to the lack of
backstage space, as our stage manager's report shows). Under normal circumstances you cannot base your calculations on the assumption that you will get a full house. Add to this the Special
Sections, which took up two or three hundred seats each evening,
and you have the reason for the "Kurfürstendamm prices at the
Communist Theater" which certain sectors of the press got so
worked up about. The seating capacity of the auditorium regulated
our prices policy.

The Dramaturgic Office
and the Dramaturgic Collective

Since the adaptation of texts was of prime importance for our theater the choice of dramaturgs was crucial.[2] After lengthy deliberation and numerous personal interviews I decided to appoint Wilhelm Herzog, the former editor of *Forum*, the candidate who also had the support of Otto Katz, the front-of-the-house manager. We took the view that the dramaturg's task should not be limited as it was in other theaters to drawing up the repertoire, making suggestions for casting the plays, looking for new scripts and cutting superfluous passages in the texts. What I required of a dramaturg in our special predicament was that he be able to cooperate creatively with myself or with the author. Our dramaturg had to be able both to rework texts in the light of our political standpoint and to work out new scenes to suit my ideas for the production, and to help to shape the script.

Although I knew all about Herzog's political and literary past— he was one of the generation of bourgeois men of letters whose protests against the status quo amounted to the proclamation of pure intellectualism—I was taken in by his plan to write a political revue which was in fact to form our first production.

As I explain elsewhere, nothing came of this. And nothing was also what came of having Herzog as dramaturg. Even before the theater opened he proved to be so incompetent that I called in Gasbarra, my old comrade-in-arms from the days of the *Red Revue*, to take over the job. A few months later, when the volume of work became too much for him, we took on Leo Lania as well.

But setting up a dramaturgic office alone was not enough to satisfy me. It is part of my view of life that work must always be a matter of cooperation with others. I have always tried to see that this conviction was incorporated into some sort of formal organization. Collective effort is rooted in the very nature of the theater. No other art form, with the exception of architecture and orchestral music, relies so heavily on the existence of a community of like-minded people as does the theater.

Even at the Volksbühne the nucleus of a collective had been formed. This was particularly true of the actors, and a section of them moved to the Piscator-Bühne as a body. But there were also members of the management, two or three on the artistic committee—I am thinking of Holitscher, Wolfenstein and Zwehl, among others—who had the practical experience and the theoreti-

2. The following paragraphs: "Since the adaptation. . . . to satisfy me" were inserted in 1963.

194

cal clarity around which a larger independent body—and this was how I imagined the scripting collective—might crystallize.

Productive cooperation

There is a common belief whose inherent validity is rarely questioned anymore. It runs: the more independence you achieve, the more you have to rely on forces which you did not have to take into consideration at all when you occupied a lower station in life: instead of being your own master you serve an anonymous multitude of forces.

There seems to be general agreement that this process is indispensable in the theater, and so a director who is determined to make it alone along lines which the intendant finds alarming will constantly be reminded that when it is his turn to hold a responsible post, he will be the first to recognize that his suggestions are impracticable and that compromises—taking the public into consideration, taking the problems of the day-to-day running of the show into consideration—are essential if the theater is to survive. At this point I must confess that, having become an independent general director in my own right, I find this line of argument even less comprehensible than I ever did before. In fact, I discover every day that my new independence opens more and more possibilities up for me—not in the sense that I am liberated from all influences or stimuli or requirements and left to do as I like, but rather in the direction of putting together with a clear aim in view a structure which incorporates all valuable forces according to objective and ideal criteria. The literary collective, the whole setup imbued with the principles of our view of the world, all this creates a community and makes the purest and safest self-scrutiny possible, cuts out any gratuitous flourishes and makes the general director just as much a part of the whole as the director and the actor, the author as much as the dramaturg.

A young theater that still has to make its name, an organization that still has to feel its way in, naturally takes greater toll of the total strength of the people involved than a theater which has built up the organization it needs over a period of time. But even at this early stage the principle of collective cooperation proves to have great advantages and takes considerable physical and moral burdens from the shoulders of the director and general director. The cogs mesh like a well-designed machine, and from this theater which we have based on our principles there emerges a kind of collective directorship: the production style gets simpler and more obvious all the time, the filmmaker, the dramaturg, the literary advisor, the stage designer get to know the latest ideas in the director's mind as soon as they occur to him and this enables them to contribute their support more easily and fully than was possible in the old theater. So the director in charge of the operation finds himself entrusted with one sole task, that of ensuring that his "empire" is properly coordinated, and that his collaborators are in the right place at the right time. In contrast to the dictatorial principles of the normal run of theaters which make the director as unfree as his subordinates, the principle of a democratic community dedicated to one idea constantly furnishes proof of its own productiveness and of its human and artistic significance.

Unfortunately, the work of the collective failed to come up to my expectations and did not meet the needs of the theater.[3] The very foundation of the thing was dogged by misunderstanding and embarrassment. Besides the men named above we had reached understandings with Balázs, Johannes R. Becher, Brecht, Döblin, Herzog, Lania, Walter Mehring, Mühsam, Toller and Tucholsky.[4] Without thinking, Lania had described himself as the "head" in a press notice about these arrangements. What he meant to call himself was head organizer, naturally, but it took all Otto Katz's diplomacy to placate the irate members. Herzog in particular was annoyed, and declared he would refuse to work under somebody else's orders. Brecht, who was a constant visitor at the Theater am Nollendorfplatz in these early days and took a close interest in all our preparations, strutted up and down the stage shouting, "My name is my trademark, and anybody who uses it must pay for it!"

I don't remember whether a proper working session was ever held after the inaugural assembly at which Erich Mühsam, Wedekind's literary buddy and an anarchist of old, read out a constitution which he had himself drawn up in minute detail. On the other hand, the individual members of the collective did in the course of the season make useful suggestions, and many of them were willing to sacrifice their own time unstintingly in order to play a part in our work. This experiment was an essential part of our first year at the Piscator-Bühne, and I hope to repeat it more successfully at some future time. And when all was said and done, several authors took away ideas and suggestions made in the collective and used them in the quiet of their own studies, spontaneously returning to themes and problems that had been placed before the collective and pursuing and developing them. Erich Mühsam wrote his *Judas* on the basis of one such idea, and Walter Mehring wrote *The Merchant of Berlin* (with which the second Piscator-Bühne on Nollendorfplatz was subsequently to be opened), Lania wrote his play *Boom*, Döblin wrote a drama of the problems of modern marriage (*Die Ehe*, pub. 1931), with which (as a doctor) he was thoroughly familiar.

3. The following paragraphs: "Unfortunately, the work . . . thoroughly familiar." were inserted in 1963.
4. Bela Balázs was a left-wing journalist and film critic. Johannes R. Becher (1891–1958) was an Expressionist poet, a communist who immigrated in 1933 to the Soviet Union and was later a prominent man of letters in the German Democratic Republic. Walter Mehring (b. 1896) was a journalist and writer of satirical songs and cabaret sketches.

196

Guidelines for the Dramaturgic Collective at the Piscator-Bühne

I. The dramaturgic collective at the Piscator-Bühne is a body of friends of the theater. They are comrades who share a spirit of revolution and a concern for artistic matters, and are willing to supervise the program and achievements of the theater, to make their advice available to the management and to bear collective responsibility for the Piscator-Bühne.

II. The collective will be free to appoint its own members, who will be selected solely for the theoretical contribution that they can make to the theater's standards and principles. As a rule, resignations will be a matter of comradely agreement and open discussion on all sides. They will, if possible, be submitted only after agreement has been reached, and they will never be in a form that might give offense. The expulsion of a member against his will can be effected only at an extraordinary meeting called for the purpose and attended by at least ten members, of whom seven (of every ten) vote for expulsion.

III. The collective will distribute the tasks that fall within its competence, such as drawing up and reaching agreement on the repertoire, organizing the Studio, editing the program notes, and so on, at its discretion to special subcommittees of suitable persons appointed by mutual agreement. In special cases it will bring decisions before the full collective. Membership of the collective will be honorary, and the collective will be free to arrange its work as experience decrees, unhampered by restrictive regulations.

IV. All the activities of the collective and its committees will on principle be voluntary, the members to have equal rights and to bear a personal responsibility within the framework of collective responsibility. The initiative and individuality of each member will be given enough scope to keep him satisfied with the work, provided that this is consistent with the concept of a collective united in comradeship and in a political line. The main burden of work will rest on the shoulders of the committee members. The collective will meet at least three times monthly to receive and discuss reports from subcommittees, and on a fourth occasion to hear a report from the management of the Piscator-Bühne on the theater's achievements and plans.

Proposal from Erich Mühsam

The Studio

The work of the second collective within the theater, the Studio, was much more rewarding, probably largely because it was carried out by members who were young and full of enthusiasm.

The plan to set up a Studio was born when we realized that if a new theater is to develop a style of its own, the author, the actor, the technical advisor and the musical director must all be equally

197

involved in the process. This inner involvement, the organic inter-growth of all the components of the theater, can be prepared in theory in advance, but it can be actually achieved only in the course of practical work. The normal working of a theater, the obligations it must meet—once it has been plugged into the circuit of social effectiveness—leave little time for self-clarification and experiment. In such a situation the Studio assumes the function of a laboratory in which the members of the theater and anyone else who is in any way involved can put their ideas to the test in practice, can learn to see the whole field of theater from every angle, helping and complementing each other's work in the process. The object of the Studio is not to explore some play or other fully, but to apply and control the principles of our theater in carrying out some concrete task.

In the Studio the actors are freed from the loose form of a mere contractual relationship and become part of a collective, with the same rights and obligations as the author, the musical director, the director, and the film technicians, and this group then selects the play it will produce, fixes the line the production will follow in comradely discussion, chooses a suitable director and a cast for the play and goes to work;—and the final product at the end of this work—the performance—is no more important than the weeks of preparation themselves, during which a clear and firm will has crystallized out of the theoretical discussions and on the basis of experiments with the material, the actors and the technical equipment.

In the Studio the actor achieves an intimate relationship with the stage itself, he sees the strengths and weaknesses of the play as he confronts it with the reality of performance. The director can see to what extent his intentions can be realized in terms of the stage, the actor is liberated and made part of the experiment. Where in the normal course of running a theater the staging of a play is predetermined by the date fixed for the first night, by which time it must be ready, which means that from the very outset you are preparing, as it were, a fair copy, in the Studio a play can be submitted to a virtually infinite process of adaptation and constructive rewriting. The plays which are produced in the Studio are therefore chosen with definite ideas in mind. They are in part works whose dramatic content has yet to be put to the test. A drama or comedy may have something in its problem, or form, or language that is worthwhile, although the play as a whole does not have either the maturity or the formal unity that would permit a performance in the evening repertoire. In a case like this the Studio gives the author a chance to submit his play to a thorough scrutiny and adapt it accordingly. In some cases the main emphasis is on literary experimentation; in others it is a matter of helping a writer who is fundamentally in sympathy with our theater and our view of the world to clarify his ideas and understand his own mind, and of showing him by means of a play which is in principle misconceived, the way which he ought to go according to his own convictions, and which he may have missed in this particular work. In this case the Studio should fertilize a writer's work and put him on the right lines, but there are other cases where a compact, well-constructed work is chosen because it offers a chance to try out young actors and a new style of acting.

So the uncommitted nature of the Studio is a necessary prerequisite if it is to work freely. It does not function under the direct control of the management, but they share a community of spirit. It must quite consciously be a playground, an arena for preparatory work. To this end courses are held for the members of the Studio and there are lectures covering all the essential political and intellectual problems of the day, but at the same time there are speech courses, courses on learning a part, courses on physical training. The subjects offered at any given time are determined by the play which is then being prepared.

Minutes of the Inaugural Assembly of the Studio

October 16, 1927

The meeting was attended by all the members of the theater who had a definite contract and was opened by Piscator, who made a few remarks about the aims of the Studio and the tasks facing it.

The intention is to lead the members out of the loose form in which they are contractually bound to the theater into a spiritual partnership wholly dedicated to the theater and the ideas behind the theater. Since spiritual partnership cannot be conjured up overnight, some preparations must be made. The Studio will provide preparation for everybody. Its aim, then, is to create a perfect theater, a responsive instrument with which to express our view of the world. Since our view of the world is activistic, our actors must be educated to activism. In addition to this the Studio has a number of other tasks:

1. Thorough training of the whole personnel;
2. Thorough training of each individual;
3. Experimentation with acting techniques;
4. Literary experimentation;
5. Political experimentation;
6. Political propaganda.

199

To enable work to start as soon as possible the directors suggest that three groups be formed. The grouping will in no way be an evaluation of the individuals concerned, but will merely facilitate a division of labor. Regrouping can take place at any time. The evaluation of the work shown by the classes will remain in the hands of all the members. The first practical task for class 1 will be the preparation of a performance of Sinclair's *Jailbirds* and Jung's *Homesickness*. Class 2 is to adapt fairy tales. Class 3 is to cooperate with Piscator in preparing an amnesty demonstration and a Max Hölz demonstration.

The second task facing the Studio is the organization of daily classes in physical training and voice for everyone to participate in. Political and literary lectures will be arranged to acquaint the members with the political concept and the literary material of our theater. The members of the dramaturgic collective and any other sympathizers are to be encouraged to attend these lectures. In all the classes, but especially in class 3, there will be an introduction to learning parts in a new, experimental manner.

The Studio will start building up a library from its own funds and from contacts which will be made with publishing houses; this library will particularly feature material relating to the plays in the repertoire.

The three classes will elect a three-man governing body and a separate committee for each production, consisting of a director, an actor, a dramaturg, etc. The groups will be interlinked by the exchange of members.

Class 3 is a teaching studio, designed entirely for training young actors. It will be divided into a school section and a production section. The director suggests the following subjects of instruction for the school: learning an individual part and learning company work, stylistic studies, foreign languages, dramatic theory, theater history, stage design, costume studies, film instruction, and the requisite physical training and special training. The subjects on the curriculum will be grouped around whatever play is being produced at any given time. Every aspect of the productions will be prepared by members of the teaching studios themselves, right down to the technical details. The theater will provide teachers for the third class. The members of the third class are asked to prepare a weekly schedule immediately, and to submit requests for teachers for each subject to the management. Whenever possible, students who share our artistic and political convictions will be accepted for the third class. A general governing body for the whole Studio is to be elected from the combined membership of the three classes, the directing and the dramaturgic groups, and this body will share the practical work and allocate the working space.

Top left: (From left to right) Russian soldier (Erich O. Peters); Trotsky (Oscar Sima); Lenin (Alexander Granach). *Center left*: Czar (Erwin Kalser); Czarina (Tilla Durieux). *Below left*: Grand Duke Pavlovich (Richard Duschinski); Dr. Lizawer (Leopold Lindtberg); Minister Dobrovolsky (Gerhart Bienert).

Rasputin by Alexei Tolstoy.

The segments of the hemispherical stage.

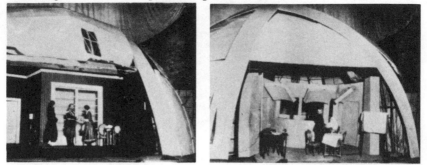

Center segment, lower half: Room in Tsarskoe Selo. Czarina, Czar, Vyrubova (Sybille Binder). Side segment, lower half: Czar's Headquarters.

Arched segment with triangular segment above. Nightclub in St. Petersburg. Gypsy chorus. Left: Vyrubova and Minister Dobrovolsky. Center segment, opened above and below: Second Congress of the Russian workers' and soldiers' councils. Bolsheviks seize power. Above: Lenin, Trotsky, Russian soldier.

Lunacharsky, then People's Commisar for Education, with Piscator at a rehearsal for *Rasputin*.

Film for *Rasputin*.

Last shot of the prologue. Rasputin's shadow (top screen) growing behind the figure of the Czar (on the top segment of the hemisphere).

Below: Scene in the Czar's palace. Czarina, her confidante Vyrubova, Minister Protopopov. Simultaneously on top screen: Execution of the Czar's family. *Right*: Data on calendar.

Max Pallenberg

Above: Technical wagon of Thespis. Seated, Piscator; in front of him, Tilla Durieux, Max Pallenberg and Paul Wegener. Cartoon from *Simplicissimus*, 1928, on the rape of the actor by the machinery.

Left: Wilhelm II's legal action against Piscator. Publicity by the grace of God. Piscator: "HE is the better strategist after all. Fabulous, the way he has mounted this publicity campaign for me!" (From *Ulk*, 1928).

Top: Under arrest in the chapel. Padre (Szöke Szakall), prisoners. Dummies by George Grosz. Set carried on by conveyor belt. *Center:* On the way to the front. Schwejk talks a sergeant into the ground. In the railway car dummy soldiers. *Below:* Finale for Schwejk which was given only once. Mutilated veterans parade before God (on the conveyor belt).

Top left: Schwejk and the medical officer (cartoon).

Top right: Schwejk before the judge (background projection).

Center left: Country policeman's yard. Policeman (Oscar Sima) (background projection).

Center right: On the parade ground.

Overhead view of conveyor belts with screen borders.

Singing Jailbirds by Upton Sinclair.   Piscator-Bühne
Director: Ernst Lönner. Designer: Traugott Müller

Above: Jail scene (dream). Red Adams (Alexander Granach), Nell (Renée Stobrawa).

Center: scene in the "tank" (mob cell).

Below: Dream scene (gauzes for projections).

INTRODUCTION

The Piscator-Bühne was to open with *Down Around the State Prosecutor (Rund um den Staatsanwalt)* by Wilhelm Herzog, but it became clear that Herzog's script would not be ready in time, so Piscator decided to put on Toller's *Hoppla, Such is Life!* instead. Herzog's play was given at a matinee in the Theater des Westens on May 6, 1928, and was dismissed as "a barren string of disordered, falsely presented facts" (H. Ihering) and as "a dry, witless, interminable diatribe against the SPD" (F. Hussong).

Toller wrote *Hoppla* in the spring of 1927 with Piscator in mind and listed subjects for film at the appropriate points in the stage directions. The play was, in part, based on Toller's life, and the central character, Karl Thomas, relived the author's experiences: war and revolution, treason trial, death sentence commuted to imprisonment for seven years. Thomas's contempt for Kilmann, his revolutionary comrade who became an SPD minister, reflects Toller's comments on associates who threw in their lot with the Weimar Republic.

Although Piscator recognized in *Hoppla* a scenario to which he could apply the techniques of political theater, he had reservations about the style and about the character of the hero, whom he saw as a romantic anarchist, and these were modified with Toller's active collaboration. The effect was to be factual and documentary, so lyrical and Expressionist speeches were cut. Politically misaligned speeches, a worker's explanation that he is voting for Kilmann because his daughter's kind employer thinks he is sound, or Thomas's list of personal motives for becoming a revolutionary (nagging wives, etc.) were eliminated. Other cuts simply served to keep up the pace of the production.

Piscator objected to the figure of Thomas because his commitment to the revolution was emotional, rather than lucid and practical. Toller had conceived him as a student, whose comrades sniped at his bourgeois background in the opening prison scene, and Piscator tried to offset this by deliberately miscasting the role with a proletarian type of actor, Alexander Granach. The original ending, a neatly contrived irony which made no specific political point, was altered. It had shown Thomas rushing back to the asylum, where it became clear to him that the mentally ill were no more mad than the politicians and the military, with the latter a menace to mankind. He sees that the patient, practical work of party members like Eva Berg and Kroll is the right course. This new lucidity makes him a danger to the state for the first time, rather than just an awkward dreamer, and the psychiatrist locks him up. The promptbook in the Deutsche Akademie der Künste, East Berlin, contains the following ending:

> Eva Berg: He doesn't answer.
>
> (Hectic tapping and projected words, then silence.)
>
> Rand: Hanged!!!
>
> Frau Meller: Is that true?
>
> Kroll: He shouldn't have. That's no way for a revolutionary to die.
>
> Eva Berg: He was broken by life.
>
> Frau Meller: Damned world! It must be changed. [Which Piscator quotes below as, "There is only one thing to do, hang yourself or change the world."]

So the play which opened with film of the war ended with the mother figure in the solid, communist group asserting the need for a change.

Piscator discerned in the play a cross section of society, and Traugott Müller built a set which reflected this. A scaffolding 25 feet high, 35 feet wide and 10 feet deep was built on rails on the revolving stage (Photo 43). It was divided vertically into three sections, the outer ones having three cubicles one above the other, while the center one was an undivided shaft surmounted by a dome. External stairs at the sides and back afforded entrances at each level (Photo 13). A screen 25 feet by 35 feet could be lowered in front for film and black-and-white gauzes for projections. The acting areas were backed by translucent, cloth-covered screens, some of which hinged upward to allow projection from the rear, while others could be rolled forward to mask off part of the cubicle. The tall screen at the back of the shaft could be both pushed forward and hauled up into the flies.

The promptbook enables the production to be visualized in detail. A film prologue by Curt Oertel showed a close-up of a general's tunic covered with medals, cut to clips of infantry assaults, advancing tanks, shellfire, machine guns, wounded men, rows of crosses, an army in retreat, abandoned weapons, then cut back to a huge hand ripping the medals off the general's chest. Karl Thomas appeared intermittently among the soldiers in the film. Then the screen went up, the gauzes came down and the prison scene with Thomas, Kilmann, and the condemned revolutionaries was acted in the center section between a back projection of prison walls and a front projection of barred windows, overlaid with film of an outsize sentry marching back and forth.

This scene was followed by the key film of the evening, a recapitulation of Thomas's lost years showing inflation, Ruhr risings, events in the Soviet Union, Mussolini in Italy, Sacco and Vanzetti, Hindenburg's election as president, the stabilization of the Weimar Republic, all accompanied by Edmund Meisel's music.

After the intermission at the end of the second act, Kate Kühl, a well-known singer in political cabaret, sang Mehring's title song, and this was followed by a sequence of scenes in a hotel in which spotlights were cross-faded swiftly from cubicle to cubicle, picking out one group of guests or employees after another, until Kilmann was shot, and the assassin and Thomas made their getaway down the external stairs on the right, which had been revolved to face the audience.

The fourth act was followed by a ballet choreographed by Mary Wigmann, in which dancers with phosphorescent skeletons painted on their tights, an allusion to Toller's earlier *Transfiguration*, danced a Charleston in ultraviolet light.

The short last act showed the original revolutionaries in prison again, this time in separate cells between which they tapped messages in code, while the projected words glided across the gauze. The play ended with Thomas's suicide, as has been indicated.

In rehearsal much time was devoted to examining the social and political attitudes implicit in the characters. The dedicated Communists, Kroll (Ernst Busch), Frau Meller (Renée Stobrawa) and Eva Berg (Sybille Binder), were cast as proletarian types to be soberly played, though Ihering noted that the last-named was too mondaine for the part. The scene in which Eva was reunited with Thomas and rejected his revolutionary outburst, telling him the times required patient groundwork, was played unsentimentally, slower than the fast pace of the rest of the production. Kilmann (Oskar Sima), the SPD minister, affected a patronizing self-assurance, and the scenes in his offices were presented ironically, to expose the corruption of the Republic which had been infiltrated by reactionaries. The War Minister strode swiftly through the waiting room, ignoring all present, while Pickel (Paul Graetz), a comic provincial lobbyist, stood sharply to attention and pinned his Iron Cross to his jacket. The actors were to understand that they were presenting a gallery of contemporary types, whose political affilia-

203

tions and relative social merit in the context of the production were to be made clear. The political context of Toller's play was further clarified by articles in the program.

Alexander Granach (1890–1945) as Karl Thomas found little favor with the critics at the time, but it was a performance which lived on in theatrical memories. Granach was a Ukrainian Jew who acted in Yiddish before coming to Berlin. He had played Shylock, Kragler in Brecht's *Drums in the Night*, the Cashier in Kaiser's *From Morn to Midnight*, as well as Mephisto and Mosca in *Volpone*. Here is how Leopold Lindtberg remembers him:

> "He had a wide range of contrasting means at his disposal, yet his approach to a role was never cool, never permitted him to step aside from it. Everything had to be played against the emotional dynamics of his early Expressionism. He became a key actor in Piscator's company, where his rhetorical fire made the cold fire of Piscator's . . . analytical productions glow. Karl Thomas and Lenin were peaks in his career. His acting was fueled by passionate political involvement, erupting in sound and fury in his Expressionist phase, but now sharp, concentrated, dialectical. He never . . . succumbed to dogma . . . needed no theories . . . for he knew what it was to work sixteen hours for a pittance, and had been in strikes when he was a baker's apprentice."
>
> (Cat. of the A. G. exhibition, Akad. d. Künste Berlin, 1971, p. 14)

Yet on the whole the critics passed over the acting briefly, and clearly saw neither quality nor novelty in it at first sight, though Ihering mentioned that the actors seemed uncomfortable among the scaffolding of the stage.

For Toller the production of *Hoppla* was a chastening experience, and he observed ruefully in *Quer Durch* (1930) that he was living in an age of middlemen. The public wanted stars and sensational novelties devised by ingenious directors, not plays. Of *Hoppla* he says:

> "I am sorry that I gave in to the current fashion and remodeled the structure of the play, substituting a structure suggested by the director. The form I had aimed for was stronger than the one shown on the stage. I have only myself to blame, but I have learnt my lesson, and today I would prefer a director who failed to bring out all that is in a play to one who put in too much of his own." (p. 292)

Toller then quotes a ponderous appeal to the audience which Piscator wished to give to Karl Thomas after the murder of Kilmann as an example of Piscator's "tightening up of the script," and denies that "a voluntary return to the asylum" was, as Piscator claims below, one of his three possible endings.

Because of postponements at the Nollendorftheater the first performance of *Hoppla* took place at the Hamburg Kammerspiele. Leipzig and Frankfurt followed, all using Toller's original ending, but it is Piscator's production that is remembered.

XVII
CONFRONTATION WITH THE TIMES
Hoppla, Such is Life!
September 3 to November 7, 1927

When we chose our opening play we did not rely on available, ready-made scripts. We wanted to do what people had always been asking us to do and open with a play which had been written in close collaboration with our own intellectual group. This was to be Wilhelm Herzog's *Down Around the State Prosecutor (Rund um den Staatsanwalt)*. As far as the subject was concerned the play would have been a significant contribution to our overall program, a kind of grand political revue. It embraced the whole period of the Revolution, and was to pick out a single figure of interest with whom the motive forces of the age could be demonstrated. The subject provided an opportunity to analyze the nature of the November Revolution, and to show all the factors involved in its rise and fall; in other words, this revue was to give us a chance to work out problems of historical importance whose impact on the present was considerable. When the play was commissioned, Herzog was given a sizable advance. His first scenes arrived in July, while I was away on holiday. I was greatly disappointed. They contained none of the things we had discussed together and amounted to nothing more than a dry, lifeless and undramatic reproduction of the historical documents. I could just as well have run *Vorwärts* and the *Rote Fahne* together and shaped the result into a play on the stage. (For example, there were stage directions by Herzog such as: "A bacchanal then ensues" or "There is an exchange of witty cracks.") Herzog's failure and the very short time that was left forced us to abandon this work for our opening show and choose a new one.

A draft Toller had submitted in the spring more or less fitted the bill for the revue as we had originally envisaged it. The basic idea was to take a revolutionary who has been in a lunatic asylum for eight years and confront him with the world of 1927.

This was another idea which afforded the possibility of giving a social and political outline of a whole epoch. But the documentary material was overlaid with poetic lyricism, as was always the case in Toller's work. All our efforts in the subsequent course of the work were directed towards providing the play with a realistic substructure. You cannot prove a single point against the bourgeois world order if your evidence is inaccurate, and it is always inaccurate when the emotions play a decisive role. Even at the very first reading in my old house in Oranienstrasse, the figure of the "hero," Karl Thomas, came under heated attack. His character was accused of being too passive and ill-defined. Toller tends to impose the burden of his own feelings on such characters, and these are subject to the restless fluctuations which are typical of artists, particularly if they have been through as much and suffered as much as Toller. This is only natural.

Both elements, the documentary and the emotional or lyrical, are essential in drama. Yet for us, for the purposes of our theater, feelings must be clearly fitted into the overall pattern, the spectator must be able to see them from all sides as if they were under a bell jar; for our purposes, even feelings must be pressed into service as evidence to support our world view. We cannot allow them to posture independently.

In my case this requirement emanates from political convictions but other people with different views have made the same demands for other reasons. The work of writers with pedagogic and philosophical leanings can no longer be a mere reflection of the writers themselves, the time for art of the ego is past. Only when the relationship of the author to his figures is impersonal and objective will he be able to clarify their meaning, their value, their intellectual structure.

Our analysis of Toller's hero had inevitably produced the conclusion that we incorporated in the staged version. (Toller himself later repudiated this conclusion; and remember, Schiller constantly altered the endings of his plays.) But with the play as it stood, I fail to see to this day what other ending we could have used. The decision was taken only after long debates and interminable suggestions.

The hero of Toller's play, Karl Thomas, was a postwar revolutionary who was condemned to death after the Revolution had been put down.[1] In 1919, shortly before the hour at which he was to be executed—along with his friend Kilmann, who had also been condemned to death—he was pardoned. Karl Thomas goes out of his mind, is committed to a lunatic asylum and drops out of sight for eight years until 1927, when he returns to an entirely new world. His friend Kilmann has made his peace with the new regime and has been made a government minister; his former girlfriend has become a political agitator. When he reappears on the scene, she takes him in for a while but eventually turns him out onto the street. Karl Thomas becomes a waiter. In his desperation at the times, he conceives a plan to shoot Kilmann, who is now a reactionary. A right-wing radical student beats him to it, but Karl Thomas comes under suspicion and is arrested and put back in the lunatic asylum; he hangs himself at the moment at which his innocence is established. . . .

Three endings for *Hoppla*

Arrest	Escape	Arrest
Police station	Voluntary Return to Prison	Police station
Committal to Lunatic Asylum		Lunatic Asylum
Lydin scene to: Masses march past	From the conical masks[2] cut on film to officer's chest, foundry, war pictures run in reverse. Instead of the Kilmann mask—a Kilmann monument.	Prison (Messages tapped on the walls from cell to cell) Thomas hangs himself.

1. The paragraph beginning: "The hero of Toller's play. . . . " was inserted in the 1963 edition.
2. The conical masks (*Trichtermasken*) used in this production had been devised earlier by Tristan Tzara, the Zurich Dadaist. They were made by twisting a piece of stiff paper into a cone and cutting eyeholes in it. The effect was like a Ku Klux Klan hood.

> As Thomas laughs and
> the last words are
> spoken a huge field
> gun appears on the
> screen and points into
> the audience.

The defeatism of this conclusion later came in for some criticism from both the radical and bourgeois camps, and at this point I can offer the following explanation.

Thomas is anything but a class-conscious proletarian. He finds it no easier to make contact with the bourgeois world than with the world of the proletariat. The theme does not plot the course of an erratic adherent of the Revolution; if it did, his suicide would be utterly misguided. Thomas is, in fact, an anarchist of the sentimental variety and his breakdown is perfectly logical. He constitutes a proof from the converse. What his case demonstrates is the insanity of the bourgeois world order.

> Two months after the first night three young proletarians in the district of Lichtenberg committed suicide because they despaired of the movement. It is certain that they did not act under the influence of the play, and it is equally certain that they had several points in common with Toller's Thomas. I can readily understand, particularly in the case of young people, that in a period of sober, unpathetic, trivial routine many should find the contrast between what they want to do and what they are actually doing quite shattering.

His counterparts, who represent the positive side of the Revolution, are Eva, Mother Meller, and above all Kroll, who represents the one hundred percent party man.

In giving the leading role to Alexander Granach, I committed a deliberate casting "error" which effectively turned that role into a proletarian type. This was my way of avoiding the standard "hero" who recurs in each of Toller's works; but at the same time I wanted to show that the petit bourgeois attitude of mind is not the exclusive privilege of the "intellectuals."

Toller's language proved to be a serious handicap in dealing with a subject which I would have preferred to analyze soberly, clearly and unambiguously in the play.

> Example:
> (During the last sentences two policemen appear. They both go up to Thomas and grab him by the wrists.)

First Policeman: Well, young man, I suppose you just found that revolver?

(A calm, factual question from which a situation can develop, because it causes a certain tension. What reply does Toller give him?)

Karl Thomas: How do I know? How do you know? Even the gunman's revolver turns against him, and the barrel spouts laughter.

(This is supposed to mean: Thomas, who intended to shoot Kilmann, the minister, himself, but was beaten to it by a Nazi student, does not yet grasp the sequence of events and feels mocked by his own revolver.)

Toller himself can see that this reply is impossible, but it does not occur to him to cut it. Instead he tries to save it with the next line:

Second Policeman: We'll have a little more respect from you, right?

His formative years lay within the period of Expressionism. I myself am well aware of how difficult it is to shake this off. And nothing is further from my mind than a repudiation of linguistic concentration. But the process of formulation must not become an end in itself. It must always be functional, it must always carry the dramatic action forward and increase the mental tension; it must never simply passively reflect itself. There were stubborn and protracted arguments with Toller on this point.

We wrestled for days with single passages. Toller scarcely ever left my apartment.[3] He had made himself at home at my desk and filled page after page at incredible speed with his huge handwriting, consigning the sheets to the wastepaper basket with equal rapidity. And all the while he kept lighting my most expensive cigars and stubbing them out again in the ashtray after a few drags. Rehearsals began on the first of August. But the script fell far short of what I required of our first programmatic play.

We had to work out a prompt-copy while work on the script was still going on.

Toller had managed to hint at a cross section of society in the choice and grouping of the settings. We had come up with a stage-set that would display this cross section and lend it precision: a multistoried structure with many different acting areas above and beside one another, which would symbolize the social order. According to the preliminary sketches, the spectator was to see this structure as a huge projection screen, on which the introductory film would run. At the moment when we cut from the filmed introduction to the first live scene, a square hole would open at the appropriate point (prisons, cut from film to cell No. 1). In this way there would be a perfect fusion of film and stage.

3. The passage: "Toller scarcely ever. . . . after a few drags" was inserted in the 1963 edition.

To achieve this, Traugott Müller, together with our stage manager Otto Richter, had devised an apparatus which linked the various flat squares to pulleys, so that they could be moved back and forward at the touch of a lever. At the same time the furniture was left collapsed on the floor and erected itself on a scissor principle after the set had opened. The actors were to make their entrances from the sides of the stage up steps, and this is what they eventually did. The main idea of developing the live action straight out of the screen action could not be made to work perfectly in practice, because the ropes failed to run smoothly. (It was because of these ropes that we christened this stage the "pulley-stage" in the notes in our first program.)

This multilevel stage is not exactly the same as the Kreisler stage. There is admittedly a certain external similarity, but they are based on diametrically opposite principles; whereas the Kreisler stage[4] as it has been used up to now does no more than make a number of sets out of the single set, the multilevel stage is a self-contained, compact acting structure, for which the proscenium opening is no more than an external impediment. The multilevel stage is actually one example of a new type of theater architecture.

"In order to create a transparent stage which can be effortlessly combined with film and projection screens, Erwin Piscator in his production of Ernst Toller's Hoppla, Such is Life! uses a mobile, multilevel steel scaffolding. Not until after the event was it discovered that directors Meinhard and Bernauer had patented a mobile, multilevel scenery-wagon which they called the Kreisler stage—but they were afterwards kind enough to consent to its use."

(Press notice, September 7, 1927)

The structure of the stage demands the extensive use of film. There was a rough outline of the film in Toller's original script. Significant additions were made as we worked through it. It was crucial to derive the fate of the individual from general historical factors, to establish a dramatic connection between Thomas's fate and war and revolution. There is one particular point where the film has an even greater measure of dramatic and functional significance; this comes at the dramatic fulcrum of the play, and touches on the central idea: the impact of today's world on a man who has spent eight years isolated behind bars. Nine years have to

4. The Kreislerbühne was devised in 1922 by Sven Gade for quick scene changes in C. Meinhard and R. Bernauer's dramatization of Die wunderlichen Geschichten des Kapellmeisters Kreisler, fantastic tales by E. T. A. Hoffmann. It was a three-storied set with cubicles, and used back and front projections.

be shown with all their terror, stupidity and triviality. Some conception of the enormities of the period has to be given. The impact will not register with its full force unless the audience sees the yawning chasm. No medium other than film is in a position to let eight interminable years roll by in the course of seven minutes.

For this "film interlude" alone we worked out a script which incorporated four hundred separate items of information about politics, economics, the arts, society, sport, fashion, etc. For the play itself we assembled a full-scale film script that called for one week of preparatory historical research. This manuscript, which was worked out in the literary office, formed the basis of the definitive scenario which was subsequently written by Curt Oertel, director of filming on *Hoppla, Such is Life!*, and Simon Guttmann. Three thousand feet of film were eventually shot for this project. Of course, only a small proportion was ever used. The forecourt, the open-air storage area, even the street in front of the Theater am Nollendorfplatz were the scene of shooting for two whole weeks. Even in the last few days before we opened, the whole building complex was lit up with the blaze of Jupiter lamps till 3:00 A.M. The scenes in the lunatic asylum and Thomas's odyssey from factory to factory were shot here; the surrender of the battleships to the committee of workers and soldiers was done on the roof of the theater.

A small group led by Victor Blum was in and out of the archives of the big film companies all the time, looking for authentic shots from the last ten years. When we spliced old and new films together for the show it was impossible to avoid a certain unevenness in the film stock.

One of the more interesting scenes from the point of view of film and acting technique was the scene with the radiotelegraphist in the hotel. Here I coupled loudspeaker announcements with spoken text and film. The film had to be synchronized, as we would say today, with both—i.e., the length of the sentences had to be measured with a stopwatch and the film cut accordingly. The X-ray film of a beating heart which so annoyed Ihering ("He—Toller—wants to show the debilitating, soul-destroying phantasms of our technical age and lets us listen on a radio station to—a heartbeat from a plane over the Atlantic. Toller is romanticizing machinery." [*Börsen-Courier*, September 5, 1927]) was based on an actual contemporary attempt to make a radiotelegraphic heart diagnosis, transmitted from an ocean liner.

Besides documentary film, I also wanted to use nonfigurative film in *Hoppla, Such is Life!*: in place of music in sound there was to be "music in movement." At the point where Thomas is talking about the conception of time represented by eight years, a black surface was to dissolve in rapid succession into lines and then into squares (ciphers for days, hours, minutes), thus expressing his conceptions. The production of this piece of film was in the hands of Ernst Koch. Lack of time prevented him from putting it together.

212

Acting Technique

I have often been criticized for not being an actor's director. The only way I can refute this accusation is by pointing to my achievements and perhaps by quoting the views of actors I have worked with.

What the critics have persisted in regarding as inadequacies in performances by actors in my productions are in reality largely discrepancies between the way the present generation of actors has been trained and the unfamiliar new architecture of the sets in which I have placed the actors. It goes without saying that actors who are accustomed to acting within the stable framework of the old bourgeois stage will be slow to find the style that suits my stage architecture. It is a matter of years of training and experience. At first my apparatus will seem strange, even hostile, to actors who are accustomed to the bourgeois stage. They feel lost amid the gigantic mechanical structures, which leave them little peace to unfold their virtuoso individual performances. They have problems in adjusting to the precision with which the film forces them to come in on their cues. Dialogue on the conveyor belt must seem quite impossible to them. But all this is only the beginning. Once they have adjusted themselves to this world they will feel that this stage is really there to help them, that it backs them up in the whole of their roles, by incorporating them into the production as a whole in a meaningful way. It is utterly ridiculous to assert that actors cannot perform in front of a projection screen because the flatness of the screen clashes with the three-dimensional nature of acting. By now this objection may have died out; but I could never see how the flatness of the projection screen differed from the flatness of the old painted backdrops. On the contrary, I have found that the effect of placing live actors against a filmed background is always lively and provocative. If a jarring note still persists at the present time, then the reason is that a definitive acting style for the new stage apparatus has not yet been worked out.

In the matter of the acting style. Style is not something that we can separate from our general conception of the nature of acting. I have explained elsewhere how I envisage the tasks facing the actor in the context of the revolutionary theater. *Hoppla, Such is Life!* was an excellent and typical example. Here the roles were sharply contrasted in terms of class: the group of class-conscious proletarians; the typical Social Democratic party official who has made it in life, represented by the figure of Kilmann; the class of the *nouveaux riches*; the liberalistic bourgeoisie; and the group from the *ancien régime,* the old aristocracy, which was represented by the figures of Count Lande and the chief of police; and finally the National Socialist. Here each role was in fact a sharply contoured expression of a social class. They were not important for their private characteristics, nor for their individual complexity, but as types, as the representatives of particular social and economic attitudes. Only two of the figures were exceptions to this: the tragic hero and the comic hero of the piece, Pickel of the petite bourgeoisie, who is in search of the ideal form for the Republic, and Thomas, the worker who wants to see the Revolution completed. When they were seen alongside these two figures who had been severed from their class roots, the binding commitments of the others were clear.

This meant that the tasks facing the actors had been defined in advance. Each actor had to be quite conscious of the fact that he represented a particular social class. I remember that a great deal of time was spent at rehearsals discussing the political significance of each role with the actor concerned. Only when he had mastered the spirit of the part in this way could the actor create his role.

Final Preparations

At the Theater am Nollendorfplatz the whole building was a hive of activity day and night during the four weeks before the premiere. Rehearsals were in progress on the stage, in the yards outside sections of the gigantic iron framework were being erected. In the offices, the script was being pieced together and transcribed, the press releases were being sent out, subscribers, advertisers and the Special Sections were being attended to, and a constant stream of visitors was building up. There was an endless succession of visits from interviewers, photographers, newspapermen, painters, actors; the telephone was constantly ringing. It was an absolute inferno of activity. Then there were fresh committee meetings daily, in which, among other things, the scripting collective was constituted, programmatic declarations were devised and edited, personal demands, complaints, differences of opinion were dealt with. There were many things which at that point could only be worked out superficially or in outline, and many things which had to be set aside as we dealt with the immediate problems we were running into with our first play.

The notes in the program were of special importance for us.

The story of this program is also linked with the Herzog case. His attitude here was typical of his whole manner of dealing with his work in

214

the theater, and after the event completely justified my removing him from his post as dramaturg. Since he was no good for anything else I had asked him to edit the first program. Three weeks passed, during which he wrote about six letters, each of which he rephrased many times. As far as he was concerned, that was the end of the job. As a result, Gasbarra, in addition to his other responsibilities, had to take on the composition of the program, because Herzog had not produced a scrap of material and there was only a week left before the opening. This did not prevent Herzog, and he was alone in this, from delivering a sharp attack on the program at the first meeting of the collective. —A similar thing happened with the programmatic manifesto which we originally planned for the theater. Gasbarra tabled a draft at a meeting and we were all quite happy with it, except Herzog, who declared that the entire formulation was out of the question. Herzog was then asked to produce a new draft within three days. On the third day, half an hour before the meeting, Herzog drifted into the theater after lunching with us to dictate his draft. The meeting had had to be postponed for an hour because he was not ready. Finally he did appear and what he read to us was Gasbarra's draft to which, in the course of one and a half hours, he had added the words "historically objective" and "documentary." —To this day Herzog feels that I treated him maliciously and perfidiously, whereas in reality it was his "way of working" that was the cause of our estrangement, which he considers to entitle him to publish private letters by way of revenge.

For it was precisely in the program notes that we saw another means of reinforcing and even increasing the effect of the performance. We did not want to be limited to a cast list and a few casual opinions along the usual lines, with perhaps the luxury of a little philological essay. Our program notes were to provide more documentary material in another form, and this was to make the political implications of the play clearer and more pointed for the audience.

The programmatic article in the first number aroused sharp controversy (it was written by Gasbarra and Lania).

The sentence: "This theater has not been founded to play politics, but to free art from politics," was singled out as a "betrayal of principle." What had in fact happened was that people had gone straight to the goal and had overlooked the path; they had taken up a position based on a concept of pure art—that is, art which has been liberated from all material restrictions and is free to develop according to its own principles, and this kind of art—must we really still stress this point?—is possible only in a classless society. Looking at it from this angle, we have to put politics, the class struggle, behind us before we can even start. But before this situation can be achieved, the theater must, as is clearly stated elsewhere in the article, "of its own accord take up the struggle against society, so that it can once again become the central cultural factor in the community."

So the incriminating opening sentence was really only an anticipation of our goal, and could be misunderstood only by those who had failed to grasp that before we could reach that goal we had to participate in the political struggle.

The Premiere

On September 3, 1927, the curtain went up on the Piscator-Bühne for the first time. After the many weeks of work my only feeling was: nothing can be changed now. The work had been done, even if it was a bit rough in many places and had not been given all the finishing touches. Even on the opening night when the first curtain was timed at 7:00 P.M., I came across Gasbarra and Guttmann at 7:45 in a basement room editing parts of the film clips which were to run upstairs at 8:00 P.M. Even during the performance I was issuing new instructions, and during the intermission I altered the lighting for a few of the scenes. At 6:45 when the public were already on their way to their seats we were still trying out the film code messages for the finale.[5]

The composition of the first-night audience was quite remarkable. *Vörwarts* (September 5, 1927) wrote: "On the one hand, the *beau monde*, who had elected to wear tuxedos and tails in honor of the evening, and their ladies who had taken their winter furs out of mothballs early and were embellished with strings of pearls which may even have been paid for—on the other hand, in plain cotton, with Wandervögel shorts and Schiller collars, healthy, suntanned boys and girls!"[6] The newspaper omitted to mention only that the latter were in fact the Special Sections, which it had previously gone to great lengths to attack and vilify as callow loudmouths. It was their actions in the auditorium that turned the first night into a political event. When the curtain fell at the end of the prison scene after Mother Meller's last words: "There is only one thing to do—hang yourself or change the world," the young proletarians struck up the "Internationale" and we all rose and sang it to the end. To the consternation of the *beau monde*, who had known that they

5. As the prisoners in their separate cells tapped on the walls the messages were projected on a gauze in front of the stage.

6. The Wandervögel were founded in 1896 as the first modern German youth movement, comparable to the Boy Scouts. The Schiller collar was a broad, floppy, open-necked collar which first came into vogue at the end of the eighteenth century.

were paying up to 100 marks for a seat in the "Communist provocateur's theater," but had never imagined that the evening could end with a political demonstration. A wave of quite perceptible consternation, sometimes pained, sometimes tinged with feigned amusement, ran through the orchestra.

We never imagined that the play would run for more than three weeks. We waited up till morning for the first editions of the papers. The press had nothing new to tell us about the play. The things they objected to were things which we had already seen and dealt with ten times more severely ourselves. —Then they came out one after another: the *Vossische Zeitung, Tageblatt, Börsen-Courier, Morgenpost, Rote Fahne,* political evaluations, aesthetic differentiations, careful considerations, and yet, all in all, in our favor. Political theater had arrived, and we went home with a feeling of complete relaxation, to catch up on our sleep after four long, hellish weeks.

"Hoppla, Such is Life"

On Saturday Piscator opened his Communist propaganda theater, because he "wants to free the stage from politics."

Art can rot! (September 5, *Nachtausgabe*)

POLITICAL EVALUATION

"We can't yet tell whether this work is a wine; what we can say is that it is a medicine. (Desired result: a medicine that has the effect of wine. First duty of the dramatist.). . . . The call for a propaganda-stage finds its fulfillment here. . . . Art with a specific lesson, my dear Sirs, will in future be very important. (Of this kind of art, too, there will be good and bad.) Try to make it good art."

Alfred Kerr (*Berliner Tageblatt*)

"Measuring with the old yardstick: an arid play, a magnificent piece of directing. But Piscator's stage calls for a new yardstick. . . . For he is now appearing openly in his own theater as an activist in the service of a political party, which can see nothing in the theater but political propaganda. . . . But precisely because he is immodest enough to force art off the tracks, he will certainly not have enough modesty to remain the propagandist of his party for long."

Monty Jacobs (*Vossische Zeitung*)

" . . . All the slogans of the last ten years, all the malicious gossip, the cries of the streets are heard again here.

"Why was this theater founded? 'To free art from politics.' Piscator is exorcizing the Devil with Beelzebub, and with politics at that. Even in Toller's own scenes he makes crude underlinings wherever possible. Toller practices gentle ridicule, Piscator lies outright. Once again film provides him with the means, which, of course, his aims proceed to desecrate. The public, about nine-tenths solid middle-class and some of it very fashionable indeed, is given to understand that it is scum, that the day of reckoning has come. That it—Hoppla, such is life—that it constitutes the dregs of a human race which is not yet, alas, totally red."

Ludwig Sternaux (*Berliner Lokal-Anzeiger*)

"Piscator's insane persecution of everything the Germans hold in honor and reverence would also be possible elsewhere—we have even seen it in *The Robbers* at the Staatstheater, or in a more extreme form in *Storm over Gotland* at the Volksbühne. But Herr Piscator provides his own interpolations, he sets up an inflammatory Communist theater quite without concern for what the author has to say. And now that he has his own theater he can do what he likes and omit what he likes. No wonder things at his theater hit heights on Saturday which are unlikely to be equaled in a hurry."

(*Hamburger Nachrichten*)

"If you were looking for a word to sum up everything that is wrong with our theater today, the word 'revue' used to spring to mind. On Saturday that word developed a comparative form: 'Piscator.' "

(*Tägliche Rundschau*)

"What is it all for? Is this the theater of the future? . . . The performance positively oozes the blatant lies of political tendentiousness. In every word, in every scene, Bolshevist agitation is trotted out in triplicate. Anything that anyone might hold in reverence is dragged in the dirt with zealous glee. Not least by Edmund Meisel's 'music,' which even turned our national anthem into a cat's concert."

(Kreuz-Zeitung)

"The opening of the Piscator-Bühne has touched off the urgent problem of our cultural development like an avalanche. Concepts like morality, religion, the uplifting of the soul, aesthetics, spiritual profundity seem to awake no resonance anymore. . . . In the face of this undermining of our cultural life, enlightenment and resistance dare not die. The Christian education of youth can play an important role here, and it is gratifying to hear more and more voices, even from the People's Party—which was initially critical of our stand—being raised in support of Keudell's proposed new school law."

(Deutsche Tageszeitung)

ARTISTIC EVALUATION

"Is it literature—is it drama—is it a dirty song, merely because it is politics? The bitter answer to this and many other questions is that it is paper, nothing but paper. . . . How unusual must Piscator's powers be, if, with such an improbable subject, he can light a flame so bright and radiant that all of us, in spite of our critical reservations, left his theater quite moved."

Felix Hollaender *(8-Uhr-Abendblatt)*

"The greatness of Piscator's achievement: he expanded the scope of our theatrical experience, time and space passed before our eyes in a telescopic vision, gripping scenes. . . . The resounding applause from the balcony may be directed primarily at the 'political aims' served by this theater. But the deafening applause from the front orchestra was for the artistic boldness of the task the director had taken on, for his courageous and successful forays in new directions."

H. H. Bormann (*Germania*, September 5)

"The little song Mehring contributes—irresistible. . . . Edmund Meisel's searing, witty signal music—irresistible. The opening film— made by Piscator himself—irresistible."

Alfred Kerr *(Berliner Tageblatt)*

"This time Toller had his eyes on the world. But on the way to the theater that world lost its sharpness. The contours are blurred. The language pales. . . . There is none of this romanticism in Piscator. He makes no concessions. He puts Toller's 'homely' style into the steely framework of his stage-set. This structure with its movable, transparent walls, with projection screens and gauzes at the back and front of the stage is highly effective . . . a phenomenal technical imagination has done wonders."

Herbert Ihering *(Berliner Börsen-Courier)*

"The way this proletarian review of current events is presented, the alertness and journalistic effectiveness with which it has been assembled, are things which are beyond the imaginations of our circles. If they only realized how powerful the artistic impact of this show will be, they would not rest till they had set up their own middle-class Volksbühne, their national contemporary theater for the struggle against the Communist theater, the cultural weapon of the proletariat."

(Deutsche Zeitung)

"Is this a topical problem play? In concept and imaginative force it certainly is. It was to be hoped that Toller would be able to deliver the dramatic word with the same kind of punch Piscator's images have. But this splendid subject has slipped through the writer's fingers. . . . Toller's friends rejoiced at this success. His political opponents took no stand. But all of them, friend and foe alike, got excited about the new Piscator-Theater."

Max Hochdorf *(Vorwärts)*

"It is no more than justice to call Piscator the co-author of the evening alongside Toller. He has achieved great things. (That technical hitches cropped up from time to time is only understandable.) A huge complicated piece of apparatus like this needs practice. But one could not miss the fertile inventiveness behind it."

Manfred Georg *(Berliner Volkszeitung)*

A cross section of the bourgeois press produced benevolent approval of the venture, with, of course, strong emphasis on its artistic merits, sometimes combined with an attempt to keep me and my theater separate from politics. In other words, a total misunderstanding of the essential causal relationship between my political view of the world and the artistic expression of that view. That the two are inseparable—that although I would naturally be able to do an "interesting" production of any random play in any random bourgeois theater, the new form of my stage, its "technicality," the introduction of film, the development of scaffolding sets, etc., would all be unthinkable without my commitment to revolutionary socialism—all this, the press, which usually looked on me personally with a certain indulgence, was at elaborate pains to ignore. We can perhaps best characterize this by saying that the bourgeois press tried to parry the political thrust aimed at itself and its own class with aesthetics, and tried to make a critical appraisal of something for which there were no established criteria, by using artistic standards borrowed from the past.

INTRODUCTION

Piscator's second production was based on Alexei Tolstoy's *Rasputin, or the Czarina's Conspiracy*, a thriller which had run successfully in Leningrad in 1924 with a bravura performance by N. F. Monachov in the title role. It was also a success in Moscow, but the German premiere at Bochum in 1926 passed unnoticed. Count Alexei Tolstoy (1882–1945), a distant relative of Leo Tolstoy, joined the Social Democratic (Marxist) Party in 1905, but at the time of the Revolution opposed the Bolsheviks and fought with Denikin's White Army. In 1923, with the approval of the authorities, he returned from exile and became a popular and wealthy Soviet writer in the thirties. His historical novels and plays show him as a gripping storyteller.

Rasputin, written in collaboration with Peter Shchegolev, was basically a melodramatic treatment of the notorious adviser's skullduggery and eventual murder set against the background of a degenerate Romanov court. Piscator and his dramaturgs decided that they would show Rasputin's individual fate in the context of European history between 1914 and 1917. Their adaptation provided a framework for a presentation of the October Revolution (just as Toller's *Hoppla* did for the German Revolution). They widened *The Czarina's Conspiracy* to embrace *The Romanovs, the War and the People which Rose Against Them.*

The original script had a prologue and ten scenes. The prologue was scrapped, the ten scenes were reduced to seven and eight new scenes were interpolated, which, apart from the "Three Emperors Scene" quoted by Piscator below, are lost, though the general scenario can be reconstructed on the basis of the program and the stage manager's notes in the Munich Theater Museum.

The following outline shows the new material in italics and indicates the original structure of the play in Roman numerals

1. Vyrubova's room at Tsarskoe Selo (I).
2. *Pub on the outskirts of Moscow showing public gloom and desperation after the reports of losses in the field (film).*
3. *Three emperors scene.*

4. *Lenin at Zimmerwalden (Switzerland) in March, 1916, the delibera-*
   tions of the revolutionary leaders counterpointing the mouthings of
   the imperialist puppets in the previous scene.
5. Rasputin's house (II) where Rasputin asserts the need for peace.
   (film: French counterattack at Verdun, Russian losses on the Düna
   and Berezina.)
6. *Three tycoons scene. The opposing arms manufacturers, Krupp,*
   Creusot and Armstrong state that they are fighting to save the Ger-
   man spirit, democracy and civilization, and freedom, respectively.
   (film: belching chimneys of arms factories.)
7. *Haig and Foch scene. Generals blandly discuss tactics against pro-*
   jections of carnage in the Western front with superimposed captions,
   such as, "Losses: half a million. Gains: 300 square kilometers."
8. *Russian deserter scene, written by Brecht, Lania and Gasbarra to*
   illustrate demoralization in the ranks.
9. Czar's headquarters (III, i & ii). Czar writes to his wife of the
   healthy and invigorating life he is leading at the front. *Projections of*
   mutilated Russian corpses.
10. *Duma.*
11. Prince Yussoupov's study (IV, i).
    Intermission
12. St. Petersburg nightclub with floor show (IV, ii).
13. Yussoupov's palace (IV, iii). Gory murder of Rasputin.
14. Czarina's room (V, i,ii,iii). Czarina plans the arrest of revolu-
    tionaries. *Film of the sealed train bringing Lenin back to Russia*
    runs overhead. Lenin acts decisively as soon as he arrives.
15. *Soviet Congress at Smolny with Lenin speaking. Soviet Revolution.*
    Internationale.

To set the action in historical perspective, a "calendar" of relevant
events was compiled by the dramaturgic office in the course of
weeks of research into available documents. When it was ready it
was combined with the visuals, newsreel and film clips which had
also been assembled in weeks of patient research. Berlin archives
and film companies were by now reluctant to release material for
the Piscator-Bühne, possibly because of pressure from the extensive, nationalistic Hugenberg empire, which controlled the UFA
film studios and a sector of the press, but the Soviet Union came to
Piscator's aid with material which had recently been used for
E. Shub's documentary *The Fall of the Romanov Dynasty.* This
covered the period from 1910, and had to be supplemented from
movies on Russian subjects and new footage shot by J. A. Hübler-
Kahla. All this material was combined in a synchronic table.

In the course of studying the material Piscator came to the conclusion that the theater of the action was the world, and might best

223

Synchronic table for *Rasputin* (act 1, scenes 1 & 2)
as collated by the dramaturgic office at the Piscator-Bühne

Time	Scene	Political Events		Russian Front	WAR Western Front	Other Fronts
		bourgeois	proletarian			
1915 January	Tsarskoe Selo Vyrubova's Room		Legion demands Liebknecht's expulsion from Reichstag.	Collapse of major Russ. offensive in Silesia and Poland. Russ. retreat in the Bukovina in full flight. Ankonisal.	Fighting at La Bassée Canal. Storming of English positions. Storming of Hartmannsweilerkopf. Battle of Soissons. (25th) Storming of Craonne Heights by Saxon regiments.	Eng. liner "Formidable" torpedoed off Plymouth—Battle of Heligoland. First zeppelin raid on Engl. East coast.
February				(– Apr.) Winter warfare in Carpathians. Winter warfare in Masuria. German offensive under Hindenburg.	(16th–Mar. 20th) Winter warfare in Champagne. Attempted Engl. breakthrough at Givenchy. N. Chapelle fails.	
March	Scene with three Russians singing.	(18th) SPD approves 3rd War Credits. Anti-war demos outside Reichstag.		(10th) Russ. Army surrounded and annihilated. 7 Gen., 100,000 men and 300 field guns captured. Sievers' suicide.	Storming of Loretto Heights.	Allied fleets attack Dardanelles. "Bouvet," "Irresistible" and "Ocean" sunk.
April				(2nd) Russ. attack on East Prussia fails. (22nd) Przemysl fortress surrenders (famine). Easter battle in Carpathians. Capture of Zwinin by Germans and Austrians. German advance on Mitau.	Battles between Maas and Moselle (Priesterwald, St. Michel and Heights of Combres). (27th) Engl. defeat at St. Julian. (22nd) Fr. defeat on the Maas Heights. (29th) Dunkirk shelled with 38cm guns.	Allied troops land at Gallipoli.

Month		Eastern Front	Western Front	Naval & Gallipoli
April				(3rd) "Lusitania" sunk.
May	(22nd) J. H. Thomas, member of Labour Party, becomes Min. for War. (23rd) Italy joins the war.	Breakthrough at Gorlice-Tarnow (Mackensen). Russ. retreat from Carpathians across the San south of the Vistula.	4th Army breaks through near Langemark. Diversive attack by French under Joffre in Artois between Arras and La Bassée, and by Engl. and Fr. between La Bassée and Armentières. (12th) Fr. divisions in action (78,300 dead and wounded at Arras)	Battle of Sedd-ul-Bahr. Attempt to storm Dardanelles overland. Engl. liners "Goliath," "Triumph" and "Majestic" sunk.
June		German army advances. Przemysl retaken. Halicz taken. Crossing of the Dniester. Lemberg taken. Russians retreat on the Bug.	Loos Lens Souchez (sugar refinery) Givenchy Neuville	
July		Major German offensive between the Baltic and the San and Bug. Battle of Narov.	(July 23rd) Only local successes.	(30th–July 6th) First battle of Isonzo. (18th–27th) Second battle of Isonzo.
August	(20th) SPD approves 4th War Credits.	(5th) Warsaw taken. (20th) Novo-Georg'evsk taken. 6 Gen., 85,000 men and 700 field guns captured at Suk on the Styr.		
September	Nik. Nicolayevich dismissed. Czar takes supreme command. (5th) Zimmerwald Conference. (29th) Peace demonstration in Berlin.	Strong Russ. thrusts on entire line (from Pripet-Styr to the Rumanian border).	Joffre's grand offensive. Autumn battle in Champagne. (–Nov. 3rd) Autumn battle for La Bassée. Autumn battle for Arras (–Oct. 23rd). (22nd): Staff conference at Calais decides on general offensive.	Engl. troops land at Suola Bay. The terrible struggle on the plain of Anaforta begins.

be symbolized by a hemisphere, and this became the basis of the set, a dome, framed with iron piping and covered with silver-coated balloon cloth. It was divided into segments with hinged flaps which opened to reveal acting areas (*Photos* 59–62), and had a crownpiece which could be taken up into the flies (*Photo* 50.) There were two overlapping front projectors trained on the dome itself, and when the crownpiece was up a screen could be lowered into the gap for back projections; in the Haig-Foch scene all three projectors were used simultaneously (*Photo* 64). There were also a front gauze and two tall side screens on which the "calendar" of data and statistics was projected. The opening sequences of the play show how these technical possibilities were handled. A band in one of the boxes played an overture by Edmund Meisel, a gong sounded, the house-lights went down, the dome revolved behind a gauze, the gauze and crownpiece were raised and the projection screen lowered in and the calendar screen on the left rolled on. A historical sequence of czars was projected on the main screen and appropriate captions such as "dies suddenly," or "dies by his own hand," or "dies insane" were flashed on the calendar screen, while on the lower part of the dome film was shown that depicted the brutalized condition of the people under the oppression of the priesthood and aristocracy. This was intended as a potted history of czarism and the Orthodox Church, and as it ended Nicholas II (Erwin Kalser) stepped onto the stage in front of a towering silhouette of Rasputin (*Photo* 65.)

The production lasted four hours and made considerable demands on the audience's concentration. The dense texture of the expanded play offered a plot set in a web of international events with dialogue which, as it was being spoken, was commented upon and often contradicted by silent film and projections, while the whole thing was being substantiated by facts and figures projected on the side screens as it went along. Hans Reimann, who was involved in the preparation of the next production, *The Adventures of the Good Soldier Schwejk*, strolled across the stage one evening in his overcoat and borsalino to see what would happen. Neither the actors, nor the audience, nor the stage manager noticed him, though the fireman seemed suspicious (Hans Reimann, *Mein blaues Wunder*, Munich, 1959, p.409).

The play ran for eight weeks, though the right-wing press was now outspoken in warning its readers that Piscator's West End admirers were signing their own death warrant. The nationalistic, conservative *Lokal-Anzeiger* sent Friedrich Hussong, its political correspondent, to cover the opening, and he made the following comment:

" . . . this public has not yet understood what it is all about, or that their necks are at stake, not to speak of their diamond tiepins and pearl necklaces, silver evening capes and gold shoes, and all the other things they need to have a night out together like this. They haven't grasped it, though the Nollendorf Soviet pressed into their hands the first number of its official bulletin with the unequivocal title, *Political Theater*, whose every contribution is a declaration of war on all those people who spend good money on seats at the Nollendorftheater, because it's the thing to do at the moment." (11.11.27)

Hussong went on to point out that Tolstoy's "relatively harmless dramatic recreation of events *(dramatische Reportage)*" had been transformed by a "virulent Bolshevik film" into a plea for world revolution. He admired the acting but dismissed the writing of the new material as puerile and the staging as derivative, "the suicidal politics of the Berlin Kurfürstendamm according to Meyerhold's prescriptions for theatrical agitation."

The critics were divided. Alfred Kerr's notice began, "Piscator has won a second, hard-fought victory," while Paul Fechter entitled his review, "Communist Fraternity Reunion." In general, it was recognized that the political message could not fail to color the evaluation of the production, and the leading critics, among them Alfred Kerr, Herbert Ihering, Bernhard Diebold and Norbert Falk, accepted this and welcomed it as a successful and coherent development of Piscator's work. Ihering wrote the following assessment in the *Börsen-Courier:*

" . . . True, there have been more rounded and complete productions. Right, there have been richer, more resonant evenings, but who would want to compare one event with another when no basis for comparison, either positive or negative, exists. This evening is a law unto itself and must be judged by its own standards.

"Which parts of it fulfill the aim of political illumination? Which don't? The parts where stage and screen clash are a failure. The masses in the Russian Revolution are more telling on film than on the stage. In the final scenes it would make for clarity, and save time, if the exchanges between Rasputin and the Czarina were counterpointed by film of the masses, rather than interrupted by actual mass entrances and exits. . . . The victory of Lenin and the Bolsheviks would be more gripping, as well as swifter and briefer . . . on film. The spoken word is hackneyed here, slogans without meaning. . . . Apart from this, Piscator hits the target. The actors are now attuned to the director's style. . . . His aims were not to get bogged down, and to work with young actors. He has succeeded by his own efforts. What a technical imagination. . . . His next task is to address himself to the right audience with the right team. More than a man of the theater. A man to shake people up."

XVIII
THE GLOBE-SEGMENT STAGE
Rasputin, the Romanovs, the War and the
People which Rose Against Them
November 12, 1927, to January 20, 1928

If *Hoppla, Such is Life!* had been a failure, we would have had to
take it off after two weeks (which indeed we expected to do after the
first night); in that case, we would not have been able to produce as
our second show such a vast and problematical work as *Rasputin*.

About the acceptance of *Rasputin:* We were well aware that we had
accepted a "blood-and-guts melodrama." What interested us was the
subject, the beginnings of the Russian Revolution. But seen for once
"from above." The decline of the ruling classes, their decay and corruption. And there was a didactic element in our choice too: we wanted to
follow a play dealing with a German revolution *(Hoppla, Such is Life!)*
with one which dealt with the Russian Revolution.

The fact that we chose to represent Russian drama of the post-
Revolutionary years with a play by an undeniable "fellow traveler"
such as Alexei Tolstoy later came in for frequent criticism.

There were good reasons for this. In contrast to today, dramatic works
reached us very infrequently. What did come out was politically problematical either because the general premises were missing (as in
Erdmann's *The Mandate (Das Mandat)*, or dealt with problems of detail
which were specifically Russian. And then other plays, the so-called
Agitkas–which may have been quite adequate over there—were too
transparent and primitive in their themes for our theater. Suchanov's

October Revolution (Die Oktober-Revolution) was seriously considered. But the huge crowd scenes around which it was constructed would have required a different theater. It was only toward the end of the season when they were too late to be of any use that we were provided with works by Kirshon, Trenyov, Ivanov, etc.[1]

Considering our public, whom we thought we knew fairly well, *Rasputin* seemed at least to offer a suitable framework. A big subject, a thrilling and interesting plot, sharp and convincing characters. The play had only one flaw, but it was a fundamental flaw, a flaw in fact which turned it into a melodrama: it dealt only with Rasputin's fate as a private person. So, interesting though the figure of the *starets* was,[2] we had to make the historical background and not "persons of interest" our point of departure. And this historical background was the fate of Europe, 1914–1917.

In the program notes for *"Rasputin"* Leo Lania explained our conception of the theme:

Drama and History

History? For us? What meaning can history have for times like these, which are themselves bursting with enormous problems, with remarkable events and destinies! The present day has no need to reawaken dead heroes; it has pitilessly desecrated its living heroes and can see itself only as the reflex of conflicting social trends and forces which are themselves more gigantic and embittered than all the wars and conflicts of times past. If we stand still in the midst of the raging turmoil of today and look back, we do so only because we see the past in terms as exclusively political as the present. Historical drama is not the tragedy of the fate of some hero or other, it is the political document of an epoch.

If we dispensed with these political documents it would mean casting to the wind experiences and discoveries which cost generations before us untold blood and sacrifice. But neither can we content ourselves with viewing history purely historically. Historical drama is not just a matter of education: only if it has a life of its own can it bridge the gap between

---

1. Vladimir Kirshon (1902–1937?) wrote plays on subjects from contemporary life, the best-known being *Bread* (1930). Konstantin Trenyov (1884–1945) wrote dramas of the Revolution and Civil War. In 1963 Piscator deleted his name and substituted Sergei Tretiakov (1892–1939), whose *Roar, China* was widely presented in Germany around 1929. Vesevelod Ivanov (1895–1963) was a pioneer of Soviet prose. His tales of guerrilla warfare in Siberia, Turkistan and Mongolia were popular in the twenties. *Armored Train 14–69* was one that we dramatized.

2. A *starets* is an elder monk in the Orthodox Church who has distinguished himself in the service of God and has been entrusted with the education of young monks and with pastoral duties among the laity. Rasputin used the title.

then and now and release the forces which are destined to shape the appearance of the present and of the immediate future.

Where does history end and politics begin? This frontier does not exist in our historical drama. The Peasants' War, the French Revolution, the Commune, 1848, 1813, the October Revolt—only in relation to the year 1927 can we experience these things. *Danton's Death (Dantons Tod)* and *Florian Geyer* tell us just as much about the time when they were written as about their historical subjects.[3] But we wish documents from the past to be seen in the light of the present moment, not episodes from times past but those times themselves, not fragments but a unified whole, history not as background but as political reality.

This basic attitude toward historical drama means a complete revision of traditional dramatic form; not the inner arc of dramatic events is important, but the most accurate and comprehensive epic account of the epoch from its roots to its ultimate ramifications. Drama is important for us only where it can be supported by documentary evidence. Film, the constant interruption of external events by projections and film clips, are a means of achieving this documentary breadth and depth; they are inserted between the acts and after decisive turns of events and provide areas of illumination as the searchlight of history penetrates the uttermost darkness of the times.

We are not concerned here with the figure of Rasputin the adventurer, nor with the Czarina's conspiracy, nor with the tragedy of the Romanovs. The idea is to create a piece of world history, where the spectator in the orchestra and balcony of this theater is just as much the hero as the miraculous Russian monk. In the trenches on the Stochod and in the Carpathians they were not mere spectators but adversaries in the great drama of the collapse of Czarism, they helped to shape the social forces from which the new Russia grew, they form a unified whole, a piece of world history: the spectator in the year 1927 and— Rasputin, the Romanovs, the war and the people which rose against them.

After we had taken up residence in the outskirts of Berlin in the first half of September so that we could work on the adaptation of the play without being disturbed by the running of the theater, we started to study the available source material.

Source Material for *Rasputin:*[4]

Maurice Paléologue (French ambassador to St. Petersburg): *An Ambassador's Memoirs.*

3. In *Danton's Death* Georg Büchner depicts events during the Reign of Terror in Paris in 1794; in *Florian Geyer* Gerhart Hauptmann deals with events during the Peasants' Revolt in the early sixteenth century.
4. In this list the English titles are used where translations exist; otherwise the original title in brackets is preceded by an English rendering.

Karl Kautsky: *Documents on the Outbreak of War (Dokumente zum Kriegsausbruch)*, based on German Foreign Office files.

S. D. Sazonov: *Fateful Years.*

Winston S. Churchill: *The World Crisis.*

Erich Ludendorff: *Memoirs, 1914–1918.*

Pavel Milyukov (former Russian foreign minister): *Russia's Collapse (Russlands Zusammenbruch).*

Wilhelm II: *Letters.*

Wilhelm II: *The Kaiser's Memoirs.*

Czarina Alexandra of Russia: *My Album (Mein Album).*

Czarina Alexandra of Russia: *My Diary (Mein Tagebuch).*

Alexandra Viktorovna Bogdanovich: *St. Petersburg Chronicles (Die Chronik von St. Petersburg): Diaries (Tagebücher).*

Anna Vyrubova: *Memoirs.*

Heinrich Kanner: *The Kaiser's Catastrophic Policies (Kaiserliche Katastrophen-Politik).*

Emil Ludwig: *Wilhelm Hohenzollern, The Last of the Kaisers.*

Lenin and G. Sinovyev: *Against the Current (Gegen den Strom).*

J. Stalin: *The Road to October: Speeches and Essays, March to October, 1917 (Auf dem Wege zum Oktober).*

N. Bukharin: *From the Fall of the Czars to the Fall of the Bourgeoisie (Vom Sturze des Zarismus bis zum Sturze der Bourgeoisie).*

I. K. Naumov: *October Days (Oktobertage).*

John Reed: *Ten Days That Shook the World.*

C. D. Mstislavsky: *Moscow: Five Days (Moskau: Fünf Tage).*

Karl Liebknecht: *Jail Sentence (Das Zuchthaus-Urteil).*

René Fülöp-Miller: *Rasputin, the Holy Devil.*

H. T. von Zancka: *Rasputin.*

Lensky: *Rasputin.*

G. Thompson: *The Czar, Rasputin and the Jews (Der Zar, Rasputin und die Juden).*

J. Kessel-Isvolsky: *Blind Rulers (Die blinden Herrscher).*

I. F. Nazhivin: *Rasputin.*

Maurice Leduet: *Nicholas II in Private (Nikolaus II intim).*

Saint-Aubien: *Biography.*

Pröczsy: *The Men of the Black Band (Die Herren von der schwarzen Bande).*

Sof'ya Fedorchenko: *Ivan Speaks.*

Kleinschmidt: *Russian History (Russische Geschichte).*

Dr. Karl Ploetz: *World History (Weltgeschichte).*

I first read the *Memoirs* of Paléologue, the French ambassador, and they in a sense formed the guidelines for our work.

The reason why this book was so valuable for me was that Paléologue did not limit himself to retailing court gossip or sketching purely Russian matters, but tried to explain every seemingly local event in terms of the international political and military scene. This book brought home to me a vision of the inevitability, of the inseparability of the events of those years. I saw that not even the smallest political ploys and moves made by Rasputin could be explained without reference to English policy in the Dardanelles or to military moves on the Western front. The concept of a globe on which all events are closely bound up with one another and are mutually interdependent took hold of my imagination.

So this reading produced two results: a framework on which to enact the drama, the globe (or at least one hemisphere), and the expansion of Rasputin's fate into a review of the fate of the whole of Europe. With these two points in mind, we set about our adaptation.

The expansion of the subject and the destruction of the originally narrow form of the drama could only be done by inserting new scenes. Three considerations enabled us to organize the enormous field involved into categories: the politico-military and economic on the one side, and the revolutionary, represented by the proletarian opposition forces, on the other side—three "currents," which had to be channeled right through the original manuscript. The first thing that was required was a chronological table of the material in which the dates of all events at the time of the play were noted. Even this task, which fell to the dramaturgic office, was much bigger than the entire preparatory work on *Hoppla, Such is Life!* We drew up a calendar. This chronological survey provided us with the points, much in the manner of a mathematical exercise, at which general political events coincided with events within the play. At these turning points in the action new scenes were inserted. A total of nineteen new scenes were added to the play's original eight, and when textually complete the play embraced the time between the beginning of 1915 and October, 1917.

The texts of the new scenes were written jointly by Gasbarra and Leo Lania. How they worked can be shown by sketching the process of adaptation of Act I.

Originally the first act of Tolstoy's drama comprised three scenes. They took place in Tsarskoe Selo in the room of Vyrubova, the confidante of the Czarina, in Rasputin's house in St. Petersburg and in the Czar's headquarters. The act closed with an air raid by German zeppelins on the Czar's headquarters.

In our adaptation the original scene in Vyrubova's room was followed by a scene in a bar in a working-class quarter of St. Petersburg which brought out the mood of despair among the masses.

The scene was intended to show the rising revolutionary wave which had taken hold of the masses in the big cities after Hindenburg's victorious German offensive and the annihilation of the Russian Tenth Army. The scene in the bar took place in March, 1915, and was thus contemporaneous with the first scene and set that scene in the atmosphere of those days. The scene which ended with the despairing workers cursing Wilhelm II led up to the "Three Emperors Scene," which later became quite famous.

Extract from the "Three Emperors Scene":

Wilhelm: Almighty, give unto Germany . . .

Franz Joseph: Our Father, lend unto the peoples of Austria . . .

Nicholas: In the name of Jesus Christ, bestow upon Russia . . .

Wilhelm: Russia, England and France have conspired against us to bring about the destruction of Germany. Hussars! The torch of war has been cast into the midst of the most tranquil peace. A crime of untold impertinence. It demands revenge and exemplary punishment. [*Speaking in another direction.*] Your Excellency, has shown me the Tenth Corps in excellent fettle, and the men's faces are glowing with satisfaction in the craft of war. I need only mention the way in which the men shouted, "Good morning"! [*Speaking in a different direction again.*] Hussars! Bring back your banners to me pure, intact and unsullied! A traitor, the man who . . .

Franz Joseph: Traitors will be executed: a Czech, eh? Aha, a Ruthenian. No, no pardon, not even to be considered. To death by hanging . . . to death by hanging . . .

Nicholas: And I? Don't I count at all? The Prime Minister has done this, the Prime Minister has done that. . . . Am I nothing at all? —My dear Ambassador, it is my wish that France should come out of this war as great and powerful as possible. I shall sign in advance whatever your Government may desire. Take the left bank of the Rhine, take Koblenz, take even more if you feel it is necessary. I have instructed my General Staff to put the march on Berlin into effect as quickly as possible.

Franz Joseph: It was not my wish. . . .

Wilhelm: I bear no responsibility for this war. It was the stupidity and clumsiness of Austria that tripped us up.

Franz Joseph: I am spared nothing. Mature consideration was given to every move. . . .

Nicholas: Perhaps a scapegoat is needed to save Russia. I shall be that scapegoat.

This scene, which Lania had written like the preceding one—wholly on the basis of historical documents—was intended to show Europe's leading monarchs as passive tools in the service of the economic interests which governed their lands, as they in fact were: dogsbodies and representatives of the economic forces which marched past in the following scenes, beside whom, by way of contrast in a further scene, we showed the figure of Lenin as the representative of the self-aware proletariat working toward the Revolution. The following scenes were also concocted from historical documents. (Extracts from Lenin's speech at Zimmerwald at the famous first Internationalist Conference, September, 1915.)

It was only after these newly interpolated scenes that the second scene of the original drama ensued; it took place in March, 1916, at the time of the big Russian offensive between the Düna and the Berezina, and of the French counteroffensive at Verdun. It takes these factors in military policy to make Rasputin's pleas for peace comprehensible, and the critics who were so amused by the political ABC that I developed in this play would, I feel, have failed in an examination on the political interconnections in the material.

In opposition to the various currents in public opinion in Russia and at the court of the Czars which were advocating peace, we introduced three industrialists into the following scene as the motive force behind the prolongation of the war, representatives of heavy industry in the shape of the Krupp, Creusot and Armstrong armament factories. This scene, too, was a montage: it contrasted the real economic needs of industry with the idealistic rallying cries and war aims of its spokesmen. This was followed by the Haig-Foch scene which showed a conference of the two allied supreme commanders at the time of the big counteroffensive on the Somme.

And only then did the original scene with the zeppelin attack on the Czarist headquarters come. To this we added the deserter scene, a short monologue which was worked out by Brecht, Lania, and Gasbarra in ten different versions (I mention this for curiosity's sake) until it seemed to us that the war-weariness of the Russian soldiers had been characterized in the way that brought it home most forcefully.

In this way the whole play was expanded. After the original ending, the outbreak of the March Revolution and the arrest of the Czar and Czarina, we added two new scenes, taking the action up to October, 1917, up to the seizure of power by the councilors which culminated in Lenin's famous speech at the second Soviet Russian Congress.

The central idea and the structure of the interpolated scenes were based on the hemispherical stage, which had a practical purpose as well as a symbolic significance. I had envisaged an acting structure which would enable us to make the many rapid scene changes that we needed without using a curtain. In lightning succession various segments of the hemisphere were to open and shut, and at the same time the whole hemisphere was to be turned into the setting for that particular scene by a picture projected on it. But, as always, the technical possibilities failed to measure up to the ideal.

I had wanted a theater machine which was versatile and elegant and worked quickly and silently, and certainly not the one which Alfred Kerr subsequently, and not without some justification, called a "trundling tortoise made of gray tent cloth." My mistrust had been aroused by the cloth which was mounted over a steel framework (it was, in fact, very expensive balloon cloth which had, over and above, been treated with an equally expensive silver coating to make it suitable for projections). But, as usual, I was forced to defer to my stage manager's expert arguments and to the financial considerations of my commercial director. It later, in fact, became clear that the doors over the individual acting segments could be mounted and moved only with the greatest of difficulty because we had used the cheaper method of construction. They constituted a constant danger (during one of the first performances one of the big doors came loose and threatened to fly off into the audience when we turned the revolving stage. Only the presence of mind of a stage hand named Arndt prevented this). Later we left out the doors altogether for the big scenes and brought the segments onto the stage already open.

The crownpiece on the hemisphere, which could be taken up into the flies on an electric hoist, was a particular problem child. Here again I had in mind to raise and lower the thing quickly and silently so as to create a special acting area on top of the hemisphere. Even today I can still see us standing fearfully with our watches in our hands when this piece was tried out for the first time. The process of raising the crownpiece to the mezzanine "quickly," as had been promised, lasted no less than seven minutes at the first attempt. Furthermore, the motor made a din like a dockside coal crane in action. And I probably stood up as always with the words which were, unfortunately, proverbial in the house: "Well, we can't put on a play with that." Outsiders who saw shortcomings, particularly technical shortcomings, had no idea of the weight of opposition we had to fight against to make even the slightest innovation in the machinery. For me, there is no doubt that it would have been cheaper in the long run, and more rational in every way, to build a new theater to our own specifications.

The combination of the hemisphere with film had one curious result. We had at first thought that the spherical surface would distort the film beyond recognition. So I had a laborious investigation made of the possibility ·of projecting the film from the mezzanine through a system of prisms mounted in a tube to counteract, at least partially, the distortion on the convex surface. This all proved to be completely superfluous. The picture which appeared on the curved surface proved to be quite lifelike and almost three-dimensional.

Besides the hemisphere, I also had a flat screen at my disposal: it was the cloth connecting the crown of the hemisphere with the acting area which was revealed when the crown was taken up into the flies. I also used a gauze in front of the set, as I had done in *Hoppla, Such is Life!*, and, finally, I had on this occasion inserted the so-called calendar.

This calendar was a canvas-covered frame, 9 feet wide and as high as the proscenium opening; it could easily be moved back and forward at the right-hand side of the proscenium arch. It owed its inception to the impossibility of covering the historical material as comprehensively as I wanted with the means provided by the stage alone. For the many military and political events which assumed a dramatic function within the play, a special instrument was necessary in order to show all these factors, if possible simultaneously, as the play was going on. The calendar was, as it were, a notebook on which we documented the events of the drama, made comments, addressed ourselves to the audience, etc. To achieve continuity of movement here, too, the text was projected in a so-called "moving script" running from bottom to top.

As in the case of *Hoppla, Such is Life!*, a huge, organized search began through the archives of the film companies. But this time we met with far greater resistance. The directors of the archives had in the meantime seen the use to which their inherently harmless film clips were going to be put. Perhaps word had even come down from above—especially in the case of the Hugenberg Enterprises.[5] On the other hand, we got very considerable help from the Russians this time, who had just assembled a film entitled *The Fall of the*

5. Alfred Hugenberg (1865–1951), press baron, built up an empire in publishing and films (UFA Films) during the Weimar Republic. "For a decade his organization fed 'national thoughts' to the masses, estranging them from the Republic and maneuvering them into the 'national opposition.' When the time came they thought Hugenberg and elected Hitler." (Peter de Mendelssohn)

Romanov Dynasty out of old newsreels. Unfortunately, this film could go no further back historically than the years 1910–1911, whereas I needed a historical outline ranging from the beginnings of Czarism to the present day as an opening, in order to contrast the seemingly abrupt outbreak of the Russian Revolution with the interminable ponderousness of the development of Czarism. So our "film squad" pounced on any film that had ever dealt with a Russian subject and in the course of a few weeks worked its way through 300,000 feet of appropriate material.

In addition to this there was the huge accumulation of material lodged in newsreels, and culture and nature documentaries which also had to be examined.

Material from Nondocumentary Films for the "Prologue":

The Rule of the Scotnini (Die Herrschaft der Scotnini): Meinert Films.
Princess and the Fiddler (Prinzessin und Geiger): UFA.
The Seventeenth Regiment of Sailors (Matrosenregiment 17): UFA.
Solo Ballerina to the Czar (Die Solotänzerin des Zaren): Meinert Films.
The Decembrists (Die Dekrabisten): Herschel-Sofar.
The Czar's Courier (Der Kurier des Zaren): UFA.
Bear's Wedding (Die Bärenhochzeit): Lloyd Films.
The Death Ship (Die Todesbarke): Prometheus.
Son of the Mountains (Der Sohn der Berge): Südfilm.
Ivan the Terrible (Iwan der Schreckliche): National Films.
Palace and Fortress (Palast und Festung): Fried Films.
The Black Eagle (Der schwarze Adler): United Artists.
Father Sergius (Vater Sergius): Ermolicff.
The Postmaster (Der Postmeister): Lloyd Films.
Revenge is Yours (Dein ist die Rache): Lloyd Films.
Resurrection (Auferstehung): United Artists.
The Fireraisers of Europe (Die Brandstifter Europas): Bruckmann.
and so forth.

The Function of the Film

Didactic film presents the objective facts, up-to-the-minute facts as well as historical ones. It gives the spectator information about the subject. Nobody can be expected to have the full list of Nicholas II's ancestors, the history of Czarism, or the significance of the Russian Orthodox Church at his fingertips. But the spectator must have them at his fingertips if he wants to understand the play. (I am, of course, disregarding those who wish to remain ignorant at any price, and consider the theater to be a little matter "avant de coucher ensemble.") The didactic film broadens the subject in terms of time and space. In order to "explain" the figure of the last of the Czars, in order to show him as the end product of a long series of generations characterized by murder, madness, double-dealing, dissoluteness and mysticism, I needed a genealogical sketch of the House of Romanov (not in order to bring "emperors and kings" into disrepute for political purposes, not as part of a "Bolshevist witch hunt"). The spectator was not to evaluate the Czar as a unique, fortuitous phenomenon. For this reason I opened the play with a "primitive history lesson," with the portraits of the Czars on which the calendar made comments like: "dies suddenly," "dies insane," "dies by his own hand." Distorted history? Incontestable facts which you can find in any history of Russia. At the end of the series a spotlight picks the figure of the last of the Romanovs out of the darkness. The film fades. Laden with the tragic burden of his house, already a symbol, Nicholas II appears, while behind him his fate, the shadow of Rasputin, grows beyond life size. In this way the foundations are laid and the points determined which will be dealt with in the further course of the play. —But the Revolution of 1917 was not to seem a unique and fortuitous phenomenon either, so the audience must be made aware that it too was the inevitable and compulsive result of a development which lasted for centuries. Poverty, famine, dejection, oppression, and revolts which had been drowned in blood had to be shown as motifs which constantly repeated themselves, becoming more powerful each time until the triumphal fanfare of 1917 rang out. This was the second part of the prologue on film and brought the audience up to the historical situation in which the play began. After the last shot, futile mass assaults by Russian regiments in the Carpathians, the stage opened; the atmosphere of the times had been created before the first words were spoken.

Dramatic film plays a part in the development of the action and is a "substitute" for the live scene. But where live scenes waste time with explanations, dialogues, action, film can illuminate the situation in the play with a few quick shots: troops' mutiny—abandoned weapons; the Revolution has broken out—a red flag on a speeding car, etc. It is inserted between scenes or imposed on scenes (simultaneously) using gauze suspended between stage and audience. While the Czarina is still pleading with Rasputin's ghost for advice, the mutinous regiments are already marching on Tsarskoe Selo (in the "old" theater this is where the messenger on horseback dashes in with his report): in this way, the scene is given a historical dimension.[6] This film which was perfectly clear and obvious in its function led on to a third category which came out more strongly in *Rasputin* than in *Hoppla, Such is Life!*, and had a new significance.

Film commentary accompanies the action in the manner of a chorus. Diebold in fact compared it with the antique chorus. It addresses itself directly to the audience, speaks to it. ("Please forgive us if we keep going back to the beginning," prologue). It draws the audience's attention to important developments in the action ("The Czar travels to the front to place himself at the head of his armies"). It levels criticisms, makes accusations, provides important facts, indeed, at times it carries out direct agitation. In *Rasputin*, film with this function was used for the calendar. Words were provided optically. When it was superimposed on a picture, new contrasts, pathetic or satirical, were produced. (In the Foch-Haig scene, above the masses storming into the battle on the Somme were the words: "Losses—half a million dead: military gain—120 square miles" or: above the corpses of Russian soldiers the authentic words of the Czar [from a letter to the Czarina]: "The life I am leading at the head of my armies is healthy and invigorating.") But the film commentary can also dispense entirely with words, as in the scene with the three industrialists. Here the film was only documentation, but had penetrating suggestiveness. The picture contrasted with the words spoken during the scene. When the representative of Krupp played his trump card: "It is a question of the salvation of the German spirit," when the representative of Creusot bellowed: "La démocratie et la civilisation doivent être défendues," when Armstrong's representative declared: "We fight for the liberation of the world"—the audience saw behind them the smoking forests of furnaces and chimneys of heavy industrial plants, and this (satirical) contrast exposed the last ramifications of the true nature of the imperialists' war. —I also used film in *Rasputin* to project Destiny into the future as I had done in *Storm over Gotland*. The film compressed the scene into its real content by showing (for the spectator) the future of the persons involved. (The family of the Czar before the firing squad on film as the "Conspiracy Scene" of the last act is played out.)

6. "The Czarina is still defiant—but the film knows better. 'Time' exists only for the Czarina—we are above time. The individual speakers are aware only of their own situation, or the situation of those nearest them. The film projected on the gauze knows the general situation, the collective situation. It is fate, the voice of wisdom. It knows everything."

Bernhard Diebold, *Das Piscator-Drama*

" . . . This is how the realistic principle and the idealistic principle alternate in Greek drama. . . . This is how the antique character scene alternates with the antique chorus . . . and in the Piscator drama the film would be the modern chorus. The difference is that the *chorus filmicus* has the realistic role, whereas the spoken scene has the idealistic speeches. The parallels lie deeper. Much deeper.

"When the antique chorus appeared as an ideal spectator, as the voice of wisdom, as the medium of Destiny, as a demon in judgment, as a collective voice of God and the people, then it built up in advance the general atmosphere for the individual drama of Orestes and Clytemnestra. . . . Exactly the same psychological function is fulfilled with the profoundest effect by the Piscator film. Here too, the chorus of the masses speaks as a collective and as Destiny. Here too, the gods and the powers of the times are first addressed in general, before the single fate of the individual speaker is enacted against the background of a fate which embraces us all."

Bernhard Diebold, Das Piscator-Drama

The Press Echo of Rasputin

The Trials

Of all the productions of this season—indeed, of all the plays I ever staged—*Rasputin* produced the loudest echo, the clearest effect. Up·until now the critics and the bourgeois public had repeatedly tried to dismiss the political aims of my productions on aesthetic grounds, and to drag the discussion down to the level of pure Art, but *Rasputin* gave them no chance to do so. The fact that this production was unequivocally evaluated as a political fact, that it exercised the minds of the politicians and even the courts more than the gentlemen from the literary reviews seems to me to indicate a positive advantage of this production and to demonstrate that this was the case where I had the opportunity to put my ideas into practice in the clearest and most trenchant form. Our grounds for staging this particular work and the form and aims of our adaptation were proved by the echo which the performance caused to be wellfounded. The theater had become a political tribune and could be considered only in political terms.

The first thing that happened was that the law appeared on the scene. In the first instance at the behest of General Consul Dimitri Rubinstein.

Mr. Rubinstein, a retired privy councilor to the Czar on finan-

cial matters and now director of a bank in Paris, objected to the way
he had been presented in the Piscator-Bühne, since he considered
that the manner in which we had characterized him constituted an
affront to his honor. We were served with an interim order which
forbade us on pain of a heavy fine to represent Mr. Rubinstein on
the stage, although Tolstoy's play had brought this figure on to the
Russian stage in hundreds of performances.

In the course of negotiations with Mr. Rubinstein's legal advisor
we agreed to have his claim dealt with through normal channels in
open court, in which the initial writ and our appeal against it
should be judged, and before which we asked permission to call as
witnesses Grand Duke Ludwig of Hesse, the banker Max Warburg,
Herr von Beneckendorff, another banker, Hindenburg, Secretary of
State Kurt Baake, the former Russian Minister of Police Bieletzky,
and the Czarina's intimate friend Anna Vyrubova. Until such times
as the courts had pronounced judgment we declared ourselves willing to let Rubinstein the banker tread the boards as plain Mr. Dimitri Ohrenstein. Herr Rubinstein wrested this concession from me
after hours of negotiations which were an amusing interlude in the
midst of the serious work in our theater. They deserve to be re-
counted in detail, and I leave Leo Lania, as the competent chroni-
cler of the Rubinstein case, to tell the story:

His Excellency Rubinstein

There is no picture of him, no photograph. Chance? Proof of how little
vanity he has? His Excellency Rubinstein, Russian State Councilor, Per-
sian Consul General, private banker to the Czar, mightiest financier in
all Russia, successively and simultaneously, Director and Chairman of
the Board of Governors of banks in Vienna, Paris and London, all his
life at the center of a web of fantastic affairs which would fill pages of
contemporary history—and not the least interesting chapters at that—
Dimitri Rubinstein was always terrified of "playing a role." Because he is
consumed by one burning passion—gambling. Titles, social position—
no more than a means to an end! The more you are able to keep in the
background, the better it is. For he is tempted by neither honors nor
popularity, by neither women nor luxury, far less by money. The big
win, the coup, adventure, the risk of bold speculations, transactions,
financial maneuvers—that is what gives his life a meaning. The setting
for such a life includes palaces and prison cells, mighty victories and
annihilating defeats. Rubinstein is perhaps the last knight of the romance
of the Stock Exchange—a swindler, nothing more, but in the grand
manner.

He began life in Kharkov. Coming from a well-to-do family, Rubinstein completed high school and went to Kharkov University. Smart beau and man of the world, brilliant dancer and gifted pianist—there is music in the family blood, and they proudly boast the most famous virtuosi among their relations—the young student was the center of the Kharkov *jeunesse dorée* and soon a well-known character in the town, a good comrade, our Mitya, who would go along with any piece of foolery. He did not take his studies very seriously, though all the professors spoke highly of his brilliant capabilities and his keen understanding, but he surprised his friends and colleagues daily with more and more grandiose plans for setting up companies and business enterprises. Until one day—the 1905 revolution was in the air—there were turbulent demonstrations in favor of an assistant professor who was being subjected to persecution, at which the young Rubinstein was so prominent and made such radical, revolutionary speeches that he was summarily expelled and had to exchange the university for a branch bank.

A few years later Rubinstein had quickly clambered, as a result of several coups which were as lucky as they were skillful, into the ranks of the financial giants of Russia and had moved to St. Petersburg, where, as Director of the Franco-Russian Bank, he lived in a princely palace, was an intimate friend of Count Witte, enjoyed the confidence of all the Grand Dukes, formed public opinion—he put his brother-in-law in a prominent position in the St. Petersburg telegraph agency—gained access through his wife to Rasputin and via him to the Imperial Court, by the outbreak of war was finance minister to Nicholas, negotiated financial transactions between the Czarina and the Grand Duke of Hesse during the war, later bought the great, arch-reactionary newspaper *Novoye Vremya*, financed the "peace party," carried on secret negotiations with German representatives in Stockholm, traveled under an assumed name across half Europe in the middle of the war, on the same mission—and gambled. Gambled on every Stock Exchange, did business in every capital—in 1916 he is regarded as the richest financier in Russia.

The Nationalist Party of the Grand Dukes strikes: Rubinstein is charged in court. He is to bear the lion's share of the blame for the run-down state of Russia's finances, he is accused of sending Russian gold abroad and, along with his friend General Suchomlinov, of collaborating with German espionage. Rubinstein is in jail and certain to be executed. Then Rasputin intervenes: no easy task, but in spite of all the opposition the *starets* gets his way, his "best Jew" is released from prison and gathers his forces to retaliate. He makes countercharges against the State Commissioners on the basis of documents passed to him by Rasputin and accuses the leading members of corruption. And Rubinstein leaves the court victorious, a high "compensation for imprisonment while innocent" in his pocket.

He has little time to rejoice at his victory. Kerensky falls, the Bolsheviks seize power. Rubinstein manages after many adventures to get to safety in Sweden. When he arrives in Stockholm, his whole fortune is reputed to be his wife's famous jewelry. His first coup partly restores the lost millions. The counterrevolutionary Army under General Yudenich is just beginning its offensive against Petrograd and all the telegraph agencies in Helsinki, Reval, Riga report that the Whites have captured Kronstadt and that Petrograd is on the brink of capitulation. Thousands of Russian émigrés in Sweden await the fall of the Soviets hourly; Czarist rubles, which Rubinstein had just bought for a song from the refugees shoot up wildly in value, and Rubinstein can sell them back to the same refugees at exorbitantly high rates. A few days later the dream dissolves. Rubinstein is familiar with telegraph agencies: they have worked well and now they can state that the first reports were false. An annihilating defeat is inflicted on the Whites before they have even had time to chalk up a single victory. Rubinstein is a rich man again and moves to Vienna.

The heroes of the Stock Exchange are twenty miles from Paris. The franc is the next objective that must be taken. At the head of the conquerors Rubinstein marches into the French capital. He plays the bear market and wins. Final victory is already assured when one morning he is wakened by a man from the French police. They cannot take a joke, Rubinstein is to go to jail, is to be deported, is to have his entire fortune confiscated—he clings to his explanation: he has not come to Paris to speculate against the franc, on the contrary he is doing all he can to support the franc. Proof?! Rubinstein—he has no choice—puts all his capital into francs, is graciously released by the police and stumbles home, a broken man. He has reached the end once again, ruined, deprived of a certain profit—the following day the franc begins to rise. Rubinstein is one of the very few who made huge gains from it, thanks to the assiduity of the Paris police.

Four weeks ago Rubinstein appeared at Piscator's office. For days he had been in the theater every evening. He had always taken a front-row seat in the orchestra and had become a well-known figure in the theater in the course of that week, for a spectator who takes such a great interest in the show doesn't crop up often. The girl at the cash desk could not get over her astonishment. "Weren't you here yesterday?" —"Yes. The production is excellent, I just have to see it again." And the doorman saluted him and ushered him to the orchestra section.

This went on for about a week until he hit upon a way of talking to Piscator.

So he marched into the manager's office, a squat little man in his forties, sharp, hooked nose over hard lips—a Jewish Napoleon—and bombarded Piscator with his quick-fire, overheated eloquence.

"None of it's true, none of it's true—this Tolstoy is a scoundrel—I'm supposed to have been a spy? Only my love of peace! Because I was against the war. Went to the Czar: Your Majesty, I said, the war is a piece of nonsense—peace, that's the right thing—and I am not going to hand over the German deposits. —Rubinstein, says the Czar, you keep

243

out of this! —I will not keep out of this, the German deposits are private property and I am not going to hand them over. I go to Paléologue, the French Ambassador, and what does he say? 'I have sold myself to the Germans.' —One more word like that, Paléologue, and I'll give you a couple of raps on the ear, said I. —I'm just a businessman, never was a politician, I want to do business, how am I supposed to do business with France if I am parading on the stage here in this Rasputin play—what does this Tolstoy know about what I did with Rasputin . . . ! How am I supposed to do business in Paris if there are reports in the papers that I am appearing here in your theater as a German spy?! Leave that out, it's not so important; 'profiteer,' if you like, but *spy*."

Piscator was amused and promised to cut the word *spy*.

The next day Rubinstein was back again. He had seen the play once more—how many times was that?—And had now decided that *profiteer* must go too. And so he argued with Piscator day after day in debates lasting hours until he persuaded him to drop the unflattering character labels which we used for him, one after the other.

This solution was to be only temporary. "Next month I'll be back in Berlin, and then we'll have our grand proceedings to judge your appeal against my interim order. Herr Piscator, I'll bring everybody along, Ministers of the Czar and Grand Dukes and Prince Yussoupov and Trepov, the minister who appears in your play and who is a colleague of mine at the moment on the Board of Governors at the bank, my best friend, in fact. What a trial it will be! You'll see how I have been slandered. Am I a politician? I am just a simple businessman! And your productions are so excellently directed, too! I know a thing or two about that!"

Will the German courts find that Mitja Rubinstein is not part of contemporary history and is nothing but a plain honest businessman?

(From *Das Tagebuch*, January, 1928)

After the comedy, the satire: Herr Rubinstein the First, Kaiser Wilhelm the Second. Herr Wilhelm was no more willing than Rubinstein to be a historical personality. He too set the wheels of justice in motion, he too obtained a temporary injunction, after we had ignored a letter from his Berlin legal advisor demanding that the figure of Wilhelm should be cut from the play.

I have explained elsewhere our reasons for inserting the figure of Wilhelm II into the drama. From the scene reprinted in this book the reader can see that there was no question of distorting the Kaiser into a caricature, but that we were aiming at an objective treatment of his personality; indeed, our objectivity was witnessed the fact that the Kaiser in the play did not speak a single sentence which we had invented, but only sentences from his own marginal notes in the military files and from his various speeches. Emil Ludwig pronounced the following judgement.

244

Wilhelm and Piscator

"The magnificent production which I saw only yesterday has turned the trivial *Rasputin* into a picture of the times in which Wilhelm II plays a less significant role than he played in real life. Only on the fringe of events does he pop out of the magical moving sphere which the great new director has turned into a symbol. There he sits for three minutes and offers prayers, reprimands and orders to the invisible Gods or court chamberlains, and every word he speaks is taken from authentic sources which have been available to the nation for years: wartime speeches and asides which were first made known by the so-called Kautsky Files, and have since become part of the historical appraisal of the outbreak of the war. At any rate every word was familiar to me when I heard it, and in most cases I could name the source.

"This demolishes any pretext for banning the play, for if I put words into the mouth of a character on the stage which he spoke in real life, I cannot thereby defame his character; in any case, the Kaiser is sympathetically presented throughout this scene; indeed, the most interesting and emotionally touching outburst of his subjectively just feelings is placed at the key point, namely, the expression of personal disappointment with his two disloyal crowned relatives, which he committed to paper in pained terms on August 1.

"The very words Piscator lets him speak could be in any war play written by 'Fridericus' to demonstrate the Kaiser's personal *bona fides* and love of peace on August 1.

"This also solves the legal problem, for when the courts dismissed the Kaiser's case against my Bismarck play in 1922 the justification for doing so was that historical figures may appeal only against being represented on the stage if there is defamation of character, which is excluded in the case of authenticated historical presentation. In the play in question the Kaiser had been on stage for almost two acts and had been talking much of the time. He had been given almost exclusively fictitious lines to characterize him as the second main figure in the play. If in this much more complicated case judgment was pronounced at the highest level in favor of the author, then there is not even room to debate Piscator's much simpler case—and an interim order can be regarded only as a piece of chicanery."

(Vossiche Zeitung, November, 1927)

I myself formulated my own attitude to the court's decision to cut the figure of the Kaiser from the play in the following declaration addressed to the court:

The topical theater, as I see it and as I practice it, cannot restrict itself to affecting the spectator artistically, that is, aesthetically, with strong emphasis on the emotional content. It has a task, and that task is to take an active part in the course of current events. And it fulfills this task by showing history as it develops. In this endeavor the theater can recognize no boundaries. It must demand the right to show all the persons in the historical development of a particular period who were decisive exponents of the social and political forces of that period. The only boundary that the topical theater can recognize in presenting such personalities is determined by historical truth. In my efforts to present a turning point in the history of Europe I had to bring the figure of the former German Kaiser onto the stage, among others, but it was remote from my intentions, remote from my entire view of life to show a distorted picture of these persons. I tried to present the aspects of his character that were of historical significance as they are documented in the accessible papers and with such accuracy that even spectators who sympathized with the ex-Kaiser could come to the conclusion only that in those fateful days of the German Empire, the direction of affairs had been placed in the hands of a man who proved to be incapable of coping with his task. In this matter I, as a historical materialist, am far from laying the whole blame solely at the feet of the former Kaiser. The complaint I make is directed not against the individual but against the system which allows such errors in its choice of a leader. I stress once again that it would have run counter to the style of the overall production to have presented single individuals in an unpleasant or insulting manner. I was concerned to present a picture of all the forces which brought about the collapse in the years 1914 to 1918, a period without parallel in European politics.

The topical theater cannot, however, claim to have fulfilled its task in every particular if it only presents historical events for their own sake. It must extract from those events the lessons they hold for the present, it acts to warn our own times by pointing out internal social and political connections, and will do its best to influence the course of development decisively. We do not conceive of the theater as a mirror of the times, but as a means of changing the times. At the same time, it is clear that the sum of the truths which make up and determine our lives is connected with that higher truth which has been considered from time immemorial to be the criterion of true art. The communication of a particular historico-philosophical insight which has emerged from the pure historical facts is for me synonymous with the ultimate demands of art. With this in mind a polemical attack on a single individual, even if that individual were the former Kaiser, would have seemed petty and senseless.

Whatever the court's judgment may be, the theater cannot allow its right to present a particular view of the world to be constricted by rights accorded to the individual personality, if it is to fulfill its task as a social factor.

The interim order was served upon us and we had no choice but to cut the role of Wilhelm II, much to the distress of the actor concerned, who bore a striking natural resemblance to Wilhelm II, had captured his voice and movements and thus cornered the market rather nicely. We staged the "Three Emperors Scene" without Wilhelm from that day on and replaced his lines with a reading of the temporary writ.

Copy

Stamp: D.R. No. 1493
Received 11.24.1927
Grande, Senior Officer of the Court
Official copy

N.
19. Q. 88 27
FINDING

At the suit of the former ruling Kaiser and King Wilhelm II of Doorn, Holland, represented by his attorney general, Colonel Leopold von Kleist, retired, of 36 Unter den Linden, Berlin W. 8,

Plaintiffs,

Representatives in Court: Karl Siebert, 78 Rathenower Strasse, Berlin N.W., and Dr. Max Alsberg, 1 Nollendorfplatz, Berlin W. 30, solicitors,

versus

Erwin Piscator, theater manager, of 83/84 Oranienstrasse, Berlin S.W. 68, Defendant,

an interim order is served to the effect that:

1. The defendant is forbidden on pain of the penalties laid down in § 888 ZPO to present in public performances of the production of the play *Rasputin* by A. Tolstoy the scenes in which the figure of the plaintiff is represented.
2. The costs of the action are to be borne by the defendant.

GROUNDS

The plea for an interim order is directed against a scene in the play in which the figure of the plaintiff has an active role on the stage along with the former Kaiser Franz Joseph and the former Czar Nicholas II.

The members of the court attended a performance on November 23, 1927, and gained the following impression:

The scene has been inserted into the original drama *Rasputin*. The make-up of the actor presenting the plaintiff is unmistakable. The plaintiff is brought into contact with the two emperors named above. The lines which the author gives them express parallel lines of thought. In that the former Kaiser Franz Joseph appears as a complete idiot and Czar Nicholas as a bigoted fool lacking any character, one is forced to conclude that it was intended that the plaintiff should be characterized in the same vein.

This constitutes an affront to the plaintiff's honor. A claim for suppression according to § 823, section 2, BGB in conjunction with § 85 ff. of the penal code and § 249 BGB has been plausibly established.

The claim also seems justified on the basis of the rights of the individual. Whether a personality who is part of recent history such as the plaintiff must allow himself to be represented on the stage is open to debate. In any event, such representation must be within the limits defined in § 23, section 2 of the law of January 9, 1907 relating to the protection of art.

The defendant makes it the express aim of his program to carry out valuable preliminary work in the theater to bring about the victory of World Revolution and better and more just relations between men. Propaganda to this end is *his full right* [author's italics] in a state based upon the principles of freedom. But this right must not encroach upon the justified interests of individual personalities.

The justified interests of the plaintiff are infringed, in that he is in this instance presented to the public in a manner calculated to satisfy curiosity and sensationalism, detrimental to the plaintiff, and quite without connection with the substance of the original drama. On this basis a case has been made for his claim according to § 23, section 2 of the law relating to the protection of art.

The necessity for the interim order is established by this analysis of the facts.

Costs allocated according to § 91 ZPO.

Berlin, November 24, 1927

County Court No. 1, Civil Chamber 4
sig. Judge: Dumcke
Issued

Berlin, November 24, 1927
(L.S.)

(Signature)
Clerk to County Court No. 1
Authenticated
sig. Siebden, Solicitor

"As a result of the court decision which was released yesterday afternoon, and according to which the Piscator-Bühne is forbidden to let the person of Wilhelm II appear on the stage, the Theater am Nollendorfplatz was filled to the last seat yesterday evening. A large number of people had to be turned away. When the words *St. Petersburg, Berlin, Vienna* were projected on the hemisphere before the monarchs scene, a large number of spectators stood up in their seats to see what was going to happen next.

"The segments opened and Czar Nicholas and Kaiser Franz Joseph were seen in the upper and lower right-hand sections as in the earlier performances, but from the left-hand segment writer Leo Lania emerged and explained to the public that the ex-Kaiser had raised objections to being represented on this stage. Lania read out the most important sentences of the interim order which had been issued by the courts that afternoon. The public, who laughed aloud at various points as the writ was read, applauded the end of this section generously. There were no further demonstrations."

(Press notice)

The interim order was not, of course, the end of the matter; on the contrary, it fanned the flames of controversy all along the line. Lawyers, politicians, writers and theater directors took up their pens to illuminate the theoretical principles and consequences of the court's decision.

At the beginning of December, the case of Wilhelm's interim order and my appeal against it were heard. The grounds for and against it were expounded once more, and once more I made an exact statement of my position, Lania and Gasbarra explained the reasons for putting the "Three Emperors Scene" in the play, and Goldberg and Jakoby, our lawyers, pointed out that the interim order was not valid in law. When we left the court that evening after hours of negotiations the fate of our appeal was not yet known. The verdict was not published until December 15. It upheld the interim order.

"In the civil action brought against Erwin Piscator by the Russian banker Dmitri Rubinstein who claims that his person appears on the stage in Tolstoy's *Rasputin* and is referred to in several scenes in defamatory terms, District Court Number Two has pronounced judgment to the effect that the Piscator-Bühne is forbidden to make defamatory statements about Rubinstein, or to represent him on the stage."

(Press notice)

The debate on the whole complex question was given fresh impetus by the court proceedings at which my appeal against Dmitri Rubinstein's interim order was heard. The Piscator-Bühne also lost its case against Rubinstein, and for a long time I, as manager of the Piscator-Bühne, was plagued by Rubinstein's and Wilhelm's lawyers for the court costs.

Piscator at rehearsal (drawing by Felix Gasbarra)

INTRODUCTION

The Piscator-Bühne's third production was an adaptation of Jaroslav Hašek's novel, *The Good Soldier Schwejk*. Hašek used the figure of Schwejk in stories as early as 1911 and worked on the novel from 1921 until his death. It was translated into German by Grete Reiner in 1926. A bowdlerized, abbreviated version in English (P. Selver) appeared in 1930, the full translation (C. Parrott) in 1974.

Max Brod (1884–1968), best-known as editor of Kafka's works, was a personal friend of the author, who was Bohemian by nature as well as nationality, and had helped with publication of the novel, and he and Hans Reimann (1889–1969), a journalist and humorist, held the rights for its dramatization and had already prepared a script, a barrack-room farce. Piscator relates how he and his team turned it into a satire on Austria-Hungary in World War I, thus coming, after dramatizing the German and Russian Revolutions, to the event which had shaped the political attitudes of his generation. The revised script was a conflation of the most telling and graphic episodes in the novel and largely consisted of passages of dialogue taken verbatim from Grete Reiner's translation.

The set devised by Piscator to bring the restless flux of Hašek's novel to the stage was simple and economical. Two pairs of white flats joined by borders stood 10 and 20 feet behind the proscenium arch, masking the flies and side stage. A conveyor belt 9 feet wide was built into the stage in front of each pair of flats, parallel to the front of the stage. At the back was a huge white backdrop. The electric conveyor belts (*Photo* 77) were controlled independently. They served as a treadmill on which Schwejk marched, and brought on props like the wooden latrine or the bar for the court scene. Large pieces like the railway car (*Photo* 71) came in from the flies. The side screens and backdrop were used for projections (the contents of letters or orders written onstage) and filmed scenery (the streets of Prague) or commentary (George Grosz's cartoons). The play opened with a Czech folk song accompanied by a hurdygurdy, then an erratic black line traveled across the screen, eventually forming the figure of a bloated Austrian general, quickly joined by a scowling, bemedaled Prussian general, then between the two a judge with a death's head and a whip, and finally an obese, unshaven clergyman balancing a crucifix on his nose. Then a corner of Schwejk's room, with Schwejk sitting in his nightshirt, puffing his pipe with a dog on his lap, traveled on from the left, while his housekeeper, Frau Müller, appeared on the second conveyor belt, ringing the doorbell loudly. Grosz's animated drawings added satirical comment to the action in this fashion throughout, and the moving props, with Schwejk marching on the spot, provided an element of visual comedy.

From George Grosz's animated cartoon for *Schwejk*

The promptbook for *Schwejk* is lost, but a typewritten transcript of the adaptation survives in the Bertolt Brecht Archive (ms. 246). The first half of the script used episodes from Books I and II of Hašek's novel and followed Schwejk's fortunes from the outbreak of war through arrest on suspicion of treason, enlistment, medical examination, military arrest, adoption by Katz, the drunken padre, and assignment to the womanizing lieutenant Lukas in settlement of a gambling debt. Lukas soon regrets his acquisition when Schwejk delivers one of his billets-doux to the wrong hands, causing both of them to be posted from Prague to the front at the end of part one.

The four scenes after the intermission followed Schwejk to the Russian front. They were subdivided into ten episodes and show

Schwejk on the train, blandly mistaking a major-general for a former drinking companion called Purkrabek, before he accidentally pulls the emergency cord. The next episode shows Schwejk, stranded on the platform at Tabor without a ticket, setting out to rejoin his regiment on foot, his celebrated Budéjovice anabasis. As Schwejk marched a film showed a country station, railway tracks, signals, a signal box, a grade crossing, then the highway, beyond which the lights of Tabor are visible. The lights change, move into the center, recede into the distance and disappear behind a hill. In the background the night sky, outlined against a hilly, wooded landscape. Cut to a map showing Budéjovice, through which the following words marched, printed in white:

"Xenophon, a general of antiquity, traversed the whole of Asia Minor and God knows where he ended up without a map. A long march, straight ahead, is known as an anabasis. Caesar's legions once reached a point in the north near the Gallic Sea without maps, and then decided to return to Rome by another route. They succeeded, too, hence the expression, 'All roads lead to Rome.' All roads lead to Budéjovice, too, or so the Good Soldier thought. Devil only knows how he came to march due west when Budéjovice was to the south."

After this projection Schwejk trudged ahead on the treadmill while a dotted line on the map projected behind him traced the erratic path which brought him right back to Tabor. The sample of stage movements on page 257 catalogs the incidents during the anabasis. The third scene showed Schwejk in a train to Budéjovice, explaining to some hungry soldiers why officers are necessary. The second part of the scene showed his reunion with Lukas, and the third showed Schwejk meting out punishment to Baloun, a soldier who had pilfered Lukas's rations.

Then came the problematic final scene. Piscator deals with the possibilities mooted by his dramaturgs and describes the first, gruesome solution which was abandoned because of the adverse audience reaction at the preview—a parade of cripples and amputees before God (*Photo* 72). He omits to tell us what was substituted, but Brecht's transcript shows Schwejk crouching with Marek behind two mounds on the battlefield:

Schwejk: I'll stick it out. . . . That's what soldiers are for. Our bones will be turned into ashes for the sugar refinery, as Lieutenant Zimmer used to say. "You sons of bitches," he would say, "you uncouth swine, you useless apes. . . . It takes a war to ensure that at least your descendants will benefit when you are dead. Your children will sweeten their coffee with sugar filtered through your bones."

Marek: We all have our problems. I'm heading for the hospital.[Off.]
[A cartoon shows a Russian swimming in a pool. A bush with the Russian's clothes hanging on it glides onto the stage. The Russian takes to his heels.]
Schwejk: I'll do my duty to the bitter end.—Look at that. A real Russian uniform. [He tries it on. A shot rings out. He throws himself flat. A Hungarian patrol appears and seizes him, talking Hungarian.]
Schwejk: How can I make this idiot understand I'm on his side? I remember Vodicka used to say to me, "Schwejk, old chap, you don't understand these Magyars."
[A shell explodes, Schwejk falls.]

At the top of the screen a procession of crosses moves toward the audience. The crosses grow larger in perspective, reach the bottom of the screen and are picked up by a gauze lowered close to the audience, downstage. The house lights go up.

The popular success of the production was due in no small measure to the shrewd characterization of Schwejk by Max Pallenberg (1877–1934). Alfred Polgar later commented:

"Unforgettable how the actor became one with the figure. He got inside its skin, its simple, sly heart beat in him. You will never see the like again."

Pallenberg had graduated from touring companies in Bohemia to the Viennese popular stage, and was predestined by his awkward appearance for comic parts in farce and operetta, though his style was rarely without underlying irony, even menace. Max Reinhardt brought him to Berlin and by 1914 he was playing classical comedy (Figaro, Harpagon, M. Jourdain). He left Reinhardt in 1920 for the rich pickings in the commercial sector which served up light comedy and bedroom farce to the nouveaux riches, and became, at 1,000 marks a night, the highest earner on the German stage, with the exception of his wife, musical comedy star Fritzi Massary. Pallenberg would also do months of one-night stands with a supporting cast of unknowns, and did so after Piscator in an innocuous version of *Schwejk*. This was clearly the wrong image for the Piscator-Bühne, so Piscator is at pains to point out Pallenberg was the obvious man for the part, for which he had in fact been engaged before the season opened.

XIX
EPIC SATIRE
The Adventures of the Good Soldier Schwejk
January 23, 1928 to April 12, 1928

The importance that the war has assumed in the literature of the last decade clearly reflects the great tensions within the social and intellectual development of Europe. Jaroslav Hašek's novel is remarkable in this context: other writers consciously "make a stand" and attempt to formulate an attitude to the war, but the war in Hašek's novel cancels itself out. The war is seen through the temperament of the plain man. Schwejk is the triumph of common sense over the patriotic cliché. Hašek and his hero Schwejk stand outside the confines of tradition and accepted ideas, they defer to no conventions, so that what we see is the common man meeting mass murder and militarism, those joint affronts to nature, on a level at which sense becomes nonsense, heroism becomes ridiculous and the divine order of existence is turned into a grotesque madhouse.

We had already presented a sketch of a decade of German history in *Hoppla, Such is Life!*, and we had exposed the roots of the Russian Revolution and the forces behind it in *Rasputin*; now, with *Schwejk*, we wanted to turn the spotlight of satire on the entire complex of the war, and to demonstrate the revolutionary power of humor. Another attraction was the chance to offer the great character actor Max Pallenberg a part calling for the whole range of his art after long, lean years of type-casting.

It was clear from the start that a dramatization of *Schwejk* must be nothing less than a faithful rendering of the novel, so the problem boiled down to putting together as many of the most striking episodes of the novel as possible, in such a way as to re-create Hašek's view of life in its entirety. Furthermore, a way had to be found of bringing Hašek's satirical comments on the episodes to life on the stage. While we were exercising our minds on the problems and principles the dramatization raised, the manuscript arrived for us to go over. It had been prepared on an earlier occasion by Max Brod and Hans Reimann, who held the rights. Our worst fears were confirmed: we were confronted not with Hašek, but with a pseudo-comic farce about an officer's personal orderly. Hašek's satire had been lost in an attempt to construct a "well-made play" with suitable "comic" effects.

Bert Brecht

What was to be done? To adapt this adaptation seemed hopeless, because Brod and Reimann started from assumptions which ran counter to our whole approach, and because the gap between their level and ours could not be bridged. But Brod and Reimann had the exclusive rights, so our hands were tied. Protracted negotiations began, time passed and we got nowhere, so that I eventually decided to do an adaptation myself with the collaboration of Brecht, Gasbarra and Lania, in the hope that Brod and Reimann, faced with a *fait accompli*, would recognize that mine was the right approach and authorize my version, which would of course be free from any suspicion of doing violence to the original author.

I moved out of Berlin, as I always did when a major project was on hand, and set up my headquarters in a little hotel and restaurant near Neubabelsberg.[1] As soon as I had clarified the principles which were to govern the dramatization, the team of collaborators I have already mentioned went into action. They were frequently joined by Max Brod and Hans Reimann, by our designer Traugott Müller, by our stage manager Otto Richter and by Otto Katz. I went into conference for hours with George Grosz, the "intellectual

1. Neubabelsberg is a village on Lake Griebnitz on the southwestern outskirts of Berlin. This paragraph (from "I moved out of Berlin . . . ") was inserted in 1963.

draftsman," as he liked to call himself, who immediately began to develop my ideas with his own peculiar brand of wholehearted objective enthusiasm. Brecht sometimes came along with his first car, an object of great wonderment, for he was the only one of us at that time to have such a vehicle, and it always amuses me to remember how often the ignition failed and we had to push him to a slope, where, a big cigar in his mouth, he would gaily roll down with a wave of his hand. And there was no lack of other distractions. I practiced marksmanship with my pistol, mostly—to the distress of the hotel owner—in the café garden among the trees. I hung a sandbag from the branches and worked off my hostility toward all who opposed me. And since I always liked to keep my people fit, I had Fritz Sommer, who acted as trainer to our Studio, come out twice a week for a rugged training session in which Lania in particular sweated many a bitter drop. Brecht watched all this from the sidelines, sitting in an open window, grinning his inscrutable grin. Grosz, on the other hand, liked to take part in these exercises and took particular delight in jogging through the woods for a quarter of an hour in his neat blue tracksuit. Many a picnicker must have thought he was seeing a bunch of escaped convicts. In the evening we got together in the comfort of the dining room and sat around a big table across which our discussion raged. Hans Reimann, whose professional sense of humor was well-known, had a particularly tough time trying (as he repeatedly did) to defend his barrack-square farce. Otherwise the work came along very well, and Brecht made his own special contribution in long lectures about the "the drag" which baffled us all for a long time until we finally realized that he meant Schwejk's march to Budéjovice. Brecht always got a big kick out of making up names for things before anyone knew exactly what was being discussed. About four weeks later we went back to Berlin with a text which formed the basis of my production.

The Theatrical Form

This was the first time we had been faced with a novel and not with a play which, whether it was good or bad, was at least conceived in terms of dialogue and scenery, and with some regard for theatrical form. A novel, furthermore, where despite the passivity of the hero there is constant movement; Schwejk is sent to prison, then discharged from prison, Schwejk follows the curate as he celebrates Mass, Schwejk is wheeled on to parade in a wheelchair, Schwejk is dispatched to the front in a train, marches for days in search of his regiment—in short, things around him are always moving, always

256

in flux. It is fantastic how the constant shifting of the plot seems to express the restless instability of war.

Sample of stage movements as used in "Schwejk"

II. 2 (Anabasis):
Belt 1 from right to left:
　　Schwejk is marching. From left to right. Singing.
On Belt 1 (from right to left):
　　Old lady is carried on standing.
　　Meeting.
Belt 1 stops:
　　Dialogue to ". . . regiment hurries."
Belt 1 from right to left:
　　Schwejk marches on.
　　Old lady travels out standing.
Belt 1 carries on milestones, trees, signposts: village of Malchin.
Belt 2 from right to left:
　　A bar travels on.
Belts 1 and 2 stop:
　　Scene to ". . . to the regiment as quickly as possible."
Belts 1 and 2 from right to left:
　　Bar travels off.
　　Schwejk marches.
On Belt 2. traveling on stage:
　　Haystack (snoring 8 sec.).
　　Scene to ". . . if they hadn't deserted."
Belt 1 runs (½ min.).
Belt 2 moves left to right.

Even when I first read the novel, long before we thought of dramatizing it, I had a mental picture of events following one another in a ceaseless, uninterrupted stream. Faced with the problem of putting this novel on the stage, this impression in my mind assumed the concrete form of a conveyor belt.

So here again the stage technique emerged ready-made from the subject of the play, or at least from what I like to call the artistic aggregate of the subject matter. The fact that this technique "symbolized" a stage of society (the dissolution and decline of a social order) was secondary and fortuitous. And the stage technique in its turn predetermined the textual shape of the play.

"P. has a technical imagination the like of which we have never seen before; he releases all the power of the stage, he wheedles out all its secrets, his conveyor belt is more than a gimmick, P. has dissolved the classical unities of time, place and space and given the dimension of the marvelous, the magical back to the theater, thanks to his inspired mastery of the most modern technical devices."

Die Welt am Abend, January 24, 1928 (Kurt Kersten)

The Dramatic Principles of the Conveyor Belt

"All previous attempts to put novels on the stage have essentially failed. In most cases they retained nothing but the figure of the hero whom they robbed of his characteristic atmosphere by placing him in a new plot and thus making him unconvincing as a character.

"It was a doubly difficult task to dramatize Jaroslav Hašek's novel. For this was not a neatly constructed whole, but a huge agglomeration of anecdotes and adventures with no adequate conclusion. Schwejk's character was established at the beginning and did not develop at all in the course of the novel. He only ever appeared in a passive, never in an active role, and he could be imagined in any possible situation except the one in which he met his end. The action of the novel was determined solely by events from 1914 till the middle of the Great War. So even when one left aside the epic breadth of the book, all its other elements conspired to defy dramatization.

"The first method we tried was dramatization in the traditional manner mentioned above. We extracted the figure of Schwejk from the novel and placed him in an action of our own invention. Predictably enough, this attempt produced nothing that could be used. We used all the best episodes in the original and still we deprived Schwejk of the atmosphere he needed. His stories and his gags were too abrupt. It was clear that they needed the build-up afforded by Hašek's involved style, and that dramatization could only shrink and diminish the events. The plot which we had superimposed on Schwejk (a love story, incidentally) also robbed Hašek's work of its political-theoretical dimension. His milieu and the people who make it work ceased to be decisive and were supplanted by the mechanical requirements of the comedy which produced its own inconsequential figures. Hašek's thrusts at the [Hapsburg] Monarchy, the Bureaucracy, the Military and the Church were thus robbed of their venom. We turned Schwejk, who takes everything so seriously that he makes it ludicrous, who obeys orders so literally that they turn into sabotage, who demolishes everything he supports, into an idiotic orderly whose witless efforts on behalf of his lieutenant eventually turn out for the best.

"The failure of this attempt—and the adapters went as far as to produce an actable play—was futher proof that this method of doctoring novels for the stage was wrong. So we abandoned the 'dramatization' of the hero and decided to stage sequences of the novel, instead of producing a play around the figure of Schwejk.

258

"There was just one single objection to this plan: the form of the present-day stage. It seemed impossible to capture the epic movement of the novel with traditional theatrical techniques. With a fixed stage, the flow of Hašek's plot was bound to be chopped up into single scenes, and this would falsify the fluid character of the novel. Piscator overcame this problem by replacing the fixed stage floor with a moving floor, and with this one skillful touch he found the appropriate staging for the epic development of the novel: the conveyor belt.

"And this solved our textual problems as well as our technical problems. The adapters no longer needed a framework other than the original story; they could limit themselves to choosing the most effective scenes in the novel and turning them into actable texts. The grouping of the action could follow Hašek's original closely, and the only problem left was how we could adequately stage Schwejk's environment, which had a decisive effect on him. And as usual, Piscator solved this question with film, but here with the difference that he had an animated cartoon made. At the beginning of each chapter where Hašek made direct general comments on his theme, Piscator projected cartoons, drawn by George Grosz. In this way he could effectively condense the forces which were opposed to Schwejk.

("It should be mentioned here that Piscator toyed for a while with the idea of making Schwejk the only figure to appear on the stage and representing all the other figures with cartoons.)

"The figures alongside Schwejk, where they had no active part in the action, were represented by dolls or puppets. Originally these were to have been much more rigidly classified according to the various class ideologies of the figures.

"Once the set and staging had been decided upon, the writers had only to compress the essentials of the novel—which at a conservative estimate takes twenty-four hours to read—into two and one-half hours without losing its particular style. (It is unfortunately impossible to spread Schwejk out over five evenings, as Piscator once suggested.) The original novel had to be radically shortened and condensed and completely rearranged in places to make it playable at all. On the other hand, we strictly avoided using any material other than Hašek's original text.

"The ending presented a special difficulty which was, in fact, never completely resolved. Hašek had died while writing the novel, without leaving any indication of a possible ending. Any ending we might contrive would seem to do violence to the original manuscript, and a natural ending was not effective theater. The controversial scene in Heaven, which in fact derived from one of Hašek's own passages, "Cadet Biegler's Dream," would have necessitated a disruptive reworking of the whole figure, since the novel did not afford all the material we would have needed. So for better or for worse, we had to adopt a compromise which was both effective theater and Schwejk-like.

"The path followed here opens extraordinary prospects for the future. The intellectual revolution going on around us is not only radically transforming purely technical materials, but is also opening up new subjects and new forms. The theater can no longer restrict itself to a dramatic form which was once produced by a particular set of social and technical conditions, at a time when these very conditions are subject to far-reaching changes. A new form of play is evolving, one which is imperfect and transitional, but rich in new possibilities. Bourgeois art-historians may set out aesthetic principles which fortify the 'purity' of their art forms against the 'vandalism' of the rising classes. Piscator has captured the revolutionary novel for the stage, an achievement worth much more than all their wordy aestheticizing."

Gasbarra (Welt am Abend, January, 1928)

The Conveyor Belt

We were also faced with new problems in acting technique. It was the first time an actor had been required to perform his entire role while he was being carried along or was walking or running. This made it imperative that the belts should function silently. During the first discussions the manufacturer accepted this basic condition. But when we heard the belts in action for the first time—on January 28, 1928—they sounded like a traction engine under full steam. The belts rattled and snorted and pounded so that the whole house quaked. Even at the top of your voice you could hardly make yourself heard. The idea of dialogue on these raging monsters was quite unthinkable. I seem to remember we just sank into the orchestra seats and laughed hysterically. There were twelve days to opening night. The technicians assured us that they could cut down the noise, but there was no longer any mention of the silent operation that we had been promised. The process threatened to be long and put the production in jeopardy. As usual, I was made to see that only a fraction of my idea could be put into practice. And in this case the problem was more difficult because in Pallenberg we had an actor of unheard-of good will who would make any sacrifice to cooperate, but he was at the same time a very temperamental artist, and naturally apprehensive about the unusual apparatus, especially if it was not even going to work. The long, hard task of modifying the belts began; it occupied every minute that I did not need the stage for rehearsals. With huge quantities of graphite, soap and lubricating oil, by strengthening the stage floor with heavy wooden props, fitting new bearings, lining the chains with felt, and putting a felt underlay beneath the whole machine, the noise was reduced to a level where it no longer drowned the text completely. Nonetheless, the actors still had to keep their voices up to make themselves heard.

The rest of the set was utterly simple. The only things on the whole stage apart from the conveyor belts were two flats joined by borders, one behind the other and a cloth screen at the back. Some of the props were carried onto the open stage by the conveyor belt, others hung in the flies, so that everything could be put in and taken out quickly. It was the cleanest, simplest and most versatile set I had ever devised. Everything went off quickly as if by clockwork.

It seemed to me that this apparatus had a quality of its own; it was inherently comic. Every application of the machinery somehow made you want to laugh. There seemed to be absolute harmony between subject and machinery. And for the whole thing I had in mind a sort of knockabout style, reminiscent of Chaplin or vaudeville.

The Ending of Our Adaptation of Schwejk

We were widely criticized in the press because our ending did not work. What was not pointed out was that we intended to stage Jaroslav Hašek's *The Adventures of the Good Soldier Schwejk*, and not a "play" with an exposition, a dramatic climax and a catharsis. Hašek had died before he could complete his work, and Vanek, the editor, had also failed to come up with a conclusion. This kind of subject can really end only with the death of the hero. So we were faced with a dilemma, and we knew it. There were endless suggestions for the ending.

Endings for Schwejk

The original ending in the Brod/Reimann version:
> Engagement of Lieutenant Lukacs and Etelka. Schwejk respectfully requests that he be godfather to the eventual offspring. .

Grosz suggests as an ending:
> Slapstick scene: "Everything in ruins."
> or:
> The characters sit around as skeletons with death's-head masks. They drink to each other's health.

Lania suggests:
> Schwejk sits in the bar waiting for Voditchka. The World War is over. But instead of Voditchka, Brettschneider appears. Conversation. Schwejk is arrested. (Compared with the old Austrian Empire, nothing has really changed. Schwejk is still the asocial man, dynamite, destructive in every social order.)

The best idea for the conclusion, all things considered: use the finale in Heaven until a solution is reached.

None of these endings really satisfied us. I found the final ending in the novel. I have, regrettably, to stress this, because the scene in question, which we did not play, later came to be regarded as Brod's brainchild, and I was accused of having cut this exciting and poetic scene for fear of the possible political effect.

The scene "Schwejk in Heaven" had been suggested by cadet Biegler's dream in Hašek's own version. The idea was that after battling with every possible human authority, Schwejk should end up facing a superhuman authority, and this authority, too, should be shown, when faced by Schwejk, to be insubstantial, nonexistent. We put the idea to Brod, who took it up gleefully, and after a thorough discussion with Gasbarra, who had worked it out in terms of staging, went off and wrote a text which pleased everybody. People later maintained that I did not stage the scene because I was afraid the effect would be too radical. The fact of the matter is that the horror of the cripples parading before God was more than the play could carry at the end.

Casting Notes for the Last Scene

Cripples before God.
Sign up legless beggars.
20 life-size dolls as extras.
5–6 real cripples.
One constantly treading on his own entrails.
One shouldering a leg.
One with his head under his arm.
Arms and legs hanging out of rucksacks, smeared with mud and blood.
Two little girls, hand in hand, with bloody faces.

We put this scene on at a private club performance for members of the Special Sections of the Volksbühne. The bloody, mutilated band of soldiers marched across the stage on the conveyor belt to the strains of the Radetzky March, led by a man who had had both legs shot away, but still painfully tried to keep in step with the rest on his stumps. God was the antagonist in this scene, and Grosz had drawn him as a horrifying grotesque, which shrank visibly in size during the conversation with Schwejk.

We saw in performance that this did not work. Brod's script for this scene was too long to start with, but could perhaps have been used if we had had another ten days to rehearse it. As it was, we had no time to stage the scene as it would have required.

This is how we came to have no final scene for the press show. So we ended with Schwejk and Voditchka making a date: "After the

Great War, at six o'clock." Not that we were satisfied with this solution. But the subject really admitted of no conclusion, and so we felt it best to break off abruptly, leaving the thing unfinished as Hašek had done.

The form which *Schwejk* assumed was certainly neither ideal nor final. As in the case of *Rasputin*, it was an embryonic dramatic form intended for the writers of future generations. Much could have been made sharper, more succinct and effective if we had had time.

The conditions under which our theater conquered new ground must not be forgotten. If we had been able to use the days and weeks that were lost in discussions with the two original adapters for positive work on the play, many things would no doubt have been different; it seems to me unjust, however, to accuse us of having missed the best passages in the novel or of having put them together ineffectively. We worked our way through the volumes of *Schwejk* over and over again for weeks, and many friends of the theater who took a literary interest in our work also helped to locate the best episodes. I do not think that we missed anything that ought to have been used, given the framework we had jointly agreed on at the start. We naturally had to leave out many scenes, simply because the performance would have run for double the three hours avail-

From George Grosz's animated cartoon for *Schwejk*

able. We hoped as we laid these scenes aside to be able to put on a second *Schwejk* the following season.[2]

By some incomprehensible indiscretion this plan leaked out to the public, and Max Brod immediately sent us a letter to stake his claim. It is doubtful whether a second installment would have had the same effect. Maybe the second part would have been no more than a collection of anecdotes, for the action had taken Schwejk from home to the front, exhausting the travel sequences required by his first "timetable."

Stage Set and Film

In *Schwejk* the role of the environment which I presented by means of film and puppets came out more strongly than in the other plays in which the figures had in the main spoken for themselves.

These puppets were not just an "artistic idea" of mine, but represented the ossified types which populated the political and social life of prewar Austria. We distinguished between a range of categories: semipuppets, puppetlike types, semihumans. And Schwejk was set against this fantastic world as the only human being. For a while I thought of taking this idea to its logical conclusion and of having Schwejk-Pallenberg appear as the only actor on the stage, the whole surrounding world being mechanized with film, puppets and loudspeakers.

I worked out the following routine to put these ideas into practice: some of the puppets were really to be lifeless dolls in horribly exaggerated poses and masks (like the grotesque puppets made by Grosz, Heartfield and Schlichter during the Dada period), whereas some were to be masked actors likewise with an exaggerated indication of their special function (e.g., police spies were to have a gigantic ear or an eye on the end of a stalk).

In the case of the puppetlike types and semihumans, the make-up and costumes were to be exaggerated. So the prison warden, for example, had a huge fist made of gauze and cotton wool which characterized him at a glance. Everything was done to make the distinction between the types obvious and clear and to exaggerate the single figures into clownlike symbols.

And for this task the only one who could possibly come to mind was my old friend George Grosz. A huge collection of drawings

2. The projected second part of *Schwejk* never materialized, but in 1943 Brecht completed his own version, *Schweik in the Second World War* (*Schweik im zweiten Weltkrieg*).

emerged from the work and attracted the interest of the authorities. The result was that Grosz and the Malik Publishing House were involved in the "Blasphemy Trial."[3] The work on *Schwejk* eventually produced three hundred separate drawings.

It was equally imperative to have the properties right for the style of Schwejk. The properties, too, had a comic function and were consequently to be exaggerated and caricatured. But here, too, unfortunately, many of our ideas were never fully developed.

The use of film was of prime importance in presenting the character of the world around Schwejk. But this time the style which the subject demanded ruled out the use of naturalistic or documentary film material. The film, too, had to conform to the element of satirical caricature in the overall production, and so, on my instructions, Grosz produced a politico-satirical cartoon in which the puppet representatives of the Army, of the Church and of the Police acted out their gruesome, comic ritual.

Grosz's main achievement in this film was not simply his inspired delineation of the types. He managed in this film to extract Schwejk or rather Schwejk's world from its historical period and establish a link with the present. The medical officers, officers, public prosecutors were figures that are still alive today in Prussia/ Germany. And so the play carried on the struggle on the political level of the day.

Marginal Notes on the Same Theme

"When John Heartfield and I invented photomontage in my Southside studio at five o'clock one May morning, we had no idea of the possibilities of our discovery nor of the thorny but successful path of its progress. As so often happens in life, we had struck gold without realizing it. It was a time when many young adventurers were setting out for the unknown land of Dada—and there are always inventions drifting ready-made in the air. Erwin was one of us at this time, though he was still a soldier, serving in the Flanders salient. He had heard about us and sent us gifts of tea to express his approval. (Those were the days of *ersatz* honey with an Iron Cross on the label, when we spread so-called war jam on our bread—all of which you could get only with ration cards.) Erwin, with the same bold toughness as his ancestor Piscatorius, the belligerent Bible translator, kept his sharp nose to the wind in his con-

3. George Grosz was fined for libeling the German army in 1920, for blasphemy and "corrupting the sense of shame and virtue innate in the German people" in 1923 (he had drawn a prostitute wearing a cross), and for blasphemy again in 1928 when he drew the crucified Christ wearing a gas mask in one of the Schwejk illustrations.

stant search for new possibilities. I know that even at that time he was carrying the complete plans for the Piscator-Bühne around with him. Do you still remember, Erwin, how, long before the Russians, you conducted the famous Dada matinee, poised as director on the top of a stepladder, while somebody bellowed a long, uncouth speech at the audience from the wings behind you? But I digress.

From George Grosz's animated cartoon for *Schwejk*

"Anyhow, Erwin made sense of putting photomontage on the stage and rearranged the old backdrops, taking away the magic and giving the stage back the vitality and action it needs. You can go into any good theater and you will see what I mean. Like many discoverers, Erwin never stands still—vestiges of the old Wagnerian longing still cling to him, and he is often to be found on the thorny path which leads to the 'total work of art' in which all the arts are united. What a dream, what a thought, what a possibility, what tremendous scope for modern stage magic. Like most men with eyes in their heads, Erwin can see what a terrible commercialized business art is today, bedeviled with shares and stock exchange quotations, and like the prophet and evangelist he is, he seeks unswervingly to put this art back on a more effective path.

"So for the graphic artist Erwin simply erected a huge drawing board covered with white paper at the back of the stage, and on this I accompany the action with hieroglyphs—I glide on and off in counterpoint to the action and underline malicious comments and asides. Erwin has in fact opened up a vast new field for graphic art, a sort of draftsman's circus, which is more attractive to today's artists than musty art for aesthetes or studio graphics for bibliophiles and the genteel educated classes.

"Here the 'Daumiers' of today can issue their warnings and paint terror on the walls. What a medium for any artist who wants to speak directly to the masses. Of course, a new drawing surface requires new methods, a new economical language of line—a real chance to educate woolly minds and chaotic hands! And the flickering touch of Impressionism is no use at all. The line has to be photogenic—clear, simple, not too thin (in case of overexposure) and hard, like the drawings and woodcuts in Gothic block-books and the lapidary engravings on the Pyramids.

"Here, young artists of today, you have a wall at your disposal. If you have something to say, use it!"

George Grosz

Naturalistic film was, of course, used as well as cartoons, especially where we had to establish the atmosphere of specific scenes, e.g. the streets of Prague, the railway journey, etc. For the street scenes, we had even sent our cameraman Hübler-Kahla to Prague. Street scenes in conjunction with the conveyor belt required a new photographic technique which presented considerable difficulties. We needed the picture to move along absolutely steadily in march time. The camera could only be mounted on a car and the bouncing of the vehicle on the uneven streets of Prague made the picture zigzag up and down constantly. The only way we could get results that even approached being satisfactory was by repeated intercutting of the best strips of film.

And finally I tried to combine naturalistic film with cartoon for the March to Budějovice and for the final battle scenes. In the "Anabasis" scene I had clumps of trees drawn on the pictures which flowed past; this brought out very strongly the notion of continuity and the hopelessness of the march. In the intervals between scenes this film led quite naturally into the drawn projections.

In the final scene—and the idea occurred to me only half an hour before the show opened, under the dreadful pressure to save our unworkable ending—I had an endless series of crosses drawn. They were projected over still shots of mutilated soldiers' bodies and came from the horizon toward the spectator. It was with some apprehension during the first night that we waited for this extraordinary effect, which had first been tried out only half an hour before. Unfortunately we waited in vain. The stills came up on the screen, though only faintly, but the moving crosses failed to appear. After the performance we discovered that the projectionist in his idiocy had in fact run the film, but without opening up the lens.

The Figure of Schwejk and Pallenberg

A matter of particularly intense dispute was whether Schwejk was a complete idiot who was unaware of what he was saying and doing and who therefore exposed the absurdity of war and of authority inadvertently, by virtue of the very simplicity of his attitude, or whether he only pretended to be simple, while in fact he was acting with a conscious aim. In any case, we were agreed that the very existence of such a person sufficed to demolish any concept of authority in Church, State, Army. Schwejk does not achieve results by attacking or rejecting existing authorities, but—on the contrary—by accepting all authority and accepting it with absolute consistency.

This was Schwejk's significance: he was not just a clown whose antics ultimately affirm the state of things, but a grand skeptic whose rigid, untiring affirmation of reality reduces reality to nullity. Schwejk, we argued, is a deeply asocial element: not a revolutionary who wants a new order, but a type without any social links who would be destructive even in a Communist society.

George Grosz

And for this role, as we saw it, there was no man in Germany other than Max Pallenberg. We have frequently been reproached by our political allies for casting Pallenberg in this role. They maintained that we were harboring the star system in our theater. I don't really know what they meant. For me there are either actors of quality or actors without talent. And in casting a particular role, there can never be any consideration other than that the man in question should be able to fill the role adequately. Whether he is a novice or a star is a matter of supreme indifference. In many cases he will be a star. Why should we not employ a man's talents, even if the commercial situation has made a star of him? Criticism is only justified here if one uses such an actor for his own sake—that is, if one creates the part to suit his personality and subordinates everything else, the interpretation, the play, the production, the direction, etc., to this end. But our case was quite the opposite. We did not put on *Schwejk* for Pallenberg's sake, we did not create the role for him, but the role and the sense of the play cried out for Pallenberg. The basic requirement can be formulated only as follows: the finest effect is achieved by the best, that is, the most appropriate casting. Especially when one has a political aim in mind as we did.

Pallenberg, who was in effect the ideal Schwejk, adapted himself admirably to the scenic and technical requirements of the play and of the company. Seen from this angle, he was not the star of our production at all in the normal sense. It took a considerable effort of mind for this kind of man, who had had his formative training in Reinhardt's school, to do justice to this new mathematical type of acting. He managed this transformation with astonishing ease and flexibility, and created a character who without exaggeration can be counted one of the immortal figures in the history of the theater.

"Pallenberg's playing of Schwejk is the central event of the evening, a magnificent rendering of a legendary folk figure, masterful enough to convince us that he really did exist in Prague. He has something of a good, innocent, long-suffering animal who does not know, cannot know, why he must suffer so much indignity. In voice and glance sometimes a touch of infinite suffering and humility, a fall guy by the grace of Peter Schlemihl, of the race of Eulenspiegel and Candide. Pallenberg has recreated Schwejk anew. It says much for Piscator that an actor of Pallenberg's unique caliber should have joined forces with him, and the restrictions Pallenberg has imposed on himself to suit the play say even more for him."

Die Welt am Abend, January 24, 1928 (Kurt Kersten)

INTRODUCTION

In February *The Adventures of the Good Soldier Schwejk* broke box-office records with receipts of between 7,000 and 9,000 marks a night, and looked set for a long run. This posed a problem, for at the beginning of the season Piscator had promised five plays to the Special Sections of the Volksbühne and seven to his own season-ticket holders *(Abonnenten)*, and now, with the season more than half over, he had staged only three productions. At the end of the season Herbert Ihering was to note that the standard German repertory season with its *Abonnenten* was incompatible with the commercial practice of long runs to exploit hits, particularly where a singled-minded political theatrical collective was concerned. Piscator had yet to discover this, to his cost. Otto Katz, his business manager, suggested taking another theater to meet their commitments and Piscator agreed, so the lease of the Lessing-Theater was secured from March 1. It was intended to open there with Leo Lania's *Boom (Konjunktur)*, which would meet another outstanding obligation, since it offered Tilla Durieux the starring part for which she had been waiting since she set up the financial backing which made the Piscator-Bühne possible.

In the event the second theater, which was intended to solve Piscator's problems, proved his undoing. *Boom*, the first play which the company had conceived and created collectively, proved to be an intractable project and the opening was delayed. Upton Sinclair's *Singing Jailbirds*, a Studio project, which had been prepared for such an emergency, went on at the Lessing-Theater as a stopgap. Receipts were poor, and it was replaced after fourteen days by *Hoppla*, which had just come back from a successful tour (Frankfurt, Mannheim, Cologne), but the public still stayed away. Meanwhile, Max Pallenberg announced that his engagement at the Piscator-Bühne would end on April 12 because of a projected South American tour, so a new production was needed for the Theater am Nollendorfplatz, and Karlheinz Martin was engaged to direct Jean Richard Bloch's *The Last Emperor (Le Dernier Empéreur)*. *Boom* finally opened at the Lessing-Theater on April 8.

Leo Lania (1896–1961) was a journalist. He had founded the first press agency *(Telegraphenagentur)* in Berlin and when he joined

Piscator had several antifascist publications to his name, among them an exposure of clandestine German rearmament in 1923. He wrote three plays about this time, *Boom* and *The Peace Conference (Die Friedenskonferenz)* in 1927 and *God, King and Country (Gott, König und Vaterland)* in 1928, and he translated Tretiakov's *Roar, China*, which was performed in twenty theaters across Germany in 1929. Lania, who emigrated in 1933, notes in a pocket autobiography in *Das Wort* (Moscow, 1937) that his books were withdrawn from commerce and pulped by the Nazis, and it has proved impossible to trace a copy of *Boom*. The promptbook is lost, so we have to rely on reviews to get an idea of the content of the play. Peter in the *Rote Fahne* gives the following impression of the action:

> "The action develops from the bottom up. Some hobos discover an oil well and sell it for schnaps and a few lire, then fight over the proceeds, which leads to the first knifing and produces the first corpse. Cutthroat trading proceeds, moving into more exalted circles, until finally France and England confront one another, rattling sabers. The League of Nations intervenes in the interest of Royal Dutch Shell.
>
> Putsch follows intrigue. A little 'revolution' is staged in the manner of the general revolts which American imperialism has stage-managed on a dozen or so occasions in Mexico and Central and South America, at the expense of the inhabitants. Trebitsch-Lincoln appears, and after a meteoric career appoints himself dictator and president, backed by international scum, penniless ex-officers and similar parasites."

Herbert Ihering sketches the same events and goes on to point out the inconsistencies in the production:

> "Three hobos come along and lie down in the noonday sun. The ground is damp, they sniff it and discover oil. They stake their claim with a board, *Soil Developments, Inc.* Other people come along and the dealing begins. The site is fenced off, shacks are built. Film: "Oil flows." The oil strike hits the headlines . . . An excellent beginning, but then comes the break. Unrest grips the local population, and an Albanian officer (in fact, a German instructor) brandishes a whip, which is wrested from his grasp by Frau Claire Barsin. With her entry and the confiscation of the whip we are back in the realm of star vehicles and star parts. The epic style is shattered, and private intrigue, concocted plot and the comedy of high society reassert themselves. Again and again Piscator and Lania try to launch the play back into the epic stream with collective themes. Frau Barsin is not epic but novelette."

As Piscator points out, the initial script was a conventional comedy with a touch of tycoonery, but as the company rehearsed it, economics and big business took over and would have engulfed the original plot, had not Tilla Durieux been playing Claire Barsin. Piscator had hitherto adapted and rewritten with sovereign abandon, as authors like Ehm Welk and Ernst Toller testified, but now he was indirectly in the hands of his backer, Frau Durieux's prospective husband. He was reduced to delegating two of his staff to coax his leading lady to accept changes in her lines, where he would normally have scrapped the entire character when it became superfluous. The play remained uneven and inconsistent.

At the end of the season Herbert Ihering appraised the position of the Piscator-Bühne, which at that point still seemed set for another season, and suggested that the first act of the play would probably have guaranteed it a modest success as an experimental piece if it had been staged in the familiar surroundings of the Nollendorfplatz. It was, after all, groping toward a dramatic analysis of economic affairs, such as was soon to exercise the mind of Brecht, whose *Wheat (Weizen,* sometimes referred to as *Joe Fleischhacker aus Chicago)*—listed for production in the Piscator-Bühne's preliminary publicity—deals with a similar subject, a wheat baron's dealings in grain on the Chicago Exchange. *Wheat* was never completed.

XX
THE COMEDY OF BIG BUSINESS
BOOM
PISCATOR-BÜHNE LESSING-THEATER
April 8 to May 3, 1928

In a conversation with Lania which had taken place about the time when we were founding our theater (I had put up Lania's *General Strike* [*Generalstreik*] for performance at the Volksbühne at the time of the English miners' strike, because the subject and the form seemed to me worthy of production), he had suggested an idea for a comedy which I liked very much. What he had in mind was to show how profiteers use revolutions, and to prove that the revolutionary idea also triumphs over the personalities who try to misuse it. The comedy with the provisional title *"Red versus White"* (*Rot gegen Weiss*) took up the events in China, and placed at the center of the action a Chinese general in England who falls into the hands of a slick manager; the latter exploits him financially as an anti-bourgeois fiend. The comic consequences of this affair, in the course of which the manager goes bankrupt, provided the backbone of the play.

The comedy proved to be unusable in the first version. The basic idea was too weak to carry the whole play and the action was un-convincing. Lania himself was dissatisfied, and decided to rework the play from the beginning, taking the available cast into consideration in the process. This was the first attempt to base a production on our theater and its requirements from the very outset: the author had a commission from the theater and was in close contact with the director and with all the possibilities and requirements of our theater from the beginning as he tackled his task.

In July we traveled down to Heringsdorf [on the Baltic] together, and while Toller, Gasbarra and I worked on the preparations for *Hoppla, Such is Life!*, Lania was busy on the revised version of *Red versus White* which now bore the title *Boom*. By the end of July two acts of the comedy were ready and when Lania read the play to us we found it excellent, especially Frau Durieux, who could see herself making a big hit in the central role. Our intention was to put on this play as our second production.

I have already explained why we decided to follow *Hoppla* with *Rasputin*. But it also emerged as we came to grips with *Boom*, and as the tasks facing our theater became clearer to us, that even the final version of the comedy was not good enough. We realized that we could not skate over the surface of the problems, that people expected us to get to the heart of the matter, and that the subject was much too serious and important to be used as mere background for a diverting idea.

This subject was oil, and once again the subject proved to be primary. It was much in people's minds at the time, because of Upton Sinclair's novel *Oil* and because of everyday politics, and it cried out to be explored in much greater depth and breadth than was done in Lania's comedy.

Lania could see this. Since he was keen to stage the play on our stage, he turned down acceptances of the existent version of *Boom* by other theaters and went to work on the play for the third time.

The more intensively we explored the subject and the problem, the greater the difficulties became. Together we worked our way through volumes of literature, statistics and industrial reports, and it gradually became clearer that the subject of *Boom* had in it the germ of an economic comedy in the grand manner, that the subject had possibilities which opened up whole new perspectives for the theater. But—it was the beginning of February and the Lessing-Theater was due to open on March first with Lania's play. An insoluble dilemma. On the one hand, there was the need to put on Lania's play, on the other hand, it was a pity to waste the subject and problem of the comedy on banal entertainment in the usual manner. A fundamental revision of the kind we had in mind would have taken many weeks or months.

The only possible result of our work was a compromise. Once again the conditions of work, the lack of time, the constraints imposed by the business side of the theater were more powerful than

274

our own wishes and intentions. Leo Lania later made the following comments on his handling of the subject and on his intentions in the program notes for the play:

The Subject

"The attempt to put topical, political and economic subjects into dramatic form faces great difficulties from the very start—especially here in Germany. Bourgeois postwar Germany, 'American' as it may choose to act, still thinks in traditional terms—apart from a small section in industry—listens with dulled nerves, and looks at real life through spectacles which have robbed their vision of its freshness. This natural shortsightedness of bourgeois intellectuals is increased by an artificial limitation, their narrow angle of vision: there are high walls built around every desk, not a glance strays past the quarto sheet of manuscript, the folio page of the book, the sketch on the drawing board and onto the street. In America students work during vacations as farmers, waiters, or telegraph operators, doctors have farms, and almost everybody who works for a living samples dozens of jobs during his working life, and has social life before his eyes from childhood. Whether it is a matter of stocks and shares, oil companies, power stations, the Stock Exchange, technology, the press or the justiciary—education and the life the individual leads ensure that every level and class of society has an exact knowledge of 'practical,' that is, public life. Soviet Russia experiences politics directly and personally as its destiny. But in Germany all things conspire to encapsulate each class and each profession, so that the individual never comes to terms in any clear or personal way with facts, events and institutions of social life. Since stocks and shares and the coal industry, technology and politics are a special preserve of a small initiated minority in this country, and since the great mass of the people, in particular the class-conscious trade unions, are denied any insight into the social organism, there is no contact between the individual and events in public life, which is precisely where a topical comedy of industrial life has to be located, unless it is satisfied with providing peripheral glosses on political and economic life from the outside."

Author and Director

"For us it is no longer enough merely to show effects, or to use politics merely as an interesting backdrop before which various psychological conjuring tricks can be demonstrated. What we want to see are not episodes from the times, but the times themselves, and we want to reach a clear understanding of them and grasp their essential internal connections as a totality. But this need to process and communicate political subjects reduces the present-day theater to limp helplessness. If in my comedy I was able to experiment along these lines it was thanks to the

275

support that I received from Erwin Piscator, both on the script and with the direction."

Dramatic Content and Stage Form

"The hero of this comedy is oil. The intention is to show the complex of economic questions which govern this subject, and to reveal the laws and the phases of its economic exploitation as well as its political side effects. I chose Albania as the setting for the play, although that country has so far been of little importance to the international oil market, because the visible stages in the international struggle can be demonstrated here from start to finish on a small scale. Trebitsch-Lincoln's connections with Albania have no documentary foundation.[1] But he is such a perfect representative of the type of adventurer who impresses his stamp on all the bloody feuds and plunderings that have afflicted the wells of Mexico, Baku and Mossul, that I took the liberty of adding a few new feats of heroism to those which history already attributes to Trebitsch-Lincoln, and of transposing his historical deeds from China and Germany to Albania. Piscator's production started from the idea that the subject and all its effects should be shown objectively in the construction of the set. The ideas and suggestions he as the director put forward helped to show me the way in which my intentions might be realized. And these intentions did not stem from spontaneous ideas or the inspiration of the moment; they sprang from the ideas which governed this theater and the task it has set for itself. Fertilized by the theater and by our collective cooperation, this comedy came into being."

Although we were worn-out with the hectic struggles during the first half of the season, we clenched our teeth and went to work. At first all seemed to be going well. The first act came along very well with our joint efforts, and it became apparent that by starting with the subject "oil" we could achieve not merely a deeper analysis of the content, but had the chance to develop an entirely new form of comedy. I wanted to expose the "struggle for oil" from the roots up, and this is how I came to base my production on a progressively constructed set which was built in close conjunction with the action. Starting with an empty stage—the naked earth—the oil rush provoked by the chance discovery of an oil well was to develop from the tiniest beginnings to the proportions of an avalanche, a sequence was to be enacted before the eyes of the audience which

1. Ignaz Timotheus Trebitsch-Lincoln (1879–1943) was a notorious political adventurer. Born in Hungary, preacher in New York, Liberal member of Parliament in England in 1910, mixed up in sensational spy revelations in 1915 and held under arrest until 1918. Involved in the Kapp *Putsch* in Berlin in 1920. Autobiography: *The Greatest Adventurer of the Twentieth Century. The Truth about My Life.*

would show all the technical processes in the production of oil. From the discovery of the oil well to the preparations for drilling, from the construction of the drilling derricks to the marketing of oil as a commercial product, the action—rivalry, murder, profiteering, corruption, revolution—was to unfold before the spectator and to involve him in all the machinations of the politics of international oil.

But only in the first act did it prove possible to put our insights into practice. In the second act we had to find a way to link up with the action of the original comedy, because the main role would otherwise have been entirely lost from sight. This contradiction proved to be insurmountable. The new version turned the power of oil into the sole hero and central role, and yet the central role of the heroine, which was rooted in the comedy version, but scarcely functioned as anything more than an episode in the new play, had somehow to be saved. Compromises at every turn. As always, the compromises had to be paid for.

The first thing that happened was that the premiere of *Boom* had to be postponed once more, at first for fourteen days and then for four weeks. In the meantime, a show had to be improvised in the Lessing-Theater (see p. 293). The rehearsals for *Boom* itself, much hampered by the need to rewrite the script daily, made halting progress and came to a complete standstill when Tilla Durieux fell ill and could not attend rehearsals.

In the interim I worked with Lania on the film accompaniment, which was to have quite a special function in the play this time and was edited from quite a different point of view.

I developed the action dynamically on the stage, and this gave the scaffolding set and the props a significance of their own; the film, too, was not only to sketch and extend the background of the play, was not to be mere illustration, but was to provide a "framework" for the comedy in the truest sense of the word.

This journalist's comedy was to develop out of the newspaper, that is to say, the entire stage opening was closed by a sheet of newsprint, a cloth which, like a newspaper, was divided into columns, each of which corresponded to a particular set on the stage. While on the stage the struggle between the rival groups, between the Italian and the French oil companies raged around the oil well, the press war between France and Italy raged on the cloth, showing the contradiction in world politics by means of animated cartoons and captions. In this way I achieved extraordinary simplicity and conciseness of action and was able to outline events with textbook clarity. The sheet of newsprint was constantly pushed forward or

277

taken away or broken open at different points to reveal the stage, and the action began just at the point at which the newspaper commentary had left off. At the end, when the newspaper went up in flames, the Albanian revolution had reached its climax and set fire to the oil wells.

It seems to me that with the production of *Boom*, which is one play I cannot be accused of overloading with apparatus or encumbering with technical devices, we achieved the most polished performance of the whole season in terms of simplicity of staging and fluidity of form.

The Political Limits of Objectivity

With *Boom* we ventured for the first time into the territory of present-day international industrial politics. The question was a delicate one for us because it touched on the position of the Soviet Union in the political and economic struggle for markets for oil: it touched on the Soviet relations or conflicts with the American and English companies which produced and sold oil, and on the Soviet position as a competitor within the capitalist international economy.

If the play had concerned itself with this problem alone, there might have been a chance of illuminating every corner and eliminating any ambiguities. We could have shown that the Soviet Union pursued a capitalist policy in international trade precisely to maintain its significance for the international workers' movement. As it was, this problem was linked with a plot involving a national revolution in an oil-producing area in which the Soviet Union appeared on the one hand as an economic factor, and on the other as a revolutionary factor. In the next to last version of the play, which we called the "Borodin version," the female lead appeared as the representative of the Russian Naphtha Syndicate and as a secret political agent of the Third International. The malicious or ignorant could conclude from this double role that the Soviet Union provoked national revolutions in order to get its hands on the oil under favorable conditions. There were very serious objections to this version in the dramaturgs' office, which was also a political office in our setup. If I tried at first to ignore these objections and went on rehearsing this version until the evening before the premiere, it was because I hoped that our well-tried pedagogic style of staging would enable us to show the Soviet motifs properly and avoid ambiguity.

This hope was not fulfilled. What then happened on the evening of the dress rehearsal was that the figure of Frau Barsin appeared to condemn Soviet policy as dishonest and two-faced in front of an assembly consisting mainly of political personalities, representatives of the KPD, the Soviet Trade Mission and the Soviet Embassy, that I had brought together for the purpose. It proved to be quite impossible, without doing great harm to the Soviet Union, to represent in a single figure two spheres which the Soviet Union had made every effort to keep separate. The very opposite of what we had intended with this production would have happened, an event which would have had unforeseeable consequences for the theater. I was clear in my own mind that it would be better to close the theater than to allow a performance which would have permitted even the slightest doubts about our theater's political standpoint.

The dress rehearsal ended at 3:00 A.M. on April 7, 1928. The critics gathered in the manager's office at the Lessing-Theater, a room which smelled as musty as if the windows had not been opened once since Otto Brahm's times.[2] On all sides, and most spiritedly from the lady representing the Communist Party, the Borodin-version was declared to be impossible. The representative of the *Rote Fahne* made it known that, to his personal regret, he was going to be forced on political grounds to attack the Piscator-Bühne sharply for the first time if the play went out in the form in which we had just seen it. I quite understood the justification for these criticisms, although many of the arguments seemed to me exaggerated.

Outside the day gradually dawned, the day on which the premiere would later take place. Pale, our faces marked by sleepless nights, unwashed, unshaven, completely exhausted by a task which had scarcely left us time to eat or sleep for three weeks, we now had a fully rehearsed play on our hands in which scarcely any alteration was possible and which, despite this, we could not put on. It was the most serious test of our nerves since our theater had opened. Lania had a nervous breakdown. The only man who seemed at ease, indeed even in high spirits, was our old friend Bert Brecht, sucking eternally at his black cigar with a leather cap pulled jauntily over his forehead. He could see a possibility of transforming the function of the entire role of the female lead at short notice and offered to go to work on the spot with Lania and Gasbarra. Postponement of the opening night for at least two days would be necessary before he would attempt it, and it was still doubtful whether Frau Durieux would agree to this alteration. It was, in fact, a frightful thing to ask her to do, to change entirely a role which she had already built up along particular lines. Otto Katz and Frl.

2. Otto Brahm was director of the Lessing-Theater from 1904 to 1912.

Wellhöner took on the thankless task of persuading Frau Durieux that a revision was necessary.

By now it was 5:00 A.M. A magnificent spring day had dawned outside. I cursed my profession once again. A burden lay upon us which we were scarcely able to bear any further. When I reflected that there was only a week left before Karlheinz Martin was supposed to stage *The Last Emperor (Le Dernier Empéreur)*, I would dearly have liked to run away to a place where I would have heard and seen no more of the theater. Instead, we drove to my apartment, where we worked on a new version of the Barsin character till the afternoon. The fact that the figure had previously represented the Third International and the Russian Naphtha Syndicate, but was now to appear as a representative of the South American ABC states who had only *pretended* to be a Soviet agent, was not without its comic aspects. This solution enabled us to let the text of the role stand right to the end, and to finish off with an "ingenious and surprising twist." I must say that I did not feel too good about all this. The play, apart from the first scenes, suffered from the thinness of its dialogue and the weakness of its individual scenes and this conclusion was bound to turn it into more of a pure comedy. But what was left for us to do, if we wanted to save the production at all? In one last piece of forced labor which used up our last reserves of strength, the central role was rewritten to take into account its new function. Although Frau Durieux was also suffering from acute nervous strain, she stuck it out with admirable self-discipline to the day of the performance. If we failed at the time to give her adequate recognition for her willingness to make any sacrifice that might save the performance, it was only because of the strain and overwork that the conditions at the time imposed on us.

The echo that *Boom* awakened in the general public was just as full of contradictions as had been the case with the other productions that season. What is interesting is that the right-wing press, which in the past had never tired of branding our performance as dull and tedious now suddenly attacked the "Super-Broadway" and the "operatic gags" in this show.

Der Tag wrote:

> "Piscator is producing 'Super-Broadway.' Moscow, Hollywood and all the boulevard-comedy of an effete Europe are combined in one final culmination. The whole world is a gigantic loony bin. The world revolution needs the help of operetta to coax people to join it."

And the *Lokal-Anzeiger:*

> "Courths-Mahler in Piscator's theater.[3] There is still a future here. This is the way out of Toller's cul-de-sac. A touch of genius as bold as it is ingenious, the Piscator-Bühne is now determined to follow Frau Hedwig Courths-Mahler's star."

The *Deutsche Zeitung* found it all "very boring." The *Tägliche Rundschau* wrote: "soporific . . . the Piscator-Bühne is twitching in the last stages of senile decay." The *Berliner Börsen-Zeitung* is an exception on this occasion:

> "Leo Lania's attempt to write a comedy of big business deserves a good deal more attention than all the potboilers which attempt to add a slightly different nuance to things that have already been shown a million times."

And, indeed, the economic experts, among them, for example, Morus in the *Weltbühne,* handled the play with much more justice than the gentlemen in the literary periodicals, who admitted that they were not competent to judge the political and economic questions with which the play dealt, but nonetheless never hesitated for an instant to dismiss the mechanism of international profiteering which was shown in *Boom* as phony and the product of the fevered imagination of a writer who had no grasp of the real problems. The political angles were on this occasion placed in the foreground by the democratic press.

For the *8-Uhr-Abendblatt* the comedy was not revolutionary enough:

> "I do not reject Piscator's repertoire because it is too revolutionary—I reject it because he lacks total revolutionary conviction. He is a fanatical compromiser; to reduce the matter to a concise formula, he is a reactionary who dulls our artistic conscience. It is not the bourgeois public that must beware of him—it is rather those who are working for a logical development and who have made that their life's work. It is they who must closely examine his very questionable methods."

Felix Hollaender saw the following reactionary element in the comedy: "Herr Lania has no wish to displease the bourgeoisie; he

3. Hedwig Courths-Mahler (1867–1950) was author of such novels as *I'll Never Leave You* (*Ich lasse dich nicht,* 1915). Her name was synonymous with trivial, sentimental best sellers.

has the finish contrived by a very clever woman whose charm and genius for business manage to create a community of interest between capitalist America and Soviet Russia." How wrong this objection is has been shown in the preceding pages, where I have explained the reasons for changing the end of the comedy in deference to political requirements.

The *Vossische Zeitung* took it amiss that "the public enjoyed the confidence tricks of Trebitsch-Lincoln and laughed at them. This was pure bourgeois pleasure of the sort usually derived from operettas or French farce. It is the aim of the Piscator-Bühne to turn bourgeois citizens into Communists. Is not the effect of his theater rather to turn Communists into bourgeois citizens? If the two classes have the same favorites and the same pleasures—and pleasure is always a form of property—must they not fall into each other's hands? If both sides laugh, it means the end of the class struggle, and Herr Piscator is the father of social peace."

The *B.Z.* pointed out that the play offered "ideas and experiments which are stimulating, which escape from the dull routine in which the theater would otherwise ossify. It is not a case of just being different. Not merely technical and mechanical innovation."

Vorwärts found that, "the idea of making Trebitsch-Lincoln into a comic and satirical captain in the farce of international profiteering is worth a fortune. Leo Lania, who had the courage to do this, has rendered German drama as great a service as Schiller with *William Tell* and *The Maid of Orleans (Jungfrau von Orleans)*. The play, the director and the actors provided a more interesting spectacle than anything we have seen in Piscator's theater to date. It was more theatrical and more lively than last winter. The message was not overloaded. The dramatist, the director and the actors are still experimenting, but it seems that they have moved a step toward the theater that we want, the theater whose techniques and convictions are related to our times and which is more than fatuous entertainment."

Kerr, Ihering and the critic in the *Rote Fahne* touched on the basic principles and problems of the subject.

"So go and see it: you will not be amused, but you may come out cleverer. That is the important thing. Let us have no more talk of poets."
Alfred Kerr

"An epic subject of gigantic proportions. The history of the beginnings of a war in speculation and big business. A small cause, a gigantic effect. In the hands of Scribe a glass of water.[4] Today the discovery of an oil well. In Scribe, private intrigue; today, the struggle between industrial groups. It is clear that differently constituted group conflicts cannot be presented with the techniques of plays of courtly intrigue.

"Lania's *Boom* has traveled the distance between a glass of water and an oil well. An excellent beginning. A beginning from nothing. A pantomime first sets out the theme; and epic commentary continues it. The style has emerged at the same time as the subject. An exemplary piece of cooperation between script writers, director, stage designers, actors. If the comedy had expanded from this point and had embraced ever-widening circles, then what would have emerged would not have been a masterpiece, or one peculiar high-quality performance but something more important: a blueprint for future stage works grouped around a complex, a ground plan for group plays, a scenario for collective fates.

"But then a gap appears. A similar process to the recent Eisenstein film.[5] The times cry out for the epic treatment of major topical subjects, the theater and the cinema reorganize; they revitalize their modes of expression. But the old stage and film conventions demand their rights and impede the new beginnings with their old conventions. Piscator's production is the most solid thing he has done this season."

Herbert Ihering

"There can be no question that the problem approached here is a thousand times more important, a thousand times more topical than the love-pangs of some beautiful soul, or the psychological dislocations of lyrical youths or other 'human problems' that are dealt with zealously and fully in bourgeois literature. It takes all the stupidity of bourgeois men of letters to find this subject "boring" and "sober," whereas we are supposed to be interested in discovering the feelings of boy X at killing his father or Lady Y after her seventeenth adultery, or of sex-killer Z as he goes about his business.

"All this is funny, gripping, colorful, lively. All this has a healthy, biting sharpness: sulphuric acid which eats into the oily pacifist phrases and the evangelical messages of the League of Nations, and unmasks the swindle and unscrupulousness of the capitalist system with grotesque sharpness. From these elements and in this play something like a witty political caricature with a touch of opera and revue could emerge if only . . .

4. Eugène Scribe (1791–1861), prolific Parisian writer of well-made conversation pieces, his best-known the comedy, *A Glass of Water (Un Verre d'Eau)*, to which Ihering alludes.

5. Shortly before reviewing *Boom* in the *Berliner Börsen-Courier* (4.11.28), Ihering had reviewed Eisenstein's *Ten Days That Shook the World* (4.3.28), in which he also discerned artistic regression. The intrusion of official historiography made it "a pathos-laden celebration rather than an epic work of art."

"If only the theme: struggle for oil, gigantic imperialist conflicts, basis for the coming world war, were not so great, so comprehensive and so shattering that whenever Lania and Piscator attempt to come to grips with it their creative control breaks down!

"So what emerges is: one cannot capture decisive problems of today's world in a plot whose conception has a touch of the operetta. This is the decisive point."

Rote Fahne, Berlin, April 12, 1928

Boom ran for no more than four weeks to dwindling audiences. The end of the first stage of my theater began to announce itself.

INTRODUCTION

The Piscator-Bühne Studio was set up in October, 1927, to provide a framework within which the techniques of political theater could be explored and developed. It offered theory courses and practical exercises. The former were nominally under Piscator's supervision and covered various aspects of acting and staging. The classes were conducted by senior members of the company and were open to the whole company as well as to interested outsiders. According to the Studio's progress report at the beginning of December Frl. Wellhöner's voice class and Erwin Kalser's stage-craft had begun, whereas the classes of stars like Tilla Durieux and Alexander Granach had not, and there are no other records of how this side of the Studio developed, apart from Franz Jung's jaundiced account in *Der Torpedokäfer*, where he suggests the top actors turned a blind eye to the Studio's activities, in particular physical training. For the practical exercises the Studio was initially split into three groups: an experimental production unit to stage Jung's *Homesickness (Heimweh)* and Sinclair's *Singing Jailbirds*, a fairy tale research unit, and a political demonstration unit. The organization was informal and members moved freely from one unit to another; members of all groups were involved in the two productions, and it was Busch and Lindtberg from the second unit who eventually performed in a Max Hölz demonstration. To Piscator's regret, play production came to dominate the Studio's activities and by the end of the season it had shown four productions in public.

The first was *Homesickness*, which was presented as a matinee at the Nollendorfplatz on January 8, 1928. It was directed by Leonhard Steckel (1901–71), an actor who was to have a distinguished career after 1933 in Zurich, where he was the first German Galileo and the first Puntila in Brecht's *Galileo* (1943) and *Baron Puntila and his Man Matti* (1947), respectively, as well as director of, among others, Brecht, Frisch and Dürrenmatt. *Homesickness*, in four acts, showed four situations involving "homeless people." A local girl dances with a Malayan in a Rotterdam bar, pleading for "one more night." When she sits down, exhausted, he dances on, alone and impassive. A phonograph blares. Three sailors brawl. Blackout. Lights up on sailor holding unconscious Malayan. Blackout. Girl cries out, "Rudolf." Body falls. Girl laughs shrilly. Sounds of running, panting. Sailor, "I've got you this time . . . "

Sound of window shattering. "Light falls in streams." End of act. In act 2 Rudolf, the European manager of a tropical copra station, passes his mistress, Lina, to his successor Jan, then tries in act 3 to arrange for the reluctant geisha Wong to come back to Europe with him. Back at the bar in act 4, the barman, alone, converses with voices off, among them Lina. Was he the one who abandoned her in Sydney, where Rudolf has told us he picked her up?

It is hard to see what these scenes from desperate affairs in foreign parts could offer the Piscator-Bühne, and F. Engel observed that Jung had "more of a feel for decorative visual, and sensitive acoustic effects than for creating people." *(Berliner Tageblatt,* 1.9.28) The noises off—chains, sirens, monsoon rains, an accordion—reminded him of Marinetti.

Jung had ideas of injecting exotic color into his script:

> "The action of the play is less important, just enough to make it comprehensible. A sailor, whom we meet again later in Hamburg, drifts from port to port toward home. . . . At his ports of call the characters speak different languages, and I had engaged Russian, Mongolian, Indian and Mexican actors, mostly extras from the film studios, to speak their own languages through the German dialogue. The theme was homesickness, emptiness. There were to be variety acts, a dance troupe, a Japanese sword dance, Chinese jugglers, a male quartet and a soapbox orator from Hyde Park as interludes. Outside the theater a military band, inside a quartet singing Schubert's *Heimweh* with Eichendorff's lyrics. During the play muted loudspeakers would play 'I'll Be Loving You, Always.' There were to be other little provocations, like advice to the women to try free love."

Jung places the blame for the play's failure on Piscator and his aides who, he says, at the last minute cut the exotic extras, the miscellaneous acts and the provocative touches. The critics made little sense of the one-hour performance. Ihering observed that homesickness was a private emotion and had no place on the committed stage. Only Heartfield's set attracted favorable comment. The proscenium arch was filled by a projection screen with a small aperture into which box sets were revolved—a waterfront bar could thus be embedded in a projection of crumbling dockside houses, or a South Seas hut in waving palms *(Photos 93 & 94)*.

The second production was Upton Sinclair's *Singing Jailbirds,* an anticapitalist play based on the California marine workers' strike in 1923. Red Adams, leader of the "Industrial Workers of the World," dies from police brutality in jail. Realistic scenes with his interrogation and trial and the workers' response are punctuated by his fevered dreams, flashbacks to the experiences which made him a union man. His martyrdom steels the workers' resolve. In the background workers and prisoners intermittently chant socialist songs with the audience joining in. For the finale the audience sings the workers' anthem:

"Solidarity for ever!
Solidarity for ever!
Solidarity for ever
And the union makes us strong!"

Piscator failed to get the workers' organizations to provide him with the (unpaid) massed choir which would have made the play effective agitation, and the production which opened at the Lessing-Theater on March 1 was flat and monotonous; even Edmund Meisel's music failed to excite. Traugott Müller's two-tier set and the use of film by Ernst Lönner, the director, were derivative and mechanical in the worst sense (Photos 78–80), whereas, as we have seen, the sets for Piscator's major productions crystallized the idea of each play in a telling mechanical image. Red Adams was played by Alexander Granach with cool precision. The play went on as a stopgap while Boom was being rehearsed and failed to attract Piscator's public to the Lessing-Theater. For the normal audiences there, who were accustomed to polished, intellectually respectable entertainment, it was a crude offering and had to be taken off after ten days.

Erich Mühsam's Judas was produced at the Nollendorfplatz on April 29 for the author's fiftieth birthday. Mühsam (1878–1934) was a radical publicist and had organized a munitions workers' strike in Munich in January, 1918, and was active alongside Ernst Toller and Gustav Landauer in organizing the Munich Soviet. Like Toller he was sentenced to fifteen years in jail, and it was there that he wrote Judas, which was based on the 1918 strikes. Mühsam died in Oranienburg concentration camp.

The Judas of the play is a composer, Raffael Schenk, who has his best friend, a pacifist professor, arrested when he needs an incident to inflame the workers' feelings. Their revolt is suppressed by arms, and he shoots himself. It was a straightforward, naturalistic piece, out of date by 1928, but with a direct message which was brought out by Leopold Lindtberg's clear, spare, unsentimental direction. (A year later Lindtberg also directed Mühsam's Sacco and Vanzetti, with Ernst Busch as Vanzetti, for the November Gruppe which had been formed by Alexander Granach.) Ihering praised the workmanlike unity and dedicated spirit of this production, necessary encouragement for the company which was in financial trouble by now. An attempt to revive *Judas* in June after the collapse of the Piscator-Bühne flopped.

The Studio's final production was a late-night performance of *The Holy War (Der heilige Krieg)* by Otto Rombach (b. 1904) at the Nollendorfplatz on May 22. Felix Gasbarra opened the proceedings with a speech on the aims of the Studio, which he saw as a laboratory for new acting and directing, and for the exploration of new subjects. Then came the play which Rombach describes in his memoirs (*Vorwärts, rückwärts, meine Spur,* 1974) :

> " . . . a lady who needed money engaged a former lieutenant as a tourist guide to the battlefield. . . . He describes tank warfare, and a tank rolls on. . . . Tourists arrive and he recounts how he knocked out a tank with a grenade as it came out of the smoke screen. He clambers on the tank and it all comes back. . . . Terror. He urges pacifism. . . . New tourists support him. Another argues, but he seems to triumph. . . . "

At the crucial point, when he seemed to triumph, the curtain failed to fall, and when it did the audience loitered, unsure whether that could possibly be all. It was, and the reviews were impatient and devastating.

All four plays, though they dealt with proletarian figures, were restricted in scope and opened up none of the wider economic and social issues which were the main thrust of Piscator's work, so the Studio's work broke no new ground, though it was good for the younger members' morale. And, of course, in the long run it pointed the way to the Dramatic Workshop, which Piscator founded in 1938 in New York.

XXI
THE YEAR OF THE STUDIO

The idea of having a Studio had almost become reality at the Volks-bühne, and now that we had a theater of our own it was implemented as a matter of course. As it was first conceived it was to be called the Young Volksbühne and was to be an activist cell within the Volksbühne. In our own house conditions were rather different. Our theater itself now fulfilled the function that was to be allocated to the Studio in the framework of the Volksbühne. So I now felt that the Studio's primary job was in the field of script editing. It was not to be expected that the trainee managers and directors would develop our technical or political principles faster than our main theater, which was experimental in every particular. What was expected of them was that they would be able to work out scripts in terms of stage techniques. The advantage of a studio in such a situation was that it was not inhibited by any material considerations, nor by the calls of the public nor the exigencies of our program of evening productions.

The Studio was conceived as a study group which would learn mainly from its own work. In the press the Studio was allocated the task of developing a new style of acting and trying out new methods of staging:

On the First Studio Performance at the Piscator-Bühne

"Erwin Piscator's generous idea of attaching a studio to his theater has nothing in common with the earlier experimental stages of Reinhardt and others. The difference in this workshop stage is that Reinhardt tried to establish young, untried authors, regardless of the message or political line of their work, whereas Piscator has set up his Studio on the principle that each play is an experiment intended to show where the beginnings of a new drama are to be found. At the same time he is committed to experimental acting and staging.

"Abandoned is the histrionic stylization of the role (the subjective approach) which is still usual today. In its place the objective exploration of the role (objective approach). In this way the danger of vapid, mechanical performances, the abuse of 'personal signatures' will be avoided."

This was in part correct, for it was intended that the Studio should take up any new ideas that might emerge intuitively or fortuitously during rehearsals in the main theater and turn them into a "school" style. It was not a matter of drilling imitators, but of taking any valuable developments we might chance upon and setting them down in a fully developed form once they had been submitted to a process of repetition and experiment.

On the Question of Style

Never in any of my productions did I allow myself to be governed by a particular style in the aesthetic sense of the concept. Style was always a secondary consideration for me at any given moment, and I was always concerned to get the most—that is, the optimum objective impact—out of any effect that the subject seemed to offer. (An effect which should, if the subject has been well-chosen, be identical with the political effect.) I would utilize any means I could to achieve such effects, intensifying theatrical means and bringing in other means from outside the theater. It was inevitable that in the course of time a characteristic manner of handling these means should develop, and a "style" should evolve. Many people confused the style with the means and called it "technical," but many recognized, quite rightly, that the style was inseparably linked with our basic political principle, and that "the idea produced the appropriate style."

". . . Technical devices as a mode of expression. . . . In this polytechnical framework the most modern media of expression are put to work. . . . They come from the sphere of the semiartistic and of the demimuses: there are fragments and seminal ideas from the film, from the revue, from dance, from jazz, from the loudspeaker. But whereas these sub-arts previously served the realm of amusement, here they are sobered up, objectified, purified: arranged by the organizing hand according to a higher principle, the idea."

Bernhard Diebold, *The Piscator Drama*

It was, of course, agreed in advance that the Studio should not view its task from a formal aesthetic point of view, but that the motive force in its work should be the will to politics. Oddly enough, the Studio was politically less committed than the Piscator-Bühne. It is difficult to find an explanation for this, unless one is prepared to accept the notion that young people lack political maturity and readily fall victim to a serious overestimation of formal concepts.

The Studio brought out four productions in the course of the season (Franz Jung: *Homesickness*, Upton Sinclair: *Singing Jailbirds*, Otto Rombach: *The Holy War*, Erich Mühsam: *Judas*).

At first I considered public performances of Studio work to be of no importance. The preparations, the work on the play seemed more important than the finished product. But my views changed. I have no reproaches to make to individuals or groups. I know myself how regular performances drain one's energy, and I know that the Studio's gradual development suffered in this way, and that no one was to blame. But it also seems to me that the students and beginners were more interested in appearing in a role in front of the press than in the basic reality of working and learning. The same goes for the writers and everybody else concerned.

To come to the plays. *Homesickness* had been chosen in response to a suggestion from the management. Franz Jung was one of the earliest to try out revolutionary effects in his plays. The Proletarisches Theater had been responsible for the production of his first plays. We expected much of him, but he was an unsettled character and flitted from one thing to another, setting up strange office enterprises, managing match factories, dabbling in journalism and business deals, all of which prevented him from reaching maturity. We were vaguely in contact with him all through the years. His mining drama *Annemarie* had, at my instigation, been accepted by the Volksbühne for a matinee performance. My depature from the Volksbühne put an end to that prospect. Now that I had a theater of my own available, I felt obligated to give him a chance. The play itself was alien to me. All the plays he had written in the interim— *Business Deals (Geschäfte)*, *Legend (Legende)* and *Homesickness* were the products of his decline and everything in them hinged on vague gestures, incomplete sentences and half-spoken words.

You had the impression of someone moving his lips to utter his last thoughts without producing an audible word. It came as a great blow to me to hear Jung explaining the meaning of *Homesickness*, and pointing out what meant most to him.

"When a production is given on the stage it is essential to put aside stylized sets and achieve the closest possible approximation to photographic reality. In *Homesickness*, I have attempted to loosen the traditionally rigid manner in which the emotional content of the dramatic presentation is communicated to the audience. Tension and relief must grip the audience directly, without necessarily being built up cumulatively in the course of the action. To achieve this end we must explore new modes of presentation (Chinese actors instead of German ones) and emphasize the use of rhythmic transitions involving mime and music, among other things.

"The play is not to be seen in the light of normal dramatic values, and it offers an opportunity of fulfilling some of the aims of the Piscator Studio as stated above."

Franz Jung

For the audience and the representatives of the press it was an easy matter to stand up at the end, shake their heads and declare the Studio's first experiment a failure. For us, the important thing was to have confronted Jung with the realities of the theater once again (and for this reason we had allowed him a completely free hand with the actors and the director); the result—if there was any—could emerge only with time.

This is not to say that the performance of *Homesickness* had no positive qualities. Steckel, who directed it, had placed the decor and the technical arrangements entirely in the hands of John Heartfield, who achieved excellent results with projections which enabled him to work with the kind of photographic material he knew so well. In the final estimate, the effect of the performance was aesthetic and nothing more. This proved that the means I had devised, collected from a variety of sources and put together, to achieve political effects, failed to work when they were not directed to the right end, even at the stage when they were beginning to add up to a "style." So it was precisely in *Homesickness* that I recognized that any attempted reforms that did not emanate from a central concept, from a world view or from a political will, would be utterly misguided.

"When he chose Franz Jung's *Homesickness* as the opening production for his Studio, Erwin Piscator remained loyal to an author who deserves a chance to experiment: even on the days before he made his reputation, when he was producing proletarian theater in the district of Wedding and elsewhere, he put on Jung's tendentious proletarian play *The Kanakans (Die Kanaker)*. With the use of crude homemade and yet utterly gripping resources. He expanded the folkplay on the proletarian movement by inserting a dialogue between Wells and Lenin. As a dramatist

Jung has not developed. But Piscator has developed the principles of a new art of the theater on the basis of his world view and has left the primitive hints once indicated in Jung's *Kanakans* far behind. If the production set out to put Jung's dramatic production into perspective, then, leaving aside the clapping and booing of supporters and opponents, it achieved its aim."

Lutz Weltmann (*Das blaue Heft*, February 1, 1928)

The second play which I had planned to do back in the Volkstheater was Upton Sinclair's *Singing Jailbirds*. Here was a play with which we could test politically just how far we could go with revolutionary agitation in front of our specific audience, and what the effect would be. The play was unambiguous and had the kind of primitiveness which speaks out of the facts of life and is often more powerful than calculated formulations. It was based on the revolutionary songs of the American worker, and could be done with crowds. It was a play that I would have liked to direct myself. The preparations for *Boom* prevented this, so after some thought the direction was finally handed over to Ernst Lönner, a young assistant who had already staged the play in Vienna at the Sozialistisches Theater. From the very outset this play was prepared with an eye to an evening performance, since it was doubtful at this advanced point whether *Boom* could be ready on the appointed date. For this reason we cast it in part with actors who had only indirect links with the Studio, a measure which should be comprehensible in view of the huge costs of an evening at the Lessing-Theater which the play had to cover.

A special film was assembled for the play, but it was later found to be largely unnecessary.

Bernhard Diebold was not entirely wrong when he wrote (in the *Frankfurter Zeitung*, March 3, 1928):

"This time the film does not quite fit. Except at the start, when the screen provided a background of a huge crowd of 100,000 heads. That created space and an expanded world. Otherwise the film was mere decoration. *Ersatz décor.* Skyscrapers, then landscapes, then prison bars. But without much of the dramatic function it had had in *Hoppla, Such is Life!* or *Rasputin*. Or else with the banal function of a superfluous illustration, like a pseudo-Wagnerian leitmotif. Adams thinks of his wife—and the screen immediately gives us a "woman-motif." Or Adams in his delirium imagines there are rats in the jail—and the rat-motif promptly appears on the screen and wags its curly tail."

The other stage devices were also used too schematically. But this would have done no harm if the songs had really carried the play as I had imagined: a flood of song through the whole house, the auditorium drowned in song, rows of men posted everywhere, on the balconies, at the back of the orchestra, in the corridors. Unfortunately, the marshaling of these choirs was a total failure.

The play was agitation and it was supposed to have the effect of agitation. All the proletarian organizations should have felt that this performance was in their cause. Nothing seemed more natural than that they should contribute and help to make the performance into a piece of real propaganda for our idea. So we turned to a number of organizations like the Communist Party and the *Rote Frontkämpferbund* to supply us with two hundred comrades for the choirs for *Singing Jailbirds*. First of all the Trade Union Section of the Party declared, "It is contrary to the trade union principles of the Party to have unpaid workers taking part in theatrical performances." (Oddly enough, this principle was never mentioned when it was a matter of my doing a show for the Party.) After we had finally managed to overcome this hurdle, we were given letters of recommendation that were supposed to make the various organizations send us their members. Only a fraction of the two hundred we had asked for ever appeared. They started off by demanding the normal fee for their appearance. At this point we took on normal extras, but only in numbers that the theater could afford. These were the events that involved us in legal proceedings which spread our name as exploiters and profiteers throughout the entire press.

(In fact the seventy volunteers demanded fees which had not been arranged and could not be met, at least not in the financial state of our theater at that time. A rehearsal which was begun in a restaurant and continued in the theater was to be paid as two rehearsals, every evening rehearsal was to be paid at double the daytime rate. In addition to which they threatened to strike if we did not pay 5 marks instead of the 3.50 we had agreed on. They rejected an offer to call in a free trade union to arbitrate.)

The damage done to the production by the lack of huge choruses was considerable. The bourgeois press rejected the play almost unanimously, partly, no doubt, on political grounds. On the other hand, for all those who sensed the real world of torture and suffering behind the events on the stage, inadequately performed though they were, Alfred Kerr formulated the following pronouncement:

"Regardless of the artistic quality, you sense a way ahead. A desire for progress. A crank wrote this, a half-wit wrote it, a semiskilled writer wrote it . . . but a brother wrote it. We must be thankful to him."
Berliner Tageblatt, March 2, 1928

From this performance it emerged that for our theater a naïve, responsive proletarian public was essential, a public without preconceived ideas who would let the facts—the essentials of the events on the stage—get to them. And precisely this audience was missing, had to be missing to some extent, because it had no money to come to the theater. After fourteen days we had to take the play off because it was not covering costs. Since *Boom* was not yet ready we put *Hoppla, Such is Life!* on the repertoire again in the hope of recouping at least the running costs of the theater.

The Holy War (Der heilige Krieg), a play by Otto Rombach, a young writer from Frankfurt, proved a complete failure. The play was in the form of a monologue and dealt with the breakthrough of a fanatical rejection of war in an officer who is recruited by the industrious daughter of a capitalist as a tourist guide for the battlefields of France.

The basic idea was good, but it had not been developed in dramatic, scarcely even in coherent verbal terms. Even the mass march with red flags at the end could not conceal this. I had attended several rehearsals, but had purposely refrained from interfering with the work, because it was important to me that the Studio should learn by its own mistakes. And not only the Studio, but the author, too, who complained bitterly to us afterward because the play was not a success. A fundamental misunderstanding of what the Studio was all about.

The fourth play to be presented to the public as a Studio production was Erich Mühsam's *Judas*, which was performed for the author's fiftieth birthday. The latter was a play which used sound theatrical means, without any pretensions, to set the Judas problem in the context of the workers' movement, using characters drawn from the Munich Soviet.[1] A clear-cut, appealing production emerged. Voices in the press afterwards wondered why the play had not been included in the evening repertory long ago. I should like to point out here, with great personal respect and sympathy for Mühsam, who had shared imprisonment in Nieder-Schönfeld with Toller, and had written the play there, that the type of drama which an active political theater requires must, in my opinion, be based on quite different subjects and written in a different form. What we have here is the transference of an individual psychological problem, a spiritual conflict in spite of its political motivation,

1. The Bavarian Democratic and Socialist Republic was proclaimed on November 8, 1918, under Kurt Eisner. Eisner was assassinated in April, 1919, and the government left Munich. On April 7 the Independents set up a Soviet Republic which was brushed aside and replaced by a Communist Soviet Republic on April 9. This was in turn wiped out by the right-wing Free Corps, aided by Prussian and Württemberg troops. In the ensuing White Terror hundreds of workers, including all the Communist leaders, were summarily shot.

into the atmosphere of the movement. A drama in the traditional sense, a variation on an individual case. Mühsam will not fail to understand when I say that I think this is wrong. In his *Sacco and Vanzetti* he took a step forward in the one direction which I consider to be fruitful, toward a great historical subject. Political drama must, if it is to fulfill its pedagogic aim, make documentary evidence its point of departure, and not the individual. On the contrary, it must maintain the most impersonal, "objective" attitude to the characters in the subject, not in a neutral sense, but in the sense of a materialistic conception of history.

Projection for *Judas* (Director: Lindtberg; designer: Veli Samih)

Judas was so well received by the public that the Emergency Group decided to put it in the evening repertoire. Unfortunately their hopes of covering their running costs with it were mistaken. The takings were so small that the cast, amounting at this time to about sixty people, were paid no more than 4 marks each for ten days' acting.

As I said at the beginning, the idea of the Studio embraced more than just public performances. A timetable had been drawn up with fixed hours for voice lessons (Gustav Müller and Frl. Wellhöner), stage studies (Erwin Kalser), design (Traugott Müller), script editing (Gasbarra, Leo Lania), languages and general subjects (art, art history, literature and so on). I laid great stress on physical training for the members of the Studio, indeed for all members of the company. Fritz Sommer's training session was made compulsory. Muscular control, clear purposeful movements, such as sport alone can achieve, seemed to me to be essential accomplishments for the modern actor. I myself passionately love boxing, even if it is not exactly appropriate in my profession and sometimes leads to differences of opinion.

All in all, the first year of the Studio produced elements from which a systematically organized school, as we understood it, could have developed, had not the economic catastrophe brought all further work in our theater to an abrupt end.

Even so, the work of the Studio and the community of members was not without lasting effect. The "Young Actors' Group" which played in Berlin and then toured Germany with Lampel's *Revolt in the House of Correction (Revolte im Erziehungshaus)* had come into being in the Studio.[2] A play by Lampel *(Putsch)* had been in the course of preparation at the Studio, and *Revolt* had been in our hands, but only at a time when the theater had virtually ceased to exist in practical terms.

Report of the Studio's Third Group

    I.   Speech Training
        Frl. Wellhöner's speech-training class takes place daily between 11:30 A.M. and 12:30 P.M., after the physical training lesson. Each student will have two sessions of two hours each week.
    II. Learning a Part and Company Work
        1. Frau Durieux, on the advice of her doctor, has withdrawn her offer to give instruction on how to learn a part.
        2. Herr Granach has promised to take a class, but has so far been prevented from doing so by hoarseness and film commitments. He would like to work on an older, well-known play (perhaps Wedekind) with the third group.
        3. Dr. Kalser's course (stagecraft) has begun. There have been two classes so far. At the suggestion of Dr. Kalser, older material (Strindberg, Wedekind, Chekhov) is being used. The group has doubts about the value of this work and wishes to be

---

2. Peter Martin Lampel (1894–1965) lived in a house of correction in order to write a report on the condition of incarcerated boys. The dramatized version aroused wide interest and led to reforms. Productions followed in London, Paris and Warsaw. Its sequel, *Schoolboys (Pennäler)*, was staged in 1929 after the police had banned his other Zeitstück, *Poison Gas over Berlin*.

advised whether this form of teaching is what was intended under the heading "experimental study of a part."

III. Production of a Play

The search for a play has not yet produced a final result. The last play to come up for consideration was *The Barber of Rosslagen (Der Barbier von Rosslagen)*, a comedy by Wellenkamp. Director: Lindtberg.

IV. Members Engaged on Group I Productions

Those involved are:

Greif and Samih in *Homesickness*, Frank, Löbinger, Kostendi, Greif, Oberländer in *Singing Jailbirds*.

V. Membership

Obscurities in the membership and official and unofficial changes in the constitution of the membership have moved the group organizers to propose that the conditions of membership should be regularized. The organizers suggest that in doing this the following rules should be laid down:

1. That only members who have given the impression in interview that they will benefit from courses related to acting and performance should be allowed into such courses.

2. That visiting members (i.e., those not under contract) shall either be given full membership or excluded entirely, and that their membership in the Studio should not depend on whether or not they happen to be appearing as extras.

December 1, 1927, signed:

Heinz Greif, Heinz Oberländer, Lotte Löbinger (Group Leaders).

Progress Report of Group II up to December 1, 1927

1. Preparatory work on the projected performance of a fairy tale, which was to be the group's first task.

2. Participation of some of the members (Busch, Genschow, Löhner, Weisse) in a performance of *Mother (Mutter)* as part of the tenth anniversary celebrations of the German Communist Party (KPD).

3. Participation of some of the members (Busch, Genschow, Lindtberg) at a matinee dedicated to Max Hölz on November 27.

4. From Group II, Dammert, Busch, Lindtberg, Weisse are involved in rehearsals for *Jailbirds*.

5. After a number of plays had been read and discussed it was decided that Group II would use P. M. Lampel's *Putsch* for its first performance; the cast which has been submitted provides every member of the group with a worthwhile task.

6. In the course of the same discussion Herr Haenel was appointed to the group's working committee in place of Herr Löhner, who had withdrawn.

7. The classes in physical training were attended regularly by members of Group II. The matter of the voice training has not yet been cleared up.

For the working committee: Haenel, Lindtberg, Lilo Dammert

INTRODUCTION

In the first half of the season the Piscator-Bühne's energies had been concentrated on two major productions, *Hoppla* and *Rasputin*, and the company went into 1928 on a wave of popularity. The Studio's first production, Jung's *Homesickness*, was shown at a matinee on January 8. *Schwejk* opened on January 23 to critical and public acclaim and box-office receipts reached record levels, which for a time masked the fact that production costs had already outstripped income. The company's fortunes were soon to change. On the assumption that *Schwejk* was set for an extended run, Otto Katz persuaded Piscator to lease the Lessing-Theater from March 1. Shortly afterward Pallenberg announced that he would be leaving *Schwejk* on April 12, so Piscator needed two new productions in quick succession. The first night of *Boom* was postponed, and the Studio production of Upton Sinclair's *Singing Jailbirds*, which had been prepared as a stopgap, went on at the Lessing-Theater on March 1. It was taken off after fourteen days as a loss. *Hoppla*, which had just returned from a successful tour, was substituted, but failed to attract the public. *Boom* eventually opened on April 10, and it too ran at a loss. On April 6 Erich Mühsam's *Judas* was staged by the Studio at the Nollendorfplatz.

Meanwhile Karlheinz Martin had been engaged to direct Jean Richard Bloch's *The Last Emperor* at the Nollendorfplatz. The play was a historical romance in the French vein, in which Ihering discerned traces of Eugène Scribe and Edmond Rostand. Prince Roger is recalled from a cruise to take the throne on the death of his father; he tries to democratize the regime, but founders on the opposition of a conservative clique which resents his illegitimate birth. Any resemblance to the fall of the Hohenzollerns, which might have been suggested by the title, was fanciful and oblique. Martin had an all-star cast and employed Piscator's techniques skillfully—Prince Roger's eye fell on the picture of an old flame, and a filmed flashback to the affair in question came up on the screen—but to no political purpose. The result was a smooth, routine production which would have done credit to one of the more ambitious commercial managements, but was out of place at the Piscator-Bühne, where it opened on April 14. The critics dismissed it as imitation Piscator, and it was a financial failure.

At this point the company's financial problems came to a head. Negotiations to extend the lease of the Theater am Nollendorfplatz for a further four years were broken off because the necessary 100,000-mark guarantee could not be found. A 120,000-mark loan had to be raised to cover wages and salaries. *Boom* and *The Last Emperor* ran at a loss until the beginning of May, when the tax authorities filed a bankruptcy suit. The Lessing-Theater was subcontracted to Emil Lind for a summer season, while Erwin Kalser, one of Piscator's actors, staved off the end briefly at the Nollendorfplatz with Marcel Achard's *Marlborough Goes to War*. The play was a boulevard comedy debunking war and heroics in the figure of the Duke of Marlborough (1650–1722), who is immortalized in the French folk song "Marlbrough [sic] s'en va-t-en guerre," which give the piece its title. Kalser had already presented the drama for the Volksbühne at the Theater am Schiffbauerdamm in March, 1926. At the end of May the Theater am Nollendorfplatz was also handed over to Lind, who opened on June 1 with a military comedy, Roda Roda's *Headquarters on the Hill (Feldherrnhügel)*. Lind used Piscator's actors, the theaters remained in Piscator's name, and his cut from Lind's profits went toward paying the Piscator-Bühne's debts until he gave up the leases on June 15. Some of his actors then formed the Actors' Emergency Group, a collective which was not responsible for its former employer's debts, and revived the Studio production of Mühsam's *Judas* in an effort to keep political theater alive, but the public, bourgeois and proletarian alike, ignored them.

Writing eighteen months after the collapse of his dream, Piscator is still too involved to resist the temptation to blame the company's failure on the inadequacies of Otto Katz's financial control. If this seems distasteful it is worth remembering that Piscator had contacted his friend Willi Münzenberg after the collapse and had arranged a job for Katz in Münzenberg's book business. In 1930 the tax authorities tried to recover 100,000 marks of the Piscator-Bühne's unpaid taxes from Katz, and Münzenberg sent him to Moscow where he worked in the film section of Meschrabpom. After a nomadic life in the communist cause, Katz was executed after a show-trial in Czechoslovakia as a Trotskyist in 1952.

XXII
THE COLLAPSE

I now come to a chapter which marks one of the stations of the cross borne by a reluctant theater director. I say reluctant because I never had any ambition to fill this post but was always forced to do so unwillingly under the pressure of circumstances. The causes of the collapse can be seen from various points of view, depending on one's attitude toward this theater. It goes without saying that in attempting to explain these causes in the following lines I have tried to keep my considerations purely objective. But human errors and external circumstances go hand in hand. Today, separated from events by eighteen months, I can see how closely one thing is tied up with another, and this makes it difficult to weigh the guilt or innocence of single individuals exactly.

"Berlin's youngest and undoubtedly most active theater, the Piscator-Bühne on the Nollendorfplatz, is in financial difficulties. The fact that the public is only discovering this now does not mean that these difficulties have only just arisen. On the contrary, these problems have existed for a long time and were on the way to being solved. Promising negotiations with new financial backers were in progress. Then demands for unpaid taxes led to bankruptcy proceedings, and a meeting of all the company's creditors was called.

"The meeting of creditors decided that the state of the Piscator-Bühne Company Limited should be examined by a committee of assessors chosen by the meeting, and that the bankruptcy proceedings should be withdrawn. It now looks as if the bankruptcy proceedings have in fact been terminated. The unpaid taxes amount to only 53,000 marks of a total deficit of 450,000 marks. Against this the assets amount to 223,000 marks."

(Press notice)

Let us first examine my personal mistakes. It is true that the productions which I directed during this one season consumed vast sums of money.

In each of these productions we were working on details of staging until the very last second. It took vast amounts of lighting, raw material, apparatus and staff to cope with artistic demands which the political basis of my work forced me to make. Everything was experimental, an exploration of unknown territory. Experiments cost money. In the theater, just as in science or technology, vast sums of money must be invested before any results are produced. Should I be blamed for setting my sights too high? For me there was only one decisive principle: our shows had to be staged as effectively, as trenchantly and as propagandistically as possible.

During the first six months everything seemed to point not only to an artistic and political but also to a financial success. I asked for the box office report every evening, and every evening I was given satisfactory information. The public crowded around the box office at the Nollendorftheater. The "Sold Out" sign became a familiar sight. *Schwejk* produced record takings of 7,000 to 9,000 marks each evening. There was nothing to suggest that the theater budget was not balanced. I had absolute confidence in Otto Katz, my business manager, to whom I had given all the rights and responsibilities which I myself had, so that I would have a man by my side looking after the venture as if it were his own. In addition, my work on the stage absorbed my time so completely that I had neither the opportunity nor the energy to examine financial matters in any detail.

So I did not oppose the takeover of a second theater for which Katz was pressing. I personally had no desire to have a second theater, but I allowed myself to be persuaded for two reasons. At the beginning of the season we had offered a season ticket for seven separate performances and had undertaken to offer the Special Sections of the Volksbühne at least five plays. But by February we had staged only three productions, and we felt it was impossible to predict how long *Schwejk* would run. We had already taken off *Hoppla* and *Rasputin* at the height of their success to keep faith with our season-ticket holders. We did not want to do the same again with *Schwejk*.

303

In addition to this, we had certain artistic obligations to Frau Durieux, apart from the fact that she had earned our gratitude by making our whole enterprise possible. The need to display her talents in a major role became more and more pressing. To this end, Lania's *Boom* with its central female role seemed an admirable choice.

The misgivings about the financial viability of the theater which had plagued me at the outset had been dispelled by our unexpected success. On the strength of the arguments adduced, I agreed, very hesitantly and not without certain premonitions, to the takeover of the Lessing-Theater.

Events followed one another quickly and fatefully.

Schwejk is running at the Nollendorftheater and *Boom* is scheduled to open on March 1. We hope that Pallenberg will continue to play *Schwejk* through the summer or at the very least until the end of May. Instead, Pallenberg declares that he can place himself at our disposal only until April 12 because of his proposed tour of South America. This creates an emergency in the Theater am Nollendorfplatz and forces us to produce a new play. It is *The Last Emperor* by Jean Richard Bloch, and I am forced to entrust the direction to a guest director, Karlheinz Martin.

Boom opens on April 10 instead of March 1. The adaptation has taken four weeks longer than had been estimated. Since our lease starts on March 1, we have no choice: we have to get a show rehearsed and on the stage at the Lessing-Theater. Our choice is *Singing Jailbirds*, a play by Upton Sinclair which has been rehearsed in the Studio and can be considered to have been prepared, in a sense, for an evening production. It is a failure. After fourteen days we have to take it off and bring back *Hoppla, Such is Life!*, which, we thought, might not yet have exhausted its appeal in Berlin. This too proves to be an error. Nevertheless we have to keep it in the repertoire until *Boom* is ready to open.

There is feverish activity in both theaters. The exhaustion of the older members of the company is compounded by the halfhearted contributions of our newer staff members. Under these circumstances we no longer have any faith in Bloch's play. The losses at the Lessing-Theater pile up like an avalanche. At the same time *Schwejk* is no longer the success it was at the outset. The takeover of the Lessing-Theater is in part to blame; the public think we have abandoned the Nollendorftheater. We have only one card left and everything is staked on it: *Boom*, an ominous title for this situation.

The Last Emperor eats up enormous resources. Martin has the best available cast, Frieda Richard, Sybille Binder, Ernst Deutsch,

Albert Steinrück; in addition to this, huge sets. A "shutter" which enables us to expand or contract the stage opening like the aperture in a camera. Films are shot especially for the play. A projector throws "stormy seas" on the screen. Martin has a perfect right to all this. Why should he not use my techniques—and who would be so bold as to refuse a guest director the facilities which he cannot do without himself? Otto Katz's proverbially amiable smile begins to look somewhat chilly. We still manage to meet all our current obligations. But what an effort.

On April 10, *Boom* opens.

On April 14, *The Last Emperor.*

Neither is a success at the box office. Hoping for a change of fortune, we keep both plays running until the beginning of May. The budget for the two plays amounts to 7,000 marks each evening. Our last resources are mobilized. Then the income tax authorities institute bankruptcy proceedings. For 16,000 marks.

"The *Piscator-Bühne* was organized with a mixed system of ticket distribution: there were the season-ticket holders, there were the Special Sections of the Volksbühne and there was the public sale of tickets at the box office; the season tickets and the Volksbühne were supposed to provide an insurance against failure and the public sale of tickets was to be the main source of income. But it turned out that these systems were not compatible with one another. The theater's expenses, the high rent, the actors' salaries, the technical apparatus demanded that any success should be exploited in the long run. The season tickets and the Special Sections of the Volksbühne constituted an obstacle to long runs. The season-ticket holders and the Special Sections who had been able to see only three plays at the Nollendorfplatz by March had to be satisfied, so the Lessing-Theater was taken over. A fateful error. The Piscator-Bühne was plunged into a crisis, not least by the organizational measures which were intended to stave off such a crisis.

"These effects were made more serious because Piscator as an artist worked in terns of experiment, not in terms of results. Piscator's method of feeling his way ahead and building up each drama afresh from the foundations took time, peace and lengthy consideration, all of which was in conflict with the two-theater system. A theater which is based on a large number of different actors and a wide range of plays, which offers a varied and colorful repertoire, can afford to expand. But a theater which is based on an idea, which is working out the fundamental dramatic theory for that idea and has not overcome the lack of suitable plays, cannot afford to expand. In the Lessing-Theater the Piscator-Bühne had set up in opposition to itself!"

Herbert Ihering

305

The events which followed no longer had anything to do with the idea on which the Piscator-Bühne was based. They were only emergency measures to keep the venture going if possible. The Lessing-Theater was taken over by Emil Lind, who kept it going with an English detective play *(Number Seventeen)* with Paul Graetz in the lead.

We kept the Nollendorftheater going until May 31 with *Marlborough Goes to War* by Marcel Achard, directed by Erwin Kalser. Then we turned this house over to Emil Lind as well, who staged *Headquarters on the Hill*. With that the Piscator-Bühne had for the moment ceased to exist. As a last flicker of the old idea, the *Notgemeinschaft der Schauspieler* (Actor's Emergency Group), which was quickly formed, put on the production of *Judas* by Erich Mühsam which we had prepared for his fiftieth birthday. This could do nothing to alter the fate of our theater.

How much of the guilt was my own and how much should be ascribed to circumstances?

A certain change in the mood of the bourgeois public had taken place since *Singing Jailbirds*. This change of mood was connected with the image projected by the Piscator-Bühne. We had published a particular and perhaps rather too extensive program in the autumn of 1927. The beginning of our theater had been regarded by the public as the prelude to a new era in the theater. To the extent that this was objective and based on an accurate assessment of our situation, there was no possible objection. However—and this is where the crime began which was commited against our venture—we had to bear the burden of being a sensation from which one novelty after another was expected. This meant that our theater, which needed a period of placid development after the first stormy beginnings, came under public pressure so strong that no undertaking could have withstood it. I must confess that I as director was unable to withstand this pressure. I could see quite clearly how the machinery of the Berlin first-night system was gradually distorting the idea behind our theater. It could almost have been mathematically calculated that the public would turn its back on us in disappointment as soon as the sensation palled, for our public, after all, had no interest in the explanation of the depths of our problem.

"It was to be expected that the capitalist snobs from the West End of Berlin who had at first poured enthusiastically into the theater would quickly abanbon it. For these people, the 'theater of conviction' was nothing more than a literary slogan. Anybody who puts his faith in this sector of society is lost. Every venture which ever relied on its supposed literary aspirations quickly perished; Berthold Viertel's excellent *Truppe* lasted one season; the Schauspielertheater (Actor's Theater) and the Dramatische Theater (Dramatic Theater) had to close up shop very soon after they were founded. The bell had tolled for the Piscator-Bühne when the needs of the sensation-hungry public for a nice moral slap in the face had been satisfied. The proletarian public, even if they had filled every last seat in the house, could never have supported such an expensive venture. The kind of entrance money that these dispossessed sectors of society could offer would never have enabled Piscator to stage one of his big productions; at least not in this theater."

Welt am Montag, June 18, 1928

Although many people consider that *Boom* was my most mature and balanced production, I cannot help feeling that it was at that psychological moment that the bourgeois public came to the theater with demands which could not be fulfilled, or at least with their minds made up that only a stupendous new trick from the director would induce them to surrender their reserve. But *Boom* was a play in which we were concerned with the illumination of the subject, international economic relations and the problem of oil, to a greater degree than any of my previous productions. I had absolutely no extravagant ideas about the production and if a new form of stage construction did emerge, it grew organically out of the subject. I can well imagine that a certain sector of the public was disappointed by the balanced handling of the technical apparatus such as film and loudspeakers, and did not feel that the appearance of a live donkey on the stage was an adequate substitute for my failure to remove the roof of the Lessing-Theater or produce President Hindenburg on the stage in person. In fact, I could have accepted this change of mood. It would have meant that we had left the overheated atmosphere of sensationalism behind us. On the other hand, the departure of this particular sector of the audience constituted the most serious possible financial threat to the undertaking.

If the bourgeoisie finally felt that its desire for sensations had been disappointed, the spokesman of the proletariat blamed the theater because its attitude did not seem to them to be revolutionary enough.

I have already explained elsewhere that in the context of the realities of the capitalist economic system you cannot manage a theater exclusively in terms of the aims the directors have set themselves, and that the theater cannot make itself independent of its public in matters of production, since it is in the final estimate supported by cash taken at the door. There can be very few people who know me and my previous development and yet deny the strength of my will and the honesty of my convictions. But will and convictions alone are not enough to keep a theater true to a particular principle at all times if it depends on the money taken at the box office. There were critics on the Left who constantly reproached us for deviating from the straight revolutionary line, no doubt purely because of their common interest in the cause of the Piscator-Bühne; but these critics forgot that, for purely economic reasons, our repertoire had to take the bourgeoisie into consideration as well as the advanced sections of the proletariat. The lengths I went to to make sure that my work was unassailable from the political point of view is demonstrated by the case of *Boom*, where we preferred to close the theater for three days, which meant the loss of about 20,000 marks, rather than stage a production which might have proved even marginally harmful to interests of the revolutionary movement. If these spokesmen had made every possible effort to bring wide circles of the proletariat into our theater, then they would have been fully justified in demanding a more radical approach from the theater. But in this regard we were let down all along the line. We had gone as far as was financially possible to enable the proletariat to come to the theater. Are we to blame if they failed to make better use of the opportunity? Even a play like *Judas*, which was of some interest to the proletariat and for which the tickets were not more expensive than for any better-class movie, could not pay even the modest expenses of the Emergency Group, because the theater remained empty in spite of intensive advertising in all factories and organizations. This was the last experiment that the Piscator-Bühne made during that season, placing its trust in the solidarity of the masses of the workers.

Cartoon from the *Nachtausgabe*

There is no doubt that the reversal of the situation coincided with the acquisition of the Lessing-Theater. Taking on a second theater was the biggest error in the disposition of our resources that we could have committed. Nothing could be further from my intentions than to offer criticism which would cast a reflection on

Otto Katz's personal honesty or on his absolute dedication to the enterprise. There is only one thing I might blame him for—and he himself accepts this—namely, that he did not keep a close enough check on how the venture was progressing. There are very few people who are able to manage the commercial side of the theater. I know that in this particular branch of business there are innumerable operative factors which cannot all be taken into account all the time, so that the theater business is by nature a game of chance. I do not hesitate to admit that controlling my method of working was part of the business of controlling the whole enterprise. Great artistic ambitions mean equally great financial demands, grand experiments commit you to building in more and more devices to ensure success, and more and more items have to be added to the budget which has been agreed on. If the normal theater involves a heavy element of risk, this has to be doubled or trebled in the case of our theater; so the financial planning should have been twice or three times as careful and everything should not have been staked on success. Under no circumstances should an expansion of this kind have been undertaken at a time when, without my knowledge, expenditure had already outstripped income. It may even have seemed to Katz that experimentation was more important than financial viability. But he was the very man for whom the financial viability should have been more important, for he was responsible for the financial side, just as I was responsible for the experimental side. If, for example, I had been told in time what the true position of the enterprise was, I should never have agreed to take over the Lessing-Theater. As it was, I was left under the illusion that I had the most financially successful theater in Berlin right up to the very morning—I was busy working on *Boom* at the Theater am Nollendorfplatz—when I was told that wages and salaries could be met only by a personal loan on the next payday. At that moment I knew that the enterprise was financially doomed.

But other factors played their part. At this time we were on the brink of signing a contract which would have secured the Theater am Nollendorfplatz for us for four more years. To bring it into effect we would have had to put down a guaranty of 100,000 marks. The Theater am Nollendorfplatz had increased considerably in value during our season. It had become one of the important Berlin theaters again, and many directors felt it was worth bidding for. There had already been intermittent rumors in the press that the theater would be changing hands. We knew that the four-year contract that we were about to sign could be fulfilled only if we did very good business. But we had no alternative.

So at the moment when we needed all our working capital we were forced to put down this large sum if we were not to face the next year without a theater.

On June 15 I turned in the license. The Actors' Emergency Group took over from the Piscator-Bühne Co. Ltd. With the greatest personal sacrifice and with admirable discipline and devotion to duty, everybody worked on, even those who did not share our politics, to keep the venture going until its finances were cleared up.

Program for *Judas* with "Actors' Emergency Group" overprinted

Of course, we did not just let matters take their course without attempting to take countermeasures. The most pressing obligations could be met by taking up a loan of 100,000 marks. The theater's former backers had withdrawn, partly for personal reasons, and a new consortium was in the process of being formed. This consortium helped us to overcome the immediate crisis, but as a condition for putting the enterprise on a firm financial footing, it required us to make it viable using our own resources. By May 20 we had managed to pay wages and salaries in full, and in spite of a big actuarial deficit there was some hope of covering our working costs with the takings from *Number Seventeen* and *Headquarters on the Hill*.

The box-office success of both plays fluctuated greatly, but there seemed to be a pronounced upward tendency. *Headquarters* in particular did better every day. But the tax authorities felt unable to let our arrears of 16,000 marks run any longer, and opened bankruptcy proceedings. The financial structure which we had taken such pains to keep on an even keel began to rock. These proceedings and the meeting called by the creditors of the Piscator-Bühne had a catastrophic effect on business in both houses. It was as if ticket sales had been cut off. The new consortium insisted that the deficit be cleared before it could step in to help: under these circumstances, an impossible requirement. As a consequence we were forced to suggest that the actors should form an emergency group and we transferred the license to them. In conclusion it can be said that if we disregard those flaws which had their origin in the structure of the project or in matters outside our control, then all the errors we made in the second half of the season go back to one and the same source: the takeover of the Lessing-Theater. If *Boom* had come out as the successor to *Schwejk* at the Theater am Nollendorfplatz, in the wake of the first big successes, without the interlude of *Singing Jailbirds* and *Hoppla*, then it would certainly have run for six weeks with normal houses. We would have been able to prepare our next production at leisure without having to throw on one show after another in which we had little interest, merely to stay in business. The public would not have been halved, nor would our expenditures have been doubled; and the uncoordinated measures and excessive burden that was thrown on the leading members in our enterprise would have been avoided. Even the possibility of a flop could have been withstood more easily if we had limited ourselves to one theater.

INTRODUCTION

During the following season Piscator worked to set up a second Piscator-Bühne. His friend Felix Weil put up 150,000 marks and, with 50,000 marks from another source, he and Ludwig Klopfer, a man with years of experience in managing theaters in Berlin, set up a holding company whose purpose was to "run a Piscator-Bühne." An eight-month contract was signed and Piscator put down 30,000 marks as a deposit for the Komische Oper, an insignificant boulevard theater on the Friedrichstrasse (not to be confused with the postwar Komische Oper in the Behrenstrasse which housed Walther Felsenstein's celebrated opera productions). Then James Klein, the owner, died and the theater was auctioned. Piscator's company declined to bid and lost its deposit. Piscator, however, was then able to make an arrangement with Meinhard and Bernauer, the owners of the Theater am Nollendorfplatz, and on June 2, 1929, it was agreed that he could move in again, though the lease was to be in the name of Ludwig Klopfer. Piscator as an undischarged bankrupt was not eligible to hold it.

Piscator was aware that a revived Piscator-Bühne would not have the field of political theater to itself. Partly due to his own pioneering work the Zeitstück, or contemporary problem play, had caught on. Günther Weisenborn's *U-Boot S4*, a dramatization of the sinking of a U.S. submarine on prohibition duty nine months before, which had been intended for the Piscator-Bühne Studio, was staged by the Volksbühne. It followed up with Karl Kraus's *The Invincibles (Die Unüberwindlichen)*, which showed a recent case of corruption and investigative journalism in Vienna and set the seal on the development of the Zeitstück with H. J. Rehfisch and Wilhelm Herzog's *Die Affäre Dreyfus* (1930), which dealt with topical issues like anti-Semitism, caste prejudice and judicial precedures in historical framework. Barnowsky's Theater in der Königgrätzer Strasse produced H. J. Rehfisch's *The Gynecologist (Der Frauenarzt)* and took in P. M. Lampel's *Revolt in the House of Correction (Revolte im Erziehungshaus)* after its successful Sunday matinee premiere at the Thalia Theater by the Gruppe Junger Schauspieler, a company of ex-Piscator-Bühne actors under Fritz Genschow. Heinz Saltenburg's Lessing-Theater staged the same group's production of Friedrich Wolf's *Cyanide (Cyankali)*, while Lampel's *Poison Gas over Berlin (Giftgas über Berlin)* and Marieluise Fleisser's *Pioneers in Ingolstadt (Pioniere in Ingolstadt)* came out at E. J. Aufricht's Theater am Schiffbauerdamm. Piscator was now competing both with the Volksbühne and with the commercial managements.

To raise support for the projected second Piscator-Bühne, Piscator addressed a meeting of the Special Sections of the Volksbühne at the Herrenhaus to explain that his aims had not changed, that he still wanted to transform the theater from a reflection of society into a progressive, formative influence within society, and that this distinguished him from his competitors. He needed the Special Sections' support for this work. This point was taken up by the *Rote Fahne*. Durus, their theater critic, pointed out that Piscator and the Special Sections carried little weight on their own, and that Piscator would be better employed in the ranks of the proletarian-revolutionary theater. In other words, Piscator should join the Workers' Theater League (Arbeiter-Theaterbund) through which the Communist Party controlled the widespread—and mainly amateur—agitprop groups. In the following chapter, Piscator politely rejects this invitation to come under the Party's wing—yet again—and explains at length why he feels his own independent propaganda theater is right. This is the final attempt in this book to justify himself in the face of Party disapproval.

It was to be fifteen months before Piscator was able to reestablish political theater at the Nollendorfplatz, and in the interim he directed *Rivalen*, Carl Zuckmayer's translation and adaptation of Laurence Stallings and Maxwell Anderson's *What Price Glory?*, at the Theater in the Königgrätzer Strasse, which was under the management of Victor Barnowsky. There was no attempt on this occasion to expand the action, though several Piscator-effects were used to heighten the atmosphere of the battlefield. Background noises—shellfire, airplanes, machine guns, soldiers' conversations—were amplified through loudspeakers, and hand-to-hand fighting was seen as shadow play on a screen above the low-ceilinged dugout in which the action took place. Piscator still had a conveyor belt from his *Schwejk* production; he used it for the finale, when, after the triangular love story (which formed the backbone of the play) had been worked out, the men moved back into the line. The props went up into the flies, an Iron Cross was projected on the backdrop, and the cast marched on the conveyor belt to the accompaniment of a military march punctuated by hooters. This last scene was widely held to be ambiguous, though Piscator felt that he had established it as ironic rather than heroic. Herbert Ihering pointed out that the weakness lay in the script, which was shaky on ideology and amenable to any interpretation, but he thought the production offered a fine evening's theater, though the first half could have been played tighter and with more bite. Kurt Pinthus observed that the acting was astonishingly good.

> "Piscator wanted to show that he could work out a script scene by scene, phrase by phrase, word by word, like Engel or Reinhardt. He has shown what many thought was impossible, namely that he could do it."
> *8-Uhr-Abendblatt,* March 21, 1929

Fritz Kortner played Captain Flagg, Hans Albers Sergeant Quirt *(Photo 97).* Raoul Walsh's film with Victor McLaglen had run shortly before, also under the German title *Rivalen,* and Piscator's production suffered by comparison. Pinthus noted that the film had been more clearly pacifistic. Piscator's account of the critical reaction to *What Price Glory?* dwells exclusively on the controversy about the view of war presented by the play. He is concerned only to refute charges of heroics and fails to mention that the acting and directing were widely praised. The production did not break new ground, but it was the most polished application of the principles he had developed at this stage of his career.

The second Piscator-Bühne opened on September 6, 1929, with Walter Mehring's exposure of the workings of inflation, *The Merchant of Berlin.* Kaftan, an Eastern European Jew, arrives in Berlin with $100 in the lining of his cap in 1923, inflation year. For days he looks around Berlin, starving in order to keep his capital intact as its value in marks rockets, waiting for his big chance, which comes when he meets Müller, a crooked lawyer whose right-wing military connections have just bankrupted Eisenberg. Kaftan buys up Eisenberg's Eisenbank and renames it the Kaftanbank. With Müller at his elbow he is soon a billionaire speculating in war-surplus arms and scrap metal. As *the* merchant of Berlin, he changes his caftan for a morning suit and holds a reception for high society, during which the bubble bursts as the stabilization of the mark bankrupts Kaftan. His bank passes into the hands of Cohn & Co., another front for Müller and his nationalist backers.

The play, with its echoes of *The Merchant of Venice*—Kaftan has a sick daughter Jessi, who needs expensive medical care, and this gives Müller a hold over him—was written with Piscator's production style in mind, with street scenes punctuating the dealings in the offices of high finance. On Unter den Linden snatches of passing conversation give the flavor of Berlin, while, as in a novel, many of the speeches are not attributed to characters:

314

Two young girls:
—Mine's an Argentinian! What currency has yours?
—He asked if I wanted to be in pictures. Then he looked at me and said there was a touch of the duchess in my profile.
—Excuse me, miss . . .
—What does this hick want?
—Stupid whore!

We see a panorama of life in the city, and behind it secret meetings of Zionist and nationalist pressure groups. There are songs, ranging from the opening "Cantata of War, Peace and Inflation" in which a choir of workers sketch what they have suffered between 1914 and 1923 ("The war defeated our masters, the Fatherland has defeated us") and the satirical "Street Sweepers' Song" at the end of act 3, to Jessi's sentimental ballad, sung as her party piece at her father's reception.

The long script (165 pages in the original book) includes extensive narrative passages, some of them stage-directions like the description of the appearance and activities of the passengers in Kaftan's compartment as he arrives in Berlin, others satirical essays, like the sketch of the position of the Jews in Berlin since 1671.

The masterly use of the city's dialects, among them Yiddish, the broad sweep of Mehring's picture, and the rapid succession of short scenes called for smooth mechanical changes, and Piscator with Moholy-Nagy, a designer from the Dessau Bauhaus, devised a brilliant, complex mechanical set *(Photo 98)*. Two conveyor belts were set on rails which enabled them to move laterally across the revolving stage, varying the space between them. Three gantries or bridges were mounted in the flies. They could be lowered in with sets and actors on them, or they could be set at stepped levels, one behind the other, to represent, for example, Kaftan's penthouse, the reception in a room below, and the street below that. This facilitated intercut action, for example, from Cohn laughing at the news of Kaftan's ruin on one level, to the military planning on the level below to move into Berlin from Potsdam, and back to Cohn still laughing in the third act.

No prompt-copy or actor's copy of the script survives, but analysis of Moholy-Nagy's notes and sketches (Sammlung Niessen, Cologne University), which exist for the first half of the play only, corroborated by the sketch in the program, suggest that Piscator played the script mainly as written, switching the "Cantata of War, Peace and Inflation" from the end of the play to the beginning, and cutting only the pub scene (Ländliches Wirtshaus "Zum Waldkater") in act 2. A summary of the opening scenes will give an impres-

315

sion of the complex technical plot. The "Cantata" was sung by a chorus of twenty-four men with Ernst Busch taking the solo part. They floated, grouped in four rows, on two bridges 10 feet above the stage, with only their heads showing through holes in a cloth draped over them. Fade. One of the bridges, set as a railway compartment with Kaftan and the other travelers in place, came in from the flies. As the scene progressed, the stage turned through 180° and billboards and fences traveled across the conveyor belts, as if seen from a train. A film ran. At the end of the scene the compartment rose and traveled downstage, the stage turned through 90° and porters singing a proletarian song were carried downstage on the conveyor belts, which stopped parallel to the audience, and separated. A sign reading "Berlin Alexanderplatz" popped up center stage through a trap, and the compartment was lowered between the belts. The porters helped the passengers to dismount at the back, while the front belt brought on a ticket barrier. Kaftan stepped downstage through the barrier, the bridge went up, a backdrop came down to cut off a narrow forestage, a street light popped up, curtains narrowed the stage aperture which quickly filled with Alexanderplatz characters, and Kaftan had his first taste of Berlin—with colored projections by George Grosz. Later in the play there were filmed backgrounds of Berlin streets, and exchange rates, dollar signs, wage rates were projected on side screens at appropriate points. This was Piscator's most elaborate exercise in "machine theater," as he called it, and the mobile set is an impressive concept. However, the machinery which should have been swift, smooth and synchronized proved to be slow and ponderous, the script was too long (7:30 P.M. to 11:45 P.M.) and the audience's interest waned as the elaborately told story, whose course was familiar and predictable to them, lumbered on.

The Merchant of Berlin offended all shades of opinion. The press response was at best cool, at worst irate, and the production lost money from the start. It was rumored to have cost 100,000 marks, though Piscator in an interview *(Berlin am Morgen, 10.3.29)* claimed that this figure included the new equipment, the guaranty and the rent for the season. Piscator was soon at odds with his codirector, Klopfer, whose main concern was to keep the theater on a sound business footing. When Piscator named Leopold Lindtberg to direct the next production, Klopfer appointed Heinz Goldberg, a Volksbühne man who had never worked with Piscator. At the beginning of October, in spite of a vote of solidarity from the actors, Piscator walked out and took his name off the enterprise, leaving the "Theater am Nollendorfplatz" in the hands of Klopfer. *The*

316

Merchant of Berlin closed on October 15, and the second Piscator-Bühne, whose only other production had been a revival of Piscator's Staatstheater production of Schiller's *Robbers* for a school matinee on September 14, ceased to exist.

XXIII
SURVEY OF ACHIEVEMENTS AND PROSPECTS

In Kortrijk in Belgium I stood on the steps leading up to the Town Hall. A gray October day hung low over the flat, square marketplace. Platoon after platoon marched past. The British had pushed back the Ypres salient. Then, suddenly, the square was empty and silent. A woman with an umbrella rounded a corner just as a shell hit the house above her. The house collapsed with a tremendous crash and a cloud of dust hung where it had just stood. The square was still and lifeless. Then the woman, whom I had completely forgotten, walked out across the square, still carrying her umbrella, and disappeared around the corner.

I cite this example for my own sake. I did not see the lady's face. She walked like a sleepwalker. She must have been surprised that she could still walk.

The catastrophe of the final collapse took me equally unawares. I, too, am surprised that I can still walk. And I walk on, the noise of the crash still in my ears, and behind me the cloud of dust from the wrecked house. Because even if circumstances are thousand times stronger than men, men still have a touch of destiny in their being. For when all is said and done, I have struggled, and tenaciously, too, for intellectual causes. The "commercial side" of things is only a means to an end for me.

I can scarcely be more careful. No matter how circumspect you are in your handling of commercial matters, you cannot totally free

"The Locarno of the Berlin Theaters Bankruptcy Conquered"
"Piscator is building an antique theater on the Kurfurstendamm (beside the Theater der Komiker) Caryatids: Alfred Kerr and Karl Kraus." (From the satirical magazine *Simplicissimus*, 1928)

Drawn by Th. Th. Heine

theatrical productions from their effect. Under normal circumstances, the question of whether a show will do good business is borne in mind during the production. But under no circumstances can my productions make any concessions to the box office.

Fifteen months have passed since I have been forced to close the Theater am Nollendorfplatz, fifteen months of hard, exacting work away from my real profession. Business negotiations, conferences, committees, calculations, everything is now being dealt with in tiresome detail; and all this, had it happened a year ago, could perhaps have saved the enterprise. But every new project collapses, there are deaf ears everywhere. A banker says, "Now, what would

319

they say at the Stock Exchange if I lent you money?" Three times I have been on the brink of setting up a new theater, but each time the financial edifice has collapsed. Finally, friends who are interested in my work are tempted by the offer of the Komische Oper. The enterprise is set up with every possible contractual security. The first installment of the rent is paid in the form of a mortgage. The most experienced lawyers preside over the birth. But all in vain. James Klein, the owner of the Komische Oper, goes bankrupt and the house is put up for sale. My group declines to take part in the auction. We lose the house—and not only the house, but the first payment (which amounted to 30,000 marks) as well.

The theater recedes into the distance again. —Preparations can be made with only half our energy, for nothing is certain. We do not dare to sign contracts, either with the dramatists or with the actors. Then we are offered the Theater am Nollendorfplatz again. Compared with the Komische Oper, a great relief. The equipment is all there, and the staff is already accustomed to our way of working. The advantages of this prospect seem to us to outweigh any superstitious objections. Negotiations go on all through the day from five in the afternoon until two in the morning. On the next day we are sitting again in the old rooms which represent a decisive slice of all of our lives. Business gets under way. The political theater takes up the struggle again.

At that time I was without liabilities; today I am burdened with experience and with debts amounting to 50,000 to 60,000 marks, for which I am personally responsible. The problems have not grown any smaller. The amount of work is huge and the task gigantic. But the goal which is the theme of this book—political theater, which places its work in the service of the proletarian class's struggle—is still as firmly fixed in our minds as ever. In all my publications and declarations I have always made it unmistakably clear that any theater which I manage serves neither to produce "art" nor to do "business." I have repeatedly stressed that a theater for which I am responsible must be revolutionary (within the limits that its commercial situation prescribes) or nothing at all. The bourgeoisie may listen to these utterances with a bittersweet smile and retire behind a protective barrier of artistic evaluations. But the proletariat should, one might say, have learned in the course of these ten years what the theater can mean as an organ of propaganda for their movement. One expects support and cooperation. The Special Sections remained true to us, in the forefront the Working Committee with comrades Jahnke, Stein, Berndt, Bork,

Brie, Schirrmeister and Zscheile, who stood by us through thick and thin. And as our theater began to take shape once more I felt bound to offer them an account of our activities—they know that results can be achieved only with active cooperation, with positive criticism, with real help from the side of the workers' organizations.

. . . When I entitled this evening's discussion "an account of our activities" it was, more than anything else, to help me to clarify the scope, significance and development of our basic theatrical idea. But to you, the Special Sections, to the whole public, I want to explain the events which have taken place since the declaration in the Herrenhaus so that we can proceed unburdened to new work.

The only way I can see to make a conclusive statement is by comparing my own development with what has happened around me, and following this up with the motto with which I began my production of *Rasputin*: "We must constantly go back to the beginning." It is, in addition, necessary to range far afield in order to establish just how unchanged my views on artistic and political matters have remained over the last ten years. I am not sentimental. But when I think of the charges laid by objective and less-than-objective opponents, I am astonished how rapidly people's assumptions change, how quick people were to discover that I had assumed my convictions solely for the purpose of doing good business, artistic business, how quickly they tried to label me as a speculator. . . . If they think I have now been "cured" of my political ideas, they are wrong. On the contrary: I see more and more clearly that only absolute consistency can produce the political and at the same time the artistic effect we need. Yet, with the difficulty of the task, I need political and moral credit to enable me to work on a long term basis. Not every production, especially with the lack of a body of drama suitable for our theater, will be unassailable on every flank. What remains decisive is that the direction of our advance is unchanged. This evening I have tried to show that for ten years I have done nothing but the work which my political convictions require.

From a lecture in the Herrenhaus, March 15, 1929

The Situation in 1929

It is impossible to appraise our theater in its entirety without at the same time undertaking an exact analysis of the general social and political situation. This analysis alone would fill a whole book. So I must limit myself here to a few brief points. The first period of the Piscator-Bühne lay in a relatively stable, undisturbed situation. The second period of the Piscator-Bühne, the period we are now moving into, looks much less undisturbed. Proletarian organizations such as the *Rote Frontkämpfer-Bund*[1] are being harrassed, while "national" organizations are allowed to prepare their march to power quite methodically in peace. The "danger from the Right" is growing visibly. Bomb-throwing indicates a steady growth of the activity of circles who have already left Erzberger, Rathenau and hundreds of Social Democrats and Communist workers lying dead in their wake.[2] Tycoons sympathize in public with the "legal dictatorship" and the Social Democrats are quick to jump on the bandwagon. There is great tension in the world. The great army of the unemployed has not been reduced by one man, but has even grown periodically. Gigantic economic struggles lie behind us (the Ruhr uprising),[3] and even bigger ones lie ahead of us. International conferences in which bourgeois Europe tries to reconcile divergent interests and groups follow hard on one another's heels. All with almost no tangible results. The League of Nations, an international clearinghouse set up by the sovereign states to handle imperialistic demands of every sort proves to be powerless. There is a hectic rush to rearm. The subject of the next war is discussed openly and objectively everywhere as a problem of the day. A sixth of the global stage on which the fate of this generation is being enacted sticks like a thorn in the flesh of the great powers. Add to this latent upheaval which is going on daily, indeed hourly, the spiritual revolution: the breakup of traditional forms of communal life (marriage), the growing conflict between the laws as codified and the real conditions (problem of justice), the reappraisal of all scientific and philosophical beliefs, the revision of the absolute (Einstein).

The exhaustive process of rearrangement in which the new order of society is emerging, just as it did one hundred and fifty years ago, cannot leave the theater untouched. In fact, within the last three years a change has made itself felt. Even the bourgeois theater has taken a new attitude to the problems of the times. Art theater is

1. The *Rote Frontkämpfer-Bund* was a Communist paramilitary association.
2. Walther Rathenau (1867–1922), the ablest politician to emerge from the Weimar Republic, was the target of right-wing criticism which became especially virulent when Rathenau as foreign minister concluded the Treaty of Rapallo (1922) with Soviet Russia. In June, 1922, he was shot at close quarters and then blown to bits with a grenade. Matthias Erzberger (1875–1921) advocated an armistice during World War I. He became finance minister in the Weimar Republic and was then assassinated as a "traitor" by two ex-officers who belonged to the *Organization Konsul*, the same terrorist group which later killed Rathenau.
3. In January, 1919, workers' and soldiers' councils took charge of the Ruhr and decided to socialize the coal mines under democratic control. The Prussian government—the mines were state property—sent in right-wing Free Corps units. There was a general strike and a state of siege was declared, but by April the episode fizzled out.

beginning to die off. It is scarcely possible to hold the line of pure art (the line of defense of political reactionaries) any longer. The public is no longer interested in it, not even the bourgeois public. Perplexed at the problematic nature of its own existence, it is beginning to ask the theater, too, for answers to politico-social questions.

After the first season of the Piscator-Bühne, a perceptible move to the Left could be observed in the repertories of the Berlin theaters. Ahead of everyone else the Volksbühne took up the Piscator-Bühne's line. Under pressure from the Special Sections it put on plays which at least attempted to come to terms with current questions. But even the avowedly commercial theaters suddenly showed an interest in topical drama. This raises an issue on which our standpoint must be clearly defined. The one world view from which political theater could spring, the political impetus whose unambiguous aim was the reorganization of society, became big business. Dramatists with a nose for success picked up the scent of topical drama. Certainly not to bring down the social order, which paid them fat royalties. Certainly not in order to make the workers' cause their own. Topical theater, the drama of current events, political theater became commercial. It goes without saying that I draw a clear dividing line between this kind of theater and my own, otherwise the essence of all my work would be falsified. It is one thing for a theater to turn topical problems into "art"; it is another thing for a theater to take art and use it in the struggle to achieve important political results. It is one thing to entrust a great and technically accomplished actor with a social accusation, in the hope that he will produce a great performance; it is another thing to use a great actor's performance to drive home a social accusation. The aim which regulates a theater's intentions will always be decisive. And in marginal cases it will always be necessary to scrutinize the person staging the show and take his past and his former attitudes into consideration; his creditworthiness must be established before judgment is made.

My participation in a production like *What Price Glory?* (March, 1929, at the Theater in der Königgrätzer Strasse) has been severely criticized. I must confess that I would neither have accepted this play for my own theater, nor would I have produced it in this form. Financial circumstances forced me to take on the play and stage it at relatively short notice. Many of its ambiguities could have been avoided. Even so, I still do not consider the play to be a glorification of war and I never did see it in this light. To regard the soldiers' march on the conveyor belt at the end of the play (to the front line once more) as an apotheosis of absolute devotion to duty can only be the result of a total misinterpretation of my intentions. On the contrary, I wanted this ending to express the hopelessness, the suffocating inevitability of such a march, which is part of my own experience. Besides, there is a battle scene in the play itself in which I attempted to show that I had suddenly developed a taste for the trenches. After all I had done, I could at least have expected my personal credit to be higher, instead of which I received warning calls which managed to turn a mere "sin of omission" into a full-scale lapse in my political convictions.

But the economic recovery, which is naturally not a matter of mere chance and, besides its social impact, has a deeper political meaning, also took the tension out of the air. Political theater emerged from the sensational stage. It is no longer evaluated as the *dernier cri* of a public which can be excited only by gunfire, spinning bullets and revolutionary anthems. It has lost its "attraction" as an exhibition piece, greatly to the advantage of its true purpose. People will perhaps see, even in wider bourgeois circles, that the Piscator-Bühne requires quite a different evaluation from the entertainment branch, that it does not absorb new objects and spew them out as art, but is really concerned to clarify or solve these questions.

This creates a new relationship between us and our public. It will be a more peaceful relationship. But it will also be a parting of the ways. The best, most self-reliant and unprejudiced circles will stand by us; the fellow travelers, the merely curious will stay away.

But where does the proletariat, that section of the public who ought to see this theater as an expression of its own will, come into all this? Like a red thread running through this book, through the history of my undertakings runs the realization that the proletariat, whatever the reason may be, is too weak to support a theater of its own. This has in no way changed; on the contrary. The situation of the working classes has deteriorated so much that even the Special Sections will go forward to the 1929/30 season with depleted numbers. We still stand where we have always stood as an advance post cut off from the main body of the army, and we have to see to it that we draw the strength which will keep us going from the territory which we have already conquered (intellectually). So our need for the moral and political support of the working class is even greater. I feel I can justly demand that all my reasons, all the limiting factors in the situation, all the objective difficulties, including even the question of playwriting should be taken into consideration, before an attack is mounted upon me from this quarter. The enterprise as it exists today has not been knocked together quickly with anything we could lay our hands on. It has grown organically from the smallest beginnings, and its growth is due solely to the significance of the idea behind it. People today who advise us to go back to halls, to "return" to the working class are forgetting that all previous undertakings of this sort collapsed and not by chance. They are forgetting above all that neither the development of a theater nor that of a man can be turned back at will. Others accuse me of having an "overly technical" style of production. They consider Stanislavsky to be more revolutionary because his naturalistic mode of presentation corresponds to the condition of the proletariat. A gigantic error! The fact that the intellectual revolution in the theater coincides with a renewal of its technical resources is not mere chance. I feel I have demonstrated adequately in this book that the technical advances developed organically out of the intellectual advances. Furthermore, it seems quite ludicrous to maintain that the theater of the proletariat should not make use of the latest technical achievements. —Finally, some of my fellow Communists doubt the honesty of my convictions and, basing their conclusions on a few superficial facts, call me a renegade motivated by personal ambition and lust for profits. Is there any truth in this?

I am not afraid to throw this topic open to the public and expose my private life. There is no private life for me in this sense.

Because of my manner of working I became more and more identified with every achievement in our theater. I had to carry everybody's share. I became the leading exponent of a movement and had to accept the disadvantages with the advantages. When this happens you are bound to be included in certain judgments, and even people who do not know you get a picture which is naturally only partly true. (It is a curious feeling to read judgments and evaluations of yourself and to see your picture in the papers. You see a figure to the right or to the left of you who resembles you but is not in fact you yourself.) Karl Kraus has me speaking Berlin dialect in one of his essays. I am not a Berliner, so the dialogue he puts into my mouth rings false. So does the supposition that what took place on the stage during my *Robbers* was effeminate. There are others who think I am a tall man with a full beard. At one time I am supposed to have escaped from a sailor's revolt in Kiel. The analyses of my mind are just as wrong as these matters of supposed fact. Friends can evaluate such judgments, but readers and strangers cannot. Where a particular person represents a cause the judgment passed on the person affects the cause at the same time; nobody takes into consideration that the person sees an ideal in his cause which he himself may not automatically be able to live up to. The idea represents a goal, which the individual naturally falls short of. The contradictions between affairs at any given time and this goal affect even our private lives.

We are not living in a Communist state. The identity between the social situation and the artist's work which exists in Russia must of necessity be absent in our case. We come into daily contact with concepts, situations and people who are far removed from our ideal aims, and yet we cannot ignore them; indeed, we must work and cooperate with them. The inevitable result is a deep gulf between the life we live and the life we would wish to live.

A sentimentalist could call these conflicts tragic. A Marxist can only seek to convince himself that this situation, for better, for worse, is necessary.

The unknown standing in the ranks along with many others lives a different life from a well-known figure. At that time I was living in furnished rooms; I was not well-off. But I was in the grip of the ideas of the day, and I placed my profession at their service, without any intention of improving my personal position. My personal position merged into and became identical with the hopes which the proletariat pinned on the victory of their revolution. (Or did people think that I had my eye on the post of Comrade Director of the Red State Theater?) In this great proletarian revolution, one man was a minute component, and the movement regulated all our actions. Individual instincts were either voluntarily repressed or suppressed by force. At that time I learned how relative our evaluation of the individual was, and I must say that I have never experienced greater satisfaction than when I abandoned my personality and gave myself up to the mass movement.

This all changed when I was forced to climb within my profession from one rung of the ladder to the next: I became famous, developed an image in individualistic bourgeois terms. People treated me as a special kind of man, one director among others, someone with talent, some people would go so far as to say stature.

Nothing can be done about this. My activities as theater manager and producer bring me into the limelight. I have to play the role of entrepreneur. I have to accept criticism based on purely aesthetic principles. I earn more money. My "social status rises." I give up my furnished rooms. I am required to live up to my position. I take a five-room apartment of my own close to the Central-Theater. At the beginning the curtains are red flags, and an old billiard table turned upside down serves as a dining table. But later the furnishings improve, enabling the *Nachtausgabe* to write: "In a petit bourgeois setup in the Oranienstrasse sits the Communist Piscator.

. . ." On the ground floor in this house was a cheap bar: the whole house stank of alcohol, which in certain circumstances I do not find unpleasant, being no teetotaler. When my lease on the apartment ran out, Gropius, who was at the time drawing up plans for the new theater, said he was prepared to decorate an apartment which had been found for me in the Katharinenstrasse (fourth floor, five rooms) on modern principles. Instead of doors with panels and applied ornamentation, flush doors were fitted; the rooms were painted white and equipped with steel furniture. But even while the apartment was in its original condition, people in the know were whispering that Piscator was building a castle in Grünewald.[4] Old proletarian friends would swear blind they had just seen me drive past in a Rolls-Royce. (As a schoolboy I did once have a bicycle.) —And so when Stone, our theater photographer, took pictures of the apartment and published them against my will in *Dame,* a women's magazine, my condemnation was complete. How can a man like that claim to be a Communist? I'd like to; but am I one? I would point out that there are people who put on a red tie to go to a workers' meeting and slip it off again as soon as they come out. I never did anything like that. What is known as Marxist science is not a matter of dress. Communism is not sentimental drivel; it is rooted in social conditions which we want to alter by the application of reason, and sentiment by no means plays the most important part. You don't have to appear in hair shirts if you want to understand or even preach Communism, but you should see to it that your appearance is as frank as possible. Would it not be two-faced for me to dissociate myself from things that I consider good and productive? From a rationalization of my private life? Only to make a concession to people who will attack whenever they see a vulnerable point, or even when they don't? Even as a boy I was embarrassed when I walked past workmen in my new yellow boots and fine gray suit. But could I have helped them by wearing working clothes? It goes without saying that no one is more sensitive to the contradictions in the present order of society than myself. Would I be fighting otherwise to put an end to it? This and this alone, it seems to me, is the only thing that matters.

Our Program

"You're not doing anything political anymore" a left-wing Social Democrat said to me. "Your program was too full of party politics

4. Grünewald is a select residential area near the lakes in the western part of Berlin. In fact, Piscator never paid the bill for redecorating the Katherinenstrasse flat.

for me" (a wide-spread opinion). "Not radical enough," say the Democrats for their part. "This is political theater, and we must have it, too," say the German Nationalists and the National Socialists. It is, as you see, a strange theater. But are the contradictory judgments and contradictory demands part of the state of affairs? It is precisely because political theater is, or could be, such an important factor that it provokes the most violent opinions.

But the theater is not unambiguous, and this must be admitted. It cannot be unambiguous. Even if we scored out the word "proletarian" on the front of the house and left only the word "revolutionary." (Unsatisfactory for me like everything unspoken and half-hearted.) We lack many things. First of all, plays. Besides being sharp and logical in its convictions, a play must also be a likely stage success. A mere editorial in dialogue is not enough. The theater needs theatricality. This is what makes it effective. Only then can it claim to be real propaganda. But this is territory which we must first conquer. There are signs that the productions we need are on the way. But the writers first have to learn to grasp the subject objectively and to see the dramatic potential of great but simple events. The theater demands naïve, direct, uncomplicated, unpsychological effects. Most authors assess their public wrongly. The public is in a better position to check the accuracy of everyday events than that of *Oedipus*. If the event is not quite right, if its course is not shown with crystal clarity, if the bald happenings are not used as dramatic elements, then the whole work is a failure.

I think the times themselves will compel literature to take issue with them. The poet is no longer the same semitragic, semiludicrous figure that he often was fifty years ago. He no longer lives apart from events, he no longer can, nor indeed can anyone else these days; events themselves bear down relentlessly on us all. Technology has shrunk the earth. But at the same time it has connected things together. Nobody can step aside or close his eyes to the problems, even if he personally is unlikely to get his fingers burned. The whole of humanity has been brought into the picture. The remnants of old ideologies (Middle Ages, Baroque, Biedermeier,[5] even the Stone Age, which incidentally has survived into our own times in Tierra del Fuego) are rapidly melting away. In 1930 the life of every individual is being brought up to date, which may only bring it up to a modest level, but at least it provides a more realistic standard than 1850. These same individuals are the people who take their seats in the theater every evening. They may have been listening to a welcoming speech in California half an hour earlier, or they may have

5. *Biedermeier* denotes the furniture style prevalent in Germany and Austria from about 1830 to 1848. The name evokes associations of petty, middle-class dullness.

seen the latest earthquake in Japan in a newsreel the day before. Ten minutes ago they may have been reading in a newspaper about something that happened two hours earlier in Capetown. Men like these carry a vision of the world around with them, and it is not a vision dating from last year, it is an immediate one. Is literature going to dare to show them a panopticon peopled by wax figures frozen in the same pose for eternity? Can it take the liberty of ignoring the lives of these people down there while it indulges in a display of intellectual abstractions, formal arabesques, changelings from its own imagination? It must be real, real to the last detail, unreservedly true, if it wants to capture even a reflection of these people's lives. And if it is to become a motive force in their lives, how much more real and true it must be! But the outspoken truth, which takes us a stage beyond the merely topical, is revolutionary in itself. The writer who is aware of his artistic duty must, whether he will or not, become a revolutionary writer in such a situation.

More and more, a plan to take subjects from the theater to the writers has been maturing in my mind. The writer would then collaborate closely with the theater in dramatizing the subject and we would no longer accept finished plays.

The development of this type of drama takes time. In the meanwhile we have to make a start; we have to put plays on the repertoire, plays which at least present the right kind of subject to the audience. What does our repertoire look like?

Piscator's forty plays: At the meeting of the Special Sections which Piscator addressed at the Herrenhaus, particular interest was aroused by the remark that he had drawn up a short list of about forty plays for the coming season, none of which entirely satisfied all his requirements. The Piscator-Bühne had in fact compiled a collection of forty plays which were suitable for its own or for associated stages from one point of view or another, and we append this list. Several plays which have still to be completed or are at present under negotiation are omitted for obvious reasons.

The operas or plays with music in question are: *Mahagonny* (Brecht-Weill), *The Dumb Girl of Portici* (*La Muette de Portici*, Auber), *The Marriage of Figaro* (Beaumarchais); dramatized novels: *The Case of Sergeant Grischa* (*Der Streit um den Sergeanten Grischa*, Arnold Zweig), *An American Tragedy* (Theodore Dreiser), *From the White Cross to the Red Flag* (*Vom Weissen Kreuz zur Roten Fahne*, Max Hölz), *Schwejk, Part II* (Jaroslav Hašek); contemporary German plays: *The Merchant of Berlin* (*Der Kaufmann von Berlin*, Walter Mehring), *Murder in Germersheim* (*Die Bluttat von Germersheim*, Hans Borchard), *Cyanide* (*Cyankali*, Friedrich Wolf), *§218* (Credé); German historical plays: *The Last Days of Mankind* (*Die Letzten Tage der Menschheit*, Karl Kraus), *The Society for Human Rights* (*Die Gesellschaft für Menschenrechte*, F. Th. Csokor), *The Hessian Messenger* (*Der Hessische Landbote*, Walter

Gruber); Russian plays, simultaneously topical and historical: *Thundering Rails* (Kirshon), *Kronstadt* and *Armored Train 14–69* (Ivanov), *The Mill* (Bergelson), *Men on the Barricades* (*Menschen auf der Barrikade*, Béla Balázs), *Aseff* (A. Tolstoy); international topical plays: a Mexican *Oil Play* (Alfons Goldschmidt), *March on Mossul* (*Marsch auf Mossul*) and *Cattaro* (Friedrich Wolf), three versions of *Sacco and Vanzetti* (Maxwell Anderson, Leonhard Frank, Erich Mühsam), *Army without Heroes* (*Heer ohne Helden*, Wiesner); classics: *Timon of Athens* (Shakespeare), *Peace* (Aeschylus/Feuchtwanger), *The Robbers* (Schiller), *Emilia Galotti* (Lessing).

In addition to these, Piscator included all the subjects that he intended to have dramatized or to dramatize himself, such as: marriage, the press, the legal system, sport, medicine, banking, as well as historical or topical subjects like: Friedericus Rex, the French Revolution, Lenin's conversations, the colonial question, etc. To these must be added the philosophic-didactic literature Brecht was producing, like *Nothing Comes of Nothing* (*Aus nichts wird nichts*) and *Johann Fatzer*.

From *Die Junge Volksbühne*, No. 5

As these lines are printed the first battles of the 1929/30 season have already been fought, the conflict of opinion has already begun. We know our weaknesses better than any critic, we never deceive ourselves, we know exactly where the inadequacies of our work lie. Of course, at the moment when—if I lived in the Soviet Union—I would be beginning the real work of producing the play, I must, under conditions at they are here in Germany, present the play to the public—for financial reasons. Again and again the abyss widens between the idea we want to put into practice and what we can in fact achieve.

The final chapter of this book, which was written during brief pauses between the afternoon and evening rehearsals of *The Merchant of Berlin* (*Der Kaufmann von Berlin*), had not been set in print when an avalanche of "public opinion" bore down on us. On September 6, 1929, the Piscator-Bühne at the Theater am Nollendorfplatz began its second season with Walter Mehring's *The Merchant of Berlin*. All the problems, all the important aspects of political theater which we have touched on in this book were once more combined effectively in this production. The public response was stronger, more contradictory, one could almost say: more passionate, than in the case of any of my earlier productions. At the present time we are unable to foresee the consequences of this. We cannot predict the fate of the second Piscator-Bühne, but whether it is a success or a failure the problem at the center of this production, which is in fact the basic problem of political theater in general, is so important that it deserves to form the conclusion to this book.

What seemed most important and valuable in *The Merchant of Berlin*— and what made us accept the play—was the contemporary subject: "One of the most disgraceful chapters in recent German history," as we wrote in the program notes, "a period in which an 'anonymous fate' robbed the German people of almost the half of its fortune, expropriated the entire middle class, depressed the working classes below the standard of living of a Chinese coolie and condemned hundreds of thousands to an existence between life and death. This was all achieved with the aid of one of the most grandiose pieces of sleight-of-hand known to history: inflation." We knew from the start that this vast theme was only sketched in outline in the play, and that the action lacked objective substance in both the social and economic spheres. This is not intended as a rejection of Mehring. Inflation is one of the most difficult subjects that exist. Its basic causes and the mechanism by which it operates are hotly disputed even today, and political economists and politicians within the Marxist camp itself propose conflicting solutions of the problem. For months the problem of inflation was the subject of thorough economic analyses during the preparatory work on the play, and at this stage we consulted economic theorists from both the Marxist and the bourgeois camps, people like Alfons Goldschmidt, Fritz Sternberg and Morus-Lewinsohn. The more the work progressed, the more clearly we saw that a subject like this could not be dealt with in one evening and really required a whole cycle of plays.

In accordance with the subject, I saw the play from the start in three stages: a tragic stage (proletariat), a tragicomic stage (middle class), and a grotesque stage (upper classes and the military). This sociological division produced the three-tier system of staging, which we constructed with the aid of elevators and bridges. Each of these social classes was to have a stage of its own—upper, middle, lower—and the classes were to meet from time to time wherever the focus of the dramatic action demanded it. The movement of the various levels toward and away from one another created a dramatic stage space. When Kurt Kersten wrote in the *Welt am Abend* (September 7, 1929): "There were two possible ways of presenting inflation: either the financiers and tycoons of heavy industry on the one hand and the revolutionary proletariat on the other, or . . . the way in which inflation morally degrades a people, and the revolutionary movement . . . is violently put down by those who caused the inflation and are now taking a profit from it," he was perfectly right. At the beginning we, too, saw the play in this light. What he forgets is that plays of the kind he demands don't pop out of slot machines; that the proletarian-revolutionary writers whom he recommends to me are undoubtedly excellent Marxists, but have yet to come up with a single usable play. Consequently I have no choice but to take the plays that are available. We saw that the proletariat was almost totally absent from Mehring's play. This was a fault we were concerned to remedy right from the beginning of our revision of the script. To avoid destroying the play completely we hit upon the detour of constructing the economic and social foundation with long interpolated songs, such as "The Cantata of War, Peace and Inflation." In these songs the proletariat was to appear as an active factor. If there is a reproach to be made here, it can only be that once again I underestimated the difficulty of expanding the subject matter of a completed play, that I did not allow enough room for the author's artistic eccentricities and perhaps failed to take the limits of his stamina into consideration, and that I was not realistic enough when I assessed the time available. At any rate, the expansion of the play in these terms remained fragmentary. The critics in the *Rote Fahne*, the *Welt am Abend* and *Berlin am Morgen* have nothing new to tell me. I would scarcely be the man to have my name linked with political theater if I had not noticed of my own accord that the most active opponent of inflation, the proletariat, was absent from this play. My constant efforts to correct this error show how serious I felt this omission to be. (Opening Cantata, Song of Dry Bread, the Tailor's-Apprentice Scene at Leschnitzer's, the filmed statistics of wages, Song of the Three Stages at the end when only the lowest proletarian stage was left standing, etc.) It is boring, and not very convincing, to have to repeat continually that the size of the task we had set ourselves, the lack of time, and our limited resources prevented us from reaching the goal that we saw before us when we began the production.

The second fundamental weakness of the play was also clear to us. We wrote in the program notes: "A further difficulty arose: in *The Merchant of Berlin* an East European Jew stands in the center of the action. The historical circumstances make him guilty along with the others. The 'Socialism of Fools,' as August Bebel once called anti-Semitism, is perilously close. As we saw it, Kaftan belonged to the second, tragicomic stage. An advocate of capitalism who perishes with capitalism. A racketeer whose cupidity is only thinly veiled by his ethical motive, his love for his sick daughter." Mehring did not take this ethical alibi seriously, either. For us Kaftan was an exploiter, or at least another beneficiary, and his racial or religious affiliations were a matter of indifference to us. But as the public saw it, Kaftan the Jew was more prominent than Kaftan the capitalist. Anything we aimed at capitalism was bound to hit the Jews. And this was precisely what we did not want. We never wanted to lend a hand in an anti-Semitic witch hunt; for it was not the racial problem, not the relationship between immigrant Jews and indigenous Germans, but the social or class problem which was the point at issue in this play.

Objective judges like Alfred Kerr, Manfred Georg, Bernhard Diebold, Walter Steinthal and Emil Faktor (among others) did not for one moment see the slightest anti-Semitic tendency in our production. Kerr wrote, "Unpleasant play," for he knew just as we did that certain—I would almost like to say—Jewish-nationalist circles would reject the very appearance of a Jew on the stage as an attack on themselves. I can readily understand this, in view of the entire historical development of the Jews, who, having been regarded as foreigners for centuries, feel that anyone who singles them out, brings them into the limelight or even mentions the problem, must have hostile intentions. But I cannot concede that in a theater based on the principle that every truth must be uttered, certain things should remain unsaid because of potential sensitivity. —Apart from that, it seems to me that the distribution of "guilt" in Mehring's play, if we want to talk about the racial question, is quite objective and just. Nobody could be painted as more unscrupulous, demagogic or crooked than the "Christian" lawyer Müller, who stakes national slogans, the bank rate and his private love affairs one after the other, in order to climb into the realms of heavy industry at the end of the play by means of an obvious swindle. Here again, only a blinkered nationalist could reproach me with slighting my "German nationality."

The fact that after this production the liberal press considered the play to be anti-Semitic, and the nationalist press, where it was not hypocritically defending Jewish symbols and institutions, called the play philo-Semitic and me a slave of Jewry, shows how different the reactions to this question within the play were.

The ideological misconception to which both Left and Center fell victim was complicated by a misunderstanding of the role of stage machinery in *The Merchant of Berlin*. The stage set which I designed was the simplest conceivable. Two conveyor belts were mounted on the revolving stage (a technical problem which can be easily solved, under normal circumstances), and these were to be matched with three mobile bridges which could be moved up and down at the speed of elevators. This was the ideal apparatus for the play. Kaftan wandered through Berlin on these conveyoi belts just as Schwejk had in his time wandered towards Budéjovice. The revolving stage and the conveyor belts brought the streets of Berlin before the audience, scenes could be intercut by lowering new scenes from the bridges, and this would have allowed us to solve all our problems in the easiest, simplest manner. What went wrong, why did the apparatus grind up each little scene with all the power of an iron mill instead of allowing the play to flow freely? The basic fault, as I have already explained when dealing with *Hoppla, Such is Life!*, is that I have been forced to build little improvements into a form of stage architecture which has outlived its technical usefulness. The result will never be anything more than patchwork. But even if we make allowances for what is feasible, the apparatus for *The Merchant of Berlin* was ten times too heavy, too powerful and too ponderous. Who was to blame for this? Instead of a light wooden framework, I was given gigantic bridge structures made of iron girders which would have been admirably suited to a harbor installation. Instead of gliding silently up and down, they rose and fell with soul-destroying slowness, and with their motors roaring. They turned into the opposite of what had been intended, and the whole project could at best be considered only as the roughest draft of a stage which might one day exist. Will we, after our efforts, after the sacrifice of our time, after committing our money and our personalities to these prototypes, ever come into possession of such a stage?

I am assailed from all sides with the accusation that "Piscator wants to do too much." Simple plays, simple settings, in a word: old-fashioned theater is demanded of me. After all, why not? Why must we always have these monstrous productions which consume so much energy, money and time, and in which I only ever momentarily achieve what seems to me to be the true nature of theater? Our theater as it has developed in theory and practice over the course of these past years is constantly faced with quite special tasks. It is not our task to present proletarian milieu plays in a naturalistic style. We cannot turn back the development to the point from which things started fifty years ago. Even bourgeois theaters can fulfill that task nowadays, and indeed they do fulfill it. The "Young Actors' Group" is putting on *The Revolt in the House of Correction (Revolte im Erziehungshaus)* for Saltenburg, *The Brothers on the Dole (Die Stempelbrüder)* will be staged in Hartung's theater.[6] There is no need of a Piscator-Bühne for that.

6. It was F. Wolf's *Cyanide* that the group did for Heinz Saltenburg at the Lessing-Theater (9.6.29). Lampel's *Revolt in the House of Correction* opened at the

Strange as it may sound, our task is not limited to individual productions. It is almost a matter of indifference how the single productions look, what weaknesses they suffer from, what flaws they contain, whether they are complete mistakes. Our goal is to supersede bourgeois theater in terms of philosophy, dramatic theory, technique and staging. We are fighting for a restructured theater, and this must follow the lines of the social revolution. So we shall probably fail again and again, in a sense, because of the inadequacies of the situation, and because this reconstruction cannot proceed in isolation. This much I have now realized.

Do I still nevertheless believe in political theater under these circumstances, at this time and with the means at our disposal? Even in the face of the situation that has been created by our production of *The Merchant of Berlin*, my answer is yes. If one thing has proved that our theater has not yet lost its political character in spite of all the half-measures and ambiguities, in spite of the misunderstandings on the part of comrades, friends, sympathizers and objective judges of our venture, it is the cries of rage directed daily at Walter Mehring and myself from the reactionary newspapers, and the threatening and insulting letters I received every day.

"Piscator is Allowed to Incite Civil War!"

"The name Piscator is synonymous with incitement to civil war. . . . But this 'action' [in the play] is larded with venemous songs and is introduced by an oratorio bursting with hate. It goes without saying that everything which represents national stature and dignity to the normal German, as well as to the respectable German Jew, is ridiculed. . . . The apostles of provocation who in this case [of civil war] as always will try to exonerate themselves from any blame can be sure that wherever they go there will be people who will remember this filth which has made the German stage into a madhouse and a fair where the lowest vulgarity is peddled."

Der Tag, September 8, 1929

"Piscator has turned the everyday plot [of this play] into a tendentious drama against capitalism. . . ."

Nachtausgabe, September 7

" . . . A revue of puerile screeching hate. . . . Everything which is German and Christian, everything associated with uniforms, everything

---

Thalia Theater and transferred to Victor Barnowsky's Theater in der Königgrätzer Strasse (12.8.28). R. Duschinsky's *Brothers on the Dole* ran at Gustav Hartung's Renaissancetheater (1.10.29). All three were commercial managements.

which concerns Prussian-German traditions and history is turned into perfidious caricature and dragged in the mud! Potsdam with its carillon, the great King, the War Generals, our marches, our most sacred songs, our flag: 'Garbage! Sweep it up!' "

Berliner Lokal-Anzeiger, September 7–8

" .,. . So in songs which really have nothing to do with this play . . . all things military are presented in the ugliest distortions. The actions of the military are shown as a mixture of narrow-mindedness and lack of conscience. Even Frederick the Great is exposed to ridicule in an animated cartoon."

Börsen-Zeitung, September 8

" . . . It is possible to evaluate the whole thing from an artistic standpoint. . . . But if Piscator consciously wants to present political theater, then his production must be evaluated politically above all. Seen in this light, the Bolshevist agitator's latest performance is a piece of effrontery without parallel, against which the whole German people must take precautionary measures for reasons of hygiene."

Königsberger Allgemeine Zeitung, September 8

I made no special effort to attract the hatred of the right wing. Certainly not with this play in which the reaction could scarcely be shown in conjunction with its real roots, big business. But the effect deserves to be recorded. In spite of my clarity there were misunderstandings even here; the scene with the three street sweepers and the soldier's corpse has been interpreted right across the board from Right to Left as an insult to the ordinary soldier. It never entered my head to vilify the "common man," as he is called in the jargon of the circles who exploit him. Walter Mehring stated his point of view on September 13 in the *Berliner Tageblatt:*

"The angriest reaction was unleashed by a scene with a song: after the end of the weird and wonderful scenes from the inflation, three street sweepers appear and sweep everything up. They come across paper money (their devalued wages), a steel helmet (devalued power), a corpse (the corpse has been left lying, dead, devalued. 'That was once a man.'). And once again the street sweepers pronounce their angry comment, 'Garbage! Sweep it up!' (I did not write 'soldier' but 'corpse.' I did not write, 'He is tossed on a dung heap!' I am not responsible for the ineptitude of the actors during the first night. Piscator, when he read the poem, said it was the most moving, the most tragic scene in the whole play.) And anyhow, when did we start to identify the author with an objective recognition of the nonentity of all beings after death? A 'national' newspaper wrote that I poured scorn on the dead of the World War! After all that I have written, I refuse to defend myself against such slander. But I would make one reply: that war cost us twelve million lives! Look at Friedrich's book on the war and see how the corpses were thrown into mass graves. But you can't see it because it was banned, banned in every country!

    Hamlet: Dost thou think Alexander looked o' this fashion i' the earth?

    Horatio: E'en so.

    Hamlet: And smelt so? Pah. *(Puts down the skull.)*"

Where Was the Coroner?

Piscator's Disrespect for the Dead

"At the Piscator-Bühne yesterday, toward the end of a puerile and insignificant performance which we have reviewed on another page, the following scene took place: The corpse of a soldier is carried toward three street sweepers on a conveyor belt. The corpse is brightly lit and the three street sweepers sing a song telling us that the soldier has been justly murdered because he shot at people. Then the corpse is rudely heaved into a barrow and one of the street sweepers adds to the disgrace by prodding at the head of the corpse. The audience at the Piscator-Bühne, 95 percent of which is made up of wealthy capitalist or proletarian followers of Communism, could produce only thirty or forty people to applaud this scene, while the rest of the theater cried out in indignation.

We did not report the content of this vulgar scene here in order to call for the censor, although the police would have every reason to ensure that future performances of the scene do not incite disturbance of the peace. We demand that the police draw the attention of the coroner to this scene for reasons of public safety. There are murderers and defilers of corpses who cannot be made responsible for their acts within the normal concepts of legality because of the brutal nature of their instincts. The people who staged this scene, those who acted in it and those who financed it should not be surprised if they are included in the category of moral inferiority as defined in paragraph 51 of the Penal Code. It is the task of the police to take persons who cannot be held responsible for their crimes into custody for their own sake. It seems to us that the police are bound to take the appropriate action in the case of those who perpetrated or financed the defilement of the corpse at the Piscator-Bühne."

Nachtausgabe, September 7

The people who rang the bells and draped the whole of Germany with flags as not one but thousands of dead soldiers were shoveled into mass graves are the selfsame people who are using a single scene in a play not just to bring down me or my theater—this would be too small an objective—but as an opportunity to mount another attack on our weak State with renewed ferocity, and to start a fresh offensive against the masses whose will to freedom, whose progress, has always been a thorn in their flesh. They are fanning the flames of a pogrom which will affect not only me but everything which is progressive, everything which has overcome their dark malignant spirit, everything which points to the future. In the *Deutsche Zeitung* on September 10 a certain Herr Palm vituperates:

"German Piscators to the front. Erwin Piscator is awake once again. His evil spirit casts crosses in the dust. His machinery throws dead soldiers on rubbish heaps. His thought: agitation. His work: party theater instead of art. His aim: disintegration. His goal: Moscow.

"Kurt Tucholsky poisons souls with his pen. A Piscator of literature. We have before us a photograph, on it several German generals. Caption by Kurt Tucholsky: 'The zoo is looking back at you!'

"George Grosz mocks God. He sees the God of the Christians as a mere caricature. He is a Piscator with a sketchpad.

"Alfred Kerr welcomes and encourages all these Piscators. He is the Piscator of the German critics. He is full of praise every time something is torn down and 'dragged in the mud,' he supports cultural Bolshevism. Whenever religion, the Fatherland or tradition are held up to scorn he registers it as an experience, as art.

"Kerr is a type. A Yiddish type. A type from the Jewish press. The same press which decries anti-Semitism as mindless, but which praises everything else that is *anti* as a grand intellectual achievement and lends it support. A type from that press which praises everything that gallops over the feelings and the tenderest sentiments of people who think differently, and praises it as a new form of artistic expression.

"These Piscators are getting bolder. They throw their scorn in our teeth with more and more effrontery. The muck which is being thrown at us from the other side is piling higher and higher. Do we want to perish under it?

"The Piscators, their patrons and protectors work with poison gas. They have gassed the cities and are moving out slowly into the country. Rage is no longer an adequate gas mask: retaliate with poison gas of your own.

"Do not leave the muck they have thrown lying in front of you. Pick it up. Throw it back. Right into the blasphemous teeth of all these Piscators.

"Don't moan. Don't complain. Don't get angry. Don't protest. These impertinent people interpret it as intolerance. Defend yourselves. Make the name 'reaction' an honorable name.

"Drag Jews onto the stage. Show their deceitfulness. Show their destructive spirit. Show their squalid little business minds. Show the merchant of Berlin who is not from Berlin, who is living today on the Kurfürstendamm and in the villas in Grünewald. (In spite of Mehring and Piscator.)

338

"Tear them down. Stop at nothing. Mutilate their most cherished feelings as they have mutilated yours. Pay them back in the same coin. But don't forget the interest. And don't forget that in these very circles they are accustomed to demand high rates of interest.

"What a pleasure it will be to be able to pay them back at last!

"Look at the lists which the Communists intend to expropriate. The Piscators stand at the head of these lists. Show them to the people. Show their diamonds. Show their villas, show their dishonest provocation. And show the most prominent actors. The ones who 'shamelessly prostitute' themselves and their art. Show them as they luxuriate in affluence with their star salaries while thousands of other men of ability perish slowly in misery.

"You know how it must be done. Go and see *Potemkin*. Follow the example of Piscator. Throw all these Piscators on the rubbish heap. Wheel them off in barrows. Look at Grosz, read Kerr. And you will always know what is to be done and when it is to be done. Do the job well. Do the whole job. And don't forget the interest.

"Long live the reaction! The reaction against a plague which has led us back to health, back to true art.

"German Piscators to the front!"

And the *Lokal-Anzeiger*—should I consider it an honor?—puts the discussion of our performance on the front page on September 7.

Must we grant them this triumph? Will the Left look on in silence as a venture which was animated by no other desire than to fight the cause of the oppressed, the cause of tomorrow, is driven into bankruptcy? Will people realize at last that it is not nuances

Headline on the front page of the *Lokal-Anzeiger*: "Garbage! Sweep it out!"

339

which are decisive, and that even our failures are a hundred times more fruitful for future developments than are the best and most balanced performances of an epoch which has outlived its usefulness? Or will they use it to demolish our foundations and make our work impossible for years to come? Then the fate which has submerged us today will submerge every other movement which has the same aims. For it must be repeated again and again that political theater is a means, and a very delicate means within a larger process which it can help along, but for which it can never be a complete substitute. If we made a mistake, it was to get too far ahead of ourselves and our times, to want more than can be achieved within this society with the means at our disposal.

I close this book in the middle of a phase of development. No one can know what shape things will take. But the will remains. And I should like to think that one of the results of this book will be to help to unite more closely, to concentrate together, all the forces which share our desire to fight on the third, the cultural front for the breakthrough of a new epoch.

Boom by Leo Lania.   Piscator-Bühne 1928.

Designer: Traugott Müller
Drilling rigs and freestanding door.

Albanian oil region. French representative (Erwin Kalser) meets an Albanian (Leonhard Steckel).

Center left: Curt Bois as dictator.

Center right: Among the drilling rigs.

Tilla Durieux as South American oil agent.

Curt Bois as a monk on Mount Athos.

The Last Emperor by J. R. Bloch.   Piscator-Bühne 1928.
Director: Karlheinz Martin. Designer: Reinhold Schön

On board the battle-
ship, the Prince
(Ernst Deutsch)
learns that he has
been proclaimed
Emperor.

Albert Steinrück

Center right: Throne room. Empress (Frieda Richard) in conversation with Chancellor (Albert Steinrück).

Courses at the Piscator-Bühne Studio (1927/28).

Training with Fritz Sommer.

Film class at the Piscator-Bühne Studio.

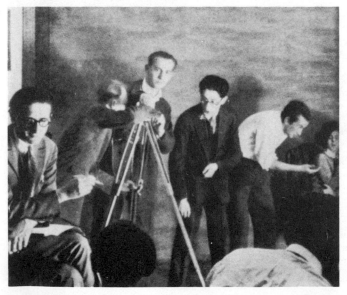

Homesickness by Franz Jung.   Piscator-Bühne 1928.
Director: Franz Jung   Designer: John Heartfield

Harbor bar, framed by a projection.

On a South Seas island (frame and background projections).

What Price Glory? by Maxwell Anderson and Laurence Stallings
Theater in der Königgrätzer Strasse 1928.

Ernst Busch (left) and Albert Venohr as
American soldiers.

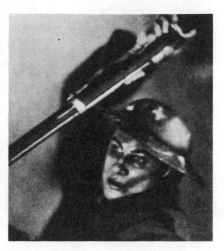

Below: Scene in a foxhole. *Left to right*: Speelmans, Berndt, Albers, Kortner.

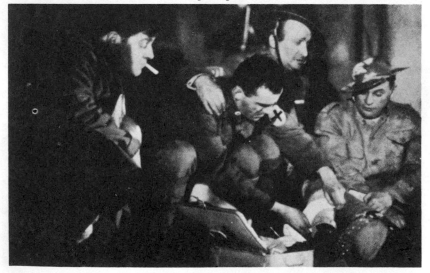

The Merchant of Berlin by Walter Mehring.

Piscator-Bühne 1929 Design: Laszlo
Moholy-Nagy

EPILOGUE

The second Piscator-Bühne was Piscator's last attempt to establish himself in a top-rank theater in the Weimar Republic, but he was still to direct three more political plays, working within actors' collectives with limited resources.

When the Piscator-Bühne folded, a group of actors re-formed as the Piscator-Bühne (Kollektiv) and rehearsed Carl Credé's § 218, *Women in Distress* (§ 218, *Frauen in Not*) for ten days in a back room in an apartment house before opening at the Mannheim Apollo Theater and playing to packed houses on a tour of Germany. The play was an exposure of the effect of the paragraph in the legal code which made abortion illegal. Medical intervention was available to the rich at a price, but the poor were forced into the hands of back-street abortionists. It was estimated that there were 500,000 to 800,000 illegal abortions a year, resulting in 10,000 deaths and 50,000 cases in need of medical attention. The play showed the fate of one of the victims which Piscator presented in intense, naturalistic scenes in two realistic workers' rooms set side by side on the stage by his designer Traugott Müller. It was an emotional play with telling effects—a piercing scream rang out as an abortion was performed behind a screen—but Piscator broke up and objectivized the action by seating some of the cast in the audience with scarcely any makeup. The minister, the doctor, the district attorney, the factory owner sat and aired their views on the law in the orchestra before climbing onto the stage to act them out. Figures stood up and discoursed on economics, without its being apparent whether this was audience participation or part of the script. The district attorney took a vote on the antiabortion law each evening. On tour they invited local figures to speak on the issue. There were special performances for doctors and lawyers. Piscator was agitating with the directness of his agitprop days, though he now had a realistic play punctuated with open debate. The production reached the Wallner Theater in Berlin on April 3, 1930, where it was performed fifty times by the end of May. From April 23 to April 27, Meyerhold's Moscow State Theater appeared in Berlin with Tretiakov's *Roar, China*, Ostrovsky's *Forest*, Gogol's *Inspector General* and Crommelynck's *Magnificent Cuckold*, and Meyerhold and Piscator met for the first time and took part in a platform discussion on political theater. § 218 toured again at the beginning of the next season and returned to Berlin to the Lessing-Theater, from which it transferred to the Wallner Theater to open the third Piscator-Bühne on October 29. Friedrich Wolf's *Cyanide*, a similar plea for the reform of § 218, was also widely performed at this time by the Gruppe Junger Schauspieler, testimony to the heat generated by the issue. The plays were subjected to demonstrations and harassment by the Catholic Center Party and by the Nazis, and § 218 was banned in Essen, Würzburg and Schweinfurt, and later the Nazi Minister Frick banned it in the whole of Thuringia.

In June, 1929, Felix Gasbarra announced that a third Piscator-Bühne would soon open at the Wallner Theater. This time the new enterprise was welcomed by the *Rote Fahne* as a real proletarian-revolutionary theater in a working-class area. Piscator now had party approval. His collective began to rehearse a stage version of Theodor Plivier's novel *The Kaiser's Coolies (Des Kaisers Kulis)*, but no agreement could be reached with the owners of the Wallner Theater, and the production was accepted by Heinz Saltenburg and opened at the Lessing-Theater on August 31. The novel, which dealt with the 1917 mutiny in the German Navy and ended with the ringleaders Kobis and Reichpietsch facing the firing squad, was not dramatized. Selected episodes were demonstrated by the actors within an explanatory framework of newsreel and cartoon film, choral commentary, and passages read by the author, who also played the part of Kobis. The production started with newsreels in which patriotic slogans alternated with the reality of the battlefield, military parades with mass graves, British statistics for arms production with German ones. This was followed by shots of ships loading coal, harbor bars, and the battle of the Skaggerak, which was then explained in a cartoon film (Svend Nolan and Albrecht Victor Blum) with little ships maneuvering on a map. The play then traced the events involving the two mutineers, and after their execution the red flag of the November Revolution was run up, and a choir explained how these events related to the present, turning history into agitation. Many elements of Piscator's epic theater recurred here—newsreel and cartoon, diagrams and statistics, narrator and choir and of course the multiple set (Traugott Müller had built a three-tier set with scaffolding). It was a production that combined elements of *Hoppla* and § 218.

The Kaiser's Coolies ran during the 1930 election campaign, when street clashes between left- and right-wing militants were daily occurrences. On September 14 the Nazis gained 6,000,000 votes and jumped from 12 to 107 seats in the Reichstag.

On October 29 the Wallner Theater opened as the third Piscator-Bühne (Kollektiv) with § 218, but by November 1 it had been put at the disposal of the Spiegelmeinschaft Berliner Schauspieler, another left-wing collective, whose three productions, supplemented by two Piscator-Bühne productions in which Piscator was not himself involved, kept the theater open while Piscator prepared his next production, his last before going into exile, Friedrich Wolf's *Tai Yang Awakes (Tai Yang Erwacht)*.

Tai Yang Erwacht illustrates the development of a Chinese factory worker to class consciousness. Her reformist illusions are dispelled by the brutality of Tschu Fu, the factory owner, and she convinces the other Communists of the need for direct action and leads the workers into the streets to fight for the revolution. Information about China provided an example for action in Germany. It was orginally a rounded, naturalistic piece, and Wolf rewrote it in the open, epic style at Piscator's instigation, as a letter from E. P. to F. W. in the Friedrich Wolf Archive in Berlin shows:

"I should like to sketch the basic idea for the production to you. . . . You have managed to put everything in, but you have kept within the closed form of drama, so that the facts are all mentioned without ever taking concrete form before us. . . . What do you think of this: The stage is open, makeup tables in the middle. Actors with European faces come on in street clothes and sit down. General conversation, then politics—reaction, national socialism, leading by analogy to foreign politics, in particular the present unrest in China.

"There is general interest. One of the actors . . . draws a map of China on his mirror, which is in fact a light which throws the map on a screen. . . . The actors make themselves up and change before the audience's eyes into the characters in the play, the Chinese . . ."

This approach was adopted and the production was worked out in demonstrative, didactic terms. The designer, John Heartfield, draped the stage and the auditorium with banners and posters— "Down with the imperialists' interventionist wars," "Fish and meat make up only 3 percent of the Chinese diet"—which turned the theater into a party meeting hall. There were bamboo bridges for entrances and exits through the audience. Film of events in China illustrated phases of the action on a screen at the back of the stage. The acting was stylized (Piscator mentioned Japanese theater as a model which offered the basic elements of acting, primal gestures well suited to propaganda) and Hans Veidt's communist dance group was engaged for the crowd scenes.

This was slogan theater, and it had the full backing of the *Rote Fahne*, which encouraged every worker and his wife to see the play,

343

but the bourgeois press rejected both the politics and their presentation. Alfred Kerr noted regretfully that the play was no more effective than the average newspaper article, and only Herbert Ihering
and Bernhard Diebold were still prepared to overlook the technical
flaws and accept the consistent political vision behind the production. Diebold reiterated his view that Piscator's style was the style of
the future:

> "Wherever the forming hand of Piscator took over from the formless
> author we saw great theater. Make no mistake, Piscator's method is a
> superb formula for a future dramatic form. It is not, however, the new
> drama itself. Make no mistake, Piscator's method is not the preserve of
> the Communist Party. Any Party could put its enthusiasms into concrete
> form on the stage using Piscator's methods."

Piscator's work during the Weimar Republic ended with his
playing in a seedy old theater in the obscurity of a working-class
quarter, deserted by the bourgeois press and public. It is worth noting that Brecht, whose work is unthinkable without Piscator's experiments, still had the ear of a broad public. He directed his own *Man
is Man* at the Staatstheater three weeks after the opening of *Tai
Yang Erwacht*. The two men's fortunes had been very different.

In 1931 Piscator went to the Soviet Union to make a film of
Anna Seghers' novel *The Revolt of the Fishermen of St. Barbara*.
He stayed there until 1936, devoting some of his time to organizing
antifascist artists in exile. Then, before Stalin's purges, he took a
business trip to the West and never returned. In Paris, with Alfred
Neumann, he prepared a dramatization of Tolstoy's *War and Peace*
which was produced in 1942 in New York, where he had set up the
Dramatic Workshop at the New School for Social Research after
his arrival in 1938. Piscator worked there, and employed some of
his old colleagues like Kalser, Rehfisch, Zuckmayer and Hanns
Eisler until the McCarthy era. He returned to the Federal Republic
of Germany in 1951, and after exhausting years as a free-lance director he was appointed Intendant of the newly built Theater der
Freien Volksbühne in West Berlin. In a sense he had come home.
This time the documentary plays which had been lacking during
the Weimar Republic began to appear, and he directed Rolf Hoch-
huth's *The Deputy*, Heinar Kipphardt's *In the Matter of J. Robert
Oppenheimer* in 1963, and Peter Weiss's *The Investigation* the following year.

Erwin Piscator died on March 30, 1966

Chronological Table
of Political and Theatrical Events

(P) = world premiere

As the war went into its third year with Piscator at the front, the first signs of a new trend in the theater were seen.

1916
Sept. 30 W. Hasenclever's **Der Sohn** (P) at the Prague Landestheater, then on Oct. 8 at Dresden Albert Theater, dir. A. E. Licho, both occasions with E. Deutsch in the title role, for which he devised the intense, hollow-eyed, emotional acting which was to make him a leading Expressionist actor.
Dec. 17 R. Schickele's **Hans im Schnackenloch** (P) at the Frankfurt Neues Theater, dir. A. Hellmer. Set in Alsace-Lorraine amid conflicting French/German loyalties, this first play to depart from jingoistic patriotism in treating a wartime problem was quickly banned by the High Command.

1917
Trench warfare at a stalemate on the Western front. Germany declares unrestricted U-boat warfare (Feb. 1) and the United States enters the war (Apr. 2). Food shortages in Germany. Independent Socialist Party of Germany (USPD) founded in April. In November, revolution and abdication of the Czar in Russia. Special seasons of new Expressionist plays open, "Das junge Deutschland" at M. Reinhardt's Deutsches Theater in Berlin, and "Das jüngste Deutschland" at O. Falckenberg's Munich Kammerspiele.

Jan. 29 G. Kaiser's **Die Bürger von Calais** (P) at Frankfurt Neues Theater, dir. J. Gottowt. Written in 1912/13, this play embodied the hope for the spiritual regeneration of mankind that was to become central to Expressionism.
Apr. 28 G. Kaiser's **Von Morgens bis Mitternachts** (P) at the Munich Kammerspiele, dir. O. Falckenberg.
June 3 O. Kokoschka's **Mörder, Hoffnung der Frauen, Hiob, Der brennende Dornbusch** (P) at Dresden Albert Theater, dir. O.

Kokoschka. These ecstatic visions in experimental Expressionism dated from 1907 to 1911, and were staged in Dresden with the encouragement of E. Deutsch, H. George and W. Hasenclever. George's performance in these one-acters earned him a contract at the Frankfurt Schauspielhaus which pioneered early Expressionism.

Oct. 27   G. Kaiser's **Die Koralle** (P) simultaneously at Frankfurt Neues Theater, dir. A. Hellmer, and Munich Kammerspiele, dir. O. Falckenberg as first play in the series "Das jüngste Deutschland."

Nov. 2   H. Johst's **Der Einsame** (P) at Düsseldorf Schauspielhaus, dir. G. Lindemann. This pathos-laden vision of the fate of the artist, featuring the dramatist C. D. Grabbe (1801–36), was widely performed and later prompted Brecht to write Baal to deflate the artist myth.

Dec. 8   P. Kornfeld's **Die Verführung** (P) at the Frankfurt Schauspielhaus, dir. G. Hartung. This production opened the remarkable Expressionist phase at the Schauspielhaus, where Intendant C. Zeiss had assembled a strong team: directors G. Hartung and later R. Weichert, writers O. Zoff, P. Kornfeld, W. Hasenclever, A. Bronnen and F. von Unruh. **The Seduction** was a key Expressionist script, exemplifying Kornfeld's assertion that drama should not deal with character and causal psychology, but should bare the depths of mind and soul.

Dec. 15   W. Hasenclever's **Antigone** (P) at Leipzig Stadttheater. The war turned Hasenclever into a political writer, and here he foxed the censors by adapting Sophocles' play as a stage vehicle for his own pacifism.

Dec. 23   R. Sorge's **Der Bettler** (P) at the Deutsches Theater, dir. M. Reinhardt. This was the first exercise in lyrical Expressionism to be seen in Berlin, where it inaugurated the series "Das junge Deutschland." The abandonment of a linear plot called for new techniques of staging, and open black spaces puntuated by a few sticks of furniture, a window frame and a door, with spotlights picking out the actors, as used here, soon became standard for Expressionist plays. E. Deutsch as the Poet established himself overnight as the Berlin specialist in cadaverous Expressionist youths.

1918

A Russo-German peace treaty is signed at Brest Litovsk (Mar. 2). President Wilson announces a Fourteen Point peace plan. In October the Hapsburg monarchy collapses, exposing Germany's south-eastern flank, and the German fleet mutinies at Kiel, marking the start of a workers' and soldiers' revolution that by Nov. 9 has reached Berlin. On Nov. 11, Wilhelm II abdicates and a cease-fire comes into effect. Ebert becomes Chancellor and the struggle between the moderate SPD and the radical USPD for control of the Left begins. In December the Spartacist League becomes the Communist Party of Germany (KPD) and Karl Liebknecht and Rosa Luxemburg found the Rote Fahne as its organ of publicity. The former court theaters become state theaters. Theater censorship ends.

Jan. 18 W. Hasenclever's **Der Sohn** at Mannheim Nationaltheater, dir. R. Weichert. This, Sorge's **Bettler** and Kornfeld's **Verführung** were the three key early Expressionist scripts, and Weichert's definitive production struck the exact style and tempo for these plays, fast and unreal, as was instantly recognized. The Son was placed center stage under an overhead spotlight, and the other characters revolved around him in the gloom, the rooms barely indicated in the black hole of the stage (des. L. Sievert). When F. Hollaender directed it for Reinhardt's "Das junge Deutschland" the effect was inhibited by the Berlin Realist tradition.

Feb. 10 R. Goering's **Seeschlacht** (P) at Dresden Schauspielhaus, dir. E. Lewinger and A. Linnebach. Set in a warship's gun turret, it was the first play to stage men under fire in wartime.

June 16 F. Von Unruh's **Das Geschlecht** (P) at Frankfurt Schauspielhaus, dir. G. Hartung. Unruh was an officer and another patriot turned pacifist in the trenches, where he composed this ecstatic antiwar scenario in 1916. It was quickly overtaken by events and when "Das junge Deutschland" revived it on Dec. 29 the critics noted that Germany already had the war behind it and was preoccupied by the revolution.

Nov. 28 G. Kaiser's **Gas** simultaneously at Frankfurt Neues Theater, dir. A. Hellmer, and at Düsseldorf Schauspielhaus, dir. G. Lindemann. This sequel to **Die Koralle** was Kaiser's most direct treatment of contemporary social problems and brought the modern industrial plant onto the stage for the first time.

1919

"Spartacus Week" sees a spontaneous rising of the Berlin workers crushed between Jan. 5 and 10 by Ebert's SPD government, for whom Gustav Noske enlists the aid of the reactionary Freikorps which are later to provide Hitler's first paramilitary units. Karl Liebknecht and Rosa Luxemburg are murdered. In Munich a Republic of Councils, in which Ernst Toller is active, is proclaimed on April 5 and by May 2 has been brutally put down by the Freikorps.

347

The Treaty of Versailles is signed on June 28. Ebert becomes President and the Weimar constitution comes into force in August. In September, K. Martin's activist Tribüne opens, stating in its manifesto, "We are committed to a standpoint and a specific direction . . . we will not play, we will be in earnest. . . ." L. Jessner becomes Intendant of the Staatliches Schauspielhaus on the Gendarmenmarkt. Brecht's first theater reviews appear in Augsburg.

Jan. 23 C. Sternheim's **1913** (P) at Frankfurt Schauspielhaus, dir. G. Hartung. Sternheim, hitherto gagged by the censors, was the only prewar writer to be taken up by the postwar theater, and this satire on the life and role of Germany's industrial magnates before the war, written in 1912/13, was the last classical Sternheim to be staged. His postwar plays lacked bite.

Feb. 27 Shakespeare's **As You Like It** at the Deutsches Theater, dir. M. Reinhardt. Long neglected in Germany as unplayable, this comedy benefited from the musical phrasing developed for lyrical Expressionism, and Reinhardt's production, though wholly at odds with the times, turned out to be "the lightest, most delicate, happiest thing he had ever done."

Mar. E. Barlach's **Der arme Vetter** (P) at Hamburg Kammerspiele, dir. E. Ziegel.

Sept. 12 W. Hasenclever's one-acters, **Der Retter** and **Die Entscheidung,** dir. K. Martin, inaugurate Die Tribüne.

Sept. 30 E. Toller's **Die Wandlung** at the Tribüne, dir. K. Martin. This production brought Berlin its first taste of the full-blooded Expressionism developed in the provinces. (Reinhardt's "Das junge Deutschland" had watered it down with Berlin Realism.) Toller and F. Kortner, who played the lead, became celebrities overnight. The actors, in grotesque makeup, moved on a low platform among skeletal props against a black background. Financial problems and ideological differences led to the abandonment of the Tribüne's activist policy by the end of the year.

Oct. 10 Shakespeare's **Cymbeline** at the Deutsches Theater, dir. L. Berger. An attempt to get away from the proscenium arch by placing the actors on a bare platform.

Nov. 28 Aeschylus's **Oresteia** inaugurates the Grosses Schauspielhaus, dir. M. Reinhardt. Reinhardt's prewar prestige was still intact, and Jessner had yet to make his mark, so the opening of this 3,000-seat arena was seen as Reinhardt's contribution to the artistic revolution, and it was on this stage that he tried to confront Jessner's challenge.

Dec. 5 G. Kaiser's **Hölle, Weg, Erde** (P) at Frankfurt Neues Theater, dir. A. Hellmer, preached a new community of mankind.

Dec. 12   Schiller's **Wilhelm Tell** at the Staatliches Schauspielhaus, dir. L. Jessner. Jessner's Berlin debut as a director marked a complete break with the pompous, declamatory, illusionistic court theater style. **Tell** was reduced to a clarion call for freedom, psychological realism was abandoned and replaced by symbolic gestures and groupings, with symbolic effects of color and lighting. As befitted a republican theater the tone was revolutionary and antinationalistic. Kortner's portrayal of Gessler make him the outstanding male actor at the Staatstheater overnight.

Dec. 15   H. Kranz's **Die Freiheit** (P) at the Philharmonic Hall, mounted by A. Holitscher and K. Martin as the first and last production of their Proletarisches Theater.

1920

Treaty of Versailles comes into force and German populations are evacuated from the ceded territories. The reactionary Kapp Putsch is quickly foiled by a general strike in support of the Republic, followed by communist risings in Saxony and the Ruhr, which the government again suppresses with the aid of the Freikorps. French occupation of the area around Mainz. The value of the mark begins to decline. Hitler proclaims his Twenty-Five Points at the Munich Hofbräuhaus. Brecht moves to Munich. The Freie Volksbühne and the Neue Freie Volksbühne merge to become the Volksbühne.

Jan. 12   A. Strindberg's **Ghost Sonata** at Königsberg Tribunal, dir. O. L. Spaun, des. O. Reigbert, with Piscator as Archenholz, the student.

Jan. 20   F. Wedekind's **Tod und Teufel** and H. Mann's **Variété** at Königsberg Tribunal, dir. E. Piscator, des. O. Reigbert.

Jan. 30   F. Wedekind's **Schloss Wetterstein** at Königsberg Tribunal, dir. E. Piscator, des. E. Piscator and F. Kaiser.

Feb. 14   R. Rolland's **Danton** (P) at the Grosses Schauspielhaus, dir. M. Reinhardt.

Feb. 17   G. Kaiser's **Der Centaur** at Königsberg Tribunal, director and designer not on record.

Mar. 12   F. Wedekind's **Der Marquis von Keith** at the Staatliches Schauspielhaus, dir. L. Jessner. Jessner's forced pace, rhythmic style and puppetlike figures against a monochrome background (white, then red) initiated a new Wedekind style in Berlin. First-nighters on the way home saw the start of the Kapp *Putsch.*

Apr. 18   W. Hasenclever's **Antigone** at the Grosses Schauspielhaus, dir. K. Martin, who had joined the Reinhardt organization at the beginning of the year.

Apr. 21   P. Kornfeld's **Himmel und Hölle** (P) at Deutsches Theater, dir. L. Berger. The house magazine, *Das junge Deutschland*, published Kornfeld's essay, *Der beseelte und der psychologische Mensch (The Man of Soul and the Psychological Man)*, outlining his theory of the drama, according to which actors, instead of demonstrating the psychology of character, were to show spiritual energy and embody mankind in ecstasy, freed from all restrictive contingencies. Berger's musically phrased production was one of the high-water marks of Expressionist theater, and Agnes Straub's playing of the Prostitute was rated one of the definitive individual Expressionist performances.

May 28   Shakespeare's **Julius Caesar** at the Grosses Schauspielhaus, dir. M. Reinhardt. Reinhardt's second attempt to adapt Shakespeare to the dimensions of the big arena. For the forum scenes the hydraulically operated stage segments were used for the first time. This was Reinhardt's last production in this theater before leaving for Salzburg.

June 3   F. von Unruh's **Platz** (P) at Frankfurt Schauspielhaus, dir. G. Hartung. This sequel to *Das Geschlecht* showed the son from the previous play attempting a revolution in the town square against the old gods. It is one of the most pathos-laden and idealistic treatments of the Expressionist themes of selfless love and the regeneration of mankind. The representatives of the old order were in grotesque garb with green faces. H. George as Schleich, wild, brutal, springing without transition from one effect to the next, gave one of the most accomplished and striking Frankfurt Expressionist performances. The erotic scenes almost caused a riot. This was Hartung's last production before going as Intendant to Darmstadt.

Aug. 22   Salzburg Festival inaugurated with H. von Hofmannsthal's **Jedermann** in front of the cathedral, dir. M. Reinhardt. Reinhardt handed his Berlin theaters over to F. Hollaender and took up residence in nearby Schloss Leopoldskron.

Oct. 5   K. A. Wittvogel's **Der Krüppel**, A. Gabor's **Vor dem Tor**, and J. Barta's **Russlands Tag** (P) at the Proletarisches Theater, organized by E. Piscator and H. Schüller.

Oct. 28   W. Hasenclever's **Jenseits** (P) at Dresden Schauspielhaus, dir. B. Viertel. Hasenclever abandoned political drama in 1917 and now turned to Expressionist spiritualism.

Nov. 5   Shakespeare's **Richard III** at the Staatliches Schauspielhaus, dir. L. Jessner. The play became a study in ruthless careerism and the Jessner steps (des. E. Pirchan) symbolized the rungs of power. Jessner extracted a powerful, high-speed performance from F. Kortner in the title role.

350

Nov. 10 M. Gorky's **Enemies** at the Proletarisches Theater, dir. E. Piscator.

Dec. 5 U. Sinclair's **Prince Hagen** at the Proletarisches Theater, dir. E. Piscator, des. L. Moholy-Nagy.

Dec. 10 C. Zuckmayer's **Kreuzweg** (P) at the Staatliches Schauspielhaus, dir. L. Berger. Jessner detected tones worth encouraging in Zuckmayer's first play, and Berger directed it as a dark, hectic Expressionist piece, full of confusions and complications. It came off after three performances and Zuckmayer went on to learn the metier by watching Jessner, Berger, Fehling and Reinhardt in rehearsal.

1921

Germany committed to high reparations repayments. Allies occupy Rhine ports. Political unrest grows, with communist risings in Hamburg and central Germany. A pro-German majority in the referendum in Upper Silesia is followed by fighting between Polish irregulars and the German home guard. J. Wirth becomes Chancellor and, with his Minister for Reconstruction W. Rathenau, embarks on a "policy of fulfillment" (of the Versailles terms). M. Erzberger assassinated by right-wing extremists.

Feb. 6 F. Jung's **Wie lange noch—du Hure bürgerliche Gerechtigkeit** (P) at the Proletarisches Theater, dir. E. Piscator.

Mar. 22 F. von Unruh's **Louis Ferdinand, Prinz von Preussen** (P) at Darmstadt Landestheater dir. G. Hartung. An Expressionist youth confronted by the problem of duty à la Kleist.

Mar. 28 F. Jung's **Die Kanaker** at the Proletarisches Theater, dir. E. Piscator, who also played Lenin.

Apr. 9 Sophocles' **Antigone** at Berlin Volksbühne, dir. J. Fehling. Fehling, hitherto an actor, went on to direct seven plays at the Volksbühne under F. Kayssler. When he rounded off the year with L. Tieck's **Der gestiefelte Kater** (Dec. 30) he was already in the front rank of directors.

Apr. 12 A. Stramm's **Kräfte** (P) at the Deutsches Theater, dir. M. Reinhardt. Reinhardt's last production of an Expressionist play.

May 6 Schiller's **Fiesco** at the Staatliches Schauspielhaus, dir. L. Jessner. The text was adapted to make it relevant to contemporary politics. Jessner's steps now came into the audience over a bridge. E. Deutsch moved from the Deutsches Theater to play Fiesco to F. Kortner's Verrina.

Sept. 26 Schiller's **Die Räuber** at the Grosses Schauspielhaus, dir. K. Martin. Martin made this arena his own in the course of the year with a series of German revolutionary dramas—G. Hauptmann's *Florian Geyer* (Jan. 5) and *Die Weber* (June 20) and Goethe's *Götz von Berlichingen* (Nov. 7). There were red flags on the thrust stage, recalling the commitment of the Tribüne in 1919.

Sept. 29 E. Toller's **Masse Mensch** at Volksbühne, dir. J. Fehling. This was Fehling's only attempt at a political play. It was intended to bring the Volksbühne, which had succumbed to middle-class taste under Kayssler, into contact with contemporary drama again. The play was an idealization of Toller's experiences during the Munich Soviet.

Nov. 7 H. von Hofmannsthal's **Der Schwierige** (P) at Munich Residenztheater, then Berlin Kammerspiele (Nov. 30), dir. B. Reich. Hofmannsthal's subtle comic celebration of the aristocratic life style that had just passed away in Vienna was torn to shreds by the—understandably—uncomprehending Berlin critics.

Nov. 11 Shakespeare's **Othello** at the Staatliches Schauspielhaus, dir. L. Jessner. Jessner's most austere and economical production. F. Kortner in the title role put the hectic go-getters of his first Expressionist phase behind him and became quieter and more differentiated, relying less on his strident voice.

Dec. 13 Strindberg's **Dream Play** at the Deutsches Theater, dir. M. Reinhardt. This production, delicately poised between fantasy and reality, and the scintillating **Orpheus in the Underworld,** which followed it on New Year's Eve, marked the temporary end of Reinhardt's activities in Berlin, a double demonstration of the light touch that Jessner could not match.

1922

Soviet-German rapprochement marked by the Treaty of Rapallo, whose architect, Foreign Minister Rathenau, is assassinated by right-wing extremists on June 24. Inflation accelerates in August, closing Düsseldorf Schauspielhaus and threatening other theaters. Actors in nonstate theaters strike in December. Expressionism in the theater moves into its second phase, idealism giving way to the black brutalism of Jahnn, Bronnen and Brecht. Brecht awarded Kleist Prize for **Trommeln in der Nacht.** *In Berlin T. Tagger opens Renaissancetheater, Piscator and H. J. Rehfisch take over the Central-Theater, and Stanislavsky's Moscow Art Theater shows Chekhov's* **Three Sisters.**

Jan. 12 P. Kornfeld's **Himmel und Hölle,** dir. R. Weichert, marks the end of the Expressionist phase at Frankfurt Schauspielhaus.

Feb. 5 H. H. Jahnn's **Die Krönung Richards III** (P) at Leipzig Schauspielhaus, dir. H. Rothe. Jahnn was a violent, wayward talent and this erotic shocker steeped in sadomasochism was his first production. It opened a phase of brutal Black Expressionism.

Apr. 22 A. Bronnen's **Vatermord** (P) at Frankfurt Schauspielhaus, dir. W. Hoffmann-Harnisch, then more importantly at Deutsches Theater Berlin (May 14), dir. B. Viertel. Paternal brutality, filial rebellion, oedipal incest marginally averted. Bronnen's first production by Moritz Seeler's Junge Bühne (which replaced "Das junge Deutschland") caused a scandal.

June 30 E. Toller's **Die Maschinenstürmer** at Grosses Schauspielhaus, dir. K. Martin. The production gained added impact from the audience's identification of Jimmy Cobbett with Rathenau, murdered six days earlier. Realistic factory set with functioning machinery by J. Heartfield.

Aug. 12 H. von Hofmannsthal's **Das Salzburger Grosse Welttheater** (P) in Salzburg Collegiate Church, dir. M. Reinhardt, an attempt at reviving religion on the stage in a sacred setting.

Sept. 28 Brecht's **Trommeln in der Nacht** (P) at Munich Kammerspiele, dir. O. Falckenberg. This was the first production of a play by Brecht, who had still to gain a foothold in Berlin. The first poetic dramatization of the fate of an individual, the returning soldier Kragler, in postwar Germany.

Sept. 29 M. Gorky's **Smug Souls** at Central-Theater, dir. E. Piscator, des. M. Frey.

Nov. 10 Shakespeare's **Macbeth** at the Staatliches Schauspielhaus, dir. L. Jessner. Kortner's realization that the title role called for subtleties beyond his former technique marked the end of his dynamic Expressionist phase.

Nov. 17 R. Rolland's **Le Temps viendra** (P) at Central-Theater, dir. E. Piscator, des. O. Schmalhausen and M. Meier, music K. Pringsheim.

1923

French troops occupy the Ruhr. A republic is proclaimed in the Rhineland, and separatists engage in an armed struggle. Inflation reaches its peak with the dollar worth 4.2 billion marks. Communist risings in Saxony and Thuringia. The abortive Hitler-Ludendorff putsch in Munich ends with the former's arrest and imprisonment. The Nazi (NSDAP) and Communist (KPD) Parties are banned. Inflation ends with the stabilization of the mark (Nov. 15). Black Expressionism is now dominant. The impoverishment of the cultured middle class hits traditional theater audiences and the tastes of the nouveaux riches make themselves felt. To combat the lowering of standards, several short-lived actors' cooperatives are formed in Berlin: H. George's Schauspielertheater, B. Viertel and R. Bruck's Die Truppe, J. Lhermann's Das Theater. Taïrov's Moscow company shows Wilde's Salomé, Princess Brambilla, *and Racine's* Phèdre *in Berlin.*

Jan. 19 L. Tolstoy's **The Power of Darkness** at the Central-Theater, dir. E. Piscator.

Feb. 1 Kleist's **Das Käthchen von Heilbronn** at the Staatliches Schauspielhaus, dir. J. Fehling. Fehling, who had made his name directing comedies at the Volksbühne, now joined Jessner to help develop a modern repertoire. His ironic, detached production of Kleist's fairy tale, long neglected as unplayable, was hit entertainment with Lucie Mannheim in the title role.

Apr. 25 Shakespeare's **As You Like It** at Lessing-Theater, dir. V. Barnowsky, with E. Bergner as Rosalind.

May 9 Brecht's **Im Dickicht** (P) at Munich Residenztheater, dir. E. Engel, des. C. Neher. This was the first production by the team of Brecht, Engel and Neher, which lasted until Brecht's death.

May 23 E. Barlach's **Der arme Vetter** at the Staatliches Schauspielhaus, dir. J. Fehling, with H. George in the title role. One of the few successful productions of Barlach's profoundly obscure plays in the twenties.

Aug. 24 H. H. Jahnn's **Pastor Ephraim Magnus** (P) at Das Theater, Berlin, dir. A. Bronnen. A provocative but short-lived piece of lurid brutalism, cut and adapted for J. Lhermann's new company by Brecht.

Sept. 18 Shakespeare's **Merchant of Venice** at the Berlin Lustspielhaus, dir. B. Viertel. Shylock was F. Kortner, who had left the Staatstheater and joined Viertel and Bruck's Die Truppe, a group formed to combat the creeping trivialization of the established theaters such as Reinhardt's.

Dec. 8 Brecht's **Baal** (P) at Leipzig Altes Theater, dir. A. Kronacher.

Dec. 27 Shakespeare's **Twelfth Night** at Lessing-Theater, with E. Bergner as Viola.

1924

Signs of a new stability in the Weimar Republic. Dawes fixes German reparations. Hitler is released from Landsberg Prison, where he had written **Mein Kampf.** *Second phase of Expressionism fades, and the plays of Claudel, O'Neill, Synge, and Pirandello are seen on the*

German stage. Reinhardt opens the renovated Theater in der Josefstadt in Vienna, and the Komödie, a fashionable boulevard theater on the Kurfürstendamm, in Berlin. Brecht and Zuckmayer are engaged as dramaturgs at the Deutsches Theater. Piscator and Rehfisch give up the Central-Theater, which passes into the hands of the Rotter brothers. Piscator moves to the Volksbühne.

Jan. 8 E. O'Neill's **The Emperor Jones** by Die Truppe at Berlin Lustspielhaus, dir. B. Viertel.

Mar. 19 Brecht's **Edward II** at Munich Kammerspiele. Directing for the first time, Brecht chose to adapt Marlowe's unruly tragedy. Like Jessner, whom he admired, Brecht wanted to strip the stucco and gilt from the classics, and his production showed the first elements of epic theater: scene-by-scene plot summaries, precise gestures, soldiers in whiteface to demonstrate fear. Brecht was already attempting to induce critical detachment in both actors and audience.

Apr. 1 Goldoni's **Servant of Two Masters,** dir. M. Reinhardt, opens Reinhardt's first theater in Vienna, "The players in the Josefstadt under the direction of Max Reinhardt." He transferred the production to Berlin on Nov. 1 to open his new Komödie am Kurfürstendamm.

Apr. 6 A. Bronnen's **Anarchie in Sillian** (P) at Deutsches Theater, dir. H. Hilpert. With its violence and eroticism, another exercise in Black Expressionism which caused a furor.

Apr. 8 F. Hebbel's **Die Nibelungen** at the Staatliches Schauspielhaus, dir. J. Fehling. Played on a bare stage with scattered cubes, the evening was carried by the powerful Kriemhild of Agnes Straub, played with telling pathos. The play stood comparison with Fritz Lang's film of the same subject which ran concurrently.

May 26 A. Paquet's **Fahnen** (P) at Volksbühne, dir. E. Piscator, des. E. Suhr, costumes T. Hecht.

Oct. 10/11 Schiller's **Wallenstein** at the Staatliches Schauspielhaus, dir. L. Jessner, with W. Krauss in the title role. Sometimes judged to be the peak of Jessner's career as director and interpreter, the production showed him moving away from the single-stranded thematic abstraction of *Wilhelm Tell* to a more objective, detailed style.

Oct. 14 G. B. Shaw's **St. Joan** at Deutsches Theater, dir. M. Reinhardt. An epic history presented with ironic detachment, it inspired similar treatments of history by F. Bruckner *(Elisabeth von England)* and C. Zuckmayer *(Der Hauptmann von Köpenick).* A triumph for E. Bergner (Joan), who had just joined the Deutsches Theater.

Oct. 29 Brecht's **Im Dickicht** at Deutsches Theater establishes E. Engel as the leading director for Brecht.
Oct. 31 O'Neill's **The Hairy Ape** at the Berlin Tribüne, dir. E. Robert.
Nov. 22 F. Gasbarra/E. Piscator's **Revue Roter Rummel** (P) tours Berlin halls, dir. E. Piscator, music E. Meisel.
Dec. 21 O'Neill's **Moon of the Caribbees** and A. Brust's **Südsee-spiel** at Volksbühne, dir. E. Piscator, des. P. Malik, music W. Zeller.
Dec. 30 L. Pirandello's **Six Characters in Search of an Author** at the Komödie, dir. M. Reinhardt.

1925
Friedrich Ebert, President of the Reich dies (Feb. 28) and Field-Marshal von Hindenburg is elected to succeed him (Apr. 26). In the summer French troops withdraw from the Ruhr, British troops from the Cologne area. The Deutschnationale (national conservatives) come into the political reckoning again and are supported by Hugenberg's Scherl press empire. The first attempts since the end of censorship to reassert bourgeois artistic values are seen. Jessner's contract at the Staatliches Schauspielhaus is extended, but not without opposition. In Berlin, Meinhard and Bernauer, the only impresarios to rival the Reinhardt theaters, sell out, and V. Barnowsky takes over the Theater in der Königgrätzer Strasse, the Komödienhaus and the Tribüne. Piscator's political revues establish him as a front-rank director, and he and Brecht make contact. Zuckmayer achieves recognition with **Der fröhliche Weinberg;** *Bronnen's streak of success holds for one last year.*

Jan. 31 H. J. Rehfisch's **Wer weint um Juckenack?** (P) at Volks-bühne, dir. E. Piscator, technical arrangements H. Sachs, with H. George (Juckenack), Gerda Müller (Lina) and G. Fröhlich (Edmund Walter).
Feb. 27 Shakespeare's **Coriolanus** for the Deutsches Theater at the Lessing-Theater, dir. E. Engel. Engel's approach had much in common with Brecht's version of **Edward II** (1924) and proved to be an early shot in the forthcoming battle to establish a modern manner for staging the classics. F. Kortner in the title role.
Mar. 14 R. Leonhard's **Segel am Horizont** (P) at Volksbühne, dir. E. Piscator, des. T. Müller, with Gerda Müller, G. Fröhlich, P. Henckels, A. Wäscher, and G. von Wangenheim.
May 2 W. Schmidtbonn's **Hilfe! Ein Kind ist vom Himmel gefallen!** for the Volksbühne at Central-Theater, dir. E. Piscator.
May 16 A. Bronnen's **Rheinische Rebellion** (P) at Staatliches

Schauspielhaus, dir. L. Jessner. Bronnen's reputation was now at its peak. The play had a topical subject, the French occupation of the Rhineland, trimmed with erotic incident.

June 7 A. Bronnen's **Exzesse** (P) for the Junge Bühne at the Lessing-Theater, dir. H. Hilpert. Bronnen's most outrageous play and biggest scandal to date.

July 12 F. Gasbarra/E. Piscator's **Trotz alledem** (P) at the Grosses Schauspielhaus, dir. E. Piscator, des. J. Heartfield, music E. Meisel.

Sept. 16 H. Johst's **Die fröhliche Stadt** at Munich Kammerspiele, dir. E. Piscator, des. O. Reigbert.

Sept. 21 G. B. Shaw's **Back to Methuselah** (parts 1 & 2) at the Tribüne, dir. M. Kerb, followed by parts 3 to 5 at the Theater in der Königgrätzer Strasse, dir. V. Barnowsky, with F. Kortner, T. Durieux, and Roma Bahn. Barnowsky, recently returned to Berlin, quickly established himself beside Reinhardt and Jessner as the third power in the city's theaters.

Nov. 11 A. Strindberg's **Rausch** at Munich Kammerspiele, dir. E. Piscator, des. O. Reigbert.

Dec. 22 C. Zuckmayer's **Der fröhliche Weinberg** (P) at the Theater am Schiffbauerdamm, dir. R. Bruck, heralds the return of the Volksstück with its everyday characters and plot, and its straightforward, unintellectual appeal. Regarded by nationalist circles as provocative, it was awarded the Kleist Prize in November.

1926

*Controversy rages around the Reichswehr, whose chief-of-staff General Seekt resigns. Two changes of administration with Luther and Marx as successive Chancellors. Disguised attempts to reintroduce censorship in the guise of a pornography law are branded by Gerhart Hauptmann as the biggest threat to intellectual freedom in his lifetime. Eisenstein's **Battleship Potemkin**, released after heated debate for public showing, acclaimed by the critics as a masterpiece. Politics invades the theater. Brecht, Engel, Piscator, and Jessner attempt topical modernization of the classics. Reinhardt's twenty-fifth anniversary as a director in Berlin is celebrated.*

Jan. 17 E. Ortner's **Michael Hundertpfund** (P) at Berlin Tribüne, dir. E. Piscator, des. C. Klein, with H. George and Dagny Servaes.

Feb. 14 B. Brecht's **Baal** at the Deutsches Theater, dir. B. Brecht.

Feb. 20 A. Paquet's **Sturmflut** (P) at Volksbühne, dir. E. Piscator, des. E. Suhr, film J. A. Hübler-Kahla, with H. George (Granka Umnitsch), A. Granach (Gad), and Ellen Widmann (Rune Lewenclau).

Mar. 26 F. Hebbel's **Herodes und Marianne** at Staatliches Schauspielhaus, dir. L. Jessner. Kortner interpreted Herod as a political leader crippled by private torment as an epoch crumbled around him. The Star of Bethlehem rose at the close to symbolize the beginning of the Christian era. Redefining the classics became the theatrical theme of the year.

May 4 H. H. Jahnn's **Medea** at Staatliches Schauspielhaus, dir. J. Fehling. This brutal and violent version of the myth presented Medea as a negress (Agnes Straub) and was a late straggler of Black Expressionism.

May 21 P. Zech's **Das trunkene Schiff** (P) at Volksbühne, dir. E. Piscator, des. G. Grosz, costumes E. Suhr, music W. Zeller, with L. Steckel (Verlaine), and C. L. Achaz (Rimbaud).

Sept. 12 Schiller's **Die Räuber** at Staatliches Schauspielhaus, dir. E. Piscator, des. T. Müller, music E. Meisel, with C. Ebert (Franz), E. Faber (Karl), P. Bildt (Spiegelberg) and Maria Koppenhöfer (Amalie).

Sept. 25 B. Brecht's **Mann ist Mann** (P) at Hessiches Landestheater, Darmstadt, dir. J. Geis.

Oct. 17 F. Bruckner's **Krankheit der Jugend** (P) at Hamburg Kammerspiele, dir. M. Horwitz. Bruckner's first play owed much to Wedekind—the sexual problems of youth taken to pathological extremes and presented with heightened realism.

Nov. 10 M. Gorky's **Lower Depths** at Volksbühne, dir. E. Piscator, des. E. Suhr, with E. Kalser (Baron), H. George (Satin), A. Granach (Luka), Agnes Straub (Vassilissa).

Dec. 3 Shakespeare's **Hamlet** at Staatliches Schauspielhaus, dir. L. Jessner. This was Jessner's follow-up to Piscator's political *Die Räuber*. Sticking strictly to the text, he turned the play into a critique of the monarchy and its increasingly vociferous conservative, nationalist advocates. English commentators identified Claudius as Wilhelm II and Polonius as Bethmann-Hollweg. Kortner played Hamlet. Des. C. Neher, music E. Meisel.

1927

Marx's new administration includes the conservative right (Deutschnationale) for the first time. Industry recovers. Unemployment sinks from 1.8 million to 300,000. Foreign capital flows in. Political pressures on the theaters increase, and Jessner at the Staatstheater has to face such criticism that he manages only one production. The left-wing Special Sections are formed at the Volks-bühne, which temporarily takes over the Theater am Schiffbauer-damm. The Piscator-Bühne opens in the Theater am Nollen-dorfplatz. Reinhardt starts a four-month tour of the United States in November.

Jan. 21 H. Mann's **Das gastliche Haus** at Munich Kammerspiele, dir. E. Piscator, des. O. Reigbert.

Feb. 15 G. Hauptmann's **Die Weber** for the Theater erwerbloser Bühnenarbeiter (unemployed theatrical people), Berlin, dir. E. Piscator.

Feb. 15 F. von Unruh's **Bonaparte** (P) at Deutsches Theater, dir. G. Hartung, followed up the success of his **Prinz Louis Ferdinand** and marked his abandonment of Expressionism in favor of topical historical drama.

Mar. 23 E. Welk's **Gewitter über Gotland** (P) at Volksbühne, dir. E. Piscator, des. G. Grosz, music E. Meisel, film J. A. with H. George (Störtebecker), and A. Granach (Asmus Ahlrich), L. Steckel (Gödeke Michelsen), A. Steinrück.

Sept. 3 E. Toller's **Hoppla, wir leben!** at Theater am Nollen-dorfplatz, dir. E. Piscator, des. T. Müller, film K. Oertel, songs W. Mehring, with A. Granach (Karl Thomas), O. Sima (Renegat), L. Steckel (Psychiater) and E. Busch and P. Graetz in small parts.

Oct. 14 C. Zuckmayer's **Schinderhannes** (P) at Lessing-Theater, dir. R. Bruck. A popular comedy about a Rhineland Robin Hood.

Oct. 15 E. Lasker-Schüler's **Die Wupper** at Staatliches Schau-spielhaus, dir J. Fehling. This production, with the previous entry and G. Hauptmann's **Dorothea Angermann,** dir. M. Reinhardt, at the Deutsches Theater (Oct. 18) amounted to a concerted conserva-tive counterattack by the Berlin realist tradition against politically progressive theater.

Nov. 10. A. Tolstoy and P. Shchegolev's **Rasputin, the Romanovs, the War and the People which Rose Against Them** at the Theater am Nollendorfplatz, dir. E. Piscator, des. T. Müller (after an idea by E. Piscator), costumes T. Müller, music E. Meisel, film J. A. Hübler-Kahla, with P. Wegener (Rasputin), T. Durieux (Czarina), O. Sima (Trotsky), E. Kalser (Czar), A. Granach (Lenin), Sybille Binder (Vyrubova).

Nov. 17 Shakespeare's **Merchant of Venice** at Staatliches Schau-spielhaus, dir. J. Fehling. Kortner's Shylock, unmasking the rotten-ness of Christian ethics, electrified friend and foe in its relevance to the anti-Semitic fascism which was now grasping for power.

1928

At the Reichstag elections the KPD and SPD make gains, winning 42 percent of the vote. A grand coalition is formed which survives until 1930. The start of the depression pushes unemployment up to 2 million in the fall. The conservative groups continue to agitate for state control of cultural life. A wave of radicalism sweeps the theater with committed plays on topical issues from Bruckner, Lampel, Menzel, Weisenborn and Marieluise Fleisser. The nationalists continue to snipe at Jessner. Piscator opens a studio theater and takes over the Lessing-Theater (Mar. 1), then goes bankrupt. In the fall an ambitious independent impresario, E. J. Aufricht, takes over the Theater am Schiffbauerdamm and opens with **The Threepenny Opera.** *H. Neft succeeds Holl at the Volksbühne. Actors from Piscator's defunct company form the Gruppe Junger Schauspieler (Young Actors' Group).*

Jan. 8 F. Jung's **Heimweh** (P) by the Piscator-Bühne Studio at the Nollendorftheater, dir. L. Steckel, des. J. Heartfield, music H. Eisler.

Jan. 23 J. Hašek's **Adventures of the Good Soldier Schwejk** (P), dir. E. Piscator, des. G. Grosz, music E. Meisel, film J. A. Hübler-Kahla, with M. Pallenberg (Schwejk), O. Sima, A. Edthofer, E. J. Pröckl, S. Szakall, Elisabeth Neumann, J. Dannegger, and J. Fürth.

Feb. 4 G. Hauptmann's **Die Weber** at the Staatliches Schauspielhaus, dir. L. Jessner. Harassed by Hugenberg's nationalists who raised the matter of the State Theaters in the Reichstag, beset by flops from his directors, his own style and ingenuity exhausted, straining the patience even of sympathetic critics like Ihering, Jessner rallied an audience around himself again with this production.

Feb. 4 H. von Hofmannsthal's **Der Turm** (P) at Munich Prinzregententheater, dir. K. Stieler.

Feb. 14 G. Menzel's **Toboggan** (P) at Staatstheater Dresden, dir. J. Gielen. A Studio theater production inaugurating the series Aktuelle Bühne (Topical Stage). Literature now concerned itself with World War I, and **Toboggan** preluded a wave of realistic war plays with an antiwar message.

Mar. 1 U. Sinclair's **Singing Jailbirds** at Piscator-Bühne Studio, dir. E. Lönner, des. T. Müller.

Apr. 10 L. Lania's **Konjunktur** (P) at the Lessing-Theater, dir. E. Piscator, des. T. Müller, music K. Weill, with Tilla Durieux (Claire Barsin), Roma Bahn, Renée Stobrawa, L. Steckel, C. Bois (Trebitsch-Lincoln).

Apr. 14 J. R. Bloch's **Le dernier Empereur** (P) at the Theater am Nollendorfplatz, dir. K. Martin, des. R. Schön, music E. Meisel, film J. A. Hübler-Kahla, with E. Deutsch (Prinz Roger), A. Steinrück (Longpré), Frida Richard (Kaiserinwitwe), Sybille Binder (Marquise Pauline), P. Graetz, O. Sima, F. Genschow, A. Granach, F. Busch in a total cast of thirty-six, plus extras.

Apr. 29 E. Mühsam's **Judas** (P) by the Piscator-Bühne Studio at the Nollendorftheater, dir. L. Lindtberg, des. V. Samih.

May 5 M. Achard's **Marlborough s'en va-t-en guerre** at Theater am Nollendorfplatz, dir. E. Kalser, des T. Müller, music T. Mackeben, with O. Sima (Marlborough), Sybille Binder (Gräfin), Renée Stobrawa, E. Busch, F. Genschow.

May 7 J. Farjeon's **Number Seventeen** at Lessing-Theater, dir. H. Lotz, des. V. Samih, with P. Graetz, Roma Bahn, W. Forst, K. Hannemann, L. Steckel.

May 22 O. Rombach's **Der Heilige Krieg** (P) at Piscator-Bühne Studio, dir. H. Oberländer.

Aug. 31 Brecht's **Dreigroschenoper** at Theater am Schiffbauerdamm, dir. E. Engel, des. C. Neher, music K. Weill. After internal friction—Carola Neher, Peter Lorre and Helen Weigel left the cast during rehearsals—the first two scenes seemed to indicate a flop, when the "Kanonen-Song" galvanized the audience and turned the production into the hit of the season. Continuing his efforts to escape from culinary theater, Brecht's *Verfremdung* here involved transferring bourgeois mores into a criminal milieu.

Oct. 16 G. Weisenborn's **U-Boot S4** (P) at Volksbühne, dir. L. Reuss. Based on press reports of a collision between a U.S. submarine and a prohibition launch, this play implemented the dramatic topicality Piscator had demanded. Aggressive where Goering's **Seeschlacht** had been elegiac, it attacked the yellow press and rearmament. The last sailor went down singing the "Internationale," and the Volksbühne, in staging it under pressure from the Special Sections, now offered de facto recognition of Piscator's aims.

Oct. 23 F. Bruckner's **Die Verbrecher** (P) at Deutsches Theater, dir. H. Hilpert. Trial plays were proliferating and this one was a catalogue of miscarriages of justice. It used a variant of T. Müller's set for **Hoppla** with six rooms on two levels.

Dec. 2 P. M. Lampel's **Revolte im Erziehungshaus** (P) by the Gruppe Junger Schauspieler at Berlin Thalia Theater, dir. H. Deppe. A topical play, it started life as a report on a welfare home for boys, whose treatment it exposed with stark realism. Here theater became a public tribunal which quickly led to reform. Piscator had an option on Lampel's earlier play *Putsch*.

361

Dec. 21   C. Zuckmayer's **Katharina Knie** (P) at Lessing-Theater, dir. K. Martin. Zuckmayer's third Volksstück provoked negative criticism in Berlin. The picture of a tightrope troupe during the inflation of 1923 was adjudged maudlin, but the public loved it.

1929
Unemployment remains high and industrial unrest and support for the National Socialists grows. In February the actors protest publicly against the fall in their earnings. Several plays, among them P. M. Lampel's **Giftgas über Berlin,** *are closed by the Berlin police, which amounts to a de facto restoration of censorship. Jessner's contract at the Staatliches Schauspielhaus is finally renewed, Reinhardt returns from a tour of the United States for his last season in Berlin, and Karlheinz Martin becomes director of the Volksbühne. The Piscator-Bühne Studio is followed by the Volksbühne Studio, the Novemberstudio (organized by A. Granach) and the Studio Dresdner Schauspieler. E. M. Remarque publishes* **All Quiet on the Western Front,** *and G. Menzel's* **Toboggan** *is staged as the first of a wave of war plays. Brecht directs his first Lehrstück at Baden-Baden.*

Jan. 4   Sophocles' **Oedipus** at the Staatliches Schauspielhaus, dir. L. Jessner. Brecht considered this to be the last stage in the development of an epic style for the classics, noting that **Oedipus at Colonus,** the second half of the production, which was usually deplorably lyrical, here told a story with theatrical force.
Mar. 20   M. Anderson and L. Stallings' **What Price Glory?** at the Theater in der Königgrätzer Strasse, dir. E. Piscator, des. C. Neher, music by W. Göhr, adapted by C. Zuckmayer, with F. Kortner (Capt. Flagg), H. Albers (Sgt. Quirt), Maria Bard, E. Busch, E. Kalser and Dagny Servaes.
Mar. 30   Marieluise Fleisser's **Pioniere in Ingolstadt** at the Theater am Schiffbauerdamm, dir. J. Geis. Naturalistic and satirical scenes from provincial life in a production instigated by Brecht.
May 3   Shakespeare's **King John** at the Staatliches Schauspielhaus, dir. L. Jessner. Jessner was as much a political target as Piscator now, and the renewal of his contract hung in the balance. **King John,** which had a commentator who explained events with a map, offered further evidence that he had now adopted the expository style of New Objectivity.
May 5   K. Kraus's **Die Unüberwindlichen** (P) at the Studio Dresdner Schauspieler, dir. P. Verhoeven. A topical dramatization of a case of press and police corruption in Vienna.

July 28   B. Brecht's **Badener Lehrstück vom Einverständnis** at the
Baden-Baden music festival, dir. Brecht.
Aug. 29   R. C. Sherriff's **Journey's End** at the Deutsches
Künstlertheater, dir. H. Hilpert. An English play about World
War I.
Sept. 6   W. Mehring's **Der Kaufmann von Berlin** (P), dir. E. Pis-
cator, des. L. Moholy-Nagy, music H. Eisler, film A. Strasser,
cartoons Elwitz-Schönfeld, with P. Baratoff (Kaftan) and Tatjana
Schilskaya (Jessi).
Sept. 6   F. Wolf's **Cyankali** (P) produced by the Gruppe Junger
Schauspieler at the Lessing-Theater, dir. H. Hinrich. Abortion was
prohibited according to §218, but a back-street racket flourished.
Cyankali exposed the situation, tracing the path from unwanted
pregnancy to fatal abortion in realistic scenes. As a Zeitstück, or
topical and polemical play, it was the fulfillment of ideas advocated
by Piscator. It was quickly staged as far afield as New York, Moscow
and Shanghai.
Oct. 13   O. von Horvath's **Sladek der schwarze Reichswehrmann**
(P) produced by the Aktuelle Bühne at the Lessing-Theater, dir. E.
Fisch.
Nov. 2   Schiller's **Don Carlos** at the Staatliches Schauspielhaus,
dir. L. Jessner. Once again an objective, expository reading of the
play, but met by a chorus of criticism, among it Arnolt Bronnen on
the far right, who wrote, "We will judge Jessner not only by his
fruits, which are artistic, but also by his roots, which are political."
The beleaguered Jessner resigned in January.
Nov. 4   E. O'Neill's **Strange Interlude** at the Deutsches Künstlertheater, dir. H. Hilpert.
Nov. 9   S. M. Tretiakov's **Roar, China** at the Frankfurt Schauspielhaus, dir. P. Buch. Translated by L. Lania, this was a
Zeitstück with an international subject, revolution in China, and
an anticapitalist, anitimperialist message.
Nov. 23   Credé's **§218** produced by the Piscator-Bühne (Kollektiv)
at the Mannheim Apollo Theater, dir. E. Piscator, des. T. Müller.
Nov. 24   H. J. Rehfisch and W. Herzog's **Die Affare Dreyfus** at
the Volksbühne, dir. H. Kenter. This Zeitstück was one of the
peaks of political theater, a courtroom play which used a historical
subject to warn Germany of the imminent dangers of anti-
Semitism, caste mentality and class justice.

1930
*The world economic crisis deepens, and Brüning, the new Center
Party Chancellor, takes emergency measures to protect finance and
industry. The Reichstag is dissolved and Hitler's NDSAP increases*

its seats from 12 to 107 in the September elections. Unemployment in Germany reaches 4.4 million. The crisis hits the theaters, and sex plays and revues flourish. Ernst Legal becomes head of the Staatliches Schauspielhaus. Reinhardt directs **Die Fledermaus** *at the Grosses Schauspielhaus to mark his twenty-fifth anniversary at the Deutsches Theater. Piṣcator opens the third Piscator-Bühne at the Wallner Theater. Meyerhold visits Berlin with Tretiakov's* **Roar, China,** *Ostrovsky's* **The Forest** *and Crommelynck's* **The Magnificent Cuckold**

Feb. 16 R. Goering's **Die Südpolexpedition des Kapitäns Scott** (P) at the Staatliches Schauspielhaus, dir. L. Jessner. Jessner's first production after resigning as Intendant showed that his innovating days were over.

May 13 F. von Unruh's **Phaea** (P) at the Deutsches Theater, dir. M. Reinhardt. Unruh, first staged by Reinhardt in 1911, now turned after pacifist and republican phases to comedy.

Aug. 31 T. Plivier's **Des Kaisers Kulis** (P) at the Lessing-Theater, dir. E. Piscator, des. T. Müller. Mutinies on the *Embden* and on the French cruiser *Waldeck-Rousseau* earlier in the year revived interest in the German mutinies in 1918.

Aug. 31 E. Toller's **Feuer aus den Kesseln** (P) at the Theater am Schiffbauerdamm, dir. H. Hinrich. Where Plivier's novel was roughly adapted by Piscator for an epic production, Toller manipulated historical fact (the 1918 mutinies) to construct a coherent, clearly motivated action, which, apart from Toller's pacifism, had no party political message.

Nov. 1 F. Bruckner's **Elisabeth von England** (P) at the Deutsches Theater, dir. H. Hilpert. There was a revival of historical plays (Shaw's *St. Joan*, Werfel's *Suarez und Maximilian*, Goetz's *Gneisenau*, Unruh's *Bonaparte*) to counter the continuing vogue of Zeitstücke from the previous season.

Nov. 8 F. Wolf's **Die Matrosen von Cattaro** (P) at the Volksbühne, dir. G. Stark. Wolf analyzed the mutineers' attitudes in a rising in the Austrian Navy in 1918. He was a KPD member and in the strained political atmosphere his play seemed a rallying call. The *Linkskurve* hailed it as a Lehrstück for future revolutions, and the first night at the Volksbühne was frequently interrupted by the KPD and SPD factions haranguing each other. Though successful, the play was made available only to the radical Special Sections. Outside Berlin it was adjudged too hot a property for theaters other than left-wing collectives to handle.

Nov. 19 S. Graff and C. E. Hinze's **Die endlose Strasse** at Aachen, a pacifistic but politically neutral war play, a German response to Sherriff's *Journey's End*, which had been seen in London before it reached the German stage.

1931

With the worsening industrial and financial situation, the banks are closed in July, wages are cut, bankruptcies proliferate and an agricultural crisis develops. Unemployment reaches 5.7 million. The internal political fronts harden and street fighting becomes a commonplace. In Berlin the Kroll Opera closes and the Schillertheater is threatened with closure. Unemployed actors form collectives (Truppe 1931, Arbeitsgemeinschaft Berlin). Piscator fails at the Wallner Theater and goes to the Soviet Union to make a film. The activities of the proletarian agitprop groups are stepped up and the plays of Gustav von Wangenheim are added to their repertoire. Volksstücke come into fashion.

Jan. 15 F. Wolf's **Tai Yang Erwacht** at the Wallner Theater, dir. E. Piscator, des. J. Heartfield, choreography Jean Weidt. Wolf had difficulty getting his next play, *Die Jungen von Mons*, staged, and turned to writing full-length agitprop scripts for the Spieltruppe Süd-West in Stuttgart.

Feb. 6 B. Brecht's **Mann ist Mann** at the Staatliches Schauspielhaus, dir. E. Engel, with Helene Weigel as Widow Begbick. A wholly experimental, "demonstrative" production with a half-curtain, projections, revealed lights, half-masks. Little Galy Gay was dwarfed by the other soldiers on stilts.

Mar. 5 C. Zuckmayer's **Hauptmann von Köpenick** (P) at the Deutsches Theater, dir. H. Hilpert. This met a demand for literate drama as satiation with the journalistic Zeitstücke set in. Zuckmayer's good-humored satire on the German respect for uniforms invested the Volksstück with a degree of social criticism.

Oct. 10 R. Billinger's **Rauhnacht** (P) at the Munich Schauspielhaus, dir. O. Falckenberg, and Dec. 17 at the Staatliches Schauspielhaus, dir. J. Fehling. A dense, irrational, atmospheric play about peasant life which H. Ihering saw as "a hymn to brutal instincts and the tyranny of the senses." "Rauhnacht" is the night before Christmas Eve. As spectacles both productions were impressive, as signs of the times they were frightening.

Nov. 2 Ö. von Horvath's **Geschichten aus dem Wienerwald** at the Deutsches Theater, dir. H. Hilpert. Like Zuckmayer, Horvath cultivated an ironic version of the Volksstück, which in his definition was a play for and about the common people, written in their own idiom. **Geschichten,** a study of life in a petit bourgeois corner of Vienna about 1924, was Horvath's breakthrough in Berlin. He had, at Zuckmayer's instigation, been awarded a half-share of the Kleist Prize in the autumn.

1932

The Geneva disarmament conference fails. Unemployment in Germany reaches 6 million. Hitler runs for President but loses to Hindenburg. Chancellor Brüning resigns in June. The Nazis get 37.8 percent of the vote in the Reichstag elections in July, some of which they lose when elections are held again in September. The Rotter entertainment empire (twelve theaters in Berlin) collapses. Reinhardt hands over management of his Berlin theaters to K. Martin and R. Beer. H. Hilpert becomes director of the Volksbühne. Experimental theater flags, and the season is dominated by revivals of **Faust** *to mark the centenary of Goethe's death and of plays by Gerhard Hauptmann to mark the author's seventieth birthday.*

Jan. 16 B. Brecht's **Die Mutter** (P) at the Komödienhaus, dir. Brecht and E. Burri. After experimenting with Lehrstücke for amateurs, Brecht now adopted Gorky's novel *Mother* for professionals. It was a demonstration that human nature can be changed (i.e., revolutionized). For this propaganda piece all the elements of epic theater were mobilized: bare stage with few props, banners and slogans, revealed lights, demonstrative acting. The *Rote Fahne* proclaimed Brecht a communist writer. The Gruppe Junger Schauspieler, an offshoot of the Piscator-Bühne, was joined by actors from agitprop groups for the production. The Junge Volksbühne, as the Special Sections which had broken away from the Volksbühne were now called, provided the audience. This was Brecht's last production before emigrating.

Jan. 19 Shakespeare's **Othello** at the Staatliches Schauspielhaus, dir. L. Jessner. In contrast to his disciplined, austere production in 1921, this **Othello's** unbridled theatricality tilted the play toward comedy and highlighted Iago (W. Krauss) rather than Othello (H. George). Intellectual rigor had given way to entertainment.

Jan. 30 B. Mussolini and G. Forzano's **Hundert Tage** at the Weimar Schauspielhaus, dir. F. Ulbrich. The play, by Forzano after a scenario by the *Duce,* dealt with Napoleon's progress from Elba to Waterloo, but the premiere was newsworthy mainly because of Hitler's presence in a private box. The review in the *Völkischer*

Beobachter assured readers that the Nazis would soon clean up and revitalize the degenerate theater of the Weimar Republic.

Feb. 16   G. Hauptmann's **Vor Sonnenuntergang** (P) at the Deutsches Theater, dir. M. Reinhardt. A nostalgic celebration of the talents of Hauptmann, Reinhardt and Werner Krauss, who found in Privy Councilor Clausen one of the great roles of his career. Unpolitical theater.

Dec. 2   Goethe's **Faust I** at the Staatliches Schauspielhaus, dir. L. Müthel. Notable for G. Gründgens' breakthrough, as Mephisto, into classical roles. Hitherto he had been a suave socialite in boulevard plays and in films. In 1934 he became Intendant of the Staatliches Schauspielhaus, which he steered skillfully through the war years. W. Krauss played Faust.

1933

Hindenburg offers Hitler the chancellorship on January 30. The Communist and Social Democratic press is banned. The Nazis take 44 percent of the vote at the Reichstag elections in June. The world economic crisis recedes. The Nazis swiftly implement their policies for the theater, and Hermann Goering, Prime Minister of Prussia, appoints Weimar Intendant Franz Ulbrich as Intendant of the Staatliches Schauspielhaus. Reinhardt's Berlin theaters are confiscated. Emigration begins, F. Kortner in January, Alfred Kerr in February, Brecht in March. F. Wolf's **Professor Mamlock,** *the first play written in exile, is produced in Warsaw. Zurich becomes the center of progressive theater in German.*

Apr. 20   H. Johst's **Schlageter** (P) at the Staatliches Schauspielhaus, dir. F. Ulbrich. Johst, originally an Expressionist, had succumbed to nationalism in 1927. This play was a hymn to an early martyr to the cause, Albert Leo Schlageter, who had been condemned and executed by a French court-martial in the Ruhr in 1924 for attacks on French transport. It opened on the Führer's birthday in the presence of Goebbels and "an impressive array of German writers . . . [now all in oblivion] who had accepted invitations to Berlin." (P. Fechter). After the performance the audience sang "Deutschland über Alles" and the "Horst Wessel Lied." The ideological theater of the Nazis had replaced the political theater of the Weimar Republic.

LIST OF CONTEMPORARY PLAYS PRODUCED BY PISCATOR BETWEEN 1919 AND 1930

L. Barta: *Russlands Tag*, in *Der Gegner*, 1920–21, No. 4, repr. in L. Hoffmann and D. Hoffmann-Ostwald: *Deutsches Arbeitertheater 1918–33*, Berlin, 1961.

M. Brod and H. Reimann: *Die Abenteuer des braven Soldaten Schwejk*, adapted by Piscator, Gasbarra, Lania and Brecht, in H. Knust: *Materialien zu B. Brechts Schweyk im zweiten Weltkrieg*, Frankfurt/M, 1974.

A. Brust: *Südseespiel*, in A. B. *Dramen*, Munich, 1971.

Carl Credé: *§218, Frauen in Not*, Berlin, 1929.

F. Jung: *Die Kanaker* und *Wie lange noch. . . .* zwei Schauspiele, Berlin, 1921. *Wie lange noch . . .* repr. in H. Denkler: *Einakter und kleine Dramen des Expressionismus*, Stuttgart, 1968.

F. Jung: *Heimweh*, in *Spectaculum 26*, Frankfurt/M, 1977.

G. Kaiser: *Der Centaur*, Berlin, 1916, repr. as *Margarine* in G. K. *Werke*, Berlin 1971, vol. 1.

L. Lania: *Konjunktur*, no publication listed.

R. Leonhard: *Segel am Horizont*, Berlin, 1925, repr. in R. L. *Ausgewählte Werke*, Berlin, 1963, vol. 2.

H. Mann: *Variété*, Berlin, 1910.

W. Mehring: *Der Kaufmann von Berlin*, Berlin, 1929, repr. in G. Rühle: *Zeit und Theater*, Berlin, 1972, vol. 2.

E. O'Neill: *Unterm karibischen Mond*, Berlin, 1924.

E. Ortner: *Michael Hundertpfund*, Munich, 1929.

A. Paquet: *Fahnen*, Munich, 1923, repr. in R. Grimm and J. Hermand: *Deutsche Revolutionsdramen*, Frankfurt/M, 1970.

A. Paquet: *Sturmflut*, Berlin, 1926.

H. J. Rehfisch: *Wer weint um Juckenack?*, Berlin, 1925, rev. version in H. J. R. *Dramen*, Berlin, 1967, vol. 2.

R. Rolland: *Die Zeit wird kommen*, no German publication listed.

W. Schmidtbonn: *Hilfe, ein Kind ist vom Himmel gefallen!*, Berlin, 1910.

U. Sinclair: *Prinz Hagen*, Berlin, 1921.

U. Sinclair: *Singende Galgenvögel*, Berlin, 1927.

E. Toller: *Hoppla, wir leben!* Berlin, 1972, repr. in G. Rühle: *Zeit und Theater*, Berlin, 1972, vol. 2.

A. Tolstoy and P. Shchegolov: *Rasputin, oder die Verschwörung der Zarin*, Heidelberg, 1927. The original, before the Piscator-Bühne adaptation.

F. Wedekind: *Tod und Teufel*, in F. W. *Prosa, Dramen, Verse*, Munich/Vienna, 1972, vol. 2.

E. Welk: *Gewitter über Gotland*, Berlin, 1926.

F. Wolf, *Tai Yang erwacht*, Berlin, 1930, repr. in F. W. *Dramen*, Berlin, 1960, vol. 3.

P. Zech: *Das trunkene Schiff*, Leipzig, 1924.

INDEX